ESSAYS IN QUASI-REALISM

D1562422

ESSAYS IN QUASI-REALISM

Simon Blackburn

New York   Oxford
OXFORD UNIVERSITY PRESS
1993

Oxford University Press

Oxford   New York   Toronto
Delhi   Bombay   Calcutta   Madras   Karachi
Kuala Lumpur   Singapore   Hong Kong   Tokyo
Nairobi   Dar es Salaam   Cape Town
Melbourne   Auckland   Madrid

and associated companies in
Berlin   Ibadan

Copyright © 1993 by Oxford University Press

Published by Oxford University Press, Inc.
200 Madison Avenue, New York, New York 10016

Oxford is a registered trademark of Oxford University Press

Library of Congress Cataloging-in-Publication Data
Blackburn, Simon.
Essays in quasi-realism / Simon Blackburn.
p.   cm.   Includes index.
ISBN 0-19-508041-6; ISBN 0-19-508224-9 (pbk)
1. Realism.   I. Title.
B835..B35   1993   149'.2—dc20   92-37005

2 4 6 8 9 7 5 3 1

Printed in the United States of America
on acid-free paper

Preface and Acknowledgements

The essays collected in this volume represent a large part of the work that I have done over the years on the issues surrounding realism. Since my own approach to this matter has been sufficiently different from that of others to cause some comment, and since the articles appeared in anthologies as well as orthodox journals, it seemed justifiable to collect them together. I have prefaced them with an Introduction, hoping to do something to justify my approach, and to locate it broadly among the very different philosophical attitudes to these contested areas.

I am pleased to acknowledge the following places of first publication, and to thank the respective editors and publishers for permission to reprint the papers: 'Truth, Realism, and the Regulation of Theory' was first published in *Midwest Studies in Philosophy,* Vol V, 1980. 'Knowledge, Truth, and Reliability' was the *Henrietta Hertz Lecture of the British Academy,* 1984. 'Morals and Modals' appeared in *Fact, Science and Value, Essays in Honour of A.J. Ayer's Language, Truth and Logic,* edited by C. Wright and G. Macdonald (Oxford: Blackwell, 1987). 'Opinions and Chances' appeared in *Prospects for Pragmatism,* ed. D.H. Mellor (Cambridge: Cambridge University Press, 1980). 'Hume and Thick Connexions' appeared in *Philosophy and Phenomenological Research* (special half-centenary volume) 1990. 'Moral Realism' appeared in *Morality and Moral Reasoning,* ed. John Casey (London: Methuen, 1973). 'Supervenience Revisited' appeared in *Exercises in Analysis,* ed. Ian Hacking (Cambridge: Cambridge University Press, 1985). 'Errors and the Phenomenology of Value' came out in *Ethics and Objectivity,* ed. T. Honderich (London: Routledge & Kegan Paul, 1985). 'How to be and Ethical Anti-Realist' appeared in *Midwest Studies,* Vol XII, 1988. 'Attitudes and Contents' appeared in *Ethics,* 1988. 'Just Causes' was originally given at an Oberlin Colloquium, and appeared in *Philosophical Studies,* 1990. 'The Individual Strikes Back' appeared in *Synthèse* 1985. 'Losing Your Mind: Physics, Identity, and Folk Burglar Prevention' was part of a conference held at Greensboro, North Carolina, and appeared in *The Future of Folk Psychology,* ed. John Greenwood (New York: Cambridge University Press, 1991). 'Filling in Space' was presented at the *Analysis* half-centenary conference in Cambridge, and appeared in the supplementary volume of the journal, April 1990.

The articles are reprinted as they first appeared, with a few minor amendments to style and grammar. They are organized not chronologically, but thematically, and are divided into three main areas of metaphysics, ethics, and mind and physics. The footnotes sometimes differ from those in the originals, partly because of added cross-references to other essays in this collection. I have resisted the temptation to add more footnotes to explain why I said what I did, even in cases where I would prefer to have said something different. But to some essays I have added an addendum, pushing things further in directions that now seem to me important, often in the light of particular reactions from friends and critics.

I would particularly like to acknowledge my debt to the editors of volumes and the organizers of talks and conferences whose invitations prompted me to the painful business of writing. Among the many auditors and readers who have made valuable comments I remember Paul Boghossian, Edward Craig, Elizabeth Fricker, Allan Gibbard, Bob Hale, Paul Horwich, John Kenyon, Robert Kraut, Saul Kripke, David Lewis, John McDowell, the late Ian McFetridge, Philip Pettit, Huw Price, Geoff Sayre-McCord, Marianne Talbot, Ralph Walker, Jonathan Westphal, and Crispin Wright.

Chapel Hill, North Carolina   S. B.
December 1992

Contents

ESSAYS IN QUASI-REALISM

Introduction

In many of these essays the main protagonist is a figure I christened the 'quasi-realist'. Two routes led to this persona. One is familiar to every student of moral philosophy. There everyone learns of philosophers who take a 'non-descriptive' or non-representational view of our commitments, seeing them instead as serving some other function, such as expressing attitude, endorsing prescriptions, or, in general, putting pressure on choice and action. Such a view is thought of as 'anti-realist', and is easily contrasted with a realist, or descriptive or representational, story that says that such commitments do what they seem to do: describe what we take to be the ethical facts. But while everybody learns of this contrast, nobody, it seemed to me, really knew how to conduct the debate about such ideas (or about the inevitable second-order question: whether the alleged point of contrast is really well drawn this way, or is even intelligible). The *images* behind the opposing sides are powerful enough, and find cavalier expression in thoughts like this: the realist thinks there is truth and knowledge to be had, that ethical properties exist, that they explain things, that they are independent of us, that they are objective. The anti-realist, or here the expressivist, is presumed to deny these doctrines. This is why such a view seemed to many philosophers to imply an 'error theory' of everyday ethical thought, claiming that a substantial component of that thought is indefensible. The reasoning is that everyday ethical thought embodies a claim to truth, or to knowledge or objectivity, or to something which 'lies beyond' the opinions and sentiments that we endorse, and which those opinions might distort or represent badly. However, if this claim to objectivity is quite spurious, as it seems to be on the non-descriptive theory, then everyday ethical thought involves a kind of self-deception or fraud. But is the claim indeed spurious, on the non-descriptive story? Does the anti-realist indeed have to accept the baggage forced upon him when the debate is conducted this way?

The issue is a large one, for not only in ethics but in many spheres—law, literary theory, history, even science—there exists the same kind of radical threat. The threat is that once we see the disappearance of some favoured conception of objectivity and truth, or once we see what these amount to, we can no longer exercise judgement as before. A proper consciousness of the activity of judgement would unmask and undermine the activity itself. But is it true that an ordinary practice in good standing, like ethics or literary criticism or law or science, needs to depend upon some illusion about objectivity? The question would hinge, I considered, on whether an anti-realist story can make sense of several ideas: that truth is the aim of judgement; that our disciplines make us better able to appreciate it, that it is, however, independent of us, and that we are fallible in our grasp of it. My idea was to domesticate these high-sounding thoughts. Brought down to earth, the question is whether the anti-realist can make sense of thoughts like 'I would like to know whether bullfighting is wrong', or 'I believe that bullfighting is wrong, but I might be wrong about that', or 'Bullfighting would be wrong whatever I or anyone else thought about it'—claims asserting our concern to get things right, our fallibility, and some independence of the ethical from what we actually feel. These concerns and claims look metaphysical, and indeed many theorists are content to define their meta-ethical theory in terms of them. But looked at another way they are merely part of good ethical thought: someone incapable of them would lack a becoming modesty, rather than a metaphysical insight. Can a non-descriptive story make sense of them? That depends on what it can do with so-called 'indirect contexts', or sentences in which an ethical sentence is itself embedded, but not actually asserted. I dramatized the question of whether a non-descriptive story can indeed understand the use we make of such contexts by inventing the figure of the quasi-realist, or someone who 'starting from an anti-realist position finds himself progressively able to mimic the thoughts and practices supposedly definitive of realism'. Quasi-realism is not really another 'ism' in the sense of a position or an ideology in the same space as realism or anti-realism; it represents more an attitude of exploration of the reality of the boundaries that those 'isms' demand, and may issue in a complication or modification of the debate, as old oppositions prove incapable of carrying its weight.

Thus far the idea is simple enough, and it would be natural to suppose that any success the quasi-realist enjoys would amount to a defence of a non-descriptive theory of ethics—a defence, at least, against the charge that it can make no sense of central elements of our ethical thought and practice. It would be a welcome barrier against having to be an error theorist. But the matter quickly goes deeper than that. For if this is all that we conclude, then it seems that the quasi-realist inhabits a familiar but highly suspect philosophical world: one where we know what we mean by descriptive versus non-descriptive theories, by objectivity, or by realism versus anti-realism. Not only would many philosophers deny that we can make good sense of these oppositions, but quasi-realism can itself offer them support. For if, from the non-descriptive starting point, it is successful in capturing some propositional feature of our discourse, then that feature can no longer be used as a litmus test such that if we allow it we are realists and if we do not then we are expressivists. If it can do this for all proposed features, then there is no point at which our *use* of ethical language supports realism rather than expressivism (or vice versa); if that is so, it is tempting to conclude that the debate is unreal, since there is no methodology for conducting it.

One might then think that if the quasi-realist explains and justifies our practice with words like 'truth', 'fact', 'independence', 'objectivity', 'knowledge', and even 'description', then the position seems to have bitten its own tail: it seems not so much a buttress to anti-realism as an instrument for dismantling the entire debate. But this, I think, is premature. Suppose we honour the first great projectivist by calling 'Humean Projection' the mechanism whereby what starts life as a non-descriptive psychological state ends up expressed, thought about, and considered in propositional form.[1] Then there is not only the interest of knowing how far Humean Projection gets us. There is also a problem generated even if the mechanism gets us everywhere we could want. If truth, knowledge, and the rest are a proper upshot of Humean Projection, where is it legitimate to invoke that mechanism? Perhaps everywhere, drawing us to idealism, or nowhere, or just somewhere, such as the theory of value or modality. The difficulty and importance of thinking about this does not diminish if quasi-realism is successful, although that success will dramatically reduce the number of actual arguments to hand when we think about such issues.

It teaches us a great deal about representation and description to learn that they are so cheap to purchase that even the Humean can have them, along with truth, fact, knowledge, and the rest. This was in fact the position I found myself drawn to by the other route into the area. This arose not from an interest in value, but from realist versus anti-realist debates conducted on a wider scale and apparently in a different key, in particular as they appeared in the works of Hilary Putnam (around 1979) and Michael Dummett. Although the forum was wider, and even global if we are asked to take one view or another of all linguistic practice, it seemed to me that the same question of how much is actually defensible on anti-realist grounds was being neglected. Both Putnam and Dummett had, it seemed to me, proposed particular litmus tests, and in each case it seemed fruitful to ask whether someone might think of himself as an anti-realist, yet with a good conscience find himself involved in the intellectual practices proposed as definitive of realism. In the case of Dummett's proposal, this would have meant a defence, on anti-realist grounds, of the logical right to unrestricted classical bivalence, and with Putnam at the time, a defence of a proper contrast between what we best believe and what is true. I addressed each task in the first essay in this volume. Apart from its direction the main innovation of that essay, I think, was a firmly 'operational' approach to the notion of truth. I was certain that the anti-realist need not involve himself with the definitions of what it would be good to believe in an ideal limit, as in Peirce or Dewey, in order to give due weight to the independence of belief and truth, or to classical logical principles apparently governing truth. This was the beginning of a dislike of the straightjacket that demands for analysis, in this case analysis of the notion of truth, put on

---

1. I was interested to discover the same interest in Humean Projection in work by H. P. Grice, published in *The Conception of Value* (Oxford: Oxford University Press, 1991), esp. pp. 146–51. Grice's construction of value delineates processes strikingly similar to those suggested by my quasi-realist.

philosophical enquiry. Throughout these essays I have found it easy to resist the blunt demand for a 'theory' of truth, forcing me to come clean on whether all commitments are true or false in the same sense. What conception of truth we have is shown in the use we give the notion; that use is most interestingly visible in our logic, and in our thoughts about such matters as the point of the commitments, their independence, and our fallibility. If we can give a story explaining or justifying those thoughts, then there is no last chapter about truth waiting to be written. The same in my view is true of knowledge, and in the second essay collected here I advocated what it would now be fashionable to call a 'minimalist' theory of knowledge. One of its effects is that the issue of realism versus anti-realism cannot usefully be framed as an issue of *cognitivism* about a disputed area.[2] Wherever there is truth and a discipline for better or worse judgement, we can in principle talk about knowledge, and such talk therefore falls as well into the quasi-realist net.

This second route into an interest in quasi-realism led me to sympathise with the view that it can work to chip away venerable oppositions. Yet in the local case of ethics I retain the other sympathy: that it actually helps to give the verdict to an anti-realist direction of thought. This second view has un-doubtedly exasperated bolder spirits who mined a global 'minimalism' from these seams. Once we have the pure gold of Wittgenstein's philosophy of thought and language, Humean Projection is supposed to be an outdated base substitute: 'fool's Wittgenstein'. Wittgenstein is taken to have reconciled us to an indefinite motley of different discourses or, as they used to be called, 'language games', each with its own coordinated, unpretentious version of truth: moral truth, modal truth, arithmetical truth, and so on. There is no external idiom in which to theorise about any of this, but only the occasional need to remind ourselves that ethics is not arithmetic, modal truth is not the description of middle-sized dry goods, and so on (although why we should need reminding of this is not all that clear).

But my exploration is more thoroughly Wittgensteinian than this kind of relaxed pluralism. Wittgenstein himself cannot be seen frolicking on the streets of Paris. He is no minimalist. In all the areas that he considered in the later philosophy he relies upon a contrast between descriptive and non-descriptive uses of language. His main technique is to press a non-descriptive function for paradigmatic assertions: philosophical assertions express gram-matical rules; ethical assertions do not describe facts; mathematical assertions characteristically lay down rules of description; assertions about oneself do not describe, but have the function of avowals; and so on for religious lan-guage, expressions of certainty, and indeed everything that he treated in any detail at all.[3] One reason for missing this is that Wittgenstein did appear to hold a minimalist theory of truth (although even that simplifies the dialectical

---

2. A suggestion recently refurbished by Crispin Wright, *Truth and Objectivity* (Cambridge: Harvard University Press, 1992), chapters 3–4.

3. I assembled the case for this interpretation in an article not included here: 'Wittgenstein's Irrealism' in *Wittgenstein: Eine Neubewerhung,* eds. J. Brandl and R. Haller (Vienna: Holder-Richler-Temsky, 1990).

position in which he expresses such views). But relying on this fact ignores that minimalism about truth is entirely compatible with holding a very un-minimal theory of assertion, as is shown by the example, very familiar to Wittgenstein, of F. P. Ramsey, who is both a minimalist about truth and a quasi-realist about many categories of commitment. The point is that a thin theory of truth can consort with a thick theory of judgement, ascribing a variety of functional roles to the commitments that on the surface all get expressed by equally well-behaved indicative sentences.

Authority apart, there is something strange about maintaining that all questions are immanent, or, equivalently, that we should be minimalist about every notion that would provide a concept in which to couch a metatheory of any area. Consider, for instance, realism in David Lewis's sense, about possible worlds. In 'Morals and Modals' I begin to sketch a quasi-realist story about the modal, and although in the first instance it seems set to work better for operator treatments of modality than for possible-worlds treatments, I am not convinced that there is any insuperable obstacle to grafting quantification onto it. But put this aside, and suppose that the theory works. Then it seems to me strange to interpret the result as showing that there was never an issue about Lewis's realism. The quasi-realist will indeed be saying, with all the sincerity that Lewis can give it, that there is a possible world in which there is a talking donkey. He has his own story about why he can say that (and, importantly, about why it is a useful thing to be saying). But does the fact that he ends up saying it show that Lewis's realism is a friendly, minimal story, had for free by anyone who makes modal distinctions? Hardly, I think. Nearly everyone thought the position was incredible, and it would be strange to see it as a notational variant on something perfectly credible, so that in the end the quasi-realist's assent to modal judgement turns him into a Lewisian realist. I sum up this message by insisting that in the philosophy of these things, it is not what you end up saying, but how you get to say it, that defines your 'ism'.

What kind of evidence could there be for one story as opposed to another about the function of judgement in an area? For a given local area, the answer is plain: we garner evidence from its surroundings, or in other words from other things we think, for example about description, explanation, and representation of the world. Thus a realist must make us comfortable with a successful activity of representing the area of reality he sees us as describing; he has to make us comfortable too with the utility we find in describing it (both aspects are highly visible when we think of a realist theory of modality). Making us comfortable is not a task that is easily circumscribed, notably because many realists are comfortable with things, such as advanced epistemological powers, that offend the rest of us. Equally, of course, anti-realism must make good *its* explanations of the discourse and the role it plays in our lives, while avoiding the view that it exists because it describes a genuine aspect of reality.

Two features of this answer get some attention in these essays, but doubtless deserve more. First, even if it works for a local discourse, the wheels skid more dramatically when we try to apply it to anything more global. We cannot mount a *naturalistic* explanation of science or common sense en bloc, for there is nowhere else to stand. The prospect for framing a global debate, for example on the issue of instrumentalism versus realism in science and common sense, in these terms is not bright. In work still in progress I take up the issue of how much of a loss this is. Second, there is a background problem: Which aspects of reality are to be taken as genuine? What is a proper base from which to conduct this theorising? Quasi-realism is often charged with 'scientism' at this point, or in other words with confining genuine reality to an ontology and a set of features delineated by some favoured fundamental science, such as physics. A better basis, it is then suggested, will include much more: Why should it not include the properties and features that, on the face of it, we know about as we indulge the area in question—moral, aesthetic, causal, and modal features, for example? Is not their exclusion just a scientific, or possibly an old empiricist, prejudice?

Three of the essays collected here—'Just Causes', 'Losing Your Mind', and 'Filling in Space'—explore the issue of when we can say that a property exists, when we can invoke it in explanation, and what kind of basis explanation has in commonsense, spatially extended nature. They illustrate my characteristic liberality, for instance by allowing forms of explanation invoking ethical properties, which will surprise both moral realists and their opponents, who frame the debate centrally in terms of the explanatory import of those properties. Just as knowledge and truth can be earned, I claim, so can explanation. Roughly: properties are the semantic shadows of predicates, and a supervening judgement, whose use of predicates is protected by quasi-realism, may be cited by way of explaining all kinds of things. Views like this are of course popular in the philosophy of mind, where a similar structure exists. But my liberality over explanation does not extend to all the purposes for which explanation is required; in particular, when our project is to place ethical or modal or probabilistic discourse, that is, to understand why we go in for it and what its role is in our activities and lives, a simple explanation of our judgements as responses to the facts is markedly inferior to the longer story explaining their functional role, the reason we have them and give them the importance we do. This inferiority, I argue, is particularly visible when we think of supervenience itself: a phenomenon that requires the most careful description and explanation, if it is not simply a device for concealing problems.

I hope that these metaphysical essays exonerate me from the charge of finding the basis for explanation obvious or simple. But I am not repentant about finding it *more* obvious that a projective theory in a quasi-realist armour is an attractive theory of value and modality, than that such-and-such a selection of things and properties deserves a privileged explanatory priority. It seems to me clear that the exercise of 'placing' our propensity for value, for the normative, and for modality in a naturalistic world is philosophically urgent whatever exactly we include in the natural. It may even be that for different problems different bases in the natural can be accepted as given, so that there is no one dimension of explanatory priority.[4] For any problem there may be one useful starting point, although there is no one useful starting point for any problem.

As well as selecting some acceptable basis for explanation, a successful projective plus quasi-realist story needs to start by identifying the cast of mind voiced by the judgement under consideration, in order make out its initial contrast with straightforward belief. We have to have a sense of what we are doing in moralizing, other than describing the lie of the moral land, and similarly for the other areas. Some critics have denied that this contrast can be made out. Perhaps their weightiest point is that the cast of mind we voice is inextricably linked to the *propositional* form in which we voice it—and discuss it, learn it, ponder it and teach it. If we want to know what state of mind is voiced by an ethical or modal remark, it is most natural to locate it as simple belief, for instance that X is good, or Y impossible. To paraphrase William James, it is as if we find the trail of the Fregean serpent over all. Again, my reaction is to distinguish what we start with in the construction, and what we finish with: however irreducible and culturally particular valuing something has become, the Humean is still in business if its irreducibility and particularity is visibly the upshot of a natural process of voicing and projecting the non-representational states she starts with.

This irreducibility is also supposed to be consistent with an approach that has gained popularity in the last decade. This exploits the analogy with secondary qualities by giving a 'response dependent' or 'judgement dependent' truth-condition for moral or modal commitments, equating them in some way with remarks about us and our dispositions under some set of conditions. Such a position advances a biconditional:

$$X \text{ is } \phi \equiv \text{[some persons] are or would be disposed to [reaction]}$$
$$\text{under [circumstances]}$$

Each bracketed term is capable of indefinite variation: the persons might be me, or us, or some of us, or me or us or some of us as we actually are, or me or us or some of us as we would be after a process of improvement or idealization. The reaction might be one of stance or attitude or judgement or sensation, and in turn it might have to be identified by using the very term ϕ, acknowledging irreducibility—or it might not. The circumstances might be usual, or normal, or idealized, or disjunctive. Finally the whole equation might be presented as giving the meaning of the original, or giving its truth-condition, or doing both if we equate these, or doing neither but still somehow helping with understanding the role of the original judgement. So a proper taxonomy of such positions would be a long business, and many objections to some versions will not apply to all.

Clearly, proponents of the approach have to navigate between the Scylla

4. This seems to have been Grice's view, op. cit., pp. 102–3.

of getting the truth-conditions simply wrong and the Charybdis of getting them right, but by importing into the right-hand side the *kind* of judgement we were hoping to understand. An example of Scylla would be

X is good $\equiv$ we as we actually are would be disposed to desire X
          when we see it.

since this forgets that we are often bad, and do not always approve of what we desire, and often misapprehend things when we see them. A full rectification is to hand, but has us falling into Charybdis:

X is good $\equiv$ perfect people would be disposed to value X under
          whichever conditions it takes to understand X's value.

The reason this represents defeat is that it takes moralizing—the very activity we are trying to understand—to make the right-hand-side judgement, so all we have is an equivalence between a quick way of judging that something is good and a lengthy way of doing the same. Obviously, perfect people in the right conditions will value $X \equiv X$ is good, but this tells us nothing about what it is to identify people as perfect, or an activity as that of valuing, or conditions as right.

The response dependency theorist has to show us a useful course between Scylla and Charybdis. Yet there is every reason to doubt that the straits have to be navigated in the first place. There is no reason at all to expect that judgement that is, on the surface, not about ourselves but rather about numbers or possibilities or rights or probabilities, is usefully identified at any level as concealed judgement about ourselves. Of course we *voice* our own reactions as we talk of these things, but we *voice* our own beliefs as we say anything whatsoever, yet not all our sayings are about our own beliefs.[5] We do not constantly turn our heads sideways to look at our own reactions. Appealing again to authority we could say that this approach is un-Wittgensteinian in at least three ways. First, it seeks a kind of reduction, or a forcing of judgements that have apparently quite different functions into the one surprising mould of describing us (or me, or some of us, etc.). Second, it detects complexity and choice at the bracketed points, supposing that the folk who go about describing colours or possibilities or values have made extremely subtle, and apparently pointless, decisions about, for example, whether to make reference to ourselves rigid or not, when there is no evidence at all that such decisions ever needed making or could have been made. (This offends against the 'nothing is hidden' principle.) Third, it goes bullheaded at the issue in terms of finding truth conditions, whereas from the point of view of these papers, and from Wittgenstein's point of view equally, if you want to talk in these terms, then the best thing to say about 'X is ϕ' in the cases considered is

5. This critical comparison is urged by Huw Price in his 'Two Paths to Pragmatism' (*Response-Dependent Concepts,* ed. Peter Menzies, Research School of Social Sciences, Australian National University Publication, 1991), p. 49.

that its truth-condition is that X is ϕ—but this will not be the way to understand matters.

Another, but less easily identified, reservation comes from philosophers who want to oppose or at least soften the fact–value distinction, often in favour of giving priority to the so-called 'thick' evaluative concepts. I have views about that move that go beyond discussions in these papers.[6] But it is at this point that the famous 'rule following considerations' lurk. (It is a considerable irony of these debates that to some of us these provide a proper field for the very kind of quasi-realistic investigation that, according to others, they rule out.) A number of these essays gesture at this theme, but 'The Individual Strikes Back' is a direct commentary on the sceptical paradox and its anti-realist solution. Obviously, since quasi-realism has its home in the account it gives of normativity, it is essential to see that it might well apply to the norms governing meaning that get lost in Kripke's sceptical dialogue. Again, I believe that Wittgenstein's authority lies squarely behind this approach, contrary to the weight of commentators who seem to have been so baffled by Saul Kripke's setting of the problem.

When I started writing essays on these themes, I had not been fully struck by their sheer size. It seemed to me likely that fairly local debates, in the theory of probability or ethics, could be tidied up by a quick application of old ideas. But the introduction of the same projective theme in other areas quickly beckoned, both because of its historical importance and because modality especially seems an almost irresistible projectivist playground. Yet modality is implicated in everything we understand about the occupancy of space. The final essay in this collection confronts this problem, if only to say that things are no better for everyone else. I hope it leaves the reader tantalized, for I suppose if I have a meta-philosophical creed it is that there are too many ideologies and too few works wondering about the foundations underlying their differences.

6. I tackle the issue in 'Through Thick and Thin,' *Proceedings of the Aristotelian Society,* Supplementary volume, 1992.

I

METAPHYSICS

1

Truth, Realism, and the Regulation of Theory

In this essay I want to approach an area where our metaphysics and our theory of knowledge are apt to become scrambled. Few would deny that a general theory of what it is that marks a statement as true should have implications for the theory of knowledge—of what is necessary, or sufficient, to know such a statement. Equally a view of knowledge might carry with it a picture of the kind of thing that makes true the statements said to be known. My trouble is this: I begin to doubt whether familiar ways of characterizing debates in the theory of truth—realism vs. instrumentalism, and so on— actually succeed in marking out interesting areas of dispute. I doubt too whether, if this is so, the theory of knowledge will provide a solution, so that by looking at conflicting views of what knowledge is we might come to understand genuine metaphysical oppositions. I shall pursue these doubts through the figure of the '*quasi-realist*,' a person who, starting from a recognizably anti-realist position, finds himself progressively able to mimic the intellectual practices supposedly definitive of realism. In effect, quasi-realism is the program begun by Hume in his treatment of both causal and moral belief. I take it that its success would be a measure of the difficulty of defining a genuine debate between realism and its opponents. There are certainly images and perhaps attitudes to our discourse within a field which seem to be associated with realism, but I shall argue that unless these are given some concrete employment they represent subjects not so much for decision as for nostalgia. This concrete employment would, in effect, be a practice that a quasi-realist cannot imitate.

Some of think of ourselves as realists about some things, but as more like pragmatists, instrumentalists, idealists, or, in a word, anti-realists about others. We are happy that the world contains certain kinds of states of affairs— perhaps physical or phenomenal ones—but no more. We might not be happy with additional realms of conditional or counterfactual or moral or mental or semantic or social or mathematical states of affairs. If this is not where we would draw the line, nevertheless, we might think, there is a line to be drawn; or, even if we prefer not to draw a line, still, we think, we can understand the position of those who do. One possible response is to seek a reduction, so that although there exist no further independent facts corresponding to truths in a certain area, nevertheless there are familiar lesser states of affairs in which their truth consists. Another response is to advocate that we abandon the area of thought in question. It was pessimism about reduction, and about the existence of a distinct area of fact, making truths about what people believe or mean, which led Quine to denigrate psychological and semantic theory.[1] But the interesting issue for quasi-realism arises if we remain anti-reductionist but also are unwilling to abandon the way of thinking in question. There is no real option to abandon conditional, moral, mathematical, etc., thought, even if we become squeamish about the existence of distinct states of affairs corresponding to our beliefs in these matters. We would like to continue behaving as though there were facts, even if we feel the anti-realist pull.

But how are we to tell, from a society or a language or the conduct of an intellectual discipline, or just from our own thought, when we are in the presence of commitment to a realm of fact? One might try saying, with due emphasis and seriousness, that one thinks that there is a fact of the matter whether. . . . We are all used to debates, say, in the theory of morals, in which one side asserts this and the other denies it, and they appear to themselves and probably to us to have located an issue. But why? Two problems suggest themselves. The first is that from the standpoint of the anti-realist the assertion 'there really is a fact of the matter (often: an objective, independent, or genuine, fact of the matter) whether . . .' is itself suspicious. For if his puzzle arises from the thought that no kind of thing *could* possibly play the role of (moral, conditional, etc.) states of affairs, then he ought to translate his doubt into difficulty about what the realist *means to be asserting* when he claims that there are such things. We face the familiar philosophical trouble that in failing to imagine something we also fail to imagine what it would be to imagine it. One may have a picture of what the realist means, but I shall argue below that this is not enough.

The second problem is that it is not so clear that the anti-realist must take issue over any sentence of the kind: 'there really is a fact . . .'. This is because it may belong to a discipline to think such a thing, and it is no part of the anti-realist's brief to tamper with the internal conduct of a discipline. The point would be obvious enough if we accepted Ramsey's redundancy theory of truth: serious assertion of some statement p transforms into 'it is true that p' and 'it is really a fact that p' without any escalation of ontology or metaphysics. But part of what is at stake in accepting Ramsey's theory is whether there is a genuine issue over realism and anti-realism, and we cannot yet rely on it. Nevertheless, the threat remains that the anti-realist blandly takes over all the things the realist wanted to say, but retaining all the while his conviction that he alone gives an unobjectionable, or ontologically pure, interpretation of them. Both these feelings can arise when reading apologies for objec-

---

1. W. Quine, 'Reply to Chomsky', in *Words and Objections*, ed. D. Davidson and J. Hintikka (Dordrecht: Reidel, 1969), p. 303.

tivity and fact in, say, moral philosophy. Often nothing is conveyed except that their authors are very well-brought-up and serious people. In the face of philosophical doubt, one cannot simply ladle out objectivity and facts.

Here is an example to illustrate both these points. I might embrace an anti-realism about conditionals by thinking along these lines. Imagine a thin time slice through the universe, capturing a momentary array of regions of space manifesting properties, like a large three-dimensional photograph. Nothing in it corresponds to a conditional fact. Imagine a succession of these: things change, order appears, yet neither in a single slice nor in a succession of them is there room for a conditional fact. But our universe is just such a succession. So there are no conditional facts. Now, if we are persuaded by this Humean picture (it is no part of my claim that we should be), we lose grip not only of what a conditional fact could be but also of what somebody could *mean to be asserting,* what point he could be making, when he counters that there are indeed such things. The temptation is to rely upon simile: the realist thinks of them as like a fixative or stabilizing glue somehow explaining order. But if pictures and simile fail, as I shall argue they do, and if we cannot use them to make sense of the realist's position, there is still nothing to stop us from using conditionals in the practice of our thought, from asserting them, and, for all we have yet shown, from emphasizing our commitment to them with notions of truth and fact. We become quasi-realists in following out the discipline—appearing in as many ways as possible like realists but believing that we have saved our souls in the process.

Clearly, images of what the original realist versus anti-realist debate is about do come to mind. The realist thinks of it as though the moral order is there to be investigated like a piece of geography, that numbers are like eternal objects spread over space, that the past and the future are laid out, even now, in a state of deep-frozen existence, and so on. But the presence or absence of such images cannot define an interesting issue. It must depend on some other way of directly identifying bad realist (or anti-realist) practice, and without such a way it is irrelevant. The only serious debate arises about the propriety of *using* or *succumbing* to these images. But we do not know *what it is* to use or succumb to them. We have seen the anti-realist fearing that the realist gives an improper *role* to the realm of fact and believing that he alone gives a defensible interpretation of his utterances by seeing them in the spirit of a quasi-realist. But what is the role that is improper, and what are the contrasting interpretations? The similes and images do nothing to answer this question: in themselves, indeed, they are harmless, and until we can define a harm that they do, to lack them is to miss nothing worse than a mildly poetic sort of pleasure.

A direct description of the contentious role that a realist gives to his states of affairs is therefore needed, unless the metadebate, about whether there was ever a point at issue, is to give the verdict that there was not. Some philosophers have so concluded. Yet it is not easy to believe that such a hardy perennial has such infirm roots. I now turn to some proposals and try to relate them to what we should want to think about knowledge.

II

The debate would be on again if we could see that the quasi-realist can imitate the realist so far but no further, or alternatively that the realist must balk at certain intellectual practices of his anti-realist opponent. If we can identify a practice or thought that we can agree to be available to a realist but that even a quasi-realist must avoid, then we have identified a contentious role for the conception of fact, and in sorting it out we will be joining in what is revealed as a genuine debate. I shall discuss four such thoughts. The first is the thought that a theory to which one is committed could, even if only as a bare possibility, be false. This suggests a conception of facts as 'transcending' theory, which the pragmatists or idealist might dislike. Anti-realist schools are often supposed to accept that truth is 'theory-relative.' The second is the thought that reality must be determinate—that at any point and whatever the infirmities of theory, there is a truth of fact of the matter whether. . . . This too can appear to be a thought that a quasi-realist must deny himself. The third, which is closely connected, is that an anti-realist can, or must, make a certain equation that to the rest of us with our realist propensities appears invalid. The equation I shall try to identify is made by denying a distinction between a regulative and a constitutive status for principles, in Kant's sense.[2] The Kantian distinction between maxims of procedure in our intellectual inquiries, on the one hand, and truths known about the world, on the other, may appear tenable only if we are real realists about the world. The particular way of taking certain principles (particularly that of bivalence, I shall argue), which is forced upon us if we deny the distinction, seems to be that adopted by Ramsey.[3] Eventually I shall conclude, although tentatively, that a competent quasi-realist can make as much sense of the distinction as the rest of us, so that here there is no distinct intellectual practice separating the quasi-realist from us. The fourth and currently the most discussed view is that realism is the best way of explaining our scientific success, that the existence of facts explains the way in which our knowledge expands and progresses: here an explanatory role seems to carry with it an ontological commitment which, again, is surely problematic to the quasi-realist. All these suggestions are current in the literature. Should we accept any of them? I shall start with the first.

Putnam says

> What does show that one understands the notion of truth realistically is one's acceptance of such statements as:

> (A) Venus might not have carbon dioxide in its atmosphere even though it follows from our theory that Venus has carbon dioxide in its atmosphere. and

2. I. Kant, *The Critique of Pure Reason*, the Appendix to the '*Transcendental Dialectic.*' The importance of this part of Kant in this connection was pointed out to me by E. J. Craig.

3. F. P. Ramsey, *The Foundations of Mathematics* (London: Routledge & Kegan Paul, 1931), especially 'Facts and Propositions', p. 153, and 'General Propositions and Causality', pp. 240 ff.

(B) A statement can be false even though it follows from our theory (or from our theory plus the set of true observation sentences).[4]

But as he himself remarks, the modal facts (A) and (B) are themselves commonsense facts about the world. They are consequences of our beliefs about the ways in which we gather knowledge or (to beg no questions) form opinion. In other words, when we describe to ourselves what makes us form opinion, we will see that (A) and (B) are true. But we cannot yet rely on anti-realist views about how we gather knowledge (or opinion) being different from anybody else's. It seems possible then that the quasi-realist will intone (A) and (B) but not regard them as denoting a sellout to the opposition. And if this is permissible, then they fail to provide the necessary litmus test. To come to understand whether it is permissible, let us consider a quasi-realist attempt on ethics and then on statements made with the subjunctive conditional.

I take an emotivist starting point: we see the meaning of moral utterances as essentially exhausted by their role in expressing the speaker's attitude. I have argued elsewhere that a surprising degree of quasi-realism is consistent with that view.[5] For example, it need not be surprising that moral utterances characteristically take an indicative form. Nor need we be worried by, for example, their appearance in the subordinate clauses of hypotheticals. 'If it is wrong to allow secondary picketing, then the government has been negligent' need not be regarded as hypothesizing the existence of a state of affairs, and we do not immediately declare ourselves to be realists by using it. An emotivist can perfectly well describe the role of such a conditional: it expresses a conviction that if one attitude is to be held then so must the other be held; this conviction may itself be moral, but there is nothing to prevent an emotivist from holding attitudes to the interrelations of attitudes and to the relation of attitude and belief. In fact, he must do so, for to hold this last kind of attitude is what it is to hold a moral standard, and these too gain expression in conditionals with the moral sentence on a subordinate clause: 'if lying causes harm, then it is wrong'. For this reason we should not accept Geach's test for whether we hold an indicative sentence to have a truth-condition, if this is itself a commitment to realism.[6] It fails to give the quasi-realist a proper run. But Putnam's test seems more compelling. What could an emotivist be up to in thinking: 'perhaps there is no such thing as a right to strike, even though it follows from my moral theory that there is'? Must he deny himself such thoughts? Is he to say that truth is 'theory-relative'?

4. H. Putnam, *Meaning and the Moral Sciences* (London: Routledge & Kegan Paul, 1978), p. 34.

5. See essay 7, 8, 9 and chapters 5 and 6 of *Spreading the Word* (Oxford: Clarendon Press, 1984). In recent years authority has been added to the position by Huw Price in *Facts and the Function of Truth* (Oxford: Blackwell, 1990), by Allan Gibbard in *Wise Choices, Apt Feelings* (Cambridge, Mass.: Harvard University Press, 1990), and by Paul Grice, whose routine for construction that he calls Humean Projection is identical with the line I endorse. See *The Conception of Value* (Oxford: Clarendon Press, 1991), esp. pp. 107–111.

6. P. Geach, 'Assertion', in *Philosophical Review*, 1965, pp. 449–65. Dummett expresses reservations about the test in *Frege* (London: Duckworth, 1973), pp. 348–53.

An analogue of Putnam's theory about how our opinion is gathered would be a view about the genesis of moral attitude. Let us suppose, as seems possible, that prominent in such a story we would find a capacity to sympathize, and an imaginative capacity to put oneself in another person's place or to see what it is like from his point of view. There would no doubt be other ingredients, but these illustrate my point. Suppose too that one recognizes that these capacities vary from person to person and time to time. Suppose finally that one admires those in whom they are boldly and finely developed. All these thoughts and attitudes are perfectly accessible to the emotivist. But they seem to give him all that is needed for a concept of an *improvement* or a *deterioration* in his own moral stance. He can go beyond saying 'I might change' to saying 'I might improve'. For he can back up that possibility by drawing the change as one which from his own standpoint he would admire. But now he has the concept of a possible flaw or failure in his present standards. A simple example would be the worry that a certain attitude, or the way in which one holds a certain attitude, is not so much the outcome of a proper use of imagination and sympathy, which one admires, but is the outcome, say, of various traditions or fears which one does not. Hume, of course, has been here before us:

> A man with a fever would not insist on his palate as able to decide concerning flavours; nor would one affected with the jaundice pretend to give a verdict with regard to colours. In each creature there is a sound and a defective state: and the former alone can be supposed to afford us a true standard of taste and sentiment. If, in the sound state of the organ, there be an entire or a considerable uniformity of sentiment among men, we may thence derive an idea of the perfect beauty. . . .[7]

So the quasi-realist can certainly possess the concept of an improved standpoint from which some attitude of his appears inept, and this, I suggest, is all that is needed to explain his adherence to the acceptance of the apparently realist claim: 'I might be wrong'. I think this view is confirmed if we ask: could one not work oneself into a state of doubting whether the capacities generating moral attitudes are themselves so very admirable? The answer is that one could, but that then the natural thing to say is that morality is all bunk and that there is no pressure toward objectivity for the quasi-realist to explain. For this kind of reason we should be skeptical of John Mackie's claim that we can detect a mistake about objectivity in our ordinary moral thought.[8] For at least as far as the modal test goes we can find ourselves holding fast to emotivism yet perfectly imitating the allegedly realist thought.

Another example comes from the suggestion, again from Mackie, that counterfactual claims are best regarded as condensed arguments. Once more we might advance the Putnam test: surely I ought to recognize that it *may* be false that if Mary had come to the party she would have gotten drunk, even

---

7. D. Hume, *Collected Essays*, 'Of the Standard of Taste'.

8. J. Mackie, *Ethics* (London: Penguin Books, 1977), chapter 1, section 7. See also essay 6 in this volume.

though I know that by far the best arguments, given what we know and the supposition that she came to the party, support the view that she got drunk? Again, the suggestion is that this makes sense only if we have a realistic conception of the truth or falsity of a counterfactual. But again the defense will be that anyone can and should recognize the partial nature of any given evidential basis of argument, including our own present one about Mary; that, once we recognize that, we can permit ourselves the concept of an improved standpoint from which our present argument takes account of only part of the facts; and that this gives us a sufficient grasp of the argument's fallibility to enable us, quasi-realistically, to say that it might be true that if she had come she would have stayed sober.

When Putnam talks of his modal criterion he admits that it is possible for an anti-realist to oppose truth-within-a-theory against truth as that which would be agreed upon in the limit of investigation. Peirce and Sellars are famous for this conception of truth, and in the remarks I have just made I may appear to be approaching it. But this is not yet certain. It may be that the notion of an improvement is *sufficient* to interpret remarks to the effect that my favorite theory may be wrong, but not itself sufficient to justify a notion of the limit of investigation; if these things are each so, then the notion of a limit cannot be necessary to interpret the fear that my favorite theory is wrong.

There are bad reasons for thinking that we must possess and justify the concept of a limit toward which improved investigation must converge. Perhaps we are misled into thinking that the notion of a limit to which improved opinion must converge is necessary if we are to believe that truth can be found or finally settled, rather than be forever fugitive. But the notion of a limit is not sufficient to remove that worry; it is itself forever fugitive. And it is not necessary. The possibility of an improvement is perfectly compatible with the existence of particular certainties. We can understand the concept of an improvement even if it on occasion remains a bare or notional possibility that such an improvement should result in modification of a particular component of our views—an attitude toward textbook examples of evil or the belief in the shape of the solar system, for instance. Truth can be achieved, and in many places it has been. The second motive to define a limit may be that it alone gives value or point to the search for knowledge. But, again, it is insufficient for that purpose: it would be no particular source of pride to know that my opinion was one on which all judges would converge in the long run, unless I had already attached value to the processes that would lead them to do so. For instance, it would be by itself no merit for a house to be one on which all modern architectural design would converge. This is the element that is unattractive in Peirce's definition of truth: unless there is a value in the processes leading to convergence, there is no merit in an opinion's being true in his sense.

We then get two different cases. It may be that the virtue in the processes can only be described as their tendency to act as midwives to the truth; that this is why we appreciate, say, simplicity, elegance, the drive to unified explanation, and so on. Or it may be, as in the moral case, that we can see the virtue in increases of sensitivity, sympathy, freedom from prejudice, and so on regardless of any belief that they are instrumental in advancing a cause of truth. If the latter is true, then we can accept Nietzsche's words:

> Can we remove the idea of a goal from the process and then affirm the
> process in spite of this?—This would be the case if something were attained
> at every moment within the processes.[9]

Or, in other words, the mere idea of improvement is after all sufficient to give content to our concepts of self-doubt and of fallibility and error.

But *is* it sufficient? One might object: it is all very well to say that an attitude M could appear inept to one with an improved use of faculties generating such attitudes (call the improved use F^*). But in itself it is consistent with the possibility of a further improved use of those faculties F^{**}, which reinstates M, and so on for evermore. It is only if one is entitled to a concept of convergence toward a limit, in which M is either vindicated or not, that the modal claim makes sense. In short, it is objected that we need more than the concept of an *improved* use of the relevant faculties. Perhaps we need the concept of a *perfect* or ultimate use of them, and this is something to which the emotivist has established no right. But is this argument cogent?

It is the final conclusion that is at fault. Suppose we are wondering whether a particular view is true. The argument may establish that we need the belief in a possible improvement of opinion to a point at which it is asserted to be true, or to be false, and *beyond* which any admirable change in theory merely serves to confirm that verdict. But this is a belief that a quasi-realist may defend. And it is *not* a belief that demands that we understand the concept of a perfect or ultimate use of the relevant faculties. It is of course true that the quasi-realist may take a pessimistic view of the ease of finding such points, or of our security in believing that we have ever found them. But so may a realist. Or he may optimistically regard a large core of opinion as already in that state, and express this by saying that certainty, or even knowledge, can be had. And like anybody else, he can take into account the empirical question of whether the history of a discipline shows an increasing core of solid fact, rendered more or less immune to successive revolutions of theory, or whether it shows little or no such tendency.[10]

Two issues remain to trouble us. One, which I discuss in section IV, is the possible claim that realism is the best explanation of such convergence in opinion as we do find. The other, which I discuss in section V, is the specter of indeterminacy, or the possibility of equally rational or admirable processes generating inconsistent or incommensurable opinion even in the face of all

---

9. F. W. Nietzsche, *The Will to Power*, § 55. I owe the reference to Gordon Bearn.

10. This notion has subsequently been explored under the title of 'superassertibility' by Crispin Wright, chapter 9 of *Realism, Meaning and Truth* (Oxford: Blackwell, 1987), pp. 295–302. I should have made it clearer that the notion of opinion, and of method, that I am using here is highly abstract. In any actual situation we might do as much as is possible to improve an actual opinion without ending up at the truth, because of contingent limitations on our position or resources of investigation.

possible evidence. This is an obvious threat to the realist, who must react either by shrinking the area of fact to a point below that at which the possibility arises or by allowing that truth transcends all possible ways of knowing about it. But it is equally a threat to the anti-realist. For I would summarize the results of this section by saying that they justify the quasi-realist in a conception of truth as a regulative ideal, or a *focus imaginarius* upon which the progress of opinion is sighted. A direct result of the indeterminacy theses would be that we are not entitled to that notion. I try to cope with this threat at the end of the essay.

The net result so far is that apart from raising these two problems there is nothing in the modal claims to distinguish realism. The quasi-realist need not wallow in the unattractive or incoherent idea of truth being 'relative to theory', and if we are to find what marks him off, we must turn elsewhere.

III

The second proposal for a distinguishing test for real as opposed to quasi-realism is the thought that there must be a fact of the matter whether p or whether not-p. This takes us into the area defined by Dummett, in which the law of bivalence, that every statement is true or false, is seen as something to which the anti-realist cannot owe any allegiance. The question must be whether, in pursuit of a theory, we might quite naturally find ourselves needing to be governed by bivalence regardless of any attitude toward the existence of facts or states of affairs that the statements of our theory describe.

Dummett himself talks as though 'true' and 'false' were in some sense derivative from a fundamental division of utterances into those which it is right to make and those which it is wrong to make; acceptable and unacceptable; correct and incorrect. This alone prompts the thought: Why should not such an apparently normative division be made and rigidly applied to every possible statement, regardless of any theory of what it is, if anything, that makes a statement come down on one side or the other? We are investigating the credentials of realism as such a theory, but the *purposes* of theory may be quite sufficient to drive us to think in terms of the universal application of such a division. To take an example (I shall take more later): the discipline of moralizing may be subject to the regulative constraint that everything is either permissible or impermissible, and this may be reflected as a commitment to bivalence, which an anti-realist would therefore wish. He will happily say 'it is either true that you did wrong or false that you did wrong' as a prelude to discussion without in the least regarding himself as subject to any unfortunate lapse.

The lapse would, perhaps, be unfortunate if it involved the suspect notion of completing an essentially uncompletable task. Thus, if we need an idea corresponding to God seeing the whole of the natural number series, or seeing a completed totality of argument surrounding a very indeterminate counterfactual, or seeing the whole of physical fact before him, and if without that idea bivalence is groundless, then we might agree that it rests on suspect imagery. And the most forceful examples where we want to query it concern infinities. It is not nearly so tempting, for example, to express anti-realism about other people's sensations in terms of doubts about bivalence applied to them, because it is manifestly true of *you* that you are in pain or false of you that you are. (Wittgenstein's *Investigations,* §352 seems to me to be counseling us not to *deny* this but to regard it as simply irrelevant, as not containing within itself the key to some understanding of the meaning of pain ascriptions. Nor, therefore, is it a sensible target for suspicion, either.) But as we saw in the last section, it is not generally true that to use a concept of truth, even to describe the result of infinite or indefinite or open-ended investigation, requires the paradoxical idea of a completion of such an investigation. It requires only the concept of a point beyond which no improved perspective demands a rejection of a given previous opinion. And it may well be that serious theorizing about an opinion requires faith in the existence of such a point: to agree that the revolutions of theory may endlessly bring in and out of favor a particular opinion is just to agree that the theory is worthless or an insufficient foundation for interest in that opinion. It would be equivalent to abandoning the area of discussion.

I do not intend these remarks as more than a preliminary orientation. They certainly do not remove the necessity to investigate the detailed arguments in the theory of meaning which Dummett uses to support his position.[11] Here I can only record my scepticism about those arguments: they all seem to me to trade upon an insufficiently analysed notion of what it is to manifest understanding of a proposition or, to put it another way, neglect of the intellectual powers of the audience *to whom* one is manifesting that understanding. This systematic neglect enables Dummett and his followers to generate the astonishing conclusion that one cannot communicate what one cannot be *observed* to communicate—as though one had to manifest understanding to the most wooden or passive of possible interpreters.[12] Nevertheless, I hope my remarks are sufficient to raise a general doubt about the use of bivalence as a litmus test.

Perhaps its most obvious application comes when we have the conception of a certain realm of discourse as grounded in another, but where the grounding can fail to support either a proposition or its negation. The clearest example arises in fiction, where remarks about, say, Hamlet are true in virtue of what is written in or supported by Shakespeare's texts. There may exist nothing at all in those texts to support the proposition that Hamlet had a baritone voice, nor that he had not. It would then seem wrong to suppose that such a proposition *must* be true or false, even if it might also be wrong ever to be sure that it will not turn out to be, as more subtle readings of the text are made. But

11. My own exploration of some relevant themes is 'Manifesting Realism' in *Midwest Studies in Philosophy* (Notre Dame, Ind.: University of Notre Dame Press, 1989).

12. M. Dummett, especially in 'The Philosophical Basis of Intuitionistic Logic', *Truth and Other Enigmas* (London: Duckworth, 1978), p. 217.

bivalence does not seem to be of so much use in discriminating the ontological commitment *within* an assertion of truth of falsity. For instance, we may be convinced that in some cases there may be nothing to make a counterfactual either true or false. But we may also think that when a counterfactual *is* true, a realist account of what makes it true—a realm of conditional facts, or powers or dispositions, or even nested possible worlds—is in order and makes a genuine opposition to anti-realism. The question is whether the quasi-realist should accept commitment to bivalence as something forced upon him by the discipline or practice of theorizing, and see no sellout to realism in so doing.

Since this strategy is crucial to quasi-realism, I shall follow it through in some detail, first as though a regulative-constitutive distinction can indeed be defended, and then in the light of skepticism about it. Corresponding to that distinction we can define two senses of commitment to bivalence in an area of discourse. Such a commitment may be expressed as:

(P_1) In all cases that arise we should say: either this assertion is true, or it is false.

or as:

(P_2) We should say: in all cases either an assertion is true, or it is false.

(P_1) is regulative, in a sense in which (P_2) is apparently not, because we might see that it should be adopted as a maxim governing practice, even if we do not accept (P_2). To take a particularly simple but illustrative example, it may be that the practical requirements on a judge demand that he should obey (P_1) where the area that the assertion concerns is within his jurisdiction (say: 'this contract is valid'). He must eventually find for one party and against the other, and the requirement regulates his attitude toward the possibilities. This is perfectly consistent with believing that there are likely to exist incompletenesses in the law, or areas of discretion in which truth would not attach to just one verdict. It will be part of the judge's discipline to think of truth as attaching to just one side, which it is his task to find, but it does not follow that in his reflections on legal reality he must suppose that this assumption has any foundation in the facts. The open-ended nature of the discipline may mean that it is never in practice possible to categorize a case as one in which it was neither true that the contract was valid, nor false that it was, in which case the maxim has an imperative force equivalent to 'keep looking for reasons'; its status is exactly like the drive to a complete and unitary explanation, which Kant saw as governing science.

Using the distinction between (P_1) and (P_2), we can thus give an account of the pressure that leads Dummett to distinguish between rejecting the law of bivalence, which is something he thinks we *should* do, and rejecting the principle of *tertium non datur,* which is something he thinks we should *not* do. In other words, he thinks we should reject (P_2), but that we should not hold that there are propositions that are neither true nor false. This way of putting it depends upon an intuitionist view of the quantifiers. But without that view, we can see the attraction of a position that is *not* committed to (P_2) in an area but that *is* committed to practice in any case as though (P_2) were true and that on principle refuses to consider an independent third status for an assertion. This position is just one that thinks that on principle we should not be satisfied with less than one of the polar verdicts and that we cannot ever regard ourselves as in a position to assert that something other than one of those is correct. And that seems compatible with a general doubt about whether there will always exist facts in virtue of which just one side is correct, and even with doubt about whether there must be the points we have defined, beyond which improvement always confirms one side or confirms the other.

Although it is a digression from my main theme, I should mention that this makes it quite wrong to argue, as Professor Dworkin sometimes seems to do, as though the practice of a bivalent or polar legal system implies confidence in its completeness, in the sense of its being sufficiently grounded to provide a right answer to each question.[13] It is particularly obvious that the constraints on legal decisions make the regulative principle necessary. The fact that their practice is so regulated licenses no inference to a need to use a group's political theory, nor for that matter to use a determinate moral reality, to fill the gaps in their law that may exist after we consider all the other actions they may have taken to create that law.

The quasi-realist seems, then, to be able to accept the regulative principle, (P_1), provided that the purposes of making judgement in the area in question can be seen to demand polar verdicts. But at this point the plot suddenly thickens. For given that this is so, given that his thought is to be governed on each occasion by the application of bivalence, what is to prevent the quasi-realist from voicing acceptance of (P_2)? If it is *on principle* to be his practice to think 'either this is true, or it is false', what is to stop him from thinking 'in all cases truth falls on one side, and falsity on the other'? It is quite natural to argue, as we have done, that something more *is* involved in accepting (P_2), but it might appear at this point that it is only a *realist* who should accept the distinction. A principle may be constitutive as opposed to regulative only if there is an area of fact whose constitution it purports to describe. We cannot just accept this contrast; it is the very one whose credentials we are querying. Thus we may think there is a distinction between accepting the maxim of inquiring into nature as though every event has a cause, on the one hand, and believing it to be the case that every event has a cause, on the other. But doesn't this very distinction stamp us as realists about cause? Once one has a view of a causal (or legal, conditional, moral, etc.) fact as a thing with a distinct ontological standing, perhaps one has a notion of it simply failing to exist in a given case, and this possibility would be there even if reason commands us to comport ourselves as though there were a truth of the matter to

13. R. Dworkin, 'No Right Answer', in *Law, Morality, and Society,* ed. P. Hacker and J. Raz (Oxford: Clarendon Press, 1977).

be found. But what can an anti-realist make of all this? Surely it would be natural for him to take it that the commitment to the maxim is all that can gain expression in the universal generalization ($[P_2]$, every event has a cause, etc.), which can therefore be bought quite cheaply.

It is interesting in this connection that Kant himself, according to Bennett, can be interpreted as sometimes betraying his own distinction.[14] For although his official position is that the antinomies arise only through mistaking a regulative for a constitutive principle, he seems to have no certain view of the distinction, nor of what it means to make this mistake. One view he may have held, again according to Bennett, is that given the sort of general principles that regulative principles are, there is simply no distinction between 'accepting the advice which (one of them) embodies, and believing that it is true as a matter of fact'. This is to equate acceptance of (P_1) and (P_2). If Kant did hold this, then the diagnosis of the antinomies becomes epistemological. We are supposed to be in danger of mistaking what it is that entitles us to accept one of them: it is not an insight into reality but the 'speculative interest of reason'. However, this is an unsatisfactory contrast for the reasons we have given. There are indeed images associated with the difference between things we take from the world and things we read into it. But we do not know what it is like to employ or misemploy these contrasting images. Kant, it is true, must have thought he could explain this, for only if we think that a principle is constitutive, which on this account means that it represents knowledge of the world, can we find ourselves involved in the antinomies. But since the steps in this diagnosis are so unclear, if we want to find a distinct employment for the different ways of taking a principle, such as bivalence, we cannot rely upon Kant as having paved the way.

Ramsey is probably the best known anti-realist to have equated such pairs as (P_1) and (P_2). I think we can also regard Dummett as seeing no significant difference between them. It explains why if we start with doubts about (P_2), as he tends to do, they become doubts about the policy adopted in (P_1), and abandoning that policy prevents us from using bivalence in the course of a logical proof and demands the intuitionist modification of logical practice. The curiosity in that route is, as I have already remarked, that starting by considering (P_2) and finding doubts about its truth seems appropriate to realists, who, thinking they have a distinct conception of the existence of states of affairs corresponding to the truth or falsity of a judgement, also fear a point beyond which the facts simply do not exist. But one would expect the anti-realist to take the reverse direction and, as it were, defuse bivalence rather than reject it. This point is supported if we favor the kind of explanations of meaning that Dummett adopts. If we learn what truth is in, for example, moral or legal contexts by observing and understanding the relevant practices and if we are kept on a very tight rein in any attempt to read more into those concepts than appears on the surface, then the concept of truth that emerges is at least governed by the commitment to (P_1). This is why Dummett has

14. J. Bennett, *Kant's Dialectic* (Cambridge: Cambridge University Press, 1974), esp. p. 276.

always seemed vulnerable (as he himself recognizes) to the counter that classical mathematical practice is part of what does give a real meaning to, in particular, the concept of an unsurveyable infinite totality. I do not think such a move is met by the reply that it involves a 'holism' that threatens to make any logical practice immune to criticism.[15] In areas where the whole question is what our understanding consists in and whether it is legitimate in any case, classical logical practice may play a part in locating it, even if in other areas we have a firm enough grasp of the truth conditions of various propositions for a given practice of inference to be vulnerable to criticism. In any case, and even if I am wrong about Dummett, it appears that hesitation about (P_2) is more a mark of the realist than of his alleged opponent.

If this is so, the prospects for a litmus test look bright, even if not in the way that might have been anticipated. For the quasi-realist becomes an embarrassingly enthusiastic mimic of traditional realist sentiments, and in his very zeal we might expect him to differ from a real realist. 'In every case of legal [moral, counterfactual, etc.] dispute', we hear him say, 'there is a truth of the matter falling on one and only one side'. The very fact that for him there is nothing more to accepting (P_2) than there is to accepting (P_1) entitles him to say such a thing; the fact that for us there is some doubt about (P_2) in spite of our defense of (P_1) shows that we are different from him. This seems to be the position if our quasi-realist accepts the regulative-constitutive equation, and, as we have seen, it is plausible to believe that the only motive for refusing to accept it is the belief in a real status for facts or states of affairs.

Let us keep with the legal example. Perhaps after all it was not fair to lumber the quasi-realist with Ramsey's equation. Clearly the question is whether the *only* motive for assenting to (P_1) yet not to (P_2) is a belief about the status of legal fact which marks a realist. If it is not, then the quasi-realist may be able to imitate whatever hesitancy about their relationship we ourselves feel. In the legal case the hesitancy about (P_2) arises from our theory of grounding: the belief that a group may not have *got up to* a question such as whether a particular kind of contract is valid, and that none of its lawmaking activities or beliefs covers the ease or determines a verdict. Now there should be nothing in that theory that offends an anti-realist. He can also see judgments of legal fact as answering entirely to questions about what the group has arranged (or to questions about what the group thinks is right). It would seem *strange* then if he cannot hesitate over (P_2) just as much as we do, since he shares the theory of grounding which *we* express by saying that there can be cases in which there is no fact of the matter, but which could be decided either way with equal propriety. Now in spite of the attraction of Ramsey's view, I think the quasi-realist can admit this, *even if* he knows that on principle we must proceed as though a decision one way or the other were always to be found. The escape is to remember the strategy used in the face of Putnam's test. There we removed the apparently metaphysical implications of the modal fact by seeing it as arising from *a natural view* of the nature of our

15. Dummett, *Truth and Other Enigmas*, pp. 218 ff.

moral capacities. The parallel here is to remove the similar implications of the thought that 'even if we must all proceed as though bivalence held, it is still not true that on every legal issue there must be a right answer' by seeing it as a natural reaction to the contingent and unproblematic belief that a society is unlikely to have thought of every eventuality. As with Putnam's test, the commitment supposed to identify realism can be seen as a reflection of a piece of knowledge available to anyone, whatever his philosophy. If this is right, then it is the regulative-constitutive equation that was at fault, but the legal quasi-realist can comfortably conform to ordinary thought.

Although I think this suggests the right solution in the legal case, others may be more complex. For often, as with the example of determinism or with moral or counterfactual reasoning, the theory of grounding is not so easy to sketch. I shall follow through the case of practical reasoning. Here there is no relatively straightforward theory of grounding leading one to any particular view on bivalence. Ramsey's equation seems to be more attractive. Given that on principle we must, once we are considering the question, suppose that either there is, for example, a right to strike or there is not, what else could we be doubting if we ask whether on every moral issue truth falls on one side and not the other? Must we not see this as a natural propositional reflection of our principle of procedure? What difference could there be between obeying the maxim and believing the generalization? The threat is that by seeing no difference the anti-realist purchases commitment to the generalization too cheaply, so that his very complacency serves to distinguish him from someone with a lively conception of moral fact and hence of its possible absence. But again the matter can be, as it were, naturalized. The brief remarks I made about the genesis of moral opinion suggest that there might exist persons in whom capacities of imagination and sympathy are equally well developed but to whom parts of our morality, or the structure of our practical reasoning, seem as unattractive as theirs might appear to us. The concept of improvement that we isolated gives us then no basis from which to claim that they are wrong and we are right. The concept of truth that did allow the anti-realist to think 'perhaps I am wrong' does not allow him, in the face of such a possibility, any confidence that they are wrong. (This is why the suspicion that a foreign culture is an actual example of this naturally and properly leads us to think that we are not entitled to interfere with it. All that is needed is the admirable [moral] opinion that we have a right to interfere only if the people's sensibilities are inferior to ours; lacking this justification, it is appropriate to live and let live, or perhaps live and learn.) This is Hume's case where 'there is such diversity in the internal frame or external situation as is entirely blameless on both sides'.[16]

Thus, a reflection of proper awareness of this possibility might be: 'on some moral issues, there may be no truth and no falsity of the matter'. Then the quasi-realist can permit himself this, even while admitting that we will, in practice, be committed to bivalence, and while admitting that there is never a

16. Hume, op. cit.

point at which we can be sure that there is no improved perspective, from which at most one side will appear to be in the right. As I showed above, this is consistent with holding that sometimes there is certainty: we are entitled to certainty that no improved perspective or equally admirable perspective could much differ from us in our most fundamental attitudes. It seems then that a quasi-realist can have just the right attitude to the general principle of bivalence, which he can agonize over with the best. His attitude does not betray him in the way Ramsey's test suggested it should.

I shall not pursue the other example where Ramsey's equation or the test of adherence to bivalence might seem to be promising methods for discriminating real from quasi-realism. There is no case in which they seem to me to work. The devices I have gone through in the examples of law and morals seem to me to be equally successful in other cases, such as those of counterfactuals, conditionals, and cause. The strategy is always to see bivalence as a natural commitment within a discipline, for more or less obvious reasons, and to see the hesitation which it may be natural to feel about indeterminate cases as available to anyone who reflects either on the theory of grounding of the facts in question or on facts about the capacities enabling us to form an opinion of them. So far, then, we have no distinctive range of thought or argument that marks off either side in the original debate. We still face the problem that the issue of whether there is a *casus belli* goes against both realists and their opponents.

IV

The final suggestion differs from the other three in a fundamental respect. Each of them seized upon a relatively formal aspect of our intellectual practice—our assent to a modal claim, to a logical principle, to a form in inference. This one seizes upon an attitude we may have toward our own opinion or knowledge. Of course, our problem all along has been to determine whether a distinctive attitude really is associated with realism, and so far we have nothing but images and similes to gesture toward it. And we know that these are not enough. The purpose of the fourth suggestion is to put, in place of these, a distinct explanatory view which, it is suggested, is available only to a real realist.

The explanatory view that may be adopted by the real realist, but not by the quasi-realist, is this:

> (RR)   It is because opinion is caused, perhaps indirectly, by the fact that *p*, that it converges upon *p*.

A quasi-realist will either deny convergence or seek some other explanation for it. Notice that he need not deny or worry over science's propensity to depart as little as possible from immediately preceding theory or to seek to incorporate as much as possible of that theory into new views. Such a propensity is quite naturally explicable in other ways and requires no mention of the states of affairs making a theory true. It does not even imply that those who are in this way conservative themselves believe in convergence.

Using (*RR*) to define a realist versus anti-realist debate accords with many intuitions. A quasi-realist can mimic our formal practice with the concept of truth or fact. But surely he cannot give the facts any role in explaining our practice. To do so is to embrace their real distinct existence, or so it might seem. Again, the most famous examples of plausible anti-realism can be seen exactly as attempts to deny (*RR*) for the areas in question. Hume explains our opinion of the existence of causal connections not by our exposure to the fact of such connections but only by our exposure to regular successions of events. His main point is not to propound an 'analysis' in terms of regular succession, for he can consistently suppose the mind to inject an ingredient into its conception of causation, which is lacking from the mere idea of regular succession. His point is that there is no explanatory role for any fact beyond that of regular succession in accounting for our opinion; exposure to such succession, given natural propensities in the mind, is sufficient. Moral realism is refuted in the same way. Here, indeed, it is not just that explanation of our opinion and practice *can* be had simply in terms of natural perceptions, given our desires and needs; it is also that there are obstacles to any other explanation. A distinct explanatory mechanism, starting with a distinct moral fact, would not be reconcilable with the requirement that its output be logically supervenient on other facts, known in other ways.[17] This contrasts with all other explanatory mechanisms; our knowledge of color, for instance, is explained in ways that leave it *logically* possible that everything else should remain as it is, but color change.

In spite of these attractive examples, the test has one flaw, which suggests that although (*RR*) may be something that a realist must say, it may be possible to say it without being a realist. It would make a necessary but not sufficient condition of realism. The problem arises if a test is made to determine whether our attitude is one of real realism or not, when the opinion or theory that we are testing *itself* makes causal and explanatory claims. For example, suppose that upon exposure to a given experimental result a physicist comes to hold that it shows the decay of a radioactive atom: he holds that it is the decay that causes the result. To deny that is simply to abandon the physics. But now we have what Putnam calls internal realism as something integral to the theoretical practice, and there is simply no issue of dissent from (*RR*). There is no option to 'speak with the vulgar' by assenting to the theory, but to 'think with the learned' by denying its *own* causal and explanatory claims about the genesis of our opinion. If thinking with the learned *is* an option, it is not identified by adherence to (*RR*), and we are back on the depressing project of finding another way to determine whether there would be such a thing as assenting to (*RR*) but with that special attitude that marks one's assent as realistic or not.

17. See essay 5 for more on Hume, and essay 6 for more on the supervenience argument.

I do not think (as Putnam seems to) that this makes (RR) metaphysically useless. It maintains its role as a necessary commitment of a realist. What it does suggest is that it has no part to play in detecting a realistic attitude toward the most interesting theories: those such as our view of the external world, or the existence of the past or other minds, where to hold the theory is *ipso facto* to hold a certain explanation of our opinions. Not all theories have this kind of involvement with their own metatheory; first-order morals does not, for instance.

Yet taking (RR) as even a necessary commitment of a realist has one unattractive consequence. This is that states of affairs are only allowed if they play a part in causing opinion. Now, it seems at least possible that one would wish to be a realist about mathematics yet deny that mathematical reality is a cause of anything. Or one might wish to have the same attitude toward the reality of both the future and the past yet believe that only past states of affairs play a causal role in generating opinion. This is the obverse of the preceding trouble: (RR) is too generous to states of affairs that enter causal theories and too dismissive of the others. But it is, so far, our only prospect for the required hurdle. We might indeed try to do without mention of causation. We could offer the test of whether a theorist agrees that it is the existence of the fact that p that explains convergence of opinion upon p, leaving it unsettled whether the explanation is causal. May I say that it is the fact that two plus two equals four that explains the convergence of mathematical opinion upon the belief that it does? Or that it is the fact that people do have the right to strike that explains convergence of moral opinion upon the belief that they do? One imagines that the quasi-realist may take license to say such a thing; it will not be clear why he should not, even if it seems a particularly bold appropriation of realist vocabulary. What may be clearer is that a quasi-realist must think that there is in principle a better or more illuminating explanation of this convergence, if he remains true to his anti-realist starting point. A recognizably Humean picture of causation may go so far as to say 'it is the fact that A causes B that explains convergence of opinion that it does'. Once the mind has 'spread itself on the world', it also regards itself as reading things off the world it has projected.[18] But a Humean also holds that there is a more illuminating and economical account of the convergence. The suggestion arises that a realist, as opposed to a quasi-realist, must hold that the best, most illuminating, and economical explanation of our opinion that p must cite the state of affairs that p. Yet put like this we lose touch with the original instincts behind the positions. Might I not believe in the real, distinct existence of the external world, yet accept that the most illuminating and economical explanation of my believing in it mentions only the coherence of my experience? Or believe in your mental states, yet accept that my opinions are explained merely by exposure to your behavior? What counts as the best explanation depends on our purposes in grading explanations. It is not obvious why realism must take a very strong stand on that.

---

18. This is why any reliance on the mere feeling of objectivity, to confirm realism about, e.g., values or obligations, is pointless. See also essay 7.

V

It seems, then, that the best use to make of convergence is not as a phenomenon of which a realist has a superior explanation but rather as one in which he alone has faith. If we use our faculties properly, and reality is determinate, then surely opinion must converge. Equally, if it is decided that even in the long run opinion need not converge, then to many people this is a powerful argument—perhaps *the* powerful argument—for denying that there is a reality which that opinion is purporting to describe. Hence the importance of indeterminacy theses: it is pessimism about convergence even in the long run, even in the face of reasoning admirably from all 'actual and possible experience',—the pessimism that is expressed in indeterminacy theses—that is the most potent enemy of belief in a determinate world of moral, or psychological, or semantic, or even physical states of affairs. The lemma is that scepticism must be intolerable: truth cannot be transcendental, incapable of being achieved by any extension of reason and experience; to imagine a truth is to have some grasp of what it would be to know it. If this is accepted, then the response to indeterminacy is to deny realism. Yet indeterminacy also threatens the existence of the points that on any suggestion give the antirealist a decent surrogate for truth.

But the contemporary confidence placed in such indeterminacy theses is quite improper. For such a thesis cannot be an argument against pursuing our moral, psychological, semantic, or physical theory as best we can. And then reason does not beg but commands us to treat a conflict of theories as a sufficient proof that the truth has not yet become known; reason is not free to order a pursuit of one systematic truth and at the same time tell us that many such unities may be equally in conformity with the world; it cannot in such a way 'run counter to its own vocation'.[19] To theorize, to assert, at all is to disbelieve indeterminacy theses. Nor is reason here at war with itself, telling us to have confidence on the one hand in our correctness, or at least in our progress toward correctness, and on the other hand in the diversity of equally good opinion that could exist. For it is not observation and reason that tell a theorist in a proper discipline that he is unlikely to be effectively pursuing the truth. It is pessimism or loss of faith among philosophers in the value of science or particular sciences; the loss of the will to believe. Indeterminacy theses are a symptom of our disenchantments, not the products of our reasoning powers: here at least it is true that the owl of Minerva takes wing only with the coming of the night. In saying this, of course, I do not deny that a history composed mainly of worthless and persistent dispute may be a good reason for abandoning a particular discipline or domain of inquiry. But neither physics, nor commonsense psychology, nor the science of interpretation and translation, nor even perhaps ethics, reveals such a history. And in a case that does, induction from that history rather than the bare possibility declared in

19. Kant, *Critique,* A 651/B 679.

an indeterminacy thesis would motivate us to reject the inquiry. The boot is on the other foot: rejection of an inquiry gains expression in indeterminacy theses. It is topsy-turvy to use fear of indeterminacy to motive a modification of an otherwise rational theoretical practice.

At last, then, can we say that the quasi-realist achieves his goal? No talk of knowledge or certainty, reason or truth, no belief in the convergence of opinion; no proper contrasts between theory and reality nor between regulative and constitutive seem beyond his grasp. The realist never intended to say more than this, nor should the anti-realist have settled for less. It is true that in getting to this point our sympathies were engaged mainly on behalf of the anti-realist: I would be inclined to say that realism, in the disputed cases of morals, conditionals, counterfactuals, or mathematics, can be worth defending only in an interpretation that makes it uncontroversial. Could this be retorted upon anti-realism, from a standpoint of differing initial sympathies? If this is so, philosophy indeed leaves everything as it is. Yet there may be reason to sympathize more with the anti-realist. He has earned the concepts associated with objectivity, while his opponent merely stole them; he has founded our practices on known facts about human capacities, while his opponent invents more. Economy matters. And perhaps we feel less guilt about what we have earned—we are less vulnerable to scepticism. Or could it be that, after all, the old pictures and metaphors are important to the disputes, it mattering to us not just that people talk, behave, and practise intellectually in the same way that we do but also that they are haunted by the same ghosts?

2

Knowledge, Truth, and Reliability

The philosophy of knowledge and truth is dominated by two metaphors: that of a system of elements that correspond with particular facts in the world, and that of a raft or boat of interconnected judgements, where no element corresponds to anything external. The choice is between realism and a leaning towards a correspondence theory of truth, on the one hand, and holism, verging towards idealism, with a coherence theory of truth, on the other: the pyramid and the raft.[1] These images have complementary attractions, but neither provides a solid, stable metaphor whereby we can understand how truth connects us to the world and its facts. The first prompts the charge of foundationalism, or of the myth that we can step outside our best beliefs to estimate how well they correspond with the facts. And the second seems to disconnect the web of belief from proper control by the world, so falling into idealism or relativism. In spite of rearguard actions it is the second image that dominates philosophy today.[2] I shall have little to say to oppose that movement of opinion. But if we follow it, does it leave our concept of knowledge where we would like it to be, or does it demand, as some have maintained, abandoning the concept as the remnant of a classical but outmoded self-image?

Suppose we come to sympathize with the image of the raft through mistrust of 'the given', or through a Humean or Wittgensteinian naturalism. These make it possible to argue that we must retreat to a coherence theory of truth, and that this in turn gives a ready answer to scepticism. It brings truth down to the natural earth. We learn, on this account, that knowledge and truth are concepts that *we* use, in *our* world. Philosophies may have falsely promised us a real correspondence, in which facts impinged upon us unfiltered by our own concepts, or our own ways of classifying, or our own perception of similarities. But by seeing how false that promise is, we learn not to fall into scepticism when it is unfulfilled. We learn to feel comfortable claiming truth and knowledge within our own terms, and not to respect an alleged demand—which could be met only by an *a priori* argument—that those terms be given any foundation beyond the fact that we find them natural. I hesitate to ascribe this position to any one writer. Its characteristic

1. Ernest Sosa, 'The Raft and The Pyramid', *Midwest Studies in Philosophy* (Minneapolis: University of Minnesota Press, 1980).
2. The image seems to me common to Quine, Goodman, Putnam, Rorty, and many others.

combination of empirical (or internal) realism and transcendental idealism (or conventionalism) is, I should have thought, almost orthodox, and writers who oppose it are self-consciously fighting not just one author, but a whole tide of thought.

But somehow it doesn't seem to work as it should. For it is at least equally easy to feel that the combination destroys any right to regard ourselves as knowing—really knowing—what the world is like. This is obvious if the transcendental part—the part gestured at by thought experiments involving bent classifications, Goodman's predicates, or what are generally called the 'rule-following considerations'—issues in a kind of conventionalism. But it is nearly as bad if it issues only in a kind of naturalism. The fear that nature, whatever it may be, has grown as not so much with a mirror as with a veil or a distorting lens is not easy to exorcise. So who is right: those who find a comfortable answer to scepticism in the combination, or those who fear that it plays into the hands of the sceptic? Or are we to suppose that part of the package is a new, appropriate, concept of knowledge that itself supersedes any that permits scepticism to remain a real challenge?

My object in this essay is to approach these problems using a natural, everyday requirement of reliability. I shall start by placing that in the relatively pedestrian context of the problems with the analysis of knowledge, on which there have been so many recent assaults. The position I arrive at is a version of 'reliabilism', but one that ought not to be opposed by theories of knowledge that insist upon justification. The reason for this combination emerges in due course. The position affords an argument against scepticism, but it would be idle to pretend that it 'refutes' it: indeed, it offers a diagnosis of the permanent appeal of sceptical thoughts. This diagnosis does not depend upon a profound internal versus external reading of the sceptical concept of knowledge.[3] It sees the sceptic, certainly, as introducing a new context of inquiry, but it offers no straightforward way of dismissing that context either as illegitimate, or as involving concepts that are new and different from any in everyday use.

So I start with some observations about the concept—our concept—of knowledge. These ought to help us to see just what that concept involves, and therefore to understand how much survives the drift towards idealism.

I

The classical problem is to find the condition that adds to

> p is true
>
> and
>
> x believes p

3. Barry Stroud, *The Significance of Philosophical Scepticism* (Oxford: Clarendon Press, 1984), especially chapters 3, 4, and 5. The distinction, of course, derives from Kant and Carnap.

to give sufficient conditions for: *x* knows *p*. The standard suggestions include refinements of the requirement that *x* be justified, refinements of the requirement that *x* be situated reliably with respect to the fact that *p*, and versions of the requirement that *x*'s belief be not defeasible (meaning that further evidence ought merely to confirm the belief that *p*).[4] The chase for more-accurate versions of these conditions, and the rivalry that can develop between them, has been called Gettier's salt mine, and it can enslave us against our will. So we might start by asking why we should need an extra condition in the first place.

If the epistemic concepts earn an honest living, they must form a natural intellectual kind. Even if some multipart analysis accurately matched our judgements in difficult cases, we would still need to ask why we are interested in just *that* set of conditions. (A similar question arises when we propose complex psychological conditions for meaning, and in many other areas.) To see ourselves and each other as knowing things is to be important. But how can it be important to organize our lives around one complex of conditions rather than another? We need a role for the epistemic concepts, and the role that seems most natural is that of ranking and selecting titles to respect. We have to pick up our beliefs about the world from our senses and from each other. So we need a vocabulary to settle whether our sources are ones that themselves properly indicate the truth. This is a natural need, and it gives us the natural intellectual kind in which to place our epistemic verdicts.

So consider a subject who believes correctly that something is so. His being right gives him one title to correctness. Why isn't this enough? Because his position may not deserve respect as the *kind* of position from which one may safely accept information. A subject may believe truly by exercising defective propensities to form belief on occasions on which, by luck, he is right, or he may believe truly by exercising proper propensities, but when it is an admixture of luck, not those proper propensities, which is responsible for his being right. Given this reply, the two concepts that are anathema to each other are *knowing* and being in an unreliable, defective state, or using an unreliable propensity to form belief (the close analogy, of course, is with the agent who does the best thing by accident, but has not exercised virtue in doing so). It is natural to detect two components in a subject's epistemic virtue on an occasion. There is the amount of information at his disposal, which may be more or less adequate, and there is what he makes of it, which may involve more or less rationality, or more or less reliable propensities to use information to deliver belief. These two components need not march in step, of course. But for the moment the difficulties this could cause, and indeed the difficulties of effecting the division in any accurate way, need not concern us.

Let us say that someone in a certain state of information, and exhibiting some disposition to form belief, also possesses a degree of soundness, or

4. K. Lehrer and T. Paxson, 'Knowledge: Undefeated Justified True Belief', in *Essays on Knowledge and Justification,* ed. G. Pappas and M. Swain (Ithaca: Cornell University Press, 1978).

solidity as a source of information. We can call this a degree of value to a would-be information receiver, or IRV (information-receiver value). If this is the normative dimension, as it were, in which to place knowledge, then we would expect to be able to put the following principle down:

> *The Mirv/Pirv principle:* If two subjects each believe truly that p, the one cannot know, when the other does not, unless the former is in a position with at least as much IRV as the latter.

Since the role of the epistemic concepts is to rank sources of information, then if one source knows when another does not, it cannot be that the belief of the knowing subject is unsafe in ways that give him less IRV than the subject who does not know. This is a principle concerning belief. So there is a caveat to enter in the use of this principle: we might call it the Matilda caveat. Matilda 'told such dreadful lies it made one Gasp and Stretch One's Eyes'. When she eventually shouted that the house was on fire, 'they only answered "Little Liar" '.[5] Her *effective* IRV had disappeared with her credibility, but for all that, she knew that the house was on fire. To use the Mirv/Pirv principle properly, we must say that Matilda's report actually *had* IRV, because the belief to which it gave voice was solid, even if rational hearers might have doubted it. Ultimately, of course, we are to be concerned with problems of our own reliability, and problems of insincerity in report, or of difficulties of interpretation of our own langauge, do not arise.

The Mirv/Pirv principle comes initially as a constraint upon the missing clause in the proposals for defining knowledge, and I suggest that it guides many verdicts in contested cases. To give a simple example, consider the subject who forms a true belief well enough, but who should have done something else as well, albeit the extra thing would in fact have misled him (he believes, rightly and reliably, that the president has been assassinated, but others who did believe this have by now read the usually reliable morning papers, which deny it . . .). If we are reluctant to describe him as the only person who knows that the president has been assassinated, this is because someone who has done the extra thing has done the kind of thing that makes them a better source of information on this kind of issue.

The principle serves to rule out even powerful and plausible attempts to analyse knowledge. More important, I suggest that it explains our unease with these attempts: our sense that somewhere things are going to go wrong for them. Consider, for example, the conditional analysis of Dretske and Nozick.[6] This finds the missing clause in the two conditionals:

> If p, then x believes that p
>
> If $-p$, then it is not the case that x would believe that p.

5. Hilaire Belloc, *Cautionary Tales for Children, Selected Cautionary Verses* (London, Penguin Books, 1964), p. 32.

6. F. Dretske, 'Conclusive Reason', *Australasian Journal of Philosophy*, 1971; R. Nozick, *Philosophical Explanations* (New York: Oxford University Press, 1981), chapter 3.

The idea is that x's believing should be sensitive to the truth, so that x should be what Nozick felicitously calls 'tracking' the truth. This idea is a good one: sensitivity to truth is indeed the kind of solidity we are looking for. But its realization in the two conditionals is not so good. For a little thought will show that a person could satisfy them through possession of a defect, compared with someone else who does not satisfy them, and that, for some audiences, this defect could make him a worse informant on the kind of case in point. I shall illustrate this by a case, but it is the principle that matters.

Two freshmen, Mirv and Pirv, see the Professor in a car. They each believe, truly, that the Professor is in his own car, and they are each good at telling, in general, when propositions like this are true. Usually, for instance, when the Professor is not in his own car he drives very insecurely, and each freshman would judge that he was in an unfamiliar car. On this occasion, however, the Professor might easily not have been in his car, which was due for a service, and had he not been, the garage would have lent him a model of the same type, which would thus have been familiar to him. The only difference is that the garage model has a sticker of Mickey Mouse on the back, but the Professor wouldn't have minded that—indeed, he used to have such a sticker himself, let us say. However, Pirv comes from a puritanical and benighted part of the country, and could not bring himself to believe that anyone as distinguished as a Professor would ever own a vehicle with such a sticker. Mirv knows more about the world. But on this occasion his knowledge stands him in bad stead, by Nozick's lights. For through it he fails to satisfy the fourth condition: had the Professor not been in his own car, Mirv would have continued to believe that he was. Whereas Pirv, through ignorance and misinformation, ends up satisfying the fourth condition: had the Professor not been in his own car, Pirv would not have believed that he was. So Dretske-Nozick would have us saying that Pirv knew the Professor to be in his own car, whereas Mirv did not. This flouts the principle, for Mirv is a better source of information about such things than Pirv. He is a better-tuned car-ownership detector, using the right parts of a better system of belief about such matters.

To say that Mirv is more solid on this *kind* of issue raises the question, noticed by Goldman,[7] of how we should classify 'kinds' of proposition in order to evaluate the reliability in informants (for reliability is inevitably reliability in a *kind* of circumstance). And it raises the question of the antecedent position of the receiver of information. Someone who knows much more about a situation may rightly take information from a source who is generally worse, or who on an occasion is behaving quite irrationally, just because he knows that for particular reasons obtaining in this case, the irrationality is not involved in the informant's situation.

Compare acting as a second to a careless rock-climber, who ties the belaying knots in such a way that they might be safe, or they might not, and does not check the difference. Was the weekend safe? God might have said so:

7. Alvin Goldman, 'What is Justified Belief', in *Justification and Knowledge,* ed. G. Pappas (Dordrecht: Reidel, 1979).

perhaps all the knots the leader tied that weekend were luckily secure. His defect made no difference to your actual security. Swayed by this, we could say that, ontologically (as it were), the weekend was really safe. But you mightn't think so: there is a good sense in which you cannot ever be safe behind such a person: you oughtn't to feel safe just because you don't know, any more than the leader does, what he is actually doing (suppose his defect only comes to light after the weekend is over: breaking out in a cold sweat, you correctly say 'what a dreadful risk I took!').

The issues here are close to those that arise in any application of statistical or dispositional facts to the singular case. Is it safe to bet on Fred surviving to the age of eighty? He is a sedentary, bran-eating, slender academic . . . We rapidly come to the narrowest class with weighty statistics, yet there is no end to Fred's peculiar combination of properties. Suppose he does survive: it does not follow that it was safe to bet on it. It may have been safe for God to bet on it, just as it is safe for him to follow the unsafe leader, or safe for him to ignore an exercise of irrationality on occasions when it is not in fact affecting the truth of his belief. But it would not have been safe for us.

In the case of chance, we suppose that the weightier the reference class, the better: we say that when we know more, so narrowing the kind in which to put the single case, we have a better estimate, or are nearer to the 'true' probability. This is easy to explain in pragmatic terms: someone using the fuller information wins when betting with someone who can use only the lesser. But because the standard epistemic position is not one in which the receiver is the more knowledgeable party, we do not tailor the epistemic verdict to cases in the same way. We are not, as it were, concerned with how God might pick up information from a source: we are concerned with how *we* might. Thus we take into account causal factors that render a source more or less sound. But if flaws are involved then it is *not* the weightier position, which happens to know that the flaws are not responsible for the truth of the infor- mant's belief, that counts. There are cases in the literature which, in effect, trade on this problem. Suppose, for instance, that Pirv is told by the President of the Royal Society that the dark room he is about to enter contains a perfect holographic illusion of a vase. Suppose that, irrationally, he takes no notice of that information and believes because of a cursory glance that there is a vase there anyhow. He doesn't know that there is a vase there, even if there was (for the President was lying, deceived, or just failing to remember that the machine was off). God, or anyone knowing this much more, could safely accept Pirv's word that there is a vase there, because they know enough to discount the exercise of irrationality in the way he came by his belief on this occasion. But someone knowing no more and no less than Pirv does could not accept his word. After the operations described, Pirv is not a solid source on the matter for that person. Since the normal epistemic circumstance—the one that makes channels of information important—is that of wanting to know whether to accept information from a better-placed source, it is not these ontologically superior positions that count. Pirv did not know that there was a vase on this occasion, because there is a kind of thing he is doing—forming beliefs irrationally—and it is dangerous to accept beliefs when this kind of thing is done. Someone knowing more can say that there is a narrower kind of thing that Pirv is doing—forming beliefs irrationally when the facts are such that the irrationality does not matter—and that it *is* safe to accept beliefs when this is true. But this superior epistemic position does not dictate our verdict: the concept of knowledge would lose its utility if it did. (There is a telling temptation to go soft on this: if someone's stoutly maintained, but irrational, belief turns out to be true, we sometimes let this success alone dictate the epistemic verdict: 'funny how Beryl knew all along that Fred was . . .'. The success makes us think that there must have been a reliable kind of belief formation involved, even if it would have taken a superior being to know what it was. Compare: 'so it *was* a safe bet after all', which is usually said when it wasn't.)

Puzzle cases and disputes arise because there are different ways of classing the kinds of case in which someone is reliable: there is the question of whether the informant is in some normal causal relationship to the facts; whether he is reliable over similar kinds of case; whether he would be justified or rational in believing himself to be reliable; and finally whether his background beliefs (which in turn may be rational or not) affect his standing as an informant. And all these can come apart. If any of them fails, then there will be a way of regarding the informant that makes him into a dangerous source of belief: there will be a kind of case over which he does badly. But it would be optimistic to expect principles to settle verdicts in such cases. Because of the 'holism' of belief, there is no principled limit to the flaws that may result in our being in kinds of states that are unreliable, and disqualify us from acceptability as a source. In particular, we will always be vulnerable, if we try to isolate some natural relation that a subject has to the fact that *p*, to cases in which he is nevertheless playing Pirv to someone else's Mirv, although the other person does not bear this particular relation to the fact. This explains the progress found constantly in the literature: someone proposes a natural relation to the facts sufficient for a subject to know that *p*, and someone comes along in a generally better state (he has read the newspapers, etc.) but who through the extra virtue, making him more solid on some *kind* of case, misses the title.

II

Solidity as an authority is a matter of degree. But knowledge, on the face of it, is not. So how much solidity do we want: can knowledge tolerate chances of being wrong, or even the bare possibility of being wrong? To put the question in a closely related way, if a situation leaves it as much as barely or logically possible that one is playing Pirv to a non-knowing Mirv, does that destroy one's title? The most important initial division in the continuum of possible improvements comes where a subject is sufficiently solid to be an authority, and where any improvement in his state, or dispositions, would simply serve to sustain his belief. We could relativize this, if the possibility of different recipients with different standpoints is worrying, and say that a recipient should allow someone to know something only when anything that from his standpoint counts as an improvement merely tends to confirm the original belief. This suggestion is of course close to the familiar nondefeasibility condition on knowledge. It differs only in that I put the notion of an improvement to the fore: it does not go without saying that increases in true belief, even when reasonably used, count as improvements on a particular kind of case. There also is a caution implied in putting the question as one of whether improvements *would* sustain the verdict. It will not be to the point to go in for thought experiments in which improvements that could overthrow the belief *could* happen, but in the actual world wouldn't. This kind of stability is sometimes easily achieved. Suppose I recognize my friend by a glance at his face. I know who he is, not because weightier investigations could not be made, but because they would simply confirm what I already know. Of course, anyone whose position is as solid as this cannot play the role of Pirv to someone else's Mirv: anyone in a genuinely improved position will also know.

If we used this as a cutoff point beyond which there is knowledge, we would be importing what Armstrong called an 'external' element into the notion of knowledge.[8] I could be in an informational state, and using dispositions sufficiently well, yet not know something because, as a matter of fact, the world does afford further evidence which would undermine proper confidence in the belief. And I could be in the same state and using the same intellectual dispositions, when, on the contrary, any improvement would confirm my belief; in that case, on this proposal, I know. People are uneasy with this for several reasons: notably, it seems to cut the concept off from any problems of objective justification, and it affords altogether too cheap a victory over scepticism (provided the way we are plugged into the world *is* all right, then we know, and the sceptic cannot show that it is *not* all right).

These worries may lead us to divide the continuum higher up. At the highest point, it is logically impossible that the subject should be playing Pirv to another's Mirv. The gap between the subject's informational state and the fact believed to obtain is to be closed altogether: it is to be logically impossible that the state should exist, yet the fact not obtain. This exorcises all external elements with a vengeance: it tries to ensure that there is no element of luck, or even contingency, in the true believer's title to knowledge. Traditionally it requires that we shrink the area of fact known, potentially down to an entirely immediate given, just as the parallel motivation in the theory of ethics shrinks the exercise of real virtue down from the chancy, external world where good intentions can go wrong, to the safe realm of acts of will.

Alternatively, we might close the gap by expanding our conception of the state the believer has got himself into. The states we get into, and because of which we form beliefs, would be ones that we could not (logically) have been in had there not been a spatially extended, temporally ordered world, contain-

---

8. D. M. Armstrong, *Belief, Truth and Knowledge* (Cambridge: Cambridge University Press, 1973), p. 157.

ing the other minds, numbers, possibilities, values, and so forth, in which we all believe.

What then is our best conception of the informational states whereby we come to believe things, or to know them? Let us say that informational states, in virtue of which we form beliefs, divide into two. There are those which, as a matter of necessity, could not have existed had not the beliefs formed in the light of them been true. We can call these guaranteeing states. And there are those that do not meet this strong condition. Call these indicative states. The question in front of us is whether only guaranteeing states sustain knowledge, or whether indicative states, provided the external circumstances are right, can also do so. If we can happily see ourselves as largely possessed of guaranteeing states, the looming problems of scepticism might be thought to disappear. But can we? The 'informational state' in virtue of which a system is disposed to absorb something new can include any part of the deposit of previous times, as well as anything that could at all be thought of in terms of the impact of the immediate environment. We think of ourselves, of course, as getting into such states as a result of our physical positions and surroundings, the operations of our senses, and the use of concepts, beliefs, and expectations which, be it because of reason (unlikely) or nature (most likely) or convention (let us hope not), we find ourselves forming. These banalities do nothing to support a 'guaranteeing' conception of informational states. On the contrary, they conjure up painful images of the ways in which the world responsible for our states might not conform to the way we end up taking it to be.

A guaranteeing conception of our epistemic positions is given spurious support by a spatial metaphor. (Kant charged that it was a mistake of Locke to sensualize the understanding.[9] I think it is at least as important a mistake, and symptomatic of the same error, to spatialize it.) Thus we are often asked to pronounce upon what is manifest, disclosed, given, embraced, internal to our subjectivity, or accessible *in* our experience, or to settle issues of what we really confront or access, or what we can penetrate to, or what is transparent or open to us. The glassy blob of the mind reaches out to encompass (embrace, contain) facts, and knowledge stops at its boundaries. But then the blob cannot stop short of embracing all kinds of states of the world, for if it did it would be confined to embracing mental proxies of them, and these would so intervene that it could never know the world, nor even understand a vocabulary purporting to describe it. Whole issues, such as the realist/anti-realist confrontation as it is framed by Dummett and his commentators, are importantly distorted (or sustained) by this spatial metaphor.[10]

9. I. Kant, *The Critique of Pure Reason*, A271/B327.

10. J. McDowell, 'Criteria, Defeasibility and Knowledge', *Proceedings of the British Academy*, 1982, pp. 455–79. The damage of the spatial metaphor is seen explicitly in McDowell's argument against his opponents: he believes that if the mind does not embrace past states of affairs, the sensations of others, and so on, then it must embrace only proxies of them 'interposing' between us and them (pp. 472–74), giving rise to insuperable problems of understanding and knowledge. In the theory of thought this is the analogy of the position that we either see physical

To escape this error we might query whether the very notion of a 'state' plays us false here. Because of the interpenetration of theory and experience, and because of the temporal growth of the system of belief, it can seem artificial to analyze a response to new experience by thinking of informational states at all. Certainly, if we do, there is little better to say about them than that our state is one of being in an external world, surrounded by other minds, possessing a long past, and so on. The promise of a quick victory over the sceptic appears again, for our basic characterization of ourselves still entails that we live in the kind of world that he finds it possible to doubt. Unfortunately, we cannot retreat into dogmatism so comfortably. It will always seem a fragile response to scepticism to refuse to set the problem up in the first place—little better than announcing that the mind embraces the relevant facts after all. So perhaps the best thing *is* to get away from the spatial image as radically as possible, and this includes avoiding the protean notion of an informational state. Although I sympathize with this, the notion of a state does not have to be taken spatially, and there is no better general term to sum up the fact that at given times we are in positions (states) in which we form beliefs, and that the ways in which we do this, and their strengths and weaknesses, merit investigation.

The lowest place, as it were, at which we could claim knowledge was where our state was what I called 'sufficiently' authoritative—meaning that it made a reliable source on the kind of matter in question—and where it was actually stable. This is a possible resting point: it depends, I think, on whether we read the condition as strong enough to mean that there is no chance, or virtually no chance, or only a chance that can be dismissed, of our being wrong. Read without that understanding, the condition that belief be true, authoritative, and stable would be far too weak for knowledge. For it could coexist with a good chance of being wrong. But where we have a good chance of being wrong, we are in a kind of state that makes us unsafe sources of information. So we must read the condition so that it excludes any significant chance of being wrong. And this is the point on which I want to focus in what follows.

If we said that knowledge can exist provided there is no significant chance, or real chance, of error, then we can defend a title to knowledge in the face of an open, acknowledged possibility that the world might not be as we have come to take it to be. The sceptic is apt to complain that when this is all we have, then for all we know, things are not as we take them to be. But this is wrong, for the whole issue is whether on the contrary we can know something through being in a state that is indicative, although not guaranteeing, provided the external condition is satisfied: that we are authoritative, and the

---

objects 'directly', or we see proxies of them—sense data. Austin attacks this dichotomy at the beginning of *Sense and Sensibility:* 'In philosophy it is often a good policy, when one member of a putative pair falls under suspicion, to view the more innocuous seeming party suspiciously as well' (p. 4). Dummett's 'challenge' to realists, to explain how things that are not 'manifest' can be understood, which McDowell meets by the strategy of making more and more of the world 'manifest', seems to me to be much better met by entirely refusing the terms of discussion.

state is stable. My suggestion is that the sceptic gets away with this bare citing of possibility because of the normal implicature that we cite a possibility only if we also give it some chance of being realized. It is normally only to the point to cite possibilities that are 'relevant', and this is exactly what relevance is. So it can seem that mere possibility left open defeats knowledge, whereas in fact it may be that it doesn't, but that only real chance of error does. The externalist has it that we know because we are right, and because any improvement in our position would just confirm that we are, and because we exercise sufficient soundness to be a proper source of information on such a matter. Once this is so, the sceptical possibility can, as we naturally say, be ignored. It is the relation of this position to scepticism which I now wish to expose. For I hold that, although it may seem to cheapen knowledge, in fact it does considerable justice to sceptical doubt: it offers an explanation of the deep roots of those doubts, and it may enable us to place them even within the context of a general sympathy with 'anti-realism' or 'internalism'.

III

Reliabilists and justificationists think of themselves as forming two different camps. Now, one element in the view I have been defending supports each of them. Reliabilists appear right, in so far as the soundness we require of informants need not imply any self-consciousness on their part. They could be like good instruments, and be deemed to know things just by being rightly tuned to the truth. But although an informant need not have views about his own reliability, we need to do so. It is always a weakness to have no account of why an informant should be thought to be yielding the truth. It generates a bad *kind* of state to be in. And when our own title is in doubt, externalism does not help us unless we can properly see ourselves as reliable. To put the matter in terms of section I, when we are unable to see ourselves as forming belief reliably but nevertheless form it all the same, we are doing a kind of thing that destroys our title as authorities. We cannot suppose that the mere fact of our being right removes this taint, any more than Pirv in the Royal Society case escapes the charge of irrationality or gains the title of knowledge, just because on that occasion his belief was true.

The power of scepticism is quite underrated if it is seen as merely a forlorn attempt to shake confidence by invoking possibilities that can normally be ignored. Its real power comes with the absence of any sense of our own reliability. Crucially, we have a sense of there being a large number of possible worlds that appear as ours has done, but that contain scientific realities unlike ours, skew distributions of other minds, large elements of counterinductive truth, and so on. We might try to say, blankly, that we know that these possibilities are not realized. But can we regard ourselves as reliable on just this *kind* of point? How could I have a better than chance propensity to tell when sceptical possibilities are realized? I can do nothing more than rehearse the very considerations governing belief; if they leave open a space of possibilities, then there is nothing more to say about which possibility is realized, and nothing more than chance to determine whether I am right. Suppose that there is, for example, only one kind of world in which other minds distribute as I naturally take them to do, but many where they distribute in other, partial, ways (no other minds, ones attaching only to . . . , etc.). Suppose that there is only one kind of world that is well behaved with respect to my inductive regularities, but many that deviate in their different ways. If evidence leaves the possibility of such mavericks, how can I be better than chance at telling when they are realized?

I think it is wrong, or at least misleading, to suggest, as Barry Stroud does, that scepticism here involves taking an 'external' view of our knowledge, as opposed to an 'internal' one in which such questions do not arise.[11] At least, this is wrong if it leaves open a ready way of suggesting that the external standpoint is optional, or even that it makes no sense. And the usual metaphor of externality is dangerous in this respect. All that really happens is that normal ('internal') assessments of knowledge go on against a background of assumptions of general reliability—the generally truth-yielding nature of our procedures. But the *same* demand that there is no chance of error can be made of the procedures, even if it is only in philosophical moments that we think of raising it. Thus when Stroud diagnoses Moore as unable to hear the philosophical sceptic's question in the intended way, it is unnecessary, on my view, to suppose that there is a special, transcendental inquiry or context that Moore cannot enter. Rather, there is a univocal query—about the chance of being wrong—that is normally answered against a background of common-sense theory (and is so answered by Moore), but that can equally be raised about the procedures used in creating and sustaining that theory, or the principles upon which it seems to depend (induction, trust in the senses, etc.). I suggest that this better explains Moore's peculiarity, which is that he seems blind to the point at which any grasp of our own reliability fails us. It also gives us reason to be cautious with the metaphor of externality, for it is not as if the philosophical undertaking demands quite different tools or perspectives from the everyday assessments of chance: it just has a different topic. Similarly, our everyday financial standing may be settled by considering the credit we have at the bank; this does not rule out a sensible query about the financial standing of the bank itself.

To show the query to be improper, in the philosophical case, we would need to show that the relevant notion of 'chance' is inapplicable, when we consider what we call the 'chance' of the sceptical possibility being realized. Unless this is done, an airy assertion that there is no chance of things being like that will sound quite unsupportable, and the sceptic wins. There is only one way that I can see of respecting the possibilities but avoiding scepticism, and that is to improve the theory of truth, for modal assertions and for assertions of chance. We have to say that although there is a real space of possibilities, as the sceptic maintains, there is also no chance that any of those

11. Stroud, op. cit., chapter 4.

possibilities are realized: it is known that we are not unreliable. Are there doctrines in the theory of truth that enable us to say this?

IV

The sovereign proposal is to think of truth as some kind of construct out of our conception of the virtues of methods of inquiry and the consequences to which they lead. 'Realism', in at least one good use of the term in this connexion, thinks that we can explain the virtues of method by certifying that they are midwives to truth; 'anti-realism' sees truth as that which ought to be established, or would be established, by the best use of the best methods. The one philosophy sees the virtues of right reasoning as a precipitate from an antecedent notion of truth, and the other reverses the priority.

It is often suggested that the anti-realist direction makes for an easy dismissal of scepticism.[12] For instance, it is supposed that on the philosophy of the later Wittgenstein, our procedures and practices of ascribing pain to other people, together perhaps with the consequences we attach to such a description, determine what we mean by it. This leaves it open, it is supposed, that such ascriptions are defeasible, so that any finite evidence for the ascription can lead us to be wrong. But it is then supposed that the priority of assertibility conditions forbids us from making sense of the sceptical possibility that the world contains no consciousnesses but mine (or those of some favoured subgroup including me): stoicism, pretence, and so forth can exist only against a background of general correctness, and this correctness is supposedly guaranteed by the criterial, practice-governed conception of meaning. I find this obscure. The practice of attributing mental states to others leaves open the possibility of error in the face of finite behavioural evidence. If it leaves this possibility in each case, then even if it does not follow that it may do so in every case, still we must ask why it does *not* do so in the conjunction of individual cases—that is, as regards the world in general. The concept of virtue attached to such ascriptions may leave us quite unable to reject this bare possibility. Rejecting possibilities of error may be no part of the practice, and not entailed by the virtues or ways of reasoning that are integral to the practice.

There is another way of raising this problem. Once more, suppose we sympathize with the anti-realist priorities. Then I might be confident that the best possible system of belief about other people, formed by the most virtuous dispositions, should contain the belief that others see colours as I do. But it might *also* contain the proposition that it is possible, in spite of any of the evidence I have or could have, that they do not. It would contain this proposition if the idealized increases in information or virtue do not rule it out, or, in other words, if even a supremely virtuous cognitive agent, using information

12. For a typical assessment see Colin McGinn, 'An A Priori Argument for Realism', *Journal of Philosophy,* 1979. But see K. Winkler, 'Scepticism and Anti-Realism', *Mind,* 1985.

as admirably as possible, should still allow or respect that possibility. And perhaps he should, for perhaps none of the increases in virtue that we can imagine to ourselves would ever lead to a proper refusal to countenance it. And in that case, it will be correct to allow it—on the anti-realist's own construction, it exists. In the same way it would be correct to allow Horatio's possibility, that there may be truths which would lie forever outside our comprehension. It would be the part of virtue to admit as much. Even God would be right to doubt the guaranteed nature of what is, nevertheless, his own knowledge; it would be part of the 'final best science' (this is a truth that the final best science could not acknowledge, disproving that definition of truth, or alternatively disproving the existence of both a final best science and truth).

It will be evident then that I differ from both Putnam and Dummett in holding that the question of priority does not coincide with the issue of whether we can understand 'verification-transcendent' truth-conditions, or in other words, allow sceptical possibilities. To that, both my sides reply that we do so in so far as our practices contain as a legitimate element an enterprise of wondering whether, in the largest respects, the world is as we take it to be. This result accords with what I call 'quasi-realism', for it is another respect in which someone who approves of the anti-realist instinct over the priority of truth or virtue still ends up with the very thoughts that the realist took for his own. In turn, the suggestion casts doubt on whether we really have an issue between global anti-realism and global realism, for if each side ought to end up following the same practice, there may be nothing to dispute over. But I would urge that sometimes, in local areas, we can make sense of the divergence of priorities and even award the victory to one side. For instance, I believe that in the theory of morality, or modality, or chance, there is an advantage to the side that starts off by regarding method as fundamental. Moral and modal propositions and, most notably for present purposes, those about chance, gain their identity, and the identity of the concept of truth to associate with them, from their place in a two-sided practice—that of coming to them, on the one hand, and of using them to guide the conduct of life and thought, on the other. It is therefore particularly attractive not to try to explain their role by postulating an antecedent notion of truth to which they answer—a layer of facts about distributions of possible worlds, or of chances defined over them—but rather to explain what is to count as truth in their case by thinking of what it is for them to perform their role successfully. One might try to say that this is always the case, so that if these propositions are better understood this way, any proposition would be. But this does not follow. These propositions may find their place in steering us around the facts, as it were, rather than in describing new layers of fact, but it would not follow that it is possible for all propositions to be like that. And these propositions (and those of mathematics) share peculiarities that contrast them with others from the outset, and that make the notion of truth so problematic in their case. They have no recognized epistemology, and their truth is not the starting point of any serious explanatory theory of our experience. So perhaps they do not serve as an attractive model for a general debate.[13]

So far, things look even better for scepticism (again, remember that this is in spite of the relatively weak account of knowledge I am offering). The sceptic is not silenced by the highly abstract changeover from, say, 'metaphysical' to 'internal' realism (anyone who has ever taken the problem of induction seriously may wonder why he should have been thought to be put out by such a charge). But we are owed an account of the relevant assessment of chances, and here there is scope for a response. Suppose we put some fledgling, anti-realist thoughts about the truth about chance alongside the position in which we now find scepticism. Hume denied, rightly, that any durable good can come of extreme, or Cartesian, scepticism. But that is not the same as saying that durable good comes from disallowing the sceptical possibility. We have already urged that virtue may involve respecting general possibilities of error. But we have not yet seen that the virtuous method of forming belief about our reliability should leave us any sense of a real chance that those possibilites are realized. Can we hold the line against scepticism at just this point?

Scepticism invites us to 'stand back' and think of a logical space of possibilities, many of which accord with our evidence, but only one of which accords with the way we take actuality to be. When we do this we are apt to think that there is a real probability measure, meaning that some such possibilities have a better chance of realization than others. On an anti-realist line about chances, matters are the other way round: proper confidence itself determines what we are to say about any such measure. The ordinary considerations in favour of induction, other minds, and so on, have to give us a title to say that there is simply no chance (or dismissably small chance) of things not being as we take them to be.

Saying that there is no such chance will sound like saying that we know that a particular ticket will not win a lottery—something that is usually false, since we can have no authority on whether such an event will happen. But it is not like that. For there we have a kind of thing that does happen (individual tickets win) and our reliability over whether it is going to happen in a particular case cannot be better than chance. Here we know the chances—they supervene upon natural facts in our world. But nobody has any right to say that massive undetectable facts according with sceptical suggestions are the kinds of thing that happen: we are not flying in the face of an actual empirical kind with a given frequency of realization when we deny them any chance at all.

There is now an opening for the sceptic to ascend a level. What I am doing, he will say, is denying that there is a real 'trans-world' probability metric giving his possibilities a real chance of being actual. I am saying that chances are properly to be evaluated in the actual world, in which, I suppose,

13. Of course, essay 1 explores the possibility of generalizing. Essays 3 and 4 go into more detail about modal judgement and judgements of chance, respectively.

things like massive undetectable failures in the mentality of others, or failures of induction or memory, do not happen. But, he will complain, this is not sufficient. Suppose that the idea of trans-world chances is incoherent. Perhaps if we knew enough about the world, we could also say that there was no chance of bizarre possibilities being realized: *contingently* the chance of his possibilities is actually zero. But his claim is precisely that we do not know this much about the world: for all we know about contingent reality, the chances of (say) there being no other minds, or of the world conforming to Good-manesque bent predictions, is quite high. In other words, denying a trans-world metric on chance is not enough, for it still leaves us ignorant of the distribution of chances at our actual world. And, the sceptic continues, the chances may be pretty unfavourable.

I think this admits of no refutation, for it depends entirely upon who bears the onus of proof. If the sceptic's task were to prove that there is a chance of massive falsity in commonsense beliefs, then he fails. We can maintain, in one breath, both our normal beliefs and the corresponding title to knowledge, since there is no chance of their being false. The sceptic cannot dislodge us, since he cannot prove the existence of the disturbing, knowledge-defeating chances. On the other hand, we cannot prove against him that the relevant chances are zero—not without helping ourselves to the very contingent knowledge that he wishes to deny us.

(Perhaps there is more to be said here along these lines. I have been emphasizing the continuity between discussion of scepticism and everyday discussion of chance, albeit that the latter is heavily constrained, empirically, in a way that the former is not. Now someone might urge that this continuity is spurious: it hides the crucial difference that in the ordinary case we have *procedures* for assessing chances, but all of these, as we have seen, can be disallowed by the sceptic. Can this be used to urge that the position and the debate are indeed taking words out of the contexts in which alone they make sense, so restoring suspicion of the whole issue? I do not think so. For example, wrestling inductive procedures into an anti-sceptical shape is a perfectly recognizable activity, bound by the same rules of chance, the same kinds of arguments, that hold sway elsewhere. The trouble is that it tends not to issue in anything that impresses the sceptic.)

So all we are left with to urge against him is a refusal to accept the onus. Allowing chances, like allowing possibilities, is something that we do. Sometimes, when the actual world affords stable frequencies, doing it well is heavily constrained by natural facts. But when we think of the chance of the world being as sceptical thoughts suggest it might be, we are not so constrained. Then, we are only aiming to express the proper, best way in which confidence is to follow on from the use of the ordinary evidence in favour of commonsense beliefs. So we can properly allow the bare sceptical possibility and properly disallow any chance whatsoever that it is realized. Durable good comes from both policies. Neither flies in the face of a real, trans-world distribution of possibilities or chances, for there is no such thing.

V

This may not be a particularly glorious victory over the sceptic. I do not mind this—indeed, like Stroud, I would mind more if the victory had been gained by the kind of dismissal that refuses to acknowledge the deep legitimacy of sceptical worries. The deep roots of scepticism lie in the need to see ourselves as reliable over as many matters as possible. It is not the use of inappropriate standards, nor shifting to a different and doubtful external point of view, nor yet accepting an unbearably strong cutoff point for knowledge, which leads us to focus upon our most general methods and ask for their reliability. It is, as we might put it, not trying to hover above our boat with a new and unfamiliar set of a priori instruments of inspection; it is just using the same instruments on the same boat, but on a little-visited and basic part of its structure. Unless this is seen, scepticism will not have had an adequate answer. For that very reason the problem of knowledge, as we have inherited it, or the very subject of epistemology, should not be seen as the parochial, historical outcome of mistaken conceptions of mind or experience. It may produce stunted side-shoots because of such mistakes, but when they are lopped off the problem of knowledge remains. For, given problems such as those of observation and induction, we have no stable way of imagining a body of knowledge that protects all the exposed surfaces where the title to reliability is vulnerable and needs questioning, protecting, reconceiving.

Wittgenstein imagined that the philosopher was like a therapist whose task was to put problems finally to rest and to cure us of being bewitched by them. So we are told to stop, to shut off lines of inquiry, not to find things puzzling nor to seek explanations. This is intellectual suicide. If the philosopher is indeed like a therapist, then his task is to insist upon constant exercise: the inspection of the bindings, the exposed surfaces, the possibilities and chances, the dangerous places where a sense of our own reliability takes no place in the rest of our scheme of things.

3

Morals and Modals

I. Introduction

Conclusions properly drawn must be true when the premises are; events must unfold in accordance with natural law; people must obey the moral laws. Why do we find it so tricky to give a satisfactory philosophy of these necessities? In the first part of this essay, I suggest that it is because we have a rooted, and inadequate, conception of what is needed to establish such an understanding. This conception dominates the philosophy of modality, just as it does other areas, but it makes a genuine advance in understanding impossible. The diagnosis here is quite simple, but it is not so simple to disentangle ourselves from its influence, and to become practised with tools that are better suited to the problem.

What would a philosophical theory of logical, natural, or moral necessity be? By making judgements of necessity we say things, and these things are true or false. Perplexity arises because we think there must therefore be something which *makes* them so, but we cannot quite imagine or understand what this is. Nor do we understand how we know about whatever this is: we do not understand our own must-detecting faculty. Elucidating the truth-condition, and our access to it, is *the* goal of philosophy, to which its techniques and controversies are essentially directed. Not only is this so, but surely it has to be so, for the philosophical itch is that of finding the nature of the facts strange and incomprehensible, of failing to imagine what could make true the relevant judgements. The problem is that of the fugitive fact, and the solution is to capture the nature of the fact in an intelligible way. This answer would tell us what such truths *consist in:* the answer would be obtained by establishing the *truth-conditions* for such judgements. It would give us an 'account' of the states of affairs in which their truth consists, or of what it is that *makes* them true. The account would have an explanatory role as well: fully established, it would explain why it is necessary that twice two is four, or how it can be that natural laws exist, or why we must be nice to one another. The most direct technique would be analysis, showing, it might be hoped, that the judgements are made true by some state of affairs relatively familiar and unproblematic (by whichever standards prompted the perplexity). Another technique would be more aggressive: to suggest that the concepts involved in

52

the judgements are defective and due for replacement, so that the fugitive 'facts' were not really such, not really worth chasing after all.

Within this conception of the philosopher's quest, there is room for disagreement over detail—for instance, whether the description of the state of affairs finally fixed upon as making true the original modal judgement has to be synonymous with that judgement; whether one range of arguments or another succeeds in showing some concepts to be defective, or over what would count as an admissible reduction class for the modal claims. It is to the twists of this detail that we naturally turn when faced with the embarrassment that the head-on search for truth-conditions for modal assertions has turned up nothing at all promising. Where else is there to turn? For rejecting the problem is too much like ignoring the itch.

The modal concepts need a theory. But I do not think that they need or could possibly get a theory described, however remotely, in the terms suggested so far. In other words, I think that we have completely misinterpreted the *kind* of solution the philosophical problem needs. This may seem surprising, for I posed the problem and the kind of solution in terms deliberately bland—the kind of terms that would go quite unremarked as a preface to discussions. But I shall argue that they mislead us, and that a better way to approach the matter exists.

II. The Quasi-Realist Alternative

Let us call the direct approach the truth-conditions approach. Here is a dilemma that attends it, and that I shall exhibit quite generally for moral, natural, or logical necessity. If we ask what makes it so that A must be the case, we may be given a local proof, a proof of A from B. This is satisfactory if we already understand why B must be so (if our topic is logical necessity, there is also the status of the proof to consider). But if our concern is with the whole area, then we turn to scrutinize that understanding. Attention shifts to why B must be the case, for our philosophical concern is with necessity in general, not with A in particular. Suppose an eventual answer cites some truth F, and so takes the form: '$\Box A$ because F'. ('Because' here is taken to include constitutive variants: the truth that $\Box A$ consists in F, is made so by F, etc.)

Now, either F will claim just that something *is* so, or it will claim that something *must* be so. If the latter, there is no problem about the *form* of the explanation, for one necessity can well explain another. But, as we have seen, there will be the same bad residual 'must': the advance will be representable as 'if we see why *this* must be so, we can now see why *that* must be as well'. And there is no escape from the overall problem that way. Suppose instead that F just cites that something *is* so. If whatever it is does not *have to be* so, then there is strong pressure to feel that the original necessity has not been explained or identified, so much as undermined. For example, suppose a theorist claims that twice two must be four because of a linguistic convention, or that particles must attract each other thus because of some ongoing cosmic setup, or that we must be nice to one another because that is what God wants. Suppose it is denied that there is any residual necessity, that we *must* make just those conventions, that laws determine the consequences and continuation of the cosmic setup, or that God's wants ought to be heeded. Then in each case there is a principled difficulty about seeing how the kind of fact cited could institute or be responsible for the necessity. This is because the explanation, if good, would undermine the original modal status: if that's all there is to it, then twice two does not have to be four, particles don't have to attract each other, and we don't have to be nice to each other, even if it would be unwise not to. This is, of course, a generalization of the famous Euthyphro dilemma. Either the explanandum shares the modal status of the original, and leaves us dissatisfied, or it does not, and leaves us equally dissatisfied.

So why is the truth-conditional approach so dominant—why is this dilemma not universally recognized? Partly at least because it leaves room for work. The circle can be virtuous and explanatory. In other words, there is no embargo on finding theories of the form '$\Box p$ because F' where F stays *within* the modal sphere in question—'$\Box p$ because in all possible worlds p'; '$\Box p$ because there is a relation of necessitation between certain universals', or '$\Box p$ because $\sim p$ is impermissible', for example. Such theories can and do uncover important aspects of our thought: making the logic of modality intelligible, for instance. But from the standpoint that prompts the original problem—the dissatisfaction with the fugitive fact—by staying within the family in question, the analyses cannot do more than postpone things. Of course, at one level this is perfectly well known, for everyone agrees that it is one thing to have a possible-worlds approach to modality, for example, and quite another to have a theory of the metaphysics or epistemology of the things we say about possible worlds.

The poor prospects of the truth-conditional approach would be easier to tolerate if there were another approach. Fortunately, there is. The truth-conditional approach looks for another way of characterizing the 'layer of reality' that makes true modal utterances. The alternative starts (and, I shall urge, ends) with our making of those utterances: the thing we intend by insisting upon a necessity or allowing a possibility. We could call it a 'conceptual role' or even a 'use' approach, but neither title is quite happy, for neither makes plain the contrast with truth-conditional approaches that is needed. The conceptual role of use of a modal idiom might be just that of expressing belief in the fugitive layer of fact! If the best that can be said about our commitments is that they are those of people who believe in particular distributions of possibilities—logical, natural, or moral—then we are silenced again. But this may not be the best that there is to say: we can approach the commitments differently.

This alternative is familiar under the heading of projectivism (or sometimes, which is worse, 'noncognitivism') in ethics: this is why in setting the scene I have includes moral musts. It has been pioneered in the philosophy of natural law by Ramsey and Ayer, and my aim is to made it a recognized option in the metaphysics of modality.

Notice that this is *not* the alternative of saying that 'there are no laws of nature' (or no possible worlds), any more than projective theory of ethics involves the 'eccentric' view that there are no obligations. Instead, this approach gives its own account of what it is to say that there *are,* and, if the commitments are valuable, *why it is correct* to do so. The account has two stages. It starts with a theory of the mental state expressed by commitments in the area in question: the habits, dispositions, attitudes they serve to express. It is these that are voiced when we express such commitments in the ordinary mode: when we say that there exists this possibility, that necessity, this obligation. The second stage (which I called quasi-realism) explains on this basis the propositional behaviour of the commitments—the reason why they become objects of doubt or knowledge, probability, truth, or falsity. The aim is to see these propositions as constructions that stand at a needed point in our cognitive lives—they are the objects to be discussed, rejected, or improved upon when the habits, dispositions, or attitudes need discussion, rejection, or improvement. Their truth corresponds to correctness in these mental states, by whichever standards they have to meet. Such a theory only collapses back into realism if we are reduced to saying that correctness in modal or moral judgement is simply representing the modal or moral facts as they are. But according to my direction of theorizing, we can do better than that, and what we can do involves no irreducible appeal to a moral or modal reality. It is here that the opposition to realism lies, although I shall try to make it plain that the interest of the approach remains even if, as I also believe, there is no very coherent realism for it to be 'anti'.

It is tempting to characterize this anti-realism as an 'as-if' philosophy: we talk as if there exist moral or modal facts, when in fact there are none. This makes it sound as though, according to this approach, some *error* of expression or thought is involved in such talk—for we talk as if *p,* when in fact *p* is false. This consequence of an as-if characterization is especially tempting when we remember other areas in philosophy where such projections are supposed to be responsible for mistakes we make—pathetic fallacies, for instance. Spinoza, for example, believed that what we take to be contingency in the world is merely a reflection of our ignorance, and this diagnoses a *mistaken* belief that we have.[1] Most writers on projective theories of morals and modals mention Hume, of course, and then continue with some version of this:

> Hume's view is that we then make a mistake: we project something essentially 'inner' onto the external world, and come to the mistaken belief that the concept of necessity we have applies to propositions in virtue of the objective properties of ideas and, as a consequence of this, we mistakenly believe that modal judgements can be true or false.[2]

There is excuse for the interpretation, for Hume is not as clear as one might wish. The first passage in which he appeals to the metaphor of the mind

---

1. Spinoza, *The Ethics,* Part II, Prop. XLIV. I owe the reference to Al McKay.
2. Graeme Forbes, *The Metaphysics of Modality* (Oxford: Oxford University Press, 1985), p. 218.

spreading itself on external objects is in the context of diagnosing a mistake—the 'contrary bias' that leads people to ridicule his philosophy of causation, to suppose that, by making the 'efficacy of causes lie in the determination of the mind', Hume is reversing the order of nature.[3] But this does not show Hume admitting that, by talking of causes (or obligations or necessary relations of ideas) as we do, we make any mistake. The theorist may misinterpret the nature of our judgements, their origins, and the standards that justify them. But the first-order user of the vocabulary makes no mistake: there is decisive evidence that Hume thought he made none. This is clearest in the moral case, of course, for Hume's philosophy of natural belief is infected by the background problem that our belief in the external world in any case involves a mistake—natural and inevitable propensities of the mind that must lead us to falsehood. But there is no further mistake involved in 'causalizing'—in finding causal order in the world we take ourselves to inhabit—any more than there is in moralizing as a reaction to characters and actions.

Hume's position is best explained by separating two different applications of the notion of projection. In the one use (which I prefer) we 'project' when we use the ordinary propositional expressions of our commitments, saying that there is this causal relation, that natural law, this other obligation. In the other we project only when we adopt, as philosophers, a particular 'realist' explanation of the sphere in question. This is a quite different thing, and it is what gave the contrary bias of which Hume is indeed complaining. The space between the two uses is easily missed, especially by philosophers coming with a realist bias in the first place. For they will be only too apt to suppose that the ordinary use has, as it were, done their work for them, so that a realist ontology is the only possible explanation of the first-order usage. But this, in Hume's view and mine, is not so. And this view must be given a hearing.

How can a projective theory accompany the view that no mistake is made in talking as we do? We would only make a mistake in saying that things ought to be done, or have to be so, if *these judgements have a false content.* But if their content arises as the projectivist + quasi-realist story maintains, they do not. No error occurs in moralizing or modalizing, even if philosophers have mistaken the kind of content these judgements have. Error exists only if there is a real *mismatch* between the truth about the nature of the claims, and their content, or what we make them do in our theories of things. But no mismatch exists in the thought that '1 + 1 = 2', that bees cause stings, and so on.

Quite apart from the implication that we make some kind of mistake, an as-if description of the theory makes it appear inadequate to the depth of our commitments. It looks refutable by a kind of phenomenological reminder of the strength of our belief that there *really are* possibilities, necessities, etc. Don't you believe that there *really are* natural laws, iron proofs, genuine duties? It is not just that we talk as if there are such things! But a quasi-realist will properly say: it is not simply that we think and behave *as if* there are

3. David Hume, *A Treatise on Human Nature,* Book I, Pt. III, Sec. XIV, ed. L. A. Selby Bigge (Oxford: Oxford University Press), p. 167.

necessities: there *are*. And we are right to think that there are. The commitment, and its correct expression, should not be in question.

What then is the mistake in describing such a philosophy as holding that 'we talk as if there are necessities when really *there are none*'? It is the failure to notice that the quasi-realist need allow no sense to what follows the 'as if' *except* one in which it is true. And conversely, he need allow no sense to the contrasting proposition in which it in turn is true. He no more need allow such sense than (say) one holding Locke's theory of colour need accept the view that we talk as if there are colours, when there are actually none. This is doubly incorrect, because nothing in the Lockean view forces us to allow any sense to 'there are colours' except one in which it is true; conversely, neither need it permit a sense to 'there are actually none' in which *that* is true. Theorists *may* construct such senses: for instance, a sense in which 'there are colours' implies that colours do some work of physical explanation, or could be apprehended by more than one sense, and of course the Lockean will deny anything implying such a thing. But if the words retain an uncorrupted, English, sense, then the Lockean, and similarly the quasi-realist, holds not just that we talk and think as if there are . . . , but that there are.[4]

Then the objection might be rephrased: according to the quasi-realist, we think and talk as if there were real moral and modal *facts,* but there are none. However, this too, although it points in a better direction, invites misunderstanding. It cannot stand as an accurate diagnosis of a position, for the word 'fact' also has an uncorrupted English sense: it is a fact that there are colours, and there are many facts about them. Certainly, there is a sense in which the quasi-realist is opposed to giving an ontological status to moral and modal facts, but according to him you cannot read off this status just from the nature of our commitments, their modes of expression, or their genuine place in our thinking, even if that thinking goes on invoking talk of facts. The appearance tempts philosophers to ontological quests, puzzles, and errors, but the mistake lies with the theorist who succumbs to the temptation.

Of what then is the quasi-realist suspicious? We can see now how the problem of characterizing either realism or anti-realism becomes acute. Suppose, for instance, we are satisfied with a quasi-realist construction of modality: we see what we are doing when we modalize, and why talking of possibilities or possible worlds is a legitimate form for these commitments to take. So when a writer such as Lewis maintains the irreducible nature of the modal idiom and expresses his commitments in that idiom, he is doing no more than a quasi-realist allows. What *more* does he intend by deeming himself a realist? How is there to be space, as it were, for some extra content in any such claim? One might see illegitimate content: if a theorist held that alternative possibilities are real in the sense that we can find them in space or hold them responsible for causing various results, or if he took comfort in the thought that he could model apprehension of possibilities upon sensory apprehension. But

4. I do not have a fixed opinion on what Locke himself thought about the existence of colour. See P.A. Boghossian and J.D. Velleman, 'Colour as a Secondary Quality', *Mind*, 1989.

theorists, including Lewis, call themselves modal realists without accepting any such theses. It begins to look as if there is no way of framing an ontological or metaphysical opposition. Saying 'I believe in possible worlds, and I am (or: I am not) a realist about them' would amount to no more than accepting irreducible modal idioms, and in either form the last conjunct is quite idle.

Universal harmony is desirable, but it does not come quite so cheaply. The difficulty of characterizing the dispute shows that it is up to anyone who takes pride in announcing himself in this style to make sure that the last conjunct has a content. And in my view, many philosophers who take pleasure in calling themselves 'moral realists' have failed badly in this obligation. They have either been content to pour cold water on revisionary anti-realism of John Mackie's kind, or content to insist on the surface appearances, or content to generalize what is mistakenly seen as a late Wittgensteinian lesson, to the effect that every indicative sentence shares the same role—that of describing an aspect of the world ('our world'). The existence of the kind of theory I am describing should undercut this. But there is still room for disagreement, specifically about what in the commitments needs explaining, and about the kind of explaining modal and moral facts can themselves do.

Realist theorizing is apt to pay too little attention to the first and to make too much of the second. It worries too little about the curious place that moral and modal commitments have, about what notion of truth can be appropriate to them, about why it matters, and about how the commitments blend with others that we have. It worries less about these issues because if these commitments are beliefs, then their aim is simple truth, and this is proper depiction of the modal or moral realm. This is an application of the second tendency: to make much of the explanatory powers of the moral or modal states of affairs. A realist may betray himself, for instance, by relying upon metaphors of perception or vision to explain how we become acquainted with moral or modal fact, or by entering false theses about the creation or destruction of such facts and their dependence on others, or by supposing that the existence of such facts explains other genuine states of affairs, in the way in which one state of affairs can explain another. To suppose, for instance, that the world exists as it does because it ought to do so might be the privilege of the moral realist. To suppose that the world exists because God made it is the privilege of the theological realist. If this kind of belief is intrinsic to first-order theorizing (as in the theological case), then the kind of diagnosis of the commitments offered by a projectivist will indeed find error in the everyday practice, as well as in various philosophical interpretations of it; this is why a 'Wittgensteinian' protection of religious belief is a kind of cheat. Ordinary religious belief, thought of in an expressive way, involves the mismatch referred to above. This is also why there is very doubtfully any space for a genuine realist verses anti-realist debate about explanatory physics. But first-order theories are notably silent about the explanatory role of possible worlds or moral duties; it is left to the philosophers to inject good or bad views about that.[5]

5. Obviously, in this paragraph I ignore the possibility of the generalized quasi-realist move introduced in essay 1: the move that allows even the use of a concept in explanatory roles, but still

Once the explanations are agreed, not much is left in the words. So the universal harmony is better approached in a case like that of colour, where we feel reasonably confident of the underlying facts and the way they relate to colour perception. And then indeed it is no great matter whether we say that there are colours (and I am a realist about them) or that there are (and I am not). The space for dispute has shrunk away and can only be resurrected if false implications are read into the parenthetical remarks. It is no great trick to announce oneself in either style; the work comes in earning a right to do so. But to achieve this harmony in the modal case involves the hard work of showing how to explain modalizing in the first place, and this remains to be done.

At the risk of appearing moralistic, I shall close this section by illustrating how truth-conditional theorizing dominates our philosophical imaginations. One of the clearest expressive approaches to commitment to natural law is that of Ramsey and Ayer. Here is Ayer:

> In short I propose to explain the distinction between generalizations of law and generalizations for fact, and thereby to give some account of what a law of nature is, by the indirect method of analysing the distinction between treating a generalization as a statement of law and treating it as a statement of fact.[6]

It is, however, a little unclear from this way of setting it up quite how Ayer conceives the step from a theory of what it is to treat something as a law of nature to giving 'some account of what a law of nature is'—the ontological overtone of this suggests that the truth-conditional theory is not quite exorcized. For if the expressive theory is successful, there is no last chapter to write on what a modal fact or state of affairs is. We would know what we do and why we are correct to do it when we commit ourselves to necessities of logic, nature or action, and that would be the end. Ayer's nod towards truth-conditional hankerings is wholesale prostration in other writers. A recent example is David Armstrong. After observing that inference from the observed to the unobserved is central to our whole life as human beings, and that if there were no laws those inferences would be unreliable, he continues: 'hence the notion of law is, or should be, a central concept for epistemology. If so we will also want to enquire into its ontology. We will want to know what a law of nature is'.[7] The grip of the truth-conditional approach appears when Armstrong considers the alternative to this, which he identifies as the 'truly eccentric view . . . which denies that there are any Laws'.[8]

---

defends an anti-realist construction of it. It is not that I changed my mind between the two papers, or between then and now, but that for the purposes of this paper it is the different *direction* of a quasi-realist story that is important. Even if explanatory contexts eventually fall within the quasi-realist net, it is not right to start with them.

    6. A. J. Ayer, 'What Is a Law of Nature?', *The Concept of Person* (London: Macmillan, 1963), p. 231.

    7. D. Armstrong, *What is a Law of Nature?* (Cambridge: Cambridge University Press, 1983), p. 5.

    8. Ibid., p. 5.

Even writers as cautious as Edward Craig and Crispin Wright find it straightforward to agree on the point that, in effect, closes off projectivism + quasi-realism. The context here is that Craig had demonstrated decisively the imaginative block that faces us when we try to conceive, in proper detail, of a counterarithmetical reality. The projectivist is then poised to see this imaginative block as something expressed when we insist upon the necessity of arithmetic. But Wright commented, 'If as Craig makes plausible, we are unable to conceive of how any alternative determination might be viable, then that is how things are with us; it is a further, tendentious step to inflate our imaginative limitations into a metaphysical discovery'.[9] And Craig, acknowledging that he and Wright agree that we should not ask the imagination to do too much, concedes immediately: 'It certainly is a further step'.[10] Is it so clear that there is this further step? Only if claims of necessity are 'metaphysical discoveries', and this the projectivist will query. Again, the position is clear if we revert to the moral case: a projectivist will see commitment to an obligation as a distinctive mental state—call it a sentiment—but he will not accept any charge that we tendentiously inflate our sentiments into metaphysical discoveries (discoveries about the independent structure of the world of obligations), precisely because he denies that in our awareness of duty and obligation we are in fact making any such discoveries. (I return later to Craig's reasons, which were good, for thinking there is *a* further step—only it is not this one.)

There are aspects of the work of making quasi-realism attractive that I shall not repeat in this paper. These include its distinction from naive subjectivism, its moves to accommodate the propositional nature of ethical claims, its explanation of the syntax and semantics that go with that, and the basis for constructing a working notion of truth. My concern here is to see how this shape of theory fares with one of the other two 'musts': that of logic.

III. Policies versus Needs

We allow possibilities, rule out impossibilities, and insist upon necessities. This is not describing anything. As in Wittgenstein, attributing necessity to a proposition is not making a true or false claim about it—or at least is not to be understood that way.[11] It is more like adopting a norm, or a policy or a rule that a thesis be put 'in the archives', above the hurly-burly of empirical determination. The decision dictates how we shall treat recalcitrant evidence. This accords with the parallel with morals. The one kind of rule makes courses of thought intellectually obligatory; the other makes courses of action so. But

9. Crispin Wright, *Wittgenstein on the Foundations of Mathematics* (London: Duckworth, 1980), p. 439.

10. E. J. Craig, 'Arithmetic and Fact', in *Exercises in Analysis* ed. Ian Hacking (Cambridge: Cambridge University Press, 1985), p. 90.

11. For example, *Remarks on the Foundations of Mathematics* (Oxford: Basil Blackwell, 1956), V. 6, 4–5, p. 163. Wittgenstein *constantly* appeals to hidden difference of role underlying superficial descriptive appearances. See also essay 8, note 13.

there is a major problem: to identify any space for this rule-making. Modalizing, like moralizing, does not feel optional: it feels as though we regard '1 + 1 = 2' as necessary simply because we *must* do so, not because we have chosen to do so. Its status is more naturally seen as a product of our inability to conceive otherwise, or to *do* anything with a counterarithmetical judgement. If the necessity of propositions is in any sense conferred by us, it is still unnatural to see it as reflecting anything in which we had a choice. So notwithstanding Wittgenstein, a projectivist will be wise to look for the mental set that gains expression outside the realms of the optional (and it is vital to notice that he can do this—the denial of metaphysical realism does not usher in a 1950s embrace of free choice and conventionalism).

If attributing modal value reflected free policies and choices, it would be unclear why we should go in for it. The right attitude would seem to be that which Wright attributes to his imagined 'Cautious Man'.[12] This is the character who agrees with us on all empirical truth. He agrees with us too in accepting proofs; in arithmetic or logic, or in any more apparently metaphysical commitments, such as those determining our basic ascriptions of temporal, spatial, or causal categories, this character agrees with us. But he refuses to make modal assignments. As far as he is concerned, it is enough that we accept, say, that 1 + 1 = 2. It is unwise to go further and ascribe necessity to the proposition.

The challenge is reminiscent of Quine: would it not be better simply to register our stronger attachment to some propositions than others, and then to leave market forces to determine which ones maintain our loyalty? Even if we abandon the self-image of decision makers, we confront essentially the same problem. What would be lost if we simply did not modalize? Is it not foolish to elevate mere imaginative limitations into iron necessities?

Quine thinks that even in the case of logic we would be better off doing no such thing. Of course, in the context of positivism, Quine's strength lay not so much in opposition to modal discrimination in itself, as in his insistence that coming to the problem with notions of meaning or convention is coming with dirty hands: there can be no modally innocent appeal to conventions, or concepts or meanings or rules or languages, giving us an anterior understanding from which to explain or justify those discriminations. In other words, even if we can *say* things like 'analytic propositions are true in virtue of meaning/concepts/constraints on the application of concepts . . .' this is no help. It is no help because there is no identification of concepts, meanings, etc., which does not itself involve knowing the modal liaisons of propositions in which the concepts occur—what must be, may be, or cannot be true, if they are so. Hence, any such appeal cannot explain or justify our modal commitments: in a frequent metaphor, it keeps us within the same circle.

It may have been naive of the positivists to think that by retreating to questions of meaning we obtained a cleanhanded empiricist aproach to modality. But overthrowing that is not the same as overthrowing the modal. Indeed, the 'dirty-hands' argument is entirely two-edged: by showing how deeply the

12. Wright, op. cit., chapter 23.

modal is entrenched in any 'conceptual scheme' it makes it less likely that modalizing is left an unprotected optional extra in our thought. But so far as the present essay goes, the point to insist upon is that there is clearly an antecedent problem for any naturalistic sanitizing of the modal. This is to explain the way in which we make modal judgements—the ease with which we noncollusively agree upon them. Obviously, before we recommend that we abandon modalizing, we want to know what it involves and why we do it. Our capacity to make noncollusive modal discriminations requires explanation, whether or not it is regrettable that we do so. But curiously enough (since the task is one of naturalized epistemology), Quine's philosophy of the modal is incapable of meeting this eminently naturalistic request, and when it is buttressed to do so, it loses its appeal, doing better by becoming quasi-realistic. Or so I shall argue.

IV. Explaining Modalizing

Quine's consistent position has been that even when we think of the most elementary trivialities of truth-functional logic, the best we can say is that they are *obvious*. It is sometimes said that he changed his mind about this, and that, discussing translation from allegedly pre-logical or alternative-logical tongues, he conceded some very special status to truth-functional logic, in the determination with which we would reinterpret others as conforming to it. But in Quine's view this is no shift. It is just a consequence of the fact that we always translate so as to save the obvious.[13]

Of course, not all truths naively called necessary are at all obvious, but Quine can and does extend the explanation to those which can be proved by obvious means from obvious starting points. Here we have the famous Quinean picture in which the truths naively called necessary are those which are obvious enough to lie far away from the theatres of war in which empirical forces mould and break theories. It substitutes the one-dimensional web of

---

13. In 'Carnap and Logical Truth' (1954; reprinted in W. V. Quine, *The Ways of Paradise and Other Essays,* New York: Random House, 1966, pp. 105–106) promoting the dirty-hands argument, he wrote "The considerations which were adduced in *1, to show the naturalness of the linguistic doctrine, are likewise seen to be empty when scrutinized in the present spirit. One was the circumstances that alternative logics are inseparable practically from mere change in usage of logical words. Another was that illogical cultures are indistinguishable from ill-translated ones. But both of these circumstances are adequately accounted for by mere obviousness of logical principles, without help of a linguistic doctrine of logical truth. For, there can be no stronger evidence of a change in usage than the repudiation of what had been obvious, and no stronger evidence of bad translation than that it translates earnest affirmations into obvious falsehoods." And in *Philosophy of Logic* (Englewood Cliffs, NJ: Prentice-Hall, 1970), in the same context, again insisting upon the inevitability of our imputing classical logic to a translatee, he offers almost identical terms: "Being thus built into translation is not an exclusive trait of logic. If the natives are not prepared to assent to a certain sentence in the rain, then equally we have reason not to translate the sentence as 'It is raining'. Naturally the native's unreadiness to assent to a certain sentence gives us reason not to construe the sentence as saying something whose truth should be obvious to the native at the time. Data of this sort are all we have to go on . . ."

belief, with only a vague and pragmatic boundary between propositions that face the test of experience routinely ('contingent') and those that at worst would only face it in periods of exceptional theoretical turbulence ('necessary'). And at first sight it gives Quine his answer to the problem of explaining our noncollusive application of the notion. When we deem a proposition necessary we express our apprehension of its obvious character.

But a little thought shows that this is quite inadequate. For a great many truths are in Quine's central reservation, but would simply be classed as contingent. These are truths that are *central, certain, obvious* to everyone— that there exist trees and rocks, that houses keep off the rain, and so on. There is no prospect of these being rocked by scientific change, nor of recalcitrant experience casting doubt upon them. But we unhesitatingly class them as contingent. How is Quine to explain this difference in the modal reaction, if they are in the scientific archive, beyond the struggles of falsification and modification?

Quine admits that logic is 'built into translation more fully than other systematic departments of science. It is in the incidence of the obviousness that the difference lies . . .'.[14] It looks as if this is to be developed when he contrasts '1 + 1 = 2', which is 'obvious outright', with 'it is raining', which is 'obvious in particular circumstances'. But the point he apparently has in mind is just that 'every logical truth is obvious, actually or potentially: each, that is to say, is either obvious as it stands or can be reached from obvious truths by a sequence of individually obvious steps'.[15] This is the extension referred to above. But it is not at all clear how it relates to the incidence of the obviousness. And in any event, in a well-developed theoretical science, obviousness can similarly transmit from obvious data through obvious principles of interpretation and explanation, to bring hitherto unobvious conclusions into the fold. There is no diagnosis of our different reactions to '1 + 1 = 2' and 'there exist trees and rocks' here.

Quine's first thought about the contrast was the best: it is indeed in the incidence of the obviousness that the difference lies: 'it is raining' is obvious *only* in particular circumstances; '1 + 1 = 2' is 'obvious outright'. But 'obvious in particular circumstances' versus 'obvious outright' is a dangerously suggestive contrast: not far from 'assertible only in the light of particular experience' versus 'assertible by conceptual means alone', or *a posteriori* versus *a priori*. If the best theory of the incidence of the obviousness is that in the one case but not the other it varies with particular *contingencies*, we are left with our judgement that the truth of the one does so vary, and the truth of the other does not. This once more is what common sense would say: 'there are trees' is obvious in the light of something that, we know, could have been otherwise; not so '1 + 1 = 2'. Another way of putting it is that common sense allows that recalcitrant experience is *possible* in the one case but not the other: we could tell a story in which it came to appear to us as if there were not trees, but not

14. Quine, *Philosophy of Logic*, p. 82.
15. Ibid., pp. 82–83.

one in which $1 + 1$ is anything other than 2. But Quine cannot appeal to entrenched modal intuitions to explain the division within the obvious.

The problem, remember, is that Quine is to *explain* our modal tendencies before dismissing or sanitizing them—showing that nothing in the making of them licenses epistemology to draw any grander distinction than his. He is therefore quite within his rights to call upon his list of theoretical defects here. Perhaps it is because we are in the grip of mythical theories of ideas, or molecular theories of meaning, or use-mention confusion, that we distinguish between equally certain or obvious judgements, identically remote from the threat of overthrow: there being trees and $1 + 1$ being 2. But is it clear from a naturalist perspective that *only* a defect is involved—that there is no legiti-mate point and purpose in the distinction, within the overall class of certain-ties, between those that are necessary and those are are contingent? Surely not, and a better explanation of our propensities is easy to produce. Let us consider the matter from the opposite point of view. It is usually necessity that is the bugbear, but if we suppose that it is the distinction between the neces-sary and the contingent that requires understanding, we also can ask what we miss if we lack the capacity to deem propositions contingent. This direction of approach must be equally legitimate. In fact, I suspect there is some evidence that contingency needs more explanation to children than necessity: the initial tendency is to take everything that is so as having to be so. Suppose someone who is modally blind in this way: he sees no point or purpose in accepting any notion of *contingency*. Running the metaphysics and the epistemology in tan-dem, we can suppose that epistemologically he can make nothing of the idea that a particular judgement is *a posteriori*.[16] So he can make nothing of the idea that although there are trees there might not have been, nor that there being trees is obvious only in the light of particular experience, so that if the experience were different (or had been different), as it might be, the opposite judgement would have seemed right.

What does he miss? The case is still underspecified. This person may, perhaps like Leibniz or Spinoza, have a background theory that all apparent contingency is disguised necessity. In that case, in the marketplace, or talking with the vulgar, he could use a perfectly good surrogate for contingency—perhaps one that he may regard as suited for finite beings. Or perhaps he is like the Cautious Man, and claims to find some kind of hubris in expressing verdicts in modal language, although he makes the same distinctions and the same use of them (for instance, in distinguishing valid from invalid proofs, or reflecting on alternative possibilities) that we do. This is theoretical or philo-

16. It is beyond the scope of this paper to explore the distinction between necessity and *a prioricity*, where the one is thought as logical or metaphysical, and the other as epistemological. I believe that an 'attitude'-based theory of necessity is able to explain Kripkean intuitions about the distinction, although the story is not altogether straightforward. The difficult phenomenon to explain would be the alleged conferring of necessity upon truths that were clearly arrived at *a posteriori*. But it should be all right that, after we have discovered something ('water is H_2O') we should 'archive it' at least for *some* purposes: we do not of course regard such things as truths of logic, nor can we 'make nothing of' the thought processes of one who would deny them.

sophical scepticism, and, like its counterparts elsewhere, is supposed to coexist with normal living. Such theorists draw the same distinctions as the rest
of us, except that when they think such things as that there might not have
been trees, they will (as it were) preface their assent with a universal qualification: contingency becomes some species of *apparent* contingency, or not the
real thing. This is scepticism, or perhaps idealism, about modality, and not
what I intend. I want instead someone who does not even recognize the need
for a reinterpretation, for he cannot begin by recognizing even apparent contingency as such.

It seems plain that blindness to the *a posteriori* status of propositions is
catastrophic. To such a person, failure to realize that it is raining here now is
like failure to realize that $1 + 1 = 2$, an incomprehensible defect. He is unable
to make anything of a mode of thinking in which it is not realized that p, when
p is true, in just the way that we are unable to when p represents an elementary necessity. But what does he make of (for instance) sleep, of blindness, of
his own need for telephone directories or testimony, or of the difference that
different spatial and temporal position causes to his own information gather-
ing? How does he think of his own failures of omniscience or conceive of his
own changes of knowledge as he goes about the world? There seems no way
of answering these questions without stripping the subject of massive quanti-
ties of ordinary, nonmodal, *empirical* understanding—simple understanding
about the variation of belief with circumstance. It would be possible to fill out
the way in which the deficiency disqualifies him from interpreting others
reliably: he cannot rationalize them, seeing why various beliefs seem right to
them because he has no way of seeing how belief varies with point of view,
with use of the senses, with skill or luck. But ignorance of these things in this
context is just a *species* of ignorance of the way one thing varies with another.
The person who cannot understand how the cat's awareness of the bird varies
with whether it can see it seems little better than one who cannot understand
how the leaf's motion varies with the wind.

Conversely, if the subject has this understanding, he is in a position at least
to *imitate* modal discriminations. Crucially, he can do better than Quine suggests in making distinctions within the class of the obvious. He can make
something of a way of thought in which it is not realized that there are trees,
just as he can make something of a way of thought in which it is not appreciated that it is raining here now. Long-term confinement to treeless zones is a
kind of position he can understand, and whose impact upon a belief system he
could appreciate. He can say something *better* about 'it is raining here now'
and '$1 + 1 = 2$' than that they are equally obvious. He can say something of
what makes the former obvious, and describe people to whom it would not be
obvious; he can appreciate how there could be, or make something of, a way
of describing the world in which it is denied. Suppose he is set our task of
discriminating, among obvious truths, between those which are intuitively
necessary and those which are contingent; then he can at least approximate to
our division, by simply classing as contingent those which satisfy this condition: he can make something of ways of thought in which, for various reasons,

they are either not accepted or are even denied. Here 'make something of' will include being able to explain how such a way of thought might arise, knowing how it might be rectified, understanding the practices of those whose thought it is, and so on. This will give the subject a sense of what would count as recalcitrant experience, and what would have counted as such, even for entrenched, obvious, but contingent, certainties. And, given that there is a residual class of apparent beliefs where he cannot do this, he will have a working substitute for the necessary and the impossible.

The upshot is that blindness to the *a posteriori* character of beliefs seems impossible in subjects who have virtually any comprehension of the world. Now naturalized epistemology is largely a study of the variation of belief with circumstance. It can be done by us only when we can make something of the variation of belief involved. In some cases we can; in residual cases such as logic and mathematics we characteristically cannot. This difference can be used naturalistically to explain our tendency to make modal divisions, and it gives the explanation that Quine left himself without.

Is it an explanation that can be taken over by Quine? I believe so. Quine has no reason to oppose our discrimination of contingency; it is the remainder he dislikes. So his best path would be to accept the explanation of our propensity to modalize, but to warn us against making too much of the imaginative differences it cites. This would be to join forces with Wright's Cautious Man: our imaginative limitations are facts about us; they may gain expression in our modalizing and explain our discriminations, but they ought not to be taken as any guide to what is necessarily the case.

V. Refining Imagination

The players, then, seem to align themselves into two teams. Both admit the existence and centrality of imaginative blocks—of the fact that there are propositions of whose falsity we can make nothing. The one side, encompassing Craig, Wright, this new Quine, Forbes, and probably most others, finds something distinctive about the Cautious Man, who goes this far, but refuses to modalize. Quine recommends his modesty; Forbes thinks it would be a mistake to project imaginative limitations. Craig does not go quite so far. He indeed thinks there is a further step if we take our imaginative limitations as guides to what must be the case, namely the step of supposing that the world is transparent to our intelligence. He points out that in particular philosophical climates the belief that the world is thus transparent, or the goal of making it thus transparent, may be much more appealing than in others. In particular in the twentieth-century pragmatic climate that Quine inhabits, this belief is less prominent: it becomes enough that theory should enable us to 'anticipate and control perceivable events', and genuine intelligibility is no longer a first priority.[17] In modalizing we are being Incautious, and even if Craig finds much

17. Craig, 'Arithmetic and Fact', p. 92.

to admire in the old ideology that prompted us to be so, the sense remains that sobriety requires the more Quinean attitude. This side then thinks that the Cautious Man is distinctive in not modalizing. Either he does not possess a set of concepts that we, somewhat unaccountably, do, or he exercises proper caution in not making judgements with them.

The other side, where I feel rather isolated, queries the central doctrine of these thinkers. When we understand what the Cautious Man lacks, we shall be pleased that we have it. The central doctrine of the other team is, in Craig's words, that 'we should not infer any absolute impossibility from the limitations of our own imaginations.[18] With modifications, I suggest that there is a quite proper move or inference here; that what looks like intellectual hubris is in fact not so. The shared doctrine of the other team is that there is a chasm which the Cautious Man is admirable for not crossing. My claim is that it is only in the shadows cast by illicit hankering after a realistic, truth-conditional account of modalizing that the crossing seems so dangerous.

Craig thinks that there might be two sources for the idea that the crossing can be made. One is that meanings are sufficiently transparent to our minds, that we can know just by introspection that what we mean by some sentence can never come out false. As he rightly says, nobody can succumb to that with a clear conscience these days. The other is the assumption that our mental powers are perfectly in tune with reality, and as he again rightly says, that can only be credible within a specific philosophical climate. My source is different: I am sceptical about the assumption that we know what we mean by 'absolute necessity', or the real distribution of possibilities, in a way that allows us to contrast them wholesale with the blocks that our only ways of thinking meet. I am sceptical because I detect the influence of realism at just this point.

This scepticism will, I hope, appear less extravagant if we remember the other, easier, fields on which projectivism + quasi realism fought. The equivalent of the Craig-Wright-Quine team over morals would say: 'we should not infer any ["absolute"] obligations from the direction of our own sentiments' (for example). The equivalent of the Cautious Man would be someone who, while conducting his practical reasoning in every respect as the rest of us do, eschews the 'inference' to the proposition that we have, for instance, an obligation to our children. He can make the same deprecatory remarks about our right to think ourselves in tune with metaphysical moral reality. He can even cite theological and philosophical climates in which this pride would have seemed natural, but which no longer obtain. My reaction is that he has mistaken the nature of the judgement: by thinking of it as 'made true' by some possibly alien state of affairs he has made his scepticism inevitable; by seeing the proper function of the proposition we avoid it. On a realist account, his caution is correct, as is his refusal to moralize. But as it is he is actually missing nothing (as I put it in essay 8, 'shmoralizing'—conducting practical reasoning properly without a realistic backdrop—is just moralizing). Again, the colour case provides an easier but slightly more distant analogy: we would be wrong

18. 'Arithmetic and Fact', p. 110.

to be cautious over whether using our eyes tunes us to the real divisions and distributions of colours, because our only concept of the reality of those divisions comes from proper use of our eyes.

However, the other team has another weapon, again wielded powerfully by Craig. Following the passage agreeing with Wright that it is a 'tendentious step' to inflate our imaginative limitations into a metaphysical discovery, Craig writes:

> It certainly is a further step. In the first place, it is clear that there is a group of possibilities which no argument from premises about what we can and can't imagine could ever rule out. We might, for instance, come to be able to imagine what we can't now imagine, there may be other beings who can imagine what we can't and never will be able to imagine, and so on. . . . [I]f we close our minds to these possibilities then we make assumptions about our present imaginative capacities for which we have no warrant.[19]

To address this, we need to make distinctions within the class of the 'unimaginable'. I wrote above of propositions whose truth we cannot imagine in the sense that we could make nothing of ways of thought in which they are asserted. Now this is to be taken fairly strictly, and so taken it does not quite correspond to 'unimaginable' on an untutored reading. Suppose, for instance, I announce that I am able to show you a new primary colour, quite distinct from any mixture or shade of previous colours. You may doubt me, and you would certainly be unable to imagine what I was going to show you, if my claim is true. You might even express yourself by saying that it is impossible. but you would be unwise to have much confidence in this claim, for in some sense you can 'make something of' the possibility that I am going to do what I said. It is not as if I had said I would show you a circle with straight sides, or a true contradiction.

Let us distinguish a proposition's being 'unimaginable', in the sense that we cannot present to ourselves a sense of what it is like to experience it as true, from its being 'inconceivable', where this involves the kind of block just indicated, in which we can do nothing with the thought of its truth. It is frequently pointed out that unimaginability is a poor symptom of inconceivability, and this is correct. The cases one would adduce include these: the extra colour, the existence of infinite totalities, the bounded and shaped nature of space or time, the existence of extra dimensions, perhaps the operation of backward causation. Then there is the unimaginability of entities like the self, or of the will, and in some frames of mind, we cannot imagine the possibility even of rule-following, intentionality, and so on. The lack of fit works the other way round as well—propositions might be properly classed as impossible, although the imagination freely allows them: notoriously, the alleged possibility that I might have been Napoleon, or that Fermat's theorem might be true (or false), one of which is imaginable, although impossible.

19. 'Arithmetic and Fact', p. 90.

Our imaginative powers change and develop. The child cannot imagine the beliefs of the adult; those unacquainted with them cannot imagine the taste of claret or the work of Rembrandt. These conditions can be altered, which immediately gives us a sense of potential ways in which our own imaginations are partial. Our experience is limited, and our imaginations not much better. Just as people of limited experience have impoverished imaginations compared with us, so we must accept that there are many things of various kinds which we cannot now imagine—tastes, smells, insights, and presumably truths. This, of course, accords well with Craig's caution: it is not just a modal sceptic, but all of us, who will beware of inferring impossibility from just any imaginative failure.

Using unimaginability as a good indication of impossibility is also a mistake because it depends upon too simple a notion of the relation between experience and thought. It asks, as it were, that we should be able to see any truth in a single picture. So, for instance, if we want to think of a theoretical notion, such as that of force acting at a distance, we try to visualize the process, and, failing, are apt to find the notion suspicious. We find it hard to accept that full intelligibility can be earned by a proper place in a theory, even if we cannot visualize the happenings of the processes. Consider, for another example, the shape of space. Children find it incredible to think that space has a shape, because they try to visualize it, or in other words imagine themselves *looking* at it, which is what we normally do to observe the shape of things, and the thought experiment collapses, for the observer cannot find a standpoint from which the whole of space can be observed. But using that failure as a reason for concluding that space must be infinite would be a mistake, for it would ignore other ways in which a shape of space might be certified—ways like those a man might use to find the shape of a container in which he is confined. If these procedures certify that only certain routes in space are possible, then the right conclusion may be that space is bounded and has a shape, and we can explain why the enterprise of trying to visualize it fails. Visualizing is a poor guide to states of affairs, because not all states of affairs reveal themselves in a picture. Similarly, things may be impossible although naive imagination allows them, because naive imagination does not tell us how to describe the scenes it recreates; this is why it is so dangerous to use imagination as a guide to the metaphysics of the self.

Here we have explanations of failures of imagination. And we can conceive of superior positions from which some of our imaginative limitations could analogously be explained. When we can do that, we will not take imaginative limitations as a guide to impossibility. Now Craig in particular notices all this. This is a difference, he writes, between the case of the extra colour or difficult intermediate cases like that of extra spatial dimensions, and full-blown cases like that of a deviant arithmetic: 'An explanation of our inability to imagine the arithmetically deviant along the lines that served for colour and spatial dimensions doesn't get started; so nothing checks our tendency to project our incapacity and suppose that reality just *couldn't be like that*.[20] But Craig does not highlight the good use the projectivist can make of this difference.

Consider again the parallel with moral projectivism. We do not find it trivial to cross from a sentiment to a moral judgement. Only certain sentiments—those of a certain strength, or with certain objects, or those accompanied by sentiments about others who do not share them—form a jumping-off point. We are also conscious that there are doubtless flaws and failures in our sentiments, which are perhaps capable of explanation in the same way that we explain the defects of those who are worse than ourselves. But when the sentiments are strong and nothing on the cards explains them by the presence of defects, we go ahead and moralize. We may be aware that our opinion is fallible, but that is because we can do something with the thought of an improved perspective, even when we are fairly certain that one will not be found, and here as elsewhere commitment can coexist with knowledge that we may be wrong. The 'step' from a fully integrated sentiment of sufficient strength to the moral expression now becomes no step at all: the moral is just the vocabulary in which to express that state. Avoiding it would not be an exercise in modesty, but an impoverishing idiosyncracy of expression.

Why should it not be like this with logical necessity? We have arrived at the residual class of propositions of whose truth we can make nothing. We cannot see our failure to make anything of them as the result of a contingent limitation in our own experience, nor of a misapprehension making us think that their truth should be open to display in a way in which it need not be. We express ourselves by saying that they cannot be true—that their negations are necessary. There is the bare possibility of being shown wrong—perhaps our search into the causes of our imaginative block was inadequate, or perhaps we were under a misapprehension of what it might be for the proposition to be true. We may be uncomfortably aware of even great philosophers who mistakenly projected what turned out to be rectifiable limitations of imagination—the *a priori* has a bad history. But as Wright notices, we should have no wish to make ourselves infallible when deeming things *a priori*. We make the commitment in the light of the best we can do. There is no step, and no illusion.

VI. Naturalism and Quasi-Realism

On this account, part of what it is for us to make nothing of the truths that we deem impossible is that we cannot explain *naturalistically* our own failure to see what it would be for them to be true. When we can see how, if a proposition were true, we might nevertheless be in bad circumstances to appreciate how it might be, we release it from impossibility. It does not deserve ruling out any more. But we cannot see how, if contradictions were true or if $1 + 1 = 3$, we might be in bad circumstances to appreciate how it might be. We could

20. 'Arithmetic and Fact', p. 106.

have not even a sketch of a natural story of the block we face, because we can make nothing of the starting point.

This provides a kind of Catch 22 in our attempts to theorize about the modal. If we can see our tendency to rule out *p* as the outcome of a contingent limitation, we are already making something of the thought that *p* might be true, but that if it were, nevertheless we would not appreciate it because of something or other. And this undermines any original commitment to its impossibility. When someone starts: 'if there were an extra colour then . . .' perhaps we can understand how it might be contingent limitations that make the hypothesis hard to contemplate—but if that is all there is to it, we lose any right to regard it as impossible. On the other hand, when someone says 'if 1 + 1 = 3 then . . .' and essays to show how, if this were true, we would be in a bad position to appreciate it, the thought experiment breaks down, for we cannot properly work through what is being supposed and how we might be in a world of which it is true. But this means that there is bound to be a residual 'surd': our incapacity to make anything of the thought that some propositions are true has to be resistant to natural explanation, if it remains a good candidate for modal commitment.

The fear of an inexplicable core motivates attempts, such as the positivists gave, to remove any content from necessary truths. But we have accepted that the dirty-hands argument shows that we will not explain this incapacity by invoking uncontaminated knowledge of meaning, concepts, rules. We now find that if *any* natural explanation of our imaginative block can be given, this attacks our right to make the commitment. I think that here we get an alternative, or perhaps supplementary, explanation to that offered by Craig, of the late twentieth-century opposition to the modal. It can arise not only from a changed conception of what theories need to do, but also from a conviction that nothing escapes naturalistic explanation.

When we have thoroughly tested the sense of a hypothesis and make nothing of it, this is, in Wright's words, how things are with us. As Craig says, if the quasi-experiment of working through how it would be if *p* is done on ourselves, now, and if our attempts to work with *p* being true fail, then 'for any logical guarantee we have, that may be as far as it goes'.[21] But it goes a little further, for in the light of what we have said, it will also be so that we cannot see the incapacity as *just* one we happen to be subject to; we cannot deem it a *mere* fact about ourselves, here, now. If we could see it in that light, then that itself would destroy the modal commitment. This is why there is something bogus in Kant's theory that it is the forms of inner and outer sense that determine our *a priori* commitments. This looks illuminating because it looks sufficiently parallel to the natural explanation we might give of the imaginative limitations we can accept as no indication of impossibility—the colour limitation, for example. But it is not really parallel, for if we can make nothing of the possibility of other forms of sense, the 'fact' that ours is one way or another is not intelligible as a genuine explanatory truth. Seeing it like

21. 'Arithmetic and Fact', p. 91.

that would require thinking the other side of the boundary: understanding how it might be, for instance, that although it is compulsory for us to use classical arithmetic, with a different cast of mind it might have been compulsory to use another arithmetic. And this we cannot do.

The residual surd marks a large asymmetry between the moral and the modal. In the case of moralizing, nothing stands in the way of a complete naturalistic story of what it is, why we do it, and, quasi-realistically, why we are right to do it. But the genesis of the way of thought is similar. The moralist insists upon obligations. He rules out those who flout them, refusing approval, ignoring contrary temptations, bending his actions to conform. The modalist insists upon necessities. He rules out ways of thought that flout them, refuses theories that involve them, bends his thoughts to conform. The moralist could just issue rules and penalties, but if he becomes self-conscious he needs the moral proposition to stand as a focus for discussion and reflection, and he contemplates its truth as a way of doing so. The self-conscious modalist needs the same. But the moralist can be quite completely aware of the genesis and justification of his activity, whereas if what we have just said is true, the modalist cannot be. In the case of the modal, the phenomenon is antinaturalistic at its core.

Or is this unduly pessimistic? Some relief might be got by teasing out more aspects of the core inability to 'make anything of' a way of thought that accepts a putative impossibility. Obviously, there are enterprises of thinking through what modifications in logic are possible or what would be missing in a way of thought that consistently tried to make $1 + 1 = 3$. The business, for instance, of thinking through how a science might be built around denial of double negation, or of the distributive laws of logic (from P and Q v R, infer $(P$ & $Q)$ v $(P$ & $R)$) proceeds under the stimulus of constructivism, or of quantum mechanics, respectively. So it ought to be possible to hold both that these laws are necessarily true and that we *can* 'make something of' ways of thought that lead people to deny them. This is not a serious obstacle to the direction of this essay. What we do is take a proposed deviation and follow it until either the way of thought seems possible—and we no longer modalize against it—or it breaks down. But 'breaks down' will mean: offends against something that we suppose essential to any scheme of thought (such as some distinction of truth and falsity, some stability of content, some embargo on contradiction). Eventually we voice an inability to make anything of transgression against these norms: this is the surd that remains. If the thought processes of the deviants are eventually seen to break down, then we can get a deeper understanding of our own commitments: it is no longer so that we face an entirely blank wall when we try to explain our own attachment to these laws. This reveals the genuine scope for explanatory work, and it may do a little to moderate the antinaturalistic pessimism. We can certainly hope to show why a way of thought that is committed (say) to noncontradiction, or to supposing that not all propositions are true, or to other elementary necessities, is also committed (say) to '$1 + 1 = 2$', since we can hope to prove (relying, inevitably, on moves that we find inescapable) that if they are necessary, then so is this. This would give a complete bill of health to the modal if, as the positivists hoped, the propositions finally bearing the burden were free of genuine content, or owed their truth to some naturalistically explicable fact about us—a decision or convention, for instance. But these escapes no longer appear, and in default of a leap outside the system of necessities, the final surd seems set to remain.

Addendum

In this essay I do not press an argument against Lewis's modal realism that I did express in *Spreading the Word;* this argument nevertheless hovers in the background. This argument is that, as well as problems of saying how we get as far as possible worlds, the realist has a problem of getting us back from them: when we use a counterfactual, for instance, in pursuit of a concern with the actual world, why should we be interested if things are thus and so in a neighbouring world, or in all neighbouring worlds? It sounds like a change of subject. This argument was assailed by Bob Hale in his review ('The Compleat Projectivist', *Philosophical Quarterly* 1986). Hale in effect plays the equation between 'this wire might have been live' and 'there is a possible world in which this wire is live' backwards, pointing out that since we have excellent reason to be interested in the former, and since according to the modal realist the latter means the same, we have excellent reason to be interested in the latter.

This mistakes the nature of the problem. My concern, as usual, was explanation, and the point is that a realist construction of the neighbouring-possible-world proposition plays absolutely no role in explaining why we should be interested in the 'might have been' proposition with which it is identified. If anything, it seems to make such an interest strange or even inexplicable. It is no good replying that we are after all interested in the 'might' proposition, so we can expect the possible-world proposition to inherit that interest: the point is that the interest is not explained, and becomes harder to explain, if we give each of the claims other-worldly truth conditions. There is an immaculate treatment of this by the late Ian McFetridge in the collection of his papers, *Logical Necessity* (London: Aristotelian Society Monographs, 1990), pp. 144–46. McFetridge also correctly breaks the alleged parallel with Kripke's notorious argument against Lewis's counterpart theory.

Another puzzle with modal realism that I do not develop is that the realism seems to take the modality out. 'Necessarily $2 + 2 = 4$' and '$2 + 2 = 4$ *everywhere*' do not mean the same. But, says the realist, what if 'everywhere' means 'in all possible worlds'? The question is ambiguous. If the collection of all possible worlds were given extensionally ($w_1, w_2 \ldots$), then again the identity would be lost: someone might think that $2 + 2 = 4$ in all those worlds, without thinking of 'all those worlds' as exhausting the possible worlds. If the totality were given under some other heading than modality, the modal content would be lost. It is only if the collection is given *under the heading* of modality that the two mean the same, but we are not any further in understanding what it is to think of a set of worlds under that heading. This is no objection to using possible-worlds talk, but it shows that the idea that when we do so we refer to real things just like the actual world provides no explanation of the nature of modal commitment.

It is natural to worry whether the use of the idea of an imaginative block is a fig leaf, disguising what must ultimately be thought of in more conventionalist terms, as for example adherence to a rule of language. In a way, and for the purposes of this essay, I do not mind very much whether this is so (it would matter much more to Craig, whose campaign has been directly concerned with refuting conventionalism). In the last few lines of the essay I do indeed express pessimism for the prospects of *any* theory of why we face the blocks we do when we set about thinking in terms of impossibilities. But for my purpose it is more important that this block is identified and properly located as the source of our propensity to modalize.

4

Opinions and Chances

Ramsey was one of the few philosophers who have fully appreciated the fundamental picture of metaphysics that was originally sketched by Hume. In this picture the world—that which makes proper judgement true or false—impinges on the human mind. This, in turn, has various reactions: we form habits of judgement and attitudes, and modify our theories, and perhaps do other things. But then—and this is the crucial mechanism—the mind can express such a reaction by 'spreading itself on the world'. That is, we regard the world as richer or fuller through possessing properties and things that are in fact mere projections of the mind's own reactions: there is no reason for the world to contain a fact corresponding to any given projection. So the world, on such a metaphysic, might be much thinner than common sense supposes it. Evidently the picture invites us to frame a debate: how are we going to tell where Hume's mechanism operates? Perhaps everywhere: drawing us to idealism, leaving the world entirely noumenal; or perhaps just somewhere; or nowhere. Hume's most famous applications of his mechanism, to values and causes, are extended by Ramsey to general propositions, which to him represented not judgements but projections of our habits of singular belief, and also to judgements of probability, which are projections of our degrees of confidence in singular beliefs.

If we are to assess his views we must be sure of what counts as an argument for or against this projectivist picture. The main burden of my essay is that most ways of framing the debate underestimate the resources available to the projectivist. I think it is also clear, particularly from his 1929 paper 'General Propositions and Causality', that Ramsey himself was optimistic about those resources, in a way that has not been widely recognised.

The usual way of attacking the projectivist is this: He is saddled with a particular view of the meaning of remarks made in the area in question. This view is then shown not to correspond with some feature of the meaning that we actually give to those remarks. It is triumphantly concluded that projectivism is inadequate, and that we must adopt a realistic theory, seeing the remarks as straightforward descriptions of a part of the world that we are (somehow) able to cognize. This kind of attack is clearly worthless unless it is clear that the projectivist is indeed committed to the theory of meaning attributed to him. Yet, I shall argue, the theory of meaning to be linked with Hume's picture is variable, subtle, and obscure: if, as I suspect, it is as yet unclear what resources the projectivist has in this matter, it follows that all such attacks so far made are unsuccessful.

A couple of examples may help. It used to be thought that a subjective theory of value entailed identifying the assertion that X is good with the assertion that the speaker himself liked X. This is properly refuted by pointing out that the two have entirely different truth-conditions (or assent-conditions), and the subjectivist is discomfited. But it is now widely recognized that only a very naive subjective theory of value commits this error: a theory of value as a projection of our attitudes can adopt a much better account of what then is said by attributions of value—primarily in terms of expression of such attitudes. Again, it used to be thought (perhaps it sometimes still is) that someone who, like Hume, thinks of the world as a succession of distinct events, and who accords no real distinct existence to necessary connections between those events, must think that we mean no more than regular succession when we talk of cause. But there is no reason for saying that this is what we *must* mean when we project a certain habit of reliance on a regularity, or some other attitude toward it, onto the world. Perhaps, for example, we express some special attitude to the regularity or dignify it in a certain way, and then many stock objections to regularity theories (factory whistles blowing at the same time and so on) are entirely irrelevant. They simply draw attention to regularities that, for some reason yet to be explored, we do not dignify.[1]

But expressive theories of meaning are themselves attacked. It is probably necessary at present to distinguish two kinds of rejection. One, which I shall be coming to, joins issue over some particular aspect of meaning, such as the occurrence of the disputed remarks in subordinate clauses, to which the theory is supposed to be inadequate. The other is hostile to the whole idea of there being a debate. I have in mind the conservative, pessimistic, and perhaps Wittgensteinian view that we cannot do much with our language except speak it, or at best put down rules for buildng up meanings by establishing rules that govern the components of sentences with those meanings. But if that enterprise leaves us with such things as the placid truths that 'good' is satisfied by good things, 'chance' refers to chance, and that A, B satisfies 'x causes y' when A causes B, then we should rest and be thankful. Sometimes, indeed, it is felt that the very endeavour to find semantic structure in a rule-governed way rules out Hume's kind of theory by committing us to a *correspondence* theory of truth, as if coherence theorists, or pragmatists, or the projectivists I am interested in, must half-wittedly deny that 'London' refers to London, and so on. In fact, in constructing such a theory of semantic contribution we use our language simply to describe itself, and leave perfectly untouched the question of which metaphysics is appropriate to that use. It is puzzling to think why people

---

1. This is explored further in essay 5.

still associate the creation of a formal truth-theory for a language with particular views of truth.[2] To exorcise this temptation, imagine a formal theory of
Arabic numerals enabling us to deduce which number a sequence of digits
refers to, given axioms saying to what individual digits refer; the one essential
rule merely captures the way the position of a digit indicates the power of ten
by which it is multiplied. Does such a theory, or the interest of creating it, tell
us what it is to refer to a number, or commit us to a correspondence theory of
such a thing? Of course not. It is entirely silent on the issue, and merely uses
the notion, while telling us nothing about it.[3]

I think the argument to the contrary that confuses people goes: a correspondence theory of truth needs to identify some fundamental word-to-world
relations; Tarski's style of theory can be taken to offer the relations of reference and satisfaction for this job; hence Tarski's style of theory is, or at least
helps, a correspondence theory. This would be fine if there were independent
argument that *what it is* for words to refer to things, or things to satisfy
predicates, is well thought of in terms of correspondence. But it might just as
well be thought of in terms of the predicates taking part in a coherent system;
or being used in promoting certain ends; or in terms of the things having the
reactions of the mind projected onto them. In other words, we might just as
well argue that a coherence, pragmatist, or subjective theory needs to identify
some fundamental word-to-world relations; hence Tarski's style of theory
helps them too. This shows its irrelevance to this issue. Yet, although it gains
nothing from truth-theories, we cannot dismiss the view that Hume's theory is
not debatable. The difficulty that perplexes me is that if, as I shall suggest, the
projectivist can make perfect sense of apparently realistic practice, it is not
clear what intellectual quirks mark him off, nor what is left to fight over
except harmless images and metaphors. The interest, at any rate, comes in
seeing what he can do by way of incorporating apparently realistic practice:
this is a programme that can be called 'quasi-realism', and I see Ramsey as
one if its patrons.

Specific charges against projectivist theories will concentrate upon ways in
which our thinking about the area in question appears to accord an objective
or independent standing to the things allegedly projected. Primarily, chances,
laws, and causes (not to mention values and goods) are all things about which,
we say, we can be ignorant. Our opinions about them can be wrong, defective,
in various ways. We allow the possibility that we think of them as existing
when they really don't and that we are unaware that they exist when they
really do. We acknowledge experts, so that some person's views of, say,
probabilities, become authoritative enough to count as knowledge and to
enter into books as physical constants like values of masses and densities (and
other people's opinions are often not worth a straw). Yet even the experts
might be wrong: it is not their opinion that defines laws and chances; the laws

2. M. Platts, *Ways of Meaning* (London: Routledge & Kegan Paul, 1979).
3. This issue was also joined in *Spreading the Word*, chapters 7 and 8. The idea that truth
theories dominate metaphysics is not nearly so popular now as when this was written.

and chances would have been what they are regardless of whether people had known about them.

Ramsey is usually thought of as one of the fathers of a 'subjective' theory of probability that denies or at best struggles with such facts. On that theory, a distribution of confidence across any totality of propositions is coherent if it satisfies some very weak constraints. But those constraints allow for the most bizarre confidences and agnosticisms. Yet coherence is all that there is. As Kyburg and Smokler put it in the introduction to their 1964 collection, for subjectivism any degree of belief in any statement is permissible, but there are restrictions placed on the distribution of degrees of belief among sets of related statements.[4] Since there is nothing to be wrong about, the view has been summarized as claiming that 'sincerity is enough'. On the more modern version, which I discuss in part III, it is also mandatory to stick by opinions through time and as various kinds of observation are made. However, even this gives us no title to say that a man who announces a quite outrageous set of confidences is 'wrong'; the only vice he could display would be a kind of fickleness as time goes by. It is easy to see why this implausible theory is fostered onto a projectivist. In probability, as in the theory of value, if projection is all there is, there is surely nothing to be wrong *about*. But all this flies in the face of the objectivity of our usage and renders the theory an easy prey to criticism.

But Ramsey was well aware of the shortcomings of a purely subjective theory of laws and chances. He explicitly denies, for instance, that chances correspond to anyone's actual degrees of belief;[5] he knows that we believe in unknown laws (and he would have said the same about chances);[6] he knows that some opinions about chances are much better than others.[7] His effort is to show that these phenomena do not refute an antirealist, projectivist, theory of chances and laws, but actually are explicable given such a theory. It is the fact that he made this quasi-realist attempt that seems to me to show that Ramsey was much better aware of the resources of projectivism than many of his apparent followers (Carnap[8] being an honourable exception). How far can his programme succeed?

II

Hume forged the essential tool for the projectivist to use as he attempts to reconcile his theory with the objectivity of usage. In his great essay 'On the

4. H. E. Kyburg and H. E. Smokler, eds., *Studies in Subjective Probability* (New York: Routledge & Kegan Paul, 1964), p. 7.

5. F. P. Ramsey, *Foundations of Mathematics*, ed. R. B. Braithwaite (London: Routledge & Kegan Paul, 1931), p. 206.

6. F. P. Ramsey, *Foundations*, ed. D. H. Mellor (London: Routledge & Kegan Paul, 1978), pp. 139, 150.

7. Ibid., p. 95.

8. R. Carnap, *Logical Foundations of Probability*, 2nd. ed. (Chicago: Chicago University Press, 1962), p. 16 ff.

Standard of Taste', he points out, in effect, that it is no part of a projectivist metaphysic to claim that one projection is as good as another. Some may be inferior, some superior, and even the best may, in principle, be capable of improvement. Thus, let us take the difficult case of moral evaluations. If values are projections of a habit of forming some kind of attitude to some kinds of thing, how can I be aware that my *own* attitudes might be defective, and capable of improvement? (If we prefer societies to individuals, the question becomes: 'how can *we* be aware that *ours* are'?) The answer is that I know that people are capable of habits of projection which from my own standpoint are deplorable: they judge things of which they are ignorant, and their views are the function of fears and fantasies, blind traditions, prejudice, and so on. But then who am I to be sure that I am free of these defects? This thought is quite sufficient to enable me to understand the possibility of my attitudes improving. They ought to be formed from qualities I admire—the proper use of knowledge, real capacity for sympathy, and so on. If they are not, and if the use of those capacities and the avoidance of the inferior determinants of opinion would lead me to change, then the resulting attitudes would be not only different, but better. It is true that in saying this I am presupposing one kind of evaluation in giving sense to the possible deficiencies of the other. An attitude to the processes of attitude formation is used to give sense to the possibility not merely of change but of improvements in moral judgement. But this gives nothing an axiomatic status: at the end of a process of reevaluation, everything may have changed. The right analogy is with the rebuilding of Neurath's boat, and we know that in principle the result of that might be an improved boat. Equally we can understand and fear the possibility of deterioration. It follows that a projectivist picture of values need have little to do with the frivolities of traditional moral subjectivism ('one opinion is as good as another' and so forth). By pursuing the point we might begin to see how a projectivist can incorporate notions of truth and knowledge.

In the case of empirical judgements of chance the matter is much easier in two respects. The first is not my main concern in this paper, but it is worth noticing. Projectivism in moral philosophy is open to attack on the grounds that the reaction of the mind that is supposedly projected is itself only identifiable as a reaction to a cognized *moral* feature of the world. The specific attitudes and emotions (approval, indignation, guilt, and so on) can, it is argued, be understood only in terms of perception of right and wrong, obligations, rights, *etc.,* which therefore cannot be reflections of them. Myself, I do not think that this is true, nor do I think, if it were true, that it would refute projectivism. For it is not surprising that our best vocabulary for identifying the reaction should be the familiar one using the predicates we apply to the world we have spread. Thus, to take a parallel, many people would favour a projectivist view of the comic, and they may well be right even if our best way of describing the reaction which we are projecting onto a situation we describe as comic is 'that reaction we have when we find something funny'. I don't think a behaviourist analysis is either required or helpful, for obviously the behaviour, to someone with no sense of humour, would be incomprehensible.

In any case, a projectivist theory of probability meets no such objection. For it is easy to identify the main component projected when we attribute a good chance to an event or a high probability to a judgement: it is, of course, simply a degree of confidence.

Degrees of confidence in propositions are 'intervening variables' in psychological theory. We can know about them through interpreting the behaviour that, supposedly, they explain. The measurement of degrees of confidence is not necessarily straightforward, but this is no problem. It may even be indeterminate, very often, what a person's degree of confidence in a proposition actually is, or whether indeed he has one. But in the same way it is often not straightforward to know what a person's belief is; it may be indeterminate what his belief about some matter is, and even indeterminate whether he has one. Yet the notion of a belief is a proper theoretical concept in psychological explanation. Here we should notice that a projectivist needs no more degrees of confidence than a person has beliefs about chances; it is no part of his view that, for instance, a real number should be in principle assigned to every proposition an agent has ever thought of, representing his degree of belief in it. We need no such extravagance: often we express ourselves by saying that we have no idea what the chance is—and this attitude need not co-exist with a particular confidence in a proposition. We shall see how to interpret it on a projectivist picture later. If the whole notion of a degree of confidence were suspect, as some authors claim, then we would need at least to indicate another projected psychological state. I am inclined to suggest that it would not be fatal if, as in the moral or even the causal example, our success in doing this without using the vocabulary of chance were only partial. But, in fact, I doubt whether it would be too difficult.

The second respect in which things are easier for probability is the backing we can give to our standards for evaluating projections. We need standards for assessing projections of degrees of confidence, enabling us to say that some are better than others, that even the best may be capable of improvement, that some are worthless. But there are obvious sources for such standards: an opinion might be formed in the light of experience of observed frequencies or fit into an otherwise successful scheme of projections, and most fundamentally it might give its possessor the habit of belief in what happens and disbelief in what does not. And it is this which is the lynchpin of Ramsey's theory. We could say that it imports a pragmatic standard for evaluating projections, but this might be misleading. For it is not as though the standard is in any way optional or avoidable if we adopt different goals or purposes. It is necessary that truth count as success in judgement, and that the proportion of successes achieved by a habit of making judgements be a measure of the confidence that ought to be felt in the beliefs to which that habit leads one. The standard is mandatory.

For suppose we have a thin, Humean view of the world. What is our purpose in projecting onto it chances and probabilities? Ramsey writes that we 'judge mental habits by whether they work, *i.e.* whether the opinions they lead to are for the most part true, or more often true than those which alternative habits would lead to'. The opinions he is talking about are of course not opinions about probabilities, for that would get nowhere, but the opinions of particular matters of fact that judgements of probability will lead us to form. Fortunately the world displays patterns allowing us to have successful habits of particular belief: faced with partial or complete regularities we can form partial or complete confidence in new cases, and the world grants us success if we are careful. As Ramsey writes, the best habit of belief formation will have us forming confidence of a strength proportionate to the ratio of particular truths to falsities that the habit leads us to believe in. (For why, see section IV.) So it seems that Ramsey is going beyond mere coherence of sets of belief, in a thoroughly sensible and necessary way. That standard is too permissive, since, on the face of it, a set of beliefs may possess the virtue of coherence while having the disadvantage of enjoining confidence that things happen which never do, or that things don't happen which often do. Pragmatism must supplement coherence.

But this charge ignores the work that has recently been done on the relation between subjectivism and 'learning from experience'. This work makes it plausible to believe that a subjective theory of probability, relying only on the constraint of coherence, can show that the process called conditionalization is obligatory. It may then seem as though conditionalizing is itself a process that forces opinions to converge, and that what they converge upon is a value for probabilities in accord with observed frequencies. If all this is true, then the constraint of coherence would be *sufficient* to give the standard of evaluation that Ramsey wants. In the next section I assess this argument, and in the last I go on to develop a projective theory in more detail.

III

In the succeeding sections I shall use the standard terminology, in which a *chance setup* exists, and there is an actual or hypothetical series of *trials* that yield a stable frequency of various outcomes. The set of trials we can call A, and the outcome in which we are interested, B. There is a slight strain in adapting this terminology to, say, the chance of a person being a gin drinker, but for the moment we are not interested in any problems caused by extending the notions.

We now suppose that we have conducted a reasonably extended investigation, and in a large number of trials the proportion of Bs is tending to stabilize around some figure, p. Our problem is to give a projectivist account of the natural judgement that such evidence (in the absence of other evidence) would lead to 'the chance of an A being B is p'. But this way of putting it blurs a vital distinction. There are two sorts of chance judgement that could be made. One is local, and concerns only the chance of one of the trials being B in the set that makes our evidence. The other is not: it is a judgement that concerns other trials and has implications for our confidence in future cases. It is one thing to say 'the chance was p of one of the examples of A we have considered having been B'. It is quite another to say 'the chance is p of any A, including ones yet to be realized, being B'. The first judgement is local or restricted to the class of trials in which we already know the frequency. The second involves a prediction, or more accurately, a commitment to a particular kind of confidence in situations not yet brought about. It involves an apparently inductive step. Yet, although it will evidently be more complex to identify the thoughts that license it, I shall consider it first.

It is not surprising that a man observing and recording results from a process that generates a certain frequency of outcomes B among events A, with no discernible pattern, should come to have a degree of confidence, proportionate to the frequency of Bs among As, that an arbitrary A, such as the next one, will be B. But why *should* he? The simplest answer has two stages. First, the man has the inductive habit: he expects the process to go on generating roughly the frequency it has done so far. Second, given that this is so, he will be right to have the degree of confidence in a particular outcome identical with its relative frequency, because that is the standard for rationality. There is nothing mysterious about this second point. If the inductive expectation is right, then the relative frequency remains stable. If that is so, then a habit of adopting and acting upon any *other* degree of confidence in particular expectations would lay you open to certain loss if you are required to act out your confidence by buying or selling bets at the corresponding rate, given that your partner is someone more straightforward. It would be like having confidence other than 0.25 that a card from a shuffled pack is a heart: a hopeless position if you are required to buy or sell bets at a corresponding rate. Nor should we worry that there is anything unrealistic (undemocratic, as it were) in criticizing someone for having a set of confidences that would lead to loss if he were *required* to post odds on which he could be *required* to buy or sell bets: it is not a satisfactory defence to reply that we are not often required to gamble. The defective degrees of confidence are like bad dispositions that may nevertheless remain unrealized. They can still be criticized by pointing out what would happen if they were to be acted upon.

The two-stage answer relies on induction, and the rationality of that is left dangling. It is tempting, therefore, to hope that work on conditionalizing achieves an answer without relying on specifically inductive habits. It is not, indeed, likely that this could be so, since induction appears to be a necessary component of any answer, in that if there were no reason for expecting the process to generate the same frequency as hitherto there would indeed be no reason for expecting the next A to be a B with any particular confidence. So unless work on conditionalization provided some justification of induction, it could not provide the requisite standard.

The central argument in this area is credited variously to David Lewis and Patrick Suppes. It is, in effect, an extension of the standard Dutch book argument for coherence to an agent's probability distributions through time. The standard argument makes coherence at any one time a necessary condition of a rational distribution of confidence. The new argument, which we can call the dynamic Dutch book argument, or DDB, extends this to prevent a rational agent from wiping his slate clean at any time and forming whatever new confidences he fancies (although until Ian Hacking first made it clear, it was not widely recognized that one might do this, so that subjectivists had happily helped themselves to conditionalization anyhow).[9] The new argument is designed to prove the connection between rationality and conditionalization. Following Paul Teller we can see the DDB like this.[10] We imagine an agent with a set of beliefs at time 0, described by a function P_o giving the confidence with which every proposition in the domain is believed. A change in belief in A is described as conditionalized upon evidence E if, at time n, after E becomes known (so that $P_n(E) = 1$), $P_n(A)$ is equal to $P_o(A \ \& \ E)/P_o(E)$. That is, at time n the new confidence in A is equal to the old conditional probability of A upon E. As Teller shows, we can generalize everything to the case where E merely changes probability, but this does not matter.

Now it is quite clear that, sometimes, changes of belief that are not conditionalizations are legitimate. One may rethink a problem afresh, and come to regret one's old confidences. One may think up new alternatives. But we can avoid objections based on this by restricting ourselves to cases where nothing of this sort occurs, but where someone has *in advance,* at time 0, a settled policy or habit of not conditionalizing. In other words, one has a policy or habit that should E come about, will lead him to some confidence in A greater or less than his present confidence of A upon E. The DDB shows that a man known to have such a plan, and required to buy and sell bets according to his confidences, can be made to buy and sell bets on which he has a net loss, whatever happens, by an opponent who knows no more than him (except, perhaps, that he has the habit or policy). The general proof is complex, but its principle is quite easy to grasp. Suppose I am following a plan, or have a habit, which means that I now have a large confidence that A will occur if E does, but which enjoins that if E does occur I will only have small confidence in A. Suppose I think there is a 60 percent chance that John will play a spade and a 90 percent chance that if he does so he will be left with a court card. But, flouting conditionalization, I am settled that I will have only 30 percent confidence that John will have a court card after he has played a spade. The nub of your strategy for profit is this. You sell *to* me a bet to yield (say) 1 if he plays a spade and has a court card, and 0 otherwise. I will pay a relatively large amount for that (0.54, in fact). You plan that *if* he plays a spade you will cover that bet by buying *from* me a bet to yield you 1 if he has a court card, 0 otherwise, and you know you will be able to do that cheaply, for since I will then have little confidence in the court card, I will want little for such a bet (0.3, in fact). You then only need to arrange side bets to give you a modest profit if he does *not* play a spade, and you will profit in any event. If you can sell me bets when I am confident, and buy when I am less so, you profit. Conversely, if I had announced that although now I regard it as only 30

9. I. Hacking, 'Slightly More Realistic Personal Probability', *Philosophy of Science* 1967, pp. 311–25.

10. P. Teller, 'Conditionalization and Observation', *Synthèse* 1973, pp. 218–58.

percent probable that if he plays a spade he will have a court card, yet, I agree, if he does play a spade I will be very confident that he has a court card (I know I get excited). You buy *from* me a bet on both things now, and sell *to* me a bet on the court card later, if he plays a spade. Again, arranging side bets to cover him not playing a spade, you profit whatever happens. I ask little now for the first bet, and am prepared to pay a lot later for the bet which covers it.

It is not quite right to say that this gives an effective method of profiting from a nonconditionalizing agent. The direction of his departure from the present value of conditional probabilities (the probability of A upon E, now) must be known. If we know that he will inflate his confidence in A we can profit, and if we know that he will deflate it we can profit, but it does not follow, and it is not true, that if we know that he will do one or the other we can profit. We have to know the direction of his aberration before we know whether to buy or sell bets, but of course a general tendency in an agent one way or another could also be exploited over time.

What does this argument show? It shows that an agent known to plan a definite confidence in some proposition receives certain evidence that is either higher or lower than the value he now attaches to the conditional probability of the proposition on the evidence, can be made to lose, whatever happens, if he is required to act out those confidences. Let us agree that such a plan is irrational. Does it follow that we should expect rational confidence to converge upon frequencies, thereby bypassing the apparently inductive step? The feeling that it may have something to do with it comes like this. Suppose we antecedently hand people a number of hypotheses about the chance of an A being a B, and invite them to form a distribution of confidence among them avoiding the pathological values 0 or 1. We then amass frequencies, and since the agents must conditionalize, the posterior probabilities gradually increase for hypotheses giving the chance a value near the observed frequency, and fall away for the others. Eventually opinion converges upon a high probability for the chance being as near as possible to the observed frequency. And the value given the chance dictates our confidence in the next A being a B.

As an attempt to either bypass or cast light upon the inductive step, this argument clearly fails. It falls to a dilemma: either the original hypotheses are consistent with changes in chances over time, or they are not but relate solely to the trials already conducted. They are local in my sense of the term. If they are, then whatever our confidence that the chance of an A being a B took a certain value in generating the frequencies we have so far observed, we need inductive confidence to transpose that confidence to the future. It is no easier to argue that since the chances of an A being a B have always been good, they will continue to be, than it is to argue that since nature has always been ordered, it will continue to be so. On the other hand, if the original hypotheses describe eternal chances, so that in accepting a hypothesis concerning chance I would indeed be committing myself to a uniformity—to the probability that a stable observed frequency of As among Bs can be extended indefinitely with a similar value—then the induction is presupposed in setting up the request; it is only if we have an inductive faith in such uniformities that we should be inclined to distribute confidence over the initial finite selection of hypotheses. Otherwise we should simply point out the many other things that nature might do instead of giving a uniform chance for an *A* being a *B*.

This is easily seen if we imagine a concourse of souls in an antecedent heaven, each of whom is handed a ticket describing a different course that nature might take in the world they are about to enter. Some give eternal constancy to the relation between *A*s and *B*s, some see it as altering over time, so that although up until a certain time a certain degree of confidence in an *A* being a *B* accords with frequencies, after that time a different one does. These souls may dream up conditional probabilities for themselves, giving the world an *x* percent chance of continuing to conform to their ticket if it does so until a certain time. But unless they have an *a priori* reason for expecting the world they are to enter to favour uniformities, there is no reason for *x* to be different for those with straight tickets and for those with bent ones. And if all possible hypotheses are ticketed, then *x* must be vanishingly small, corresponding to the fact that at any time there will be an indefinite number of tickets conforming to the world up until that time, but subsequently divergent. Of course, I am not here denying that we may be able to think of a reason why *x* should be placed higher for those with straight tickets: that is solving the problem of induction. But it is quite clear that if this can be done, it is not by simply proving the virtue of conditionalizing. For *that* is something which the bent can do with the straight. In a nutshell, conditionalizing appears interesting only if we pose the problem in a way that presupposes inductive good sense. (Philosophers of a sociological and Popperean bent are liable to point out that only hypotheses about stable chances would be of interest to scientists, who would regard the others as crazy. This is true. It is true because scientists, like the rest of us, possess inductive good sense.)

It appears, then, that hypotheses about chances that carry implications for future distributions of confidence are not automatically the outcome of conditionalizing changes of opinion. Induction is needed, as indeed we might have expected. Furthermore, we can escape the unrealistic element of seeing learning from experience in terms of conditionalizing: namely, the nebulous nature of the prior distributions of confidence needed. It is usually much more natural to see our experience as putting us in mind of some hypothesis about chance, rather than merely modifying the degree of confidence with which we used to hold one. The rational man does not have to spring from the womb fully armed with an infantile probability distribution across all the hypotheses that experience teaches him to believe. But if we now turn to purely local assessments of chance, things may appear easier. Here we merely want to say that the chance of an *A* being a *B* on the trials we have conducted was *p*. Whether it remains so can be, so far as that judgement goes, entirely up to the gods, and depending on our opinion of them we can expect what we like about the next *A*. What is the rationale for such local judgements?

The connection between judgements of chance and confidence that we have relied upon has been quite simple. We have imagined judgements of chance dictating a corresponding degree of confidence: the reason why that must conform to relative frequency is evident if we demand that the confidence could be acted upon in willingness to buy and sell bets. If we imagine a closed set, like a pack of cards, any confidence in an outcome (e.g. a card being a heart) with a known frequency must conform to that frequency, for otherwise, if the confidence were acted out, loss would be certain. So it might seem as though everything ought to be very simple for local judgements of chance. We know the frequency of *A*s in our set being *B*s; the right confidence to have that an arbitrary member of the set is a *B* must conform to that frequency, so the right chance judgement must be one that expresses that degree of confidence, that is, the judgement that the chance is identical with the frequency. But the trouble is that although this may be correct in the sense that, if we knew nothing else, it would be the proper estimate of the chance, it does not follow that we regard it as true.

For there is actually no compulsion on us to identify local chances with local frequencies: we all know that there is a chance that in any finite set of trials the frequency with which an outcome actually occurred differs markedly from the *chance* of that outcome occurring. The chance of getting a *B* might have been q, even if the obtained relative frequency of *B*s was p. Here realism seems to triumph: what kind of account can a projectivist give of this modal claim? Equally we may persist in actually believing that the *A*s in our set had a chance q of being *B*, although we know that the relative frequency was p, so if we were told to bet on whether an arbitrary *A* had been a *B*, p would be the right figure to act upon. Again, what account can a projectivist give of the belief about chance, when, as in this case, it appears to diverge from the right degree of confidence to have about arbitrary members of the set?

The answer can come only from seeing the parts that induction and science play. If we think the chance of an *A* being a *B* was actually q, we think that q would have been the right betting rate antecedently to the set of trials. We can believe this because we can believe that there was or could have been a longer set of trials in which the proportion of *B*s tended to stabilize on the correct figure, q, and we believe that none of the things that affect such frequencies was different on our actual trials. This last is a scientific belief, in the sense that our causal theories of the world are what tell us whether particular factors that do influence the frequency of *B*s were present. Of course, if the figure p arose from a sufficiently long series, this in itself will be evidence that such a factor was present, whatever it may have been. But the point is that we may not be forced to think that, and it may be easier to believe the reverse. The judgement of local chance, when it diverges from actual frequency, is then an expression of the confidence that should be felt in a hypothetical situation: a situation where none of the things that, we believe, affect frequencies of *B*s among *A*s would be different from those which obtained on our trials. Similarly the modal claim expresses our fear that the hypothetical series might exhibit the different frequency q, and our actual set of trials may be a very poor indication of it. However, there is no reason to be depressed by these possibilities, for induction works, and what produces a frequency of outcomes one day is very likely to do substantially the same the next.

It seems to me that this is an account of our apparently realistic talk (in this case, modal claims and claims apparently divorcing local judgements from expressions of confidence) that yet concedes nothing to realism. Chances have not entered as real facts, capable of explaining or causing events. They remain projections, even if we are interested in spreading them not only over the actual events that have confronted us or that will confront us, but over events that could have happened as well.

In my last section I want to take up another problem that may tempt us to realism: the problem of our willingness to talk about knowledge of chance, and our subtlety in so doing.

IV

Let us suppose that the best evidence is that the frequency of Bs among As indeed approximates to p, and will keep doing so. Clearly, then, a man with the degree of confidence p has the habit of singular belief that meets Ramsey's standard: he has a degree of confidence proportionate to the number of times he is right. But there is another standard needed. For it does not follow that we should endorse this confidence, nor this judgement of chance. Consider that we may be able effectively to divide the As into two classes and rightly predict a high ratio of Bs among the CAs and a low ratio among the others. I shall call this 'effecting a partition of the As'. If this were done we would be in a better position than him in this very straightforward sense. Using our knowledge we can gamble with him and consistently win, by buying bets at a rate corresponding to p on CAs being B, and selling on $\sim CA$s. And in a variety of less mercenary ways we can see that our habit is more useful than his. It is more accurate, more efficient. It is not necessarily incorrect to say that the chance of an A being a B is p, even when effective partitions exist. We can, after all, talk of the chance of an animal being a carnivore, or of a human baby being Chinese. But if an acceptable practical application is to be made of such a remark, then the context must be one in which the participants themselves cannot easily put the subject matter into one or the other partition. If they could, then there would be something deficient about the distribution of confidence: it could effectively be improved. We might express this by saying that there is no case of an A, neither those which are C nor those which are not, on which we should accept such an estimate of the chance of it being a B. But if an acceptable single-case judgement is to follow from such a remark, then the conversational context will be one in which the participants cannot easily put the subject into one or other of the partitions. It remains true that if this can be done, the judgement of chance is deficient. (Of course, there is no implication here about negligence or otherwise in being ignorant about C.)

We here have the beginnings of a reasonably clear view of two topics that sometimes perplex analyses of probability: the rationality of seeking the narrowest reference class when we want single-case judgements, and the propriety of restricting the terminology of chance to phenomena which satisfy von Mises's second condition for an empirical collective, namely that there should be no effective selection procedure for singling out a subset of the members with a different overall frequency of the relevant property. (This is felicitously called 'the requirement of excluded gambling systems'.) To take the second issue first, if we believe that a selection procedure (corresponding to the property C in the last paragraphs) can *easily* be found, then it follows that we believe that our distribution of confidence can *easily* be improved, by the standards we have seen. While we believe such a thing we are obviously in a deficient position, and, depending on the consequences of a judgement and the degree of ease of improving our knowledge, we may wish to attach no weight to our judgement—to suspend it, in fact. The projectivist thus has excellent pragmatic reasons for confining our judgements of chance of an A being a B to reference classes for which we do not expect an easy method of partition. There is no metaphysics of randomness required. It is just that if we cannot effect a partition, a judgement of chance leads to our best possible habit. If we can, it does not.

The single-case problem is in effect the same. If you want to have a degree of confidence in the judgement of a particular philosopher that he drinks gin, the statistic of the proportion of men who drink gin helps. But that statistic can easily be refined: middle-class people, academics, academics in arts subjects, of a certain age . . . The pragmatic motive for seeking the narrowest reference class is just the same as before: a degree of confidence based solely on the wider statistic leaves its possessor in an inferior position vis-à-vis someone who can partition the class of men and attach different degrees of confidence to singular judgements depending upon the subclass in which the subject is found. Again, of course, the extent to which it is worth seeking statistics for narrower reference classes depends upon the expected benefit of the more discriminating judgement and the expected homogeneity of the reference class. If nothing much hangs on it and if our prior judgement is that gin drinking is not likely to be much different in any subsets we can think of, it may not be worth a research programme to find out. Nevertheless the point remains that unless we make our evidence as weighty, in Keynes' sense, as we can, by considering possible partitions of our class, we cannot be sure that we are properly serving the purposes of judgement, and the right think to do may be to form no opinion. A good example of such reticence comes from legal suspicion of a 'mere' statistic putting a defendant into a class with a high frequency of guilt. Unless the class is as weighty as it can be made, it would be impermissible to be confident that the defendant is guilty.[11]

It seems to me that this pragmatic perspective on these issues has a clear advantage over a realist metaphysics. Notoriously, in trying to give sense to the single-case judgement, a realist metaphysic of chance becomes tangled in

---

11. L. J. Cohen, *The Probable and the Provable* (Oxford: Clarendon Press, 1977), esp. chapter 7.

the issue of determinism. If it is determined now that I will, or will not, catch a cold next winter, it is hard to see what sense to make of talk of my propensity to do so or not, just as, if I did not die before I was thirty, it is very unclear what could be meant by saying that I had a propensity to do so. Yet I had a chance of doing so. Equally, only if a chance setup is indeterministic will it be, for a realist, true that trials on it form a collective. Otherwise, it is in principle possible to select trials with a different long-run frequency of outcomes. For the projectivist this becomes simply irrelevant. Our purpose in making judgements of chance, and the standards to use in following out those purposes, are perfectly indifferent to whatever secret springs and principles lie behind the empirical collectives that form the subjects of those judgements. When our best judgement is that we should treat the trials on some setup as forming a collective, we are entitled to project a chance and form confidence accordingly; when we suspect that we can find a partition, we should not. But there need have been nothing wrong with us if we have treated something as a collective, but at some improved state of knowledge a partition is found. Not all ignorance is culpable.

The realist is apt to be impatient with such *laissez-aller* attitudes. True, he will say, you can tell us when we talk of empirical chance, and perhaps you can give some pragmatic understanding of why we do. But for all that, we may be *wrong* to do so in some cases even when we are not culpable. Warranted assertibility is not truth. A later discovery that a trial on a chance setup A fell into a subclass with a different ratio of Bs from that shown overall would show that we had spoken falsely; but what made our remark false was not the discovery but the fact about the trial. Unless indeterminism is true, there are always such facts, in principle, forcing falsity on all attributions of chance other than 0 or 1. This argument is all the more persuasive because it cannot be avoided by mentioning warranted assertibility in the long run, the usual pragmatist substitute for truth. Once we admit that there are facts determining whether a particular outcome will occur or not, we cannot very well claim that a long run of improving investigation would not find them; and in that case determinism will entail that all chances of particular events are 0 or 1, even on this definition.

But it is the definition that is at fault. A projectivist need have no use for truth, about the chance of a single case, as the limit of the degree of confidence to which progressive omniscience would tend. He *does* need a proper account of fallibility, enabling him to admit that a particular estimate of chance might in principle be improved. This we have provided him, without any involvement in the metaphysics of determinism. This means that along with a judgement he has the concept of a standpoint yielding a possibly improved judgement. It does *not* mean that he needs the concept of a standpoint from which *all* other judgement is seen to be wrong, and this is what the unnecessary notion of the limit is attempting to import.[12]

In practice this means that although we have plenty of use for warranted,

12. See also essays 1 and 2.

defensible, careful, estimates of chances of particular events, we have less use for claims that we know such chances. The claim to knowledge entails, I think, the claim that no improved standpoint, yielding a revised estimate, is possible. To know something is to know that no judgement contradicting one's own could be really preferable. To know that the chance of an outcome on a single trial is p we would need theoretical knowledge that no partition exists. thus we are entitled to say that we know the chance of an individual outcome on an individual trial only if we are entitled to say that we know that the chance setup admits of no partition. Now we can adopt different standards for saying this. The clearest case (where, as it were, even God cannot partition the trials) is one where we know that the system is indeterministic. Yet our standards need not be so absolute. We may know that whatever God could do, there could be no practicable project of partitioning the trials. The systems on which people gamble are designed so that this is so. In such a system we have effectively ruled out the possibility of an improved judgement about any single trial, and we can properly express belief that we have succeeded in doing this by claiming knowledge of the chance. In other cases, responsible judgement is all that we want or need.

How far can our quasi-realism, our attempt to found apparently realist practice on a subjective basis, succeed? A possible stumbling block would be talk of chances as explaining events, or as themselves being things that need explanation. This would seem to invest them with some ontological standing, with a real influence on the world, which fits ill with the projectivist picture. But perhaps the appearance is deceptive, for everything will depend on the interpretation we make of such explanatory claims. Clearly, if we have a generalized antirealist attitude toward science, then chances could be as honest inhabitants of theory as any other posit can be. But even without this, once we have incorporated the notion of truth, or right opinion, there will be natural things to ask and say about why chances are what they are. We can ask what it is about the world that makes it the case that one particular distribution of confidence over propositions about some subject matter is right. And we can, in asking why something is the case, cite that some such distribution is right as part of our answer, even if this looks dangerously like giving some chances a real, causal, place. It need not be doing so, for instance, because if we endorse one distribution (say, give a 0.5 chance to heads in a coin toss) it will standardly follow that we ought to endorse others (a 0.25 chance of two heads on two trials) and it is no surprise that if asked why this is the chance on two trials, we reply by citing the first 'fact'. This is not the place to enter into all the moves a projectivist might make in tackling explanatory contexts, but their mere existence is unlikely to be much of a problem for him. The empirical part of science connects frequencies with whatever factors influence them, and our reaction to this knowledge is our talk of chance. If, in expanding such reactions, we find ourselves talking of chances explaining things and needing explanation, the proper response is to ask what we are projecting onto the world by making these remarks.

A more serious threat is that with its very success quasi-realism takes much of the impetus out of subjectivism. Responsible subjectivism is less fun. If, one by one, a quasi-realist programme takes over the things that realists used to consider their special private property, then the view that we have real metaphysical options becomes more doubtful. We all thought we knew what we meant by subjectivism, as opposed to propensity theories, frequency theories, and so on. But, if I am right, the intellectual practices supposedly definitive of these different positions can be available to all, so that the old definitions and divisions appear quite artificial.

In any case, if there is a metaphysical issue, then the subjectivists, so far as we have yet discovered, may have been right about it. But the subjectivism is not the irresponsible and therefore inefficient brand with which Ramsey is wrongly associated. It maintains standards for proper projection, and those standards go beyond coherence and beyond the dynamic coherence that I discussed. They involve a proper respect for frequencies, arising from a proper respect for induction. The main consequence of this responsibility is that subjectivism, as a metaphysic, becomes immune to a large variety of abuses. It also finds itself able to give sense to most of the thoughts that tempt us to realism. However, it maintains what can be seen as clear gains: it avoids the metaphysical problems of indeterminism, since proper single-case projections can be made when we are perfectly indifferent to that issue, and by trying to purchase realist practice from a more austere metaphysic we may come to feel more secure in that practice. There would, of course, be much more to be said if we were to expand the quasi-realist programme, particularly to cover the hypotheticals that are involved in the modal claims I discussed. But my instinct is that if there are obstacles on this route, then they afford opportunities for delightful scrambles, rather than excuses for retreat. And I think that was Ramsey's view as well.

Addendum

It may be instructive to add some notes comparing the resolutely antirealist approach sketched in this paper (and of course much more technically elaborated in works such as Jeffrey's *The Logic of Decision* (Chicago: University of Chicago Press, 1983) and Skyrms's *Choice and Chance* (Encino, Calif.: Dickenson, 1975) with the eclectic theory of David Lewis's 'A Subjectivist's Guide to Objective Chance'. Lewis believes that the practice of science requires, in addition to measures of reasonable partial belief, a notion of 'objective chance'. However, our best grip on this notion is given via our conception of what reasonable credence concerning it amounts to: the Principal Principle. This identifies the chance of an event at a world and a time as the unique degree of belief in the event that would arise from any reasonable initial degree of belief, by conditionalizing on the complete history up to the time and 'theory of chance' at the world.

This is the upbeat side (I owe the description to James Logue). It seems, initially, grist to the antirealist mill, since direct evaluations of objective chance now turn out to be the kinds of thing a subjectivist can make—provided, of course, he can access the history and the 'theory of chance'. Objective chance might stand to confidence like values stand to attitudes. In the philosophy of value we might say that the objective value of a state is or reflects the attitude you would have to it given the complete facts ('history') and theory of value. Provided that having a theory of value is something like having a sensibility, that is, a fact-in/attitude-out grinder (or having such a grinder plus proper concern for coherence and attitudes of fallibility, describable by the antirealist), all is well. It would not be well if having such a theory were having a description of a particular part of the way of the world, because the antirealist will resist the metaphysics that this seems to be bringing with it.

Lewis does not see it like this. He wants to leave objective chance as a real aspect of things, and it is instructive to see the difficulties this causes (the downbeat side). These centre around finding a coherent status for the theory of chance, or the 'history-to-chance' conditionals. Lewis himself appears to vacillate over the crucial feature of this theory already mentioned, namely whether we are to think of it as *true* or not. When it first comes in 'it may or may not be a complete theory, a consistent theory, a systematic theory, or a credible theory. It might be a miscellany of unrelated propositions about what the chances would be after various fully specified particular courses of events. Or it might be systematic . . .' (p. 96). But it rapidly transforms itself into the theory that *holds* at w, or in other words, the truth about how history determines chance at w (p. 97). The transformation is critical for the subjectivist versus objectivist opposition, of course. In the former guise the theory is naturally thought of as the subject's own set of procedures or norms for distributing confidence in the face of empirical knowledge; in the latter guise it seems more like an objective, potentially unknown and even unknowable specification of how real chances relate to real events in the particular world. Only in the latter guise does it sustain Lewis's realism about chance. It is also worth remarking that only in the latter guise does it seem the kind of thing chances might supervene upon. We do not normally think of values, for instance, as supervening on our own dispositions to value this or that, and it can falsify practical reasoning to think of them doing so (see chapter 9 for more on this. The theme is usefully taken up in Philip Pettit and Michael Smith, 'Backgrounding Desire', *Philosophical Review,* 1989).

The difficulty that I interpret Lewis's paper to be exploring is not this, but rather the problematic modal status for history-to-chance conditionals. Either they are necessary, or they are contingent. If necessary, then any two worlds sharing the same Humean mosaic (or even the same historical Humean mosaic, or set of admissible events) share the same chances. If contingent, what are they contingent upon? Lewis dislikes the first option because he cannot see belief in such conditionals as rationally compulsory. But we are fairly familiar with the idea of necessary truths that are not rationally compulsory. My own reason for disliking it would be that it appears to fly in the face of the methodology implicit in judgements of chance. We make such judgements in the light of finite evidence in accordance with various methodologies from the family of laws of large numbers. When a finite pattern is interpreted as a Bernoulli sequence in which each event has a chance p, we understand that the same pattern *could* have been the outcome of a different chance set up: a non-Bernoullian sequence in which chances change, or a sequence in which every event had a somewhat different chance than p. The history-to-chance conditionals are not treated as necessarily true. This is not the 'assertibility condition' for chances.

But if contingent, contingent upon what? The question will not trouble an antireductionist realist, content to see chance as another self-standing domain of fact, which may or may not vary with other things. It may not trouble a realist roughly of Armstrong's type, content to think in terms of universals and relations between them forming self-standing 'gridlocks' or instructions for the ways things fall out. But it rightly troubles Lewis (who doubts whether these theories can give any account of the Principal Principle, which sums up all we take ourselves to know about chance), and it troubles anyone who thinks that the Humean mosaic is all that there is. Perhaps one might think this but also think that a chance exists (how?) of there being other things that would in turn have altered the chances at the Humean world. But let us call a resolutely Humean world one where the mosaic makes up all that there is and *all that there is any chance of being.* What can history-to-chance conditionals be contingent upon in a resolutely Humean world? How could they be true in one such mosaic and not true in another identical mosaic? And if they could not so vary, we seem to be back with the necessity of history-to-chance conditionals.

The dilemma is sharp. But it should trouble Lewis only because of his realist leanings. If we jettison those we can give a perfectly good description of the way in which norms governing belief in chances should be governed by patterns in the Humean mosaic, the way in which those norms are neither rationally compulsory, nor, in the light of the large-numbers methodology, thought of as necessarily yielding the truth (the last word about chance at a world). There is no final puzzle to dispel over how chances ('the things themselves') can be contingently related to the mosaic: finding that intractable is a symptom of the truth-conditional hankerings I tried to diagnose for modality in essay 3. (My thanks to David Lewis for extensive reaction to an earlier commentary on his paper, and especially to James Logue.)

5

Hume and Thick Connexions

I. Two Approaches

Recently there has been a pronounced shift in the interpretation of Hume on causation. The previous weight of opinion took him to be a positivist, but the new view is that he is a sceptical realist.[1] I hold no brief for the positivist view, but I believe it needs replacing by something slightly different, and that at best it shows an error of taste to make sceptical realism a fundamental factor in the interpretation of Hume.

Let us call any concept of one event producing another, or being necessarily a cause or consequence of another, and that involves something in the events beyond their merely being kinds of events that regularly occur together, a thick concept of the dependence of one event on another. Then on the positivist account, Hume believes that no thick notion is intelligible. On the positivist view there is very little that we can ever understand and mean by a causal connexion between events. All we can understand and properly mean by talk of causation is that events fall into certain regular patterns, and the positivist interpretation is that Hume offered this as a reductive definition of causation. This is the famous regularity theory, summed up in the 'philosophical' definition: 'an object, followed by another, and where all the objects similar to the first are followed by objects similar to the second'.[2] The sceptical realist view denies that Hume offered any such reduction or analysis of the notion of causation. It takes seriously the many passages in which Hume appears to allow that we are talking of some thick notion of dependence of one event on another, going beyond regular succession. It takes it that Hume acknowledges that there is some such thick relation, even if it will be one about whose nature and extent we are doomed to ignorance. Hence, in John Wright's phrase, sceptical realism.

At first sight the difference between positivism and sceptical realism is reasonably clear, and it is plausible that if these are the two options then Hume is better seen as tending toward the second. But, as proponents of the

1. I have in mind Edward Craig, *The Mind of God and the Works of Man* (Oxford: Clarendon Press, 1987); Galen Strawson, *The Secret Connexion* (Oxford: Clarendon Press, 1989); and John Wright, *The Sceptical Realism of David Hume* (Manchester: Manchester University Press, 1983).

2. *Enquiry Concerning Human Understanding,* ed. Selby Bigge, section VII, part II, p. 76.

sceptical realist interpretation realize, there is one big problem, arising from Hume's theory of meaning. Sceptical realism seems to demand that we understand what it would be for one event to depend thickly upon another, even if we are ignorant of the nature of this relation; Hume seems to insist that we have no impression and hence no idea of any such dependence.

The problem here is a problem for any interpretation and can be focussed on a contradiction, to which Hume seems to be committed:

(1) We have no ideas except those that are preceded by suitably related impressions.
(2) There are no impressions that are suitably related to the idea of a thick necessary connexion between distinct events.
(3) We have an idea of a thick necessary connexion between distinct events.

The 'suitable relation' spoken of includes direct copying, in the case of simple ideas, and whatever is covered by 'compounding' in the case of complex ideas that are compounded out of simple ones.

The positivist interpretation takes Humes to be claiming that when we talk of causation we mean only something that strips out the thick element of necessity and substitutes regular contiguous succession. So (3) is false. The difficulty is that Hume apparently denies this:

> Shall we then rest contented with these two relations of contiguity and succession, as affording a compleat idea of causation? By no means. An object may be contiguous and prior to another, without being consider'd as its cause. There is a NECESSARY CONNEXION to be taken into consideration; and that relation is of much greater importance, than any of the other two above-mentioned.[3]

The central problem in interpreting Hume is coping with the contradiction. The sceptical realist strategy is to downplay the importance of the theory of understanding, so that even if Hume officially said (2), it played a negligible part in his view of causation.

II. A Doubtful Distinction

How then does the sceptical realist deal with the problem of meaning? Edward Craig and Galen Strawson draw attention to a distinction that occurs in Hume's writings.[4] When the theory of ideas threatens our idea of external existence or 'body', it is said that Hume invokes a distinction between what we can 'suppose' and what we can 'conceive', the idea being that we can coherently suppose that there are things of some sort (external objects) even when strictly we have no idea of what it is that we are supposing. Another way of putting it is that we have a 'relative' idea of things whose 'specific' differ-

---

3. *Treatise of Human Nature*, ed. Selby Bigge (Oxford: Oxford University Press, 1888), p. 77.
4. Edward Craig, op. cit., p. 124, and Galen Strawson, op. cit., chapter 12.

ence from other things we cannot comprehend. We could say that we have no
representative idea of what we talk about, but a relative or relational idea,
locating it by its role. We would talk of a 'something-we-know-not-what' that
does something or bears some relation to an aspect of the world of which we
do have an idea. This distinction solves the contradiction by distinguishing
between the terminology of (2) and (3). Hume thinks we have no representative idea of causation: we have no impression of it, and in some important
sense it remains incomprehensible, and we cannot represent to ourselves what
it is. What we do have, however, is a relational idea of it: it is whatever it is
that issues in regular successions of events or upon which such patterns depend, or whatever forces such regularities. The negative side is given in (2)
but the positive side in (3).

The texts, however, give no direct support to this interpretation of Hume.
While he does indeed use both a 'relative' versus 'specific' distinction and the
possibility of 'supposing' what we cannot 'conceive', he uses them very spar-
ingly indeed. In fact he never uses either, nor mentions either, in connexion
with causation. He never uses or mentions either in the *Enquiry* or in the
Dialogues in any context at all. This alone makes them unlikely candidates for
a central role in understanding his mature philosophy.[5] But worse, there are
warning signs to be noticed when they occur in the *Treatise*. There are four
occurrences: on pp. 67–68, p. 188 referring back to them, p. 218, and p. 241.
In none of these cases is Hume actually contrasting a specific versus a relative
idea of any one property or relation, enjoining us that we can understand a
property or object by its relations even if we cannot understand it by some
stricter standard derived from the theory of ideas. On the contrary, in each
context it is the impossibility of conceiving a 'specific difference' between
external objects and perceptions that is the focus of attention. 'Specific' quali-
fies the properties supposedly differentiating external objects from ideas, and
of these specific qualities we know and understand nothing by any standard at
all. Here are the two major passages with enough surrounding context to
matter:

> Now since nothing is ever present to the mind but perceptions, and since all
> ideas are deriv'd from something antecedently present to the mind; it fol-
> lows, that 'tis impossible for us so much as to conceive or form an idea of any
> thing specifically different from ideas and impressions. Let us fix our atten-
> tion out of ourselves as much as possible: Let us chase our imagination to the
> heavens, or to the utmost limits of the universe; we never really advance a
> step beyond ourselves, nor can conceive any kind of existence, but those
> perceptions, which have appear'd in that narrow compass. This is the uni-
> verse of the imagination, nor have we any idea but what is there produc'd.
> The farthest we can go towards a conception of external objects, when
> suppos'd *specifically* different from our perceptions, is to form a relative
> idea of them, without pretending to comprehend the related objects. Gener-
> ally speaking we do not suppose them specifically different; but only attri-

---

5. It is particularly odd that Strawson relies upon them, since he conceives of the *Enquiry* as
embodying Hume's official theory of causation.

bute to them different relations, connexions and durations. But of this more fully hereafter. (pp. 67–68)

Philosophers deny our resembling perceptions to be identically the same, and uninterrupted; and yet have so great a propensity to believe them such, that they arbitrarily invent a new set of perceptions, to which they attribute these qualities. I say, a new set of perceptions: For we may well suppose in general, but 'tis impossible for us distinctly to conceive, objects to be in their nature any thing but exactly the same with perceptions. What then can we look for from this confusion of groundless and extraordinary opinions but error and falsehood? And how can we justify to ourselves any belief we repose in them? (p. 218)

It requires some daring to take these passages as a model for sceptical realism. Hume is far—about as far as can be—from saying that we actually possess a going idea of the external world that allows us to understand, by some weak standard, what the externality is that we do not know about. Each of the two passages gives the strongest contrary impression. The first affirms idealism ('. . . we never really advance a step beyond ourselves'). The second introduces the 'supposes' versus 'conceives' distinction only while he simultaneously dismisses its effect out of hand. Its dismissal justifies Hume in describing his Philosophers (the culture whose spokesman is Locke) as actually inventing new *perceptions,* rather than inventing new things different from perceptions. This is the very opposite of the view a sceptical realist Hume should take. He should admit that a Lockean succeeds in introducing a (relative) notion of an external object as something that has various relations to our perceptions, and then go on to worry how much we know about such objects. Hume does not do this: he simply dismisses the idea that we have a set of determinate, intelligible, propositions about which, unfortunately, we shall never know the truth. It is not that we understand something, but cannot know whether it is true; it is that we give ourselves explanations that seemed to introduce an intelligible concept, but in fact fail (the demands put upon an external world independent of perception are simply inconsistent). We are in the domain of a 'confusion of groundless and extraordinary opinion' where our only hope is to abandon reason altogether. So, even when it is used, the 'specific' versus 'relative' distinction is not used as Craig and Strawson would have it used in the different area of causation, to which, as I have said, Hume never applies it.

III. Another Distinction

Before proceeding it is necessary to have in mind two things that might be asked of 'thick' causation. When we think of a causally connected pair of events, such as the impact of the first billiard ball causing the motion of the second, we want there to be a further fact than (mere) succession, or even mere regular succession of these kinds of event. We want there to be a dependency or connexion, a fact making it so that when the first happens the second

must happen. Call this the desire for a causal nexus. But now suppose we shift
our gaze to the whole ongoing course of nature. Again, we may want there to
be a further fact than mere regular succession. We feel that the ongoing
pattern would be too much of a coincidence unless there is something in virtue
of which the world has had and is going to go on having the order that it does.
We want there to be some secret spring or principle, some ultimate cause, 'on
which the regular course and succession of objects totally depends'.[6] This is
whatever it is that ensures the continuation of the natural order, that dispels
the inductive vertigo that arises when we think how natural it might be, how
probable even, that the constrained and delicate pattern of events might fall
apart. Call the desire for this further fact the desire for a straitjacket on the
possible course of nature: something whose existence at one time guarantees
constancies at any later time.[7]

A fact alleviating this vertigo has to be a very peculiar fact, for the following reason. It has to be something whose own continued efficacy through time
is subject to no possibility of change or chance of failure. For otherwise the
fact that it keeps on as it does would itself be a case of coincidence or fluke,
another contingency crying out for explanation and engendering inductive
vertigo. Some think they can point us toward a fact with this potency. Some
draw comfort from God's sustaining will (as if anything understood on the
analogy of our own mental states could be timeproof!). David Armstrong
believes that a kind of necessary, timeless, gridlock of universals will do.[8]
Galen Strawson takes comfort in fundamental forces constitutive of the nature of matter.[9]

It is easy to conflate the desire for a nexus, case by case, with the desire for
a straitjacket. But Hume (sometimes—but see below) is clear that they are
different. They are different because whatever the nexus between two events
is at one time, it is the kind of thing that can in principle change, so that at a
different time events of the same kind may bear a different connexion. Thus
suppose we grant ourselves the right to think in terms of a thick connexion
between one event and another: a power or force whereby an event of the first
kind brings about an event of the second. Nevertheless, there is no contradiction in supposing that the powers and forces with which events are endowed at
one time cease at another, nor in supposing that any secret nature of bodies
upon which those powers and forces depend itself changes, bringing their
change in its wake. Hume emphasizes this point in both the *Enquiry* and the
Treatise.[10] It is his reason for denying that the problem of induction can be
solved by appeal to the powers and forces of bodies. But it is equally a reason
for separating the question of a nexus from that of a straitjacket. Nexuses by

6. *Enquiry*, p. 55.
7. At least. It may be that its existence at one time should entail its existence at any
previous time as well. But one way of gesturing at what is wanted is to imagine God creating it by
some kind of fiat or act of law-giving, whose writ would run only into the future.
8. *What is a Law of Nature* (Cambridge: Cambridge University Press, 1983), p. 88 ff.
9. E.g., p. 91, pp. 254–55.
10. *Treatise*, pp. 90–91; *Enquiry*, p. 37.

themselves do not provide a straitjacket. The ongoing regularity and constancy even of a thick nexus between one kind of event and another is just as much a brute contingent regularity as the bare regular concatenation of events.[11] In each case we have something that can engender the inductive vertigo, or whose continuation through time might be thought to demand some kind of ground or ultimate cause or straitjacket.

The difference between a nexus holding on some particular occasions and a straitjacket guaranteeing the continuation of a pattern of connexions is easy to overlook. This is because of a lurking epistemological difficulty. Suppose one thinks that a particular nexus can be known for what it is, for instance by some observation whose content is more than the mere succession of events. One might report this by claiming to have seen that the one event *had to* happen, given the other. But if you see a 'must' in one pair of events, would you not thereby see that it will hold for every pair of some kind that the original pair enables you to identify? How could you see it without seeing something with general implications, and ones that are immune to temporal change? In other words, you will take yourself to have seen a timeproof connexion: one that rigidly governs how things could ever fall out. To put it the other way round, if things were not to fall out as expected, the original claim to have seen that the one event had to follow the other is refuted. This in turn makes it hard to see how a particular nexus could be an object of observation. Observation extends only to limited periods of space and time: how could we have within our view something that *essentially* casts its net over the whole of space and time?

This problem probably explains one puzzling feature of Hume's procedure. He repeatedly affirms that someone who has a full apprehension of a thick causal connexion would be in a position to make an *a priori* claim about the way events will fall out and what kind of event will be caused by another. He argues that because we cannot have this time-proof knowledge we do not apprehend the causal connexion, for instance in the exercise of our own will.[12] The argument seems initially to be, as Craig describes it, a muddle, since there is no evident reason why someone apprehending a nexus on one occasion should thereby know that the same nexus will obtain on another—the very point Hume himself emphasizes when arguing that powers and forces will not solve the problem of induction.[13] I suspect that Hume sees that nothing would really count as apprehension of a particular 'must' unless it carried with it implications of uniformity for the general case. It is to be (*per impossibile*) a particular apprehension, but one with the consequences of apprehending a straitjacket. Someone apprehending a straitjacket for what it is will as a

---

11. One might seek to avoid this by the verbal manoeuvre of identifying kinds of events by their causal powers, in which case it will follow that events of the same kind will bear the same causal connexions. But as Hume in effect points out, inductive vertigo then transfers itself to the contingent question of whether future events with the same sensory appearance will turn out to be of the same kind.

12. *Enquiry*, section 7, passim.

13. *Treatise*, p. 91, and Craig, p. 97.

consequence know its immunity to time and chance: he will know the timeless 'must' that it guarantees. He will be apprehending the impossibility that events should ever transpire otherwise. He has therefore a piece of knowledge that, although it took an empirical starting point in the apprehension of an individual thick necessary connexion, can be seen *a priori* to have implications for all other places and times. And it is this that Hume treats as his target, even when the issue ought to be the apparently lesser one of the particular nexus.[14]

There may be some room for manoeuvre over the lesser claim to have apprehended a particular, but not necessarily timeproof, thick connexion. One might try allowing the particular apprehension not to carry any implications for what might be present on other occasions.[15] The difficulty will be that an apprehension of a mutable thick connexion does not gives us quite what we want from knowledge of causation. That knowledge has to have a *consequence:* the subject possessing it must be prepared to foretell the one kind of event on the appearance of the other. It is not at all clear how apprehension of a particular relation obtaining at a particular place and time could automatically carry any such consequence: one might, as it were, say that this is how events are connected today, and form no expectation, and not know what to expect to happen tomorrow.

Sceptical realism might characterize Hume's position on either the nexus or the straitjacket. But unless we understand the extraordinary demands on a straitjacket we shall fail to see that realism concerning it is hardly important compared to his scepticism. Thus when Strawson opposes the Regularity Theory, with its ongoing flukes, by citing 'fundamental forces' essentially constitutive of 'the nature of matter', and invokes these to soothe away inductive vertigo, he is surely forgetting Hume's point.[16] Even if forces are taken 'to latch on to real, mind independent, observable-regularity-transcendent facts about reality',[17] they need something further in order to serve as a straitjacket. They need *necessary* immunity to change; they need to be things for which the inductive vertigo does not arise. Equally, if the 'nature of matter' is to help, then the continuation of matter must not be just one more contingency, whose falling out the same way instant after instant, time after time, is a cosmic fluke. The force that through the green fuse drives the flower might falter, and so might the fuse and the flower, but a straitjacket must not. Its immunity to change must be necessary, for if it is contingent then either it is a fluke—of any changes that might occur, none ever does—or else this regularity is itself not brute but demands some further straitjacket in the background, of which we have even less inkling. The point is that we will not locate it by ordinary talk of 'force' and its cognates. For even if Hume can countenance

14. On these issues, see also Peter Millican, 'Natural Necessity and Induction', *Philosophy* 61, 1986.

15. G. E. M. Anscombe, 'Causality and Determination', in *Metaphysics and the Philosophy of Mind* (Oxford: Blackwell, 1981).

16. Strawson, p. 91.

17. Ibid.

understanding of a thick nexus, the theoretical pressures on a straitjacket are a great deal more demanding.[18]

Hume's main interest in causation is to destroy the idea that we could ever apprehend a straitjacketing fact: we have no conception of it, nor any conception of what it would be to have such a conception, nor any conception of how we might approach such a conception. In particular we must not think of the advance of science as targeted on finding such a thing. The lesson drawn from Newton is that just as *Principia* gives us the operation of gravitational force but does not tell us what it is, so any conceivable advance in science can do only more of the same. It can put events into wider and more interesting and exception-free patterns, and that is all. 'The most perfect philosophy of the natural kind only staves off our ignorance a little longer."[19]

Would it be easy for Hume to allow us a 'relative' idea of a straitjacketing fact—a something-we-know-not-what that governs/brings about/explains the continuing order of nature? We understand this only insofar as we understand the relation of governing or bringing about. But can we understand the relation? Can Hume say the relation part of the relational idea is intelligible? The question is whether we know what governing or bringing about would be when we have no example, and indeed no conception, of the kind of fact alleged to be doing it. Hume, given his endorsement of Berkeley's theory of ideas, must say that we cannot take relational ideas (governing, forcing, grounding, issuing in, bringing about) out of the context within which they have intelligible application, and apply them without blush in contexts in which they do not.[20] We can generate the general idea only if we have particular examples. Otherwise, comprehension fails.

Nevertheless, it will be said, even if this shows that we have no idea at all of what would count either as straitjacket, or as knowledge that some kind of fact provides one, it seems plain that Hume allows that there is one, even while insisting on scepticism about its nature. Sceptical realists might be right that he allows us a 'relative' idea of such a fact, silently betraying the Berkeleyan

---

18. Strawson is probably betrayed into this conflation by using the one term 'Causation' (with a capital 'C') equally for a thick nexus and a thick straitjacket.

19. *Enquiry*, p. 31. This is the famous point where Newton said '*hypotheses non fingo*', and the point that left contemporary scientists such as Huygens and Leibniz, who had wanted to know what gravity *was* and not merely how bodies moved under its influence, feeling badly let down. Newton was quite within his rights to want more scientific understanding of gravitational attraction, and Hume does not oppose the goal. But if Newton and his contemporaries wanted a different thing—an understanding of the impossibility that events should ever fall out otherwise—then Hume stands in his way. Hume does not magnify the difference between himself and Newton, but if Newton was aiming at this superlative piece of understanding and thought that the methods of natural science might give it, then Hume is clearly opposed. He was the first to see that what Newton did was the only kind of thing that could ever be done.

20. Berkeley's rigour on this is apparent in his constant polemic against 'abstraction' and in such matters as his embargo on taking causal relations away from the domain of the will, given that it is this that is the basis of our understanding of them. More directly relevant is his insistence that if you try to introduce a 'relative notion' of matter as whatever it is that supports various properties, you mean nothing. As well as the passage quoted in the text, see *Principles of Human Knowledge*, part 1, section 80.

background. Even if this were technically correct—and we have seen how far it stretches the texts—it would still misplace the stress; this is why I originally described it as an error of taste rather than an outright mistake. The point is that Hume is utterly contemptuous of any kind of theorizing conducted in terms of such a thing. We are at the point where anything we say 'will be of little consequence to the world',[21] or in the world of 'notion(s) so imperfect that no sceptic will think it worthwhile to contend against (them)'.[22] His attitude must be the same as that he holds to an equally noumenal substratum, supporting the qualities of matter:

> But these philosophers carry their fictions still farther in their senti-
> ments concerning *occult qualities*, and both suppose a substance support-
> ing, which they do not understand, and an accident supported, of which
> they have as imperfect an idea. The whole system, therefore, is entirely
> incomprehensible. . . .[23]

He is here directly echoing Berkeley:

> Lastly, where there is not so much as the most inadequate or faint idea
> pretended to: I will not indeed thence conclude against the reality of any
> notion or existence of any thing: but my inference shall be, that you mean
> nothing at all: that you imply words to no manner of purpose, without any
> design or signification whatsoever. And I leave it to you to consider how
> mere jargon should be treated.[24]

Craig especially makes the case that there is importance in the positive claim that something-we-know-not-what exists, and the importance is sceptical: it enables Hume to destroy any pretension to finding what we might anteced-ently have hoped to understand about nature. I agree entirely that this critical aim is essential to Hume, and at least as important as the theory of understand-ing itself. But Hume enjoys this realignment without himself making any positive claim about the existence of any mysterious, straitjacketing fact or facts. The realignment of our self-image, our philosophy of what real discov-ery and understanding might be, is independent of any such assertion. We do not ourselves have to think the other side of the line to learn how tightly the line defining the limit of all possible empirical enquiry is drawn. The point is that our real engagement with the world, in our understanding and our sci-ence, and our self-image or philosophical understanding of the notions we actually use must sail on in complete indifference to any facts transcending our ideas. 'Relative' ideas of such facts play no role any more than relative ideas of many things: Cartesian egos (simple, indivisible entities whose perma-nence ensures the identity of the self); the substratum in which properties inhere; objective goods commanding the will of all those who apprehend

21. *Enquiry*, p. 155.
22. *Treatise*, p. 168. 'I am indeed, ready to allow, that there may be several qualities both in material and immaterial objects, with which we are utterly unacquainted; and if we please to call these power or efficacy, 'twill be of little consequence to the world'.
23. *Treatise*, p. 222.
24. Berkeley, *Three Dialogues between Hylas and Philonous*, dialogue 2, paragraph 121.

them, and so on. Since the actual business of making judgements about the identity of the self, or the possession of properties by things, or what is good or bad, goes on in complete indifference to these things, they play no role in our real understanding.[25] They have no use at all: nothing will do just as well as something about which nothing can be said.

IV. The Nexus

Perhaps the same is not true of individual thick connexions, that is, the particular causal nexus obtaining between specific events at a time. Don't we give every employment to such a notion? And if sceptical realists are right that Hume is not giving us a positivist reduction, do they remain in possession of the field here at least? I do not think so, for there is a third option: a truer description of Hume on ordinary empirical causation would be that he is neither a positivist nor a sceptical realist, but rather a not-so-sceptical anti-realist.[26] That is, he gives us a story explaining and even justifying our use of the vocabulary of causation, while denying that we represent a real aspect of the world to ourselves as we use it.

The outline of Hume's positive theory of causation is well known. The mind's perceptions, which form the material with which it must work, reveal only a regular succession of events. However, upon experience of such a regular succession the mind changes. It does not change by forming an impression or idea of any external property invisible in one instance alone. It changes functionally: it becomes organized so that the impression of the antecedent event gives rise to the idea of the subsequent event. No new aspect of the world is revealed by this change: it is strictly nonrepresentative, just like the onset of a passion, which which Hume frequently compares it.[27] But once it takes place we think of the events as thickly connected; we become confident of the association, we talk of causation, and of course we act and plan in the light of that confidence.

There are two separate components in this story: the contribution of the world to our apprehension, and the functional change in the mind itself.[28] These are the two aspects separated in the famous two 'definitions' of cause:

> An object, followed by another, and where all the objects similar to the first are followed by objects similar to the second.

---

25. Strawson is at pains to show that not all Hume's reference to straitjacketing facts are ironic, but I do not think he shows that they are not contemptuous.

26. Or, quasi-realist, in the sense of the essays.

27. Norman Kemp Smith, *The Philosophy of David Hume* (London: MacMillan, 1942), chapters I and II. These present convincing evidence that this comparison was the prime mover of Hume's theory of causation. It opened up the 'New Scene of Thought' of which he speaks in the 1734 letter to (probably) George Cheyne.

28. As clear a statement as any is Hume's recapitulation, *Enquiry*, pp. 78–79.

An object followed by another, and whose appearance always conveys the thought to the other.[29]

The first 'philosophical definition' describes the contribution of the world, insofar as we can apprehend it, and the second 'natural' definition describes the nonrepresentative, functional difference in the mind that apprehends the regularity. The parallel with Hume's philosophy of ethics is so far complete: again, there is a neutral starting point in the mind's apprehension of some nonethical facts, and then the onset of nonrepresentative passions ready to be voiced in our moralizing.

It is only now that complexities start, but unfortunately Hume gives less help with them than one would wish. The theory so far tells us of a nonrepresentative change, a change in the structure of our expectations, that gets expression when we deem two events to be causally connected. But it has not yet conjured up a full theory of the content of propositions about cause. It does not tell us, for example, what we are bothered about when we wonder if *A* caused *B*, what we are saying when we say that every event has a cause, or whether we can sensibly talk of unknown causes. We need more detail about the way in which cause becomes objectified so as to be spoken of as a feature of the real world, if its origin is in a feature of our own minds. Hume shows little interest in such questions, and indeed against the background of the theory of ideas, he can point only in misleading directions. He says, for example, that by a necessary connexion we 'mean' a connexion in the mind, leaving himself open to interpretation as a kind of Berkeleyan, taking the idea of necessity to be a representation of some thick connexion we are aware of in our own minds. He then has to spend Part 1 of Section VII of the *Enquiry* averting this misunderstanding.[30] In his theory of morality he similarly seems unclear whether he is saying that virtue and vice are 'nothing in the objects', but only sentiments in us, or that they are the qualities of objects that tend to arouse those sentiments.[31] What he lacks is a link between the real functional difference and the thick content to give causal judgements: the way we talk and think in terms of a projected property of things.[32] A telling point here is that in both the *Treatise* and the *Enquiry* he produces the 'two definitions' only at the end of the discussion, and in each place he does so apologetically, in effect telling us that they are not to be regarded as strict

29. *Enquiry,* pp. 76–77.

30. An interesting scholarly question, to which I do not know the answer, is why he took such elaborate care in the *Enquiry,* section VII, to distinguish his theory from Berkeley's, when the *Treatise* contains no corresponding passages. It is one of the very few cases where the *Enquiry* is fuller than the *Treatise.* Did some review or correspondence make the need evident to him?

31. His lists of virtues (e.g., *Enquiry Concerning the Principles of Morals,* appendix I, p. 258) specify the properties of people, such as benevolence, serenity, and so on, that make us love them; his official position (e.g., *Treatise,* pp. 471, 614) identifies the virtue with the sentiment itself.

32. Hume is quite prepared to allow that our common notion of cause contains defective elements—see the footnote on p. 77 of the *Enquiry.* But overall he is perfectly friendly to the way we think.

definitions. On the view I am recommending this is right: they separate the two different *aspects* of the matter—the contribution of the world, and the change in us. But they do not give us a lexicographer's analysis, and we should not expect one. There is no way of moralizing without using a moral vocabulary, and no way of causalizing without using the vocabulary of cause, efficacy, or power.

Notice, however, how many cards Hume holds in his hands. The basic theory is flexible enough to accommodate many points that are usually raised against him. Our reactions to nature are subtle: not all regularities betoken cause, and sometimes we attribute cause after miniscule experience of regularity.[33] Well and good: the basic theory need put no limits on the input to our causalizing, any more than his theory that in moralizing we voice a passion puts a limit on the input to our moralizing. On the output side, the change in the structure of our thought after we have deemed a sequence to be causal may also be complex. Its heart is that we 'make no longer any scruple of foretelling' one event upon the appearance of another. But there may be other changes. We may become willing, for example, to hold the sequence constant as we think about what would have happened if something else had happened, or what would happen if something else were to happen. Once we view a sequence as causal, it is held fixed as we conduct counterfactual and conditional deliberations. Well and good: the basic theory puts no limits on such consequences either. The theory also happily predicts the 'intuitions' that lead people to detest the Positivistic 'regularity' theory of the content of our causal sayings. Someone talking of cause is voicing a distinct mental set: he is by no means in the same state as someone merely describing regular sequences, any more than someone who appreciates some natural feature as good is in the same state of mind as someone who merely appreciates the feature. The difference in this case is in the sentiment or passion that the feature arouses, and, in the causal case, in the fixity that the sequence of events takes in our thinking. Finally, the contradiction I identified at the beginning of this essay is sidestepped by distinguishing a representative idea of a connexion, which we do not have, from a capacity to make legitimate use of a term whose function is given nonrepresentatively, which we can have.

There are, I believe, only two ways in which this kind of theory could be opposed. One is to deny that a Humean could forge the missing links between the functional difference we are expressing and the surface content of our causal judgements. The other is to deny that we have here a distinctive position, by assailing the limits on 'representation' under which Hume operates. The first attack presses the point that Hume needs to tell us what happens not just when we think that *A* causes *B*, but also when we think that there exist unknown causal connexions, that regardless of whether we had ever existed there would still have been causal connexions, and so on. We think in terms of causation as an element of the external world, and there remains a real

---

33. Hume discusses these complexities in *Treatise* I, pp. iii, xv: 'Rules by Which to Judge of Causes and Effects'.

question of how much of this thought Hume can explain and how much he has to regret. However, his prospects for deflecting this first criticism must be quite bright. For as we have seen, he is working with exactly the same ingredients in the case of ethics. Here too there is the task of explaining the apparently objective content of moral judgements given their source in the passions, but here it is much harder to believe that the problem is insoluble, and Hume certainly did not believe it to be so.

The second attack need not deny Hume his ingredients. It simply claims that we can cook with them in a different way, awarding ourselves the right to a genuinely representative concept of causation. For when should we say that we have a representative idea of a property or relation? One answer would be: when we can picture it holding, or exhibit to ourselves in imagination a scene in which the property or relation is visibly instanced. This is a natural empiricist answer and the one that leaves Hume poised to argue that we have no representative idea of thick causal connexions. For a view (or succession of other experiences: sounds, felt pressures, and so on) in which there is given a certain succession of events, and in which one event causes another, need be no different from a view in which the one event does not cause another, but in which the same succession happens anyhow. This is why we have to interpret sequences as causal, and, however automatic this act is, it is still one that needs to be performed. But empiricism nowadays sounds like prejudice: why should we not have a *theoretical* concept of a thick causal connexion, allowing that there is a step from the raw appearance of a scene to the belief that it instances such and such connexions, but also insisting that we know what it is for such connexions to exist? We have a theoretical idea of them, and the idea represents the way the world is when they are present.

The real problem with this is that it only works if we also understand the relation between the thick connexions and the ongoing pattern of events. Thick connexions make events happen; they guarantee outcomes, they issue in patterns of events, and so on. But these are terms of dependency or causation, so we understand the theory only if we understand them. And this understanding in turn is queried by the problems described above: any realist theory needs to tell us how the 'musts' present on one occasion throw their writ over others. Otherwise it fails to give us what we want from a causal understanding of the world. For all the story goes, someone might be a virtuoso at detecting particular thick connexions, yet have no idea what to expect or how to conduct counterfactual and conditional reasoning.

The net result is that any such realist theory looks extravagant. It asks from us more than we need. To see this, imagine a character we might call the Bare Humean. The Bare Humean misses out this capacity for apprehension or theory, so does indeed lack the representative idea of thick connexions that these are supposed to give us. But she goes through the functional change that Hume describes, and conducts her expectations and actions accordingly. She can be an enthusiastic natural scientist, finding concealed features and concealed patterns in nature to aid prediction. She can understand that finding ever more simplicity and ever more general patterns may be 'set us as a task', so that there will always be more to know about nature. She will need a vocabulary to express her confidences and her doubts, and to communicate them to others; she will be a virtuoso at the salient features that are usable day by day to control her world. What else does she need? Are we sure she is missing anything at all—isn't she a bit like you and me?

II

ETHICS

6

Moral Realism

I

Granted that it is correct to reply to a moral utterance by saying 'That's true' or 'That's not true', the question remains of what sort of assessment is indicated by these responses. Dummett, with whose paper this emphasis is associated, also says that a statement is false if a state of affairs obtains such that a man asserting the statement and envisaging that state of affairs as a possibility would be held to have spoken misleadingly.[1] But there are ways and ways of speaking misleadingly, of which speaking falsely is only one; and indeed not always one, as when you say something false knowing that the hearer will misinterpret it as something true. Even apart from the possibility of misleading someone only as to my beliefs or my authority, still I can mislead someone *about the truth of the subject under discussion* when a state of affairs exists, and I envisage it as a possibility (and indeed more than a possibility), and I say nothing but the truth. I would do this for example if I told an interested child that some elephants are at least twice as large as some fleas. Worse than that, in what way does a man speak misleadingly if he sincerely judges a thing to be good, envisaging the possibility that he may be wrong, according to standards of which we are aware and with which we disagree? We hold his judgement false, but I don't think we would hold him to have spoken misleadingly, unless we just meant: what he said would mislead anyone who believed it as to the truth about whether the thing is good. But then the relevant assessment of misleadingness is itself to be understood in terms of truth.

Nevertheless, perhaps some candidate for the correspondence relation other than one constructed from misleadingness exists. It is the purpose of this essay to argue that there are features of the claim that a moral judgement is true that prevent this being taken as the claim that it corresponds in any way with a state of affairs. It follows that an attribution of truth to such a judgement must involve a different sort of assessment, and it is a secondary purpose of the paper to ask what that might be, and whether it should be thought surprising that we have a form of utterance with this form of assessment. I shall call the view that the truth of moral utterances is to consist in their correspondence with some fact or state of affairs 'moral realism'; it is this view

1. M. Dummett, 'Truth', *Proceedings of the Aristotelian Society,* 1958, p. 150.

that I shall argue is false. Another way of characterizing realism, adopted by Dummett,[2] would be as the belief that for any moral proposition there must be something in virtue of which either it or its negation is true. This certainly points to the same view: the advantage in stressing that it is the existence or nonexistence of a state of affairs that determines truth or falsity, according to the realist, is that it is precisely the disparity between the logical conditions upon the existence of states of affairs, and those upon moral truth, that is to be urged in what follows.

There exist already two well-known arguments for the falsity of moral realism. Both take one feature of assent to a moral proposition and claim that this is not a feature of belief that some state of affairs obtains; whence it follows that assent to a moral proposition—which may be expressed as belief that it is true—is not belief that some state of affairs obtains, and thence that the truth of a moral proposition does not consist in the existence of any state of affairs. The features that these arguments seize upon concern respectively our attitudes and our actions.

The first argument, then, emphasizes the connection between real assent to a moral proposition and the possession of a certain attitude to its subject. At its strongest, it can be stated as follows. Belief that a thing is good entails possession of a certain attitude towards it. No belief that a thing enters into a state of affairs entails the possession of any attitude towards it. Therefore, belief that a thing is good is not belief that it enters into a state of affairs, and moral propositions must be distinguished from propositions with realistic truth conditions.

The trouble with the argument lies in the second premise. For it is not at all evident that no belief that a thing enters into a state of affairs—no belief, that is, with realistic truth conditions—can entail[3] the possession of an attitude toward its subject. Consider, for example, the belief that a person X is *in possession of the truth* about some matter. This is clearly a factual belief. But if I come to hold this belief about X, doesn't it follow that my attitude toward X alters? I become prepared to defer to X's opinion on the matter, or commend his views to other people whom I wish to inform, and each of these is quite naturally construed as possession of an attitude toward X. Again, consider the way in which one's attitude to a statement must change according to whether one believes it to be true. Finally, there are beliefs—for example, that something is alive—that may also entail the possession of an attitude, even if all that can be said about the attitude is that it is one that one feels toward things that are alive, but not toward other things. Now these examples may produce a certain impatience. All that they could prove, it may be thought, is that the notion of an attitude can be used to cover such things as a belief that something is alive, or true. Seen this way, Wittgenstein's remark, 'My attitude towards him is an attitude towards a soul. I am not of the opinion that he has a soul',[4]

2. 'Truth', p. 157.

3. I am using 'entails' throughout in the logical sense, so that 'P entails Q' strictly implies that P strictly implies Q.

4. L. Wittgenstein, *Philosophical Investigations* (Oxford: Blackwell, 1958), part II, section IV.

tells us more about attitudes than about the judgement that people have souls. Now this can only be part of the truth, for it fails to explain why Wittgenstein's remark is a good deal more intelligible than, say, 'My attitude toward the room is an attitude toward a room with a bottle in it. I am not of the opinion that there is a bottle in it', but even if this was all that my examples indicated, it is enough to topple the anti-realist argument that we are considering. For if it is correct to say that real assent to the proposition that a thing is alive, or true, or a true proposition, then even if real assent to the proposition that a thing is good entails that my attitude toward it is an attitude toward a good thing— namely one of approval—still goodness may be as much a property of a thing as life or truth.

To this it will be replied that there are features of moral approval that are not shared by my other examples of 'attitudes', that enable it to be identified independently of statement of a moral belief. These features concern the necessary consequences for our choices and actions of holding a moral position. So the second argument we are to consider hopes to find, in the connection between moral belief and the will, a proof that moral realism is false. In so doing it would hope to find a practical aspect of moral approval that will distinguish it from other examples of attitudes, and so reinstate the first argument. I shall briefly describe two difficulties into which this line of thought runs, not in order to show that it cannot be correct, but in order to show that the obstacles in the way of its proper statement are sufficiently great that a new line of attack on moral realism may be not entirely otiose.

The position, then, is that the anti-realist is to describe a connection between moral belief and the will in such a way that it is clear that moral belief necessarily has connections that no realistic belief need have. The first trap is that of simply giving a false description of the connection, making it, for example, logically impossible to do something that one believes to be wrong, or logically impossible to will something that one believes to be bad. When it is realized that these things are possible, various things may be said about the situations in which they happen. This is the second trap: the failure to identify a connection that will perform what the argument requires. For example, if the claim is made that necessarily (other things being equal) an action done contrary to a moral belief produces remorse or guilt, then unless remorse or guilt can be identified as something further than attitudes felt toward actions that the person believes himself to have performed and that he believes to have been wrong, nothing to the purpose has been achieved. It would be like proving that the belief that a proposition is true cannot be a realistic belief, because it has this connection with the will: that upon considering a past action of stating the negation of a proposition believed true, one must feel the attitude ϕ, where ϕ is that attitude felt toward the past production of falsehood.

A better approach might be to try to identify this connection by considering the place that a moral belief holds in practical reasoning. The best statement of this for the purpose of the argument would, I think, go something like this. Consider the situation in which a person X is wondering whether to do A or to do B. Suppose a person Y tells him that A is the right thing to do.

Suppose that X believes Y. Then it is logically necessary that this belief is *relevant to his decision*. On the other hand, there can be no realistic belief of which this is necessary, for, as Hume saw, the relevance of belief that some state of affairs obtains to a decision is always contingent upon the existence of a desire whose fulfilment that state of affairs affects. Now this argument, as its antiquity suggests, is not easy to assess, and I shall not say by any means everthing that ought to be said about it. But the central difficulty is clear. To say that a belief is relevant to a decision is, analytically, to say that it *ought to be taken into account if the decision is to be the right one*. So the first premise of the argument says that it is logically necessary that the belief (that A is the right thing to do) ought to be taken into account if X's decision is to be the right one. Now this may be logically necessary, but only as it is logically necessary that the belief that A is the cheapest thing to do ought to be taken into account if the decision is to be the cheapest one. In short, the production of this argument serves only as a prelude to an explanation of the analyticity above, for otherwise it merely underlines connections between moral concepts. So until such an explanation is produced, this approach cannot be said to have produced the required connection between morality and the will.

II

There are, then, obstacles in the way of disproving moral realism by considering assent to a moral proposition. What I now want to do is to present an argument against moral realism that starts directly from the notion of the truth of a moral proposition. The form of the argument is this. I shall first describe two properties of moral truth, and then try to show how, jointly, they provide an insuperable difficulty for a realistic theory. The argument is not original,[5] but so far as I know it has never received a clear or detailed presentation in print.

The first property is that of supervenience. It is widely held that moral properties are supervenient or consequential upon naturalistic ones. The general notion of supervenience is capable of various slightly different expressions. We can take first:

> (S_1) A property M is supervenient upon properties $N_1 \ldots N_n$ if M is not identical with any of $N_1 \ldots N_n$, nor with any truth function of them, and it is logically impossible that a thing that is M should cease to be M without changing in respect of some member of $N_1 \ldots N_n$.

This is equivalent to saying that a thing ceasing to be M strictly implies that it has changed in respect of some member of $N_1 \ldots N_n$. So a contraposed version says that a thing remaining the same in respect of all members of

---

5. It was given to me in conversation by Dr. C. Lewy.

$N_1 \ldots N_n$ strictly implies that it does not cease to be M. However, the notion of supervenience that we want in ethics should be slightly stronger than this, for moral properties are capable of degree, and we should, if we believe in the supervenience of moral properties, also hold that a thing cannot come to possess them, or come to possess them in a greater or lesser degree than hitherto, without changing some of its naturalistic properties. So a better version is:

> (S)   A property M is supervenient upon properties $N_1 \ldots N_n$ if M is not identical with any of $N_1 \ldots N_n$ nor with any truth function of them, and it is logically impossible that a thing should become M, or cease to be M, or become more or less M than before, without changing in respect of some member of $N_1 \ldots N_n$.

Again, a contraposed version says that a thing remaining the same in respect of all members of $N_1 \ldots N_n$ strictly implies that it remains the same in point of possession, lack of possession, or degree of M-ness.

(S) defines a notion of a supervenience of a property applying to one thing over a period of time. But we also believe that if two things are the same in their naturalistic properties, then it follows that they are identical in their moral properties, that is, have the same moral worth. This notion of supervenience can be defined:

> (S_2)   A property M is supervenient$_2$ upon properties $N_1 \ldots N_n$ if M is not identical with any of $N_1 \ldots N_n$ or with any truth function of them, and it is logically impossible that two things should each possess the same properties from the set $N_1 \ldots N_n$ to the same degree, without both failing to possess M, or both possessing M, to the same degree.

For our purposes we need not distinguish between supervenience and supervenience$_2$. It is difficult to think of a property that might be supervenient upon some others in the sense of (S) but not supervenient$_2$ upon those others in the sense of (S_2), and I can think of no argument that might be used to show that moral properties are supervenient upon naturalistic ones in one sense but not the other. So from this point, when I talk of supervenience, I shall take it to include both notions, and the claim that moral properties are supervenient upon naturalistic ones embraces the claims that they are supervenient both in the sense of (S) and in the sense of (S_2). It should be noted that (S) and (S_2) define supervenience in terms of logical impossibility, and it is a logical claim about the interrelations of sets of properties that is being made. It may, for example, be a physical impossibility that two materials be identical in their crystalline properties but one strong and the other not, or a biological impossibility that two twins come from the same ovum but one be a zebra and the other not. But neither of these impossibilities indicates supervenience in the sense that I have defined, for neither is a logical claim. Similarly, if it were only a moral impossibility that two things should be identical in naturalistic properties but different in moral worth, then moral worth would not be supervenient upon naturalistic properties in my sense. One thing, then, that must be established in defending this part of the argument is that if somebody claimed, say, that an action was absolutely identical in every respect with another, except that it was much worse; or that a feature of character like courage had changed in no way in its nature, relations, consequences, yet was of much less value than formerly; it would be a logical and not merely a moral mistake that had been made.

The other feature of moral truth that is needed to support the argument is even more commonly believed in than its supervenience. It is that the possession of moral worth is not entailed by the possession of any set of naturalistic properties whatsoever, in any degree whatsoever. This lack of entailment has often been claimed, and often disputed, and often confused with other claims, such as that moral properties are not identical with naturalistic ones, or that moral properties have no criteria in a Wittgensteinian sense. So the precise claim that is being made is this:

(E)   There is no moral proposition whose truth is entailed by any proposition ascribing naturalistic properties to its subject.

This is not the claim that moral properties are not identical with any naturalistic ones. For although such an identity would ensure an entailment both from naturalistic to moral propositions and vice versa, to suppose that the existence of the entailment would ensure the identity is simply to indulge in wishful thinking. There are counter-examples to the thesis that Fa only entails Ga if F is identical with G or some conjunct of which G is a member, which have never been satisfactorily explained away, and it cannot be confidently assumed at the outset that this would not be one of them. Of course Moore's concern in *Principia Ethica* was to disprove the thesis that there is an identity, not the thesis that there is an entailment.

Second, (E) is not the claim that there are no naturalistic properties that are *necessarily reasons* for an ascription of a moral property. To say that P is necessarily a reason for Q is[6] to say that, necessarily, coming to know P ought to increase one's confidence in Q. Now suppose that there exist naturalistic properties such that necessarily coming to know that a thing possesses such a property ought to increase one's confidence that it is good. It would by no means follow that (E) is false. For it does not follow that any statement that a thing possesses one of these properties can be given that is a conclusive reason for the thing being good, in the sense that having come to know that statement, whatever else one learns about the thing in question, one is right to be certain that it is good. Whereas if an entailment exists, that is precisely what can be done, for if P entails Q, then the conjunction of P with any proposition whatsoever entails Q. This sort of consideration should be familiar from other

---

6. With minor complications.

areas of philosophy. For example, it is very plausible to suppose that some statements about what seems to be the case to some observers are necessarily reasons for supposing certain things to be true of the external world. That is, it is plausibly supposed to be necessary, and not contingent (for what could it be contingent upon?), that something's seeming to be yellow under appropriate conditions to an apparently normal person is a reason for supposing it to be yellow. But few people are prepared to believe that such statements about what seems to be the case can entail that something is the case. A better example comes from consideration of induction. It is very plausible to suppose that, necessarily, the knowledge of the existence of certain past regularities ought to increase one's confidence in certain appropriately related predictions. Yet there is no entailment between the evidence and the prediction. Now it is no part of my purpose to claim that these positions about perception and induction are correct in affirming that some things are necessarily reasons for others while no entailment can be produced. But the evident plausibility of supposing this is sufficient to show that claims about lack of entailment must be very sharply separated from claims about lack of a necessary reasoning relationship, and that it cannot be safely assumed that argument against the latter claim will transfer to the former. *A fortiori,* one must keep the claim that, necessarily, reasons for moral judgements must come from certain areas (facts concerning human interests, for example) entirely distinct from the claim that there is an entailment from some propositions describing things in those areas, to a moral proposition.

Third, (E) is not the denial that there exist criteria, in a Wittgensteinian sense, for the ascription of moral properties. What is meant by saying that P is a criterion, in a Wittgensteinian sense, for Q is not at all clear. It certainly doesn't mean just that P is necessarily a reason for Q, for there are cases where it is plausible to suppose that one proposition is necessarily a reason for another, yet extremely unnatural to call that proposition a criterion, in any sense, for the other. Nor would anyone who believes in the necessary reasoning relationship want to express it in this way. I have already given one example where this is true, in pointing out that perhaps certain facts about the past necessarily provide a reason for certain predictions; for surely nobody would want to express this by saying that perhaps some facts about the past are criteria, in a Wittgensteinian sense, for the truth of certain predictions. Again, for at least most values of P and Q, P is necessarily a reason for the conjunction $P\&Q$. Yet surely P is not therefore a criterion, in any sense, for the truth of $P\&Q$. Or, to take a familiar case, just as some philosophers claim that someone's exhibiting certain behaviour is necessarily a reason for supposing that he is in pain, so the knowledge that some unobserved person was in pain at a certain time may be necessarily a reason for supposing that he exhibited certain behaviour at or around that time, but it is obviously not a Wittgensteinian criterion for us exhibiting that behaviour.[7]

7. Strictly speaking, the propositions that might be thought necessary are not of the form 'coming to know P ought to increase one's confidence in Q', but rather 'If the situation is (in some

Perhaps some condition limiting the type of fact with which P and Q are respectively concerned can be added to the condition that P is necessarily a reason for Q to give an acceptable sense of 'criterion'. The result would be a conjunctive definition: 'P is a criterion of Q if and only if P is necessarily a reason for Q and knowing the sort of fact that P describes is the only way of knowing propositions like Q'. This would be a plausible attempt, and one that would give the result that if P described a naturalistic fact, and Q was a moral proposition, and P was necessarily a reason for Q, then P would be a criterion of Q. But then the question of whether there are naturalistic criteria for moral propositions would in effect be the question of whether there are necessary reasoning relationships, and, as we saw, this question must not be confused with that of the truth of (E).

These preliminary remarks serve only to distinguish (E) from other claims that a naturalist might wish to dispute; the important point is that (E) denies the existence of an entailment, not of a 'logical connection' of a weaker sort, nor of logical constraint on the areas from which morally relevant considerations must be adduced. This much said, I shall postpone further discussion of (E) and (S) until I have described the difficulty that they provide for moral realism. For it will turn out that a principle in some respects weaker than (E) can serve as a basis for the argument, so that although (E), being a familiar claim to moral philosophers, may provide the clearest starting point, the anti-realist might rest his position on something less controversial.

What, then, is the difficulty for realism that the lack of entailment described in (E) and the supervenience described in (S) and (S_2) jointly promise? Suppose that we ask a moral realist to describe his position, showing it to be compatible with the lack of entailment and supervenience. He has to say that the truth of a moral proposition consists in the existence of a state of affairs, which it reports; that the existence of this state of affairs is not entailed by the existence of other, naturalistic facts; yet that the continuation of these facts entails that the moral state of affairs continue as it is. Now this may at first sight seem harmless enough, and perhaps it is not actually inconsistent, but it is very mysterious. To make the preculiarity of the view evident we can put it like this. Imagine a thing A, which has a certain set of naturalistic properties and relations. A also has a certain degree of moral worth: say, it is very good. This, according to the realist, reports the existence of a state of affairs: A's goodness. Now the existence of this state of affairs is not entailed by A being as it is in all naturalistic respects. This means, since all the propositions involved are entirely contingent, that the existence of this state of affairs is not strictly implied by A being as it is in all naturalistic respects. That is, it is logically possible that A should be as it is in all naturalistic respects, yet this further state of affairs not exist. But if that is a logical possibility, *why* isn't it a

---

respects) normal, coming to know P ought to increase one's confidence in Q'. For example, it could at best be 'If there is no reason to suppose that he is pretending or abnormal, then coming to know that he exhibited certain behaviour ought to increase one's confidence that he was in pain', which could be supposed necessary.

logical possibility that A should stay as it is in all naturalistic respects, and this further state of affairs cease to exist? If it is a logical possibility that A be as it is in all naturalistic respects, and not be good, why isn't it a logical possibility that A remain in all naturalistic respects as it was when it was once good, and yet cease to be good? The existence of the naturalistic facts doesn't guarantee, logically, the moral state of affairs, so why should their continuation give a logical guarantee of the continued existence of the moral state of affairs? Again, these questions can be put in terms of (S_2), giving the puzzle for the realist: if A has some naturalistic properties, and is also good, but its goodness is a distinct further fact not following from its naturalistic features, and if B has those features as well, then it follows that B also is good. And this is a puzzle for the realist, because there is no reason at all, on his theory, why this should follow. If the goodness is, as it were, an *ex gratia* payment to A, one to which A is not as a matter of logic entitled in virtue of being as it is in all naturalistic respects, then it should be consistent to suppose that although goodness was given to A, it was not given to B, which merely shares the naturalistic features that do not entail the goodness.

It may not, at first sight, be clear why these problems are particularly acute for the realist. If joint supervenience and lack of entailment are problematic for any theory, then it is no objection to realism that it finds them particularly hard to explain. But the situation is not like that. For although the correspondence theory of truth, of which moral realism is an instance, is often thought to be entirely vacuous, it does in fact offer a distinct picture of the truth of propositions: each proposition may be construed as asserting that a certain state of affairs exists (namely, that state of affairs in whose existence or nonexistence the proposition's truth or falsity consists). And, however grave for some purposes the circularity introduced in the parenthesis, the definite consequence is that the truth of propositions should be subject to just the logical constraints that govern the existence of states of affairs. But this is exactly what does not happen with moral truth, where we are asked to make intelligible the notion of a state of affairs subject to the constraint that its existence does not follow from the naturalistic facts *being* as they are but its continued existence follows from the natural facts *staying* as they are. Now, while I cannot see an inconsistency in holding this belief, it is not philosophically very inviting. Supervenience becomes, for the realist, an opaque, isolated, logical fact for which no explanation can be proffered.

We can now see why a claim weaker than (E) will support the argument equally well. (E) asserts that *no* proposition ascribing a degree of worth to a thing is entailed by any naturalistic proposition, however complicated. But all we need for the argument is that there are *some* propositions ascribing worth to things which are not entailed by any naturalistic proposition, however complicated. For if there are some such moral propositions they nevertheless still ascribe properties that are supervenient upon the naturalistic facts, and their supervenience is again an objectionable peculiarity for the realist. Of course, if we weaken the premise in this way, it is theoretically open to a realist to say that some moral truths are entailed by naturalistic facts, and his realism is a theory about these, and others are not, and his realism does not apply to these. But in that case the position has the disadvantage of simply postulating a large but hitherto unsuspected dichotomy in moral truths, and then leaving one half (the interesting half) of this dichotomy completely unexplained. Since this is not very attractive, the argument is just as strong if we use as one premise, instead of (E):

(E′)   There are some moral propositions that are true, but whose truth is not entailed by any naturalistic facts about their subject.

This is quite a significant strengthening of the argument, for using this premise we need not defend ourselves against the view that in some cases 'is' does entail 'ought'. All we hold in adopting (E′) is that in some cases it does not, yet that the 'ought' proposition can be a moral truth all the same. Thus J. R. Searle's well-known argument[8] that in some cases there are purely naturalistic criteria for undertaking an obligation, and that sometimes it can follow from an obligation having been undertaken that, other things being equal, it ought to be fulfilled: even if it convinces us that there is an entailment and that the 'ought' in the conclusion is a moral 'ought' (so that someone who considers the fact that he promised to do *A* irrelevant to the decision whether to do *A* or not *A* is illogical rather than immoral) this argument is beside the point. For there is no prospect at all of extending these considerations to cover all moral truths. Searle's argument, as he himself notices, can cover only moral propositions that are true because of certain *institutional* facts. When an action is described truly in the terms appropriate to an institutionalized activity ('He was clean bowled'), it would seem to follow that consequences which the rules of that activity prescribe ought to be brought about ('He ought to stop batting'). But of course no morality is going to suppose that all moral truths are, in this way, institutional. For a start, that would make it impossible to raise a moral question about the existence of the institution, and in any case there are features of human life whose lack of desirability obviously is not a matter of the rules of institutions.

Does the position sometimes called 'neonaturalism', associated with the work of Philippa Foot, advance reasons for denying (E′)? I do not think so. A central claim of this view is that necessarily certain qualities—courage, justice, temperance—are qualities by which men come to act well: because they are needed in any enterprise whatsoever, other than an accidental fulfilment of any desire or need, anyone, whatever his moral nature, has to prize them. It seems to me that there can be no need to deny this sort of claim in defending (E′). For how can this view, even when allied with the view that human harm and injury are necessarily bad and human benefit necessarily good, be used to demonstrate every moral truth? Consider, for example, the view that a state of satisfaction is a good thing only if its object is somehow appropriate, so that it adds nothing to the worth of a state of affairs if, say, somebody achieves

8. J. R. Searle, 'How to Derive "Ought" from "Is" ', *Philosophical Review*, 1964.

content or satisfaction by contemplating or creating something totally unfitting. This is an important moral view, underlying many people's discontent
with utilitarianism. And of course many people would reply that it is illiberal
and false, that although it is a pity that people should contemplate or create
unfitting things, it is nevertheless better, given that they do, that they should
be satisfied with them than not. Now, is it likely that, even allowing Foot's
claim that certain things are necessarily good, we shall find naturalistic facts
entailing that one of these views is true and the other false? I cannot see that it
is. Of course, it might be argued as follows: necessarily human benefit is good,
necessarily satisfaction is a benefit, so it follows from the fact that someone
has achieved some satisfaction that, whatever its object, something good has
come about. But this is a very weak way of trying to show the anti-utilitarian
to be illogical rather than immoral,[9] for it denies that it is even true, let alone
necessary, that all cases of satisfaction are in any morally relevant sense a
benefit to their possessors. Satisfaction at inappropriate objects is, according
to this argument, something that should not be wished upon anyone, even if
the only alternative is dissatisfaction at those same objects.

Another line would deny that the notions of truth or falsity are applicable
in these cases, where no entailment exists. It would thus be possible to deny
(E′) by denying that there exist any further moral truths beyond those that are
entailed by naturalistic facts. So neither the proposition that satisfaction is
good only if its object is appropriate nor its negation is true or false, and the
dispute between the utilitarian and his opponent is not to be construed as a
dispute about moral truth. But this is not only *ad hoc,* it is itself a serious
departure from realism. For one consequence of realism is that the law of the
excluded middle applies: either the state of affairs in which the goodness of
unfitting satisfaction consists exists or it doesn't. In the former case the proposition that such satisfaction is good is true, and in the latter case, false. The
point is that the correspondence theory seems to allow no third alternative,
and quite obviously the picture of moral truth that the realist presents would
make the description of such an alternative a most unenviable task.

It seems then that (E′) is reasonably secure, at least so far as recent
argument, which might certainly seem to be in opposition to it, is concerned.
The question now remains whether the other premise, that moral worth is
supervenient upon naturalistic properties, is indisputable. I doubt very much
whether anybody would feel entirely happy about disputing it, so even if there
is no very good argument for it that a realist need accept, it may be quite
proper to accept it as an axiom of meta-ethics. However, what can be done is
to show how certain natural ways of explaining the feature of supervenience
are not open to the realist, so that it is an objectionable factor for him but not
for others. We can also show that if, faced with this, he does try to deny the
necessity of supervenience, this can only be at the cost of making moral truths
unimportant. It has often been realized that moral realism runs this danger;

9. G. E. Moore, *Principia Ethica* (Cambridge: Cambridge University Press, 1903), chapter
VI.

what I wish to do is to show how this escape route from the argument leads directly to the danger. For an anti-realist, a natural way of explaining the supervenience of moral properties would be something like this. There can be no question that we often choose, admire, commend, or desire, objects because of their naturalistic properties. Now it is not possible to hold an attitude to a thing because of its possessing certain properties and, at the same time, not hold that attitude to another thing that is believed to have the same properties. The nonexistence of the attitude in the second case shows that it is not because of the shared properties that I hold it in the first case. Now, moral attitudes are to be held towards things because of their naturalistic properties. Therefore it is not possible to hold a moral attitude to one thing, believe a second to be exactly alike, yet at the same time not hold the same attitude to the second thing. Anybody who appears to do this is convicted of misidentifying a caprice as a moral opinion.

This line of thought is insufficient for the realist. We saw earlier that he need not refrain from talking about moral attitudes: it is just that he thinks this a less clear alternative to talking about moral beliefs. But if we rephrase the preceding paragraph in terms of moral belief, it is obviously insufficient to explain supervenience. For we obtain: we hold moral beliefs about things because of their naturalistic properties; it is not possible to hold a belief about one thing because it satisfies some condition, and, at the same time, not hold that belief about another thing that is believed to satisfy the same condition; therefore, it is not possible to hold a moral belief about a thing, believe a second to be exactly alike in all naturalistic respects, yet at the same time not hold the belief about the second thing. But this doesn't explain supervenience at all: it merely shows the realist putting conditions upon what can be *believed* to be the truth, not upon what *is* the truth. Our belief, he is saying, has to be consistent across naturalistic similarities—but this is no explanation of why, on his theory, the truth has to be. Furthermore, once we have grasped the inadequacy of his picture to account for supervenience, we may doubt his right to help himself to conditions upon belief that mean that beliefs are to be constrained as though supervenience were true. Why, that is, should a realistic theory accept that things believed to be naturalistically alike cannot be believed to be of distinct worth? Surely the condition on belief is that it should be true, and the trouble with inconsistency is that it is false: but the realist, as we have seen, offers no explanation of why this sort of inconsistency in moral belief should yield falsehood.

Finally, suppose the realist takes the apparent consequence of his position seriously, and denies supervenience. Then he holds that it is possible that the worth of, say, a feature of human life, such as courage, should alter, although its intrinsic nature, consequences, relation to our desires, and so forth remain the same. The only conclusion is that it is possible that the worth of courage should be irrelevant to our interest in it, attitudes toward it, or preparedness to urge it on our children or to criticize or commend someone for possessing it. For when moral truth is that pure there *can* be no reason for being interested in it—nothing hangs upon the worth of courage changing if its relation to everything perceptible remains the same, and no reason could possibly be given for being interested in this fact.

Moral realism, then, is false. The purpose of the next section is to introduce the consequences of this for the logic of moral discourse. For it is natural to suppose that the falsity of realism entails the falsity of any propositional account of moral discourse. For this reason many people might suppose that the results of section II could better be expressed as a disproof of the thesis that moral utterances express propositions, or of the thesis that goodness is an attribute. But this is too hasty. If propositions are what can be true, false, believed, hypothesized, or premises of arguments, or if they are what can enter into entailment relations, then it is not at all attractive to suppose that the statement 'Courage is an intrinsically good thing' expresses no proposition, even if the only natural theory about the truth of that proposition is certainly false.

III

The argument of section I showed that it is easy to overestimate the amount that we gain from talking in terms of moral attitudes rather than moral beliefs. However, in section II, I claimed that an anti-realistic theory does have a distinct advantage in being alone consistent with supervenience and lack of entailment, and I sketched a way in which a theory based on attitudes might account for the former phenomenon. However, this was just a sketch, and we must now see whether it could be successful by describing the connection that an anti-realist must draw between moral attitudes and moral predicates. The problem is this. It is easy to think that the meaning of moral predicates has been given if it is said that they are used in sentences that when uttered assertively, express the speaker's attitude to the subject of the discourse. At any rate, *if* this is true, and *if* a suitable account of the attitude is given,[10] it is easy to think that all that is needed to give an analysis of moral discourse has been done. However, it has been pointed out by J. R. Searle[11] and others that this is not so. For such a description of the use of moral sentences leaves us completely in the dark as to what happens when such sentences are used not assertively, but in less direct contexts. For example, suppose we are told that the sentence 'Courage is an intrinsically good thing' is standardly used so that in asserting it a speaker is expressing his attitude, namely approval, to courage. This does not, it is argued, enable us to construe: 'If courage is an intrinsically good thing, then organized games should be a part of school curricula', or 'No statement of the naturalistic properties of courage entails that courage is an intrinsically good thing', since in neither of these is any more value attributed to courage, nor is any attitude to it expressed. So the

10. This is a problem to which this paper makes no contribution. For an investigation of it, see Roger Scruton, 'Attitudes, Beliefs and Reasons', in *Morality and Moral Reasoning*, ed. J. Casey (London: Methuen, 1971).

11. 'Meaning and Speech-acts', *Philosophical Review*, 1962, pp. 423 ff.

problem, for an anti-realist, is that of showing how the original insight as to what is done when a moral proposition is asserted also gives him an explanation of what is done when the sentence expressing it occurs in such contexts.

There are, I think, two natural ways for the anti-realist to attempt to meet this challenge, and it can be shown that neither of them will do. The first is to suppose that in an indirect context[12] some proposition about an attitude is being hypothesized, said to be entailed, or otherwise involved. Now this is clearly unnatural, because the anti-realist is not claiming that in a direct context, when asserted straightforwardly, moral sentences express propositions about attitudes. This would be to hold a realistic theory, if the proposition expressed was supposed to be one simply claiming the existence of certain attitudes, or to fail to give a theory of moral discourse at all. If, for example, the view was that in asserting that courage is intrinsically good one is asserting that an attitude of approval to courage is *appropriate,* then this, although true, is unhelpful. For the judgement that approval is appropriate is a moral judgement, and giving it as a synonym for the original removes no problems of analysis or epistemology that the original causes. So if an anti-realist tried to answer Searle's point by saying that what is hypothesized is 'If an attitude of approval to courage is appropriate, then . . . ', no ground is gained at all, for still nothing has been done to explain how moral judgements can occur in indirect contexts. The same point applies to more complicated versions. Urmson, discussing only judgements of something as good of a kind or from a point of view, suggests that 'good' means 'satisfies a description such that no one can correctly dissent from a favourable evaluation (as of some kind or from some point of view) of an object that satisfies that description'.[13] But if this were extended to try to give a theory of moral judgement, precisely the same objection would apply: to say that nobody can correctly dissent from a favourable evaluation of a good thing is true but completely unhelpful.

The other thing that an anti-realist might try to do is to suppose that in an indirect context a naturalistic proposition is being hypothesized, said to be entailed, or otherwise involved. *Which* naturalistic proposition would, I take it, be determined by the moral views of the person who utters the sentence expressing the hypothetical, or other compound proposition. Thus take

(H) If courage is an intrinsically good thing, then organized games should be a part of school curricula.

This would be a sentence that is interpreted on a particular occasion of utterance by our knowing the moral standards of the man uttering it and supposing that he is hypothesizing that courage has the naturalistic properties that he would give as reasons for its being intrinsically good. Again, there is difficulty in reconciling this view of indirect contexts with the view that it is not a

12. I do not, fortunately, need to embark on the analysis of the notion of an indirect context. For the purpose of the argument it is just taken to embrace those contexts in which the moral proposition is expressed, but not asserted.

13. J. O. Urmson, *The Emotive Theory of Ethics* (London: Hutchinson & Co., 1968), p. 142.

naturalistic proposition that is asserted when it is said that courage is a good thing. For if you and I, with different standards, each assert (H), we have hypothesized different things, but then, unless in asserting that courage is intrinsically good we assert different things, at least one of us is construed as hypothesizing something other than what he asserts, which makes it difficult to see how *modus ponendo ponens* is valid when used on moral propositions. Also some hypotheticals will become tautologous when they have a moral antecedent and naturalistic consequent, namely those in which the naturalistic consequent gives the facts that the speaker would use as his standards for the truth of the moral antecedent. Thus, 'If courage is intrinsically good, then it is a quality by which men must act to achieve happiness' might be tautologous as uttered by me. But it doesn't look much like a tautology, for disagreement with it seems to be disagreement with a substantive moral claim, a claim about the necessary conditions of intrinsic worth of a quality, rather than the sort of disagreement about the use of words that disagreement with a tautology usually involves. In short, if an anti-realist takes this view of indirect context, he is opening himself to the classical, Moorean objection to naturalism, and the apparent sophistication of the position renders it no less vulnerable.

The trouble with both these attempts to escape from Searle's argument is that they try to answer the question of *what* is being hypothesized, said to be entailed, and so on, and we have a definite view of how to set about questions of this sort. We try to give an *analysis* of the moral proposition, and this turns out to be either incorrect or unhelpful. Instead, I propose to consider the total sentence expressing the hypothetical, or entailment, and to give a theory of what these say and why we have these locutions to say it. The nature of the theory can best be presented via an example. Consider:

(I)   No statement of the naturalistic properties of courage entails that it is an intrinsically good thing.

Here is a sentence in which the proposition that courage is an intrinsically good thing is expressed but not asserted, so what can an anti-realist theory, based on the way in which an attitude is expressed when a moral proposition is asserted, say about it? The answer is given if we extend Frege's theory of such contexts to sentences that express attitudes. Frege thought that sentences occur in contexts in which they refer to propositions that they normally express. I suggest that in (I) we refer to an attitude: an attitude is the subject of the proposition expressed by (I), and it is quite easy to see what is said about that attitude. For, according to an anti-realist, (I) is not asserting the logical independence of the existence of two states of affairs, the moral and the naturalistic. It is an expression of a fact about the moral attitude of approval toward courage, and says that nobody who fails to approve of courage while knowing all that there is to be known about it can be convicted of a logical mistake. This is a claim about the nature of the moral attitude, and the statement (I) is what I shall call a 'propositional reflection' of this claim. By a 'propositional reflection' I mean roughly any statement that, while appearing to make a factual claim about states of affairs, their interrelations, and their logic, is actually making claims about attitudes, *although* none of the propositions involved in the statement is to be analyzed into one whose subject is an attitude. I am afraid that this is probably quite obscure, and I shall not, in this essay, make the notion nearly as clear as I think it could be made, but further examples of the use of the notion should help.

If we turn again to the anti-realistic explanation of (S), we can see that it shares with the explanation of (I) the feature that an attitude—the attitude of moral approval—is said to have certain properties, and this by itself is the truth of which (S) is, in the above sense, a propositional reflection. Thus, the moral attitude is said to be necessarily held because of the naturalistic properties of its objects, and the statement of supervenience, made in terms of which differences entail which others, is a realistic-appearing way of putting the view that difference in moral attitude to two things must, logically, be justified by difference in beliefs about them. So the theory, if it works for other examples of indirect contexts, does give an account of the relation between moral predicates and moral attitudes that allows the anti-realist explanation of supervenience to be successful.

The idea fares well when we consider hypotheticals again. A hypothetical, such as (H), although it appears to be making a claim that one state of affairs exists if another does, must be taken as a propositional reflection of a claim about attitudes. This claim is that an attitude of approval to courage in itself involves an attitude of approval to organized games as part of the curriculum in every school. It does not, of course, involve this as a matter of logic, but then neither is (H) true as a matter of logic. To show that one attitude does involve the other it is necessary to show that organized games are intimately connected with the production of the quality of courage and lack other disadvantages. This is precisely what would have to be shown to verify the original hypothetical (H). If we attack the claim that one attitude involves the other ('Surely not—organized games at school promote cruelty and cowardice'), we produce just the propositions that are reasons against the original hypothetical. Clearly with moral as with natural discourse there is a variety of grounds on which an 'if . . . then . . .' proposition might be held, but this elasticity is preserved by varieties of involvement. Consider, for example, logically necessary propositions using moral antecedents: 'If you ought to divide the pound evenly among ten people, then you ought to give them two shillings each'.[14] This is necessarily true. The analysandum that refers to attitudes must therefore be necessarily true also. And 'Approval of dividing the dollar evenly among ten people involves approval of giving them twenty cents each' can easily be given a sense in which it expresses a necessary truth—namely, that one attitude cannot be *consistently* held without the other. This logical constraint upon consistency in attitude must not, of course, be thought to derive in any way from the logical interrelations of moral

---

14. An example suggested by Tom Baldwin, who most helpfully criticized an earlier version on this point.

propositions that it analyses. It is rather explained by pointing out that it is logically impossible to divide a dollar evenly among ten people without giving each of them twenty cents, so for this type of example the analysis can show in a genuinely explanatory way how the hypothetical refers to attitudes and expresses their relations.

The validity of *modus ponendo ponens* as a rule of inference is preserved by this treatment of moral hypotheticals. The question, for the anti-realist, is that of how his account of the hypothetical is to cohere with his account of straightforward assertion in such a way that '*P*, and if *P*, then *Q*' entails *Q*, where *P* is a moral proposition. The theory tells us that anybody asserting '*P*, and if *P*, then *Q*' where *P* attributes worth to a thing *expresses* his attitude to that thing, and *asserts* that that attitude involves a further attitude or belief. There is, when that has been done, a logical inconsistency in not holding the further attitude or belief. It is this logical inconsistency that is expressed by saying that *modus ponendo ponens* is valid: its validity is a reflection of possible logical inconsistency in attitudes and beliefs.

A moral proposition can be the antecedent of a hypothetical of which the consequent is not a moral proposition. Here the claim of which this form is a propositional reflection is that the attitude involves a belief, not another attitude. 'If courage is an intrinsically good thing, then it is a quality by which a man must act to achieve happiness' is a reflection of the view that an attitude of approval to courage in itself involves belief that courage is a quality by which a man must act to achieve happiness. This is a statement of one's moral standards: only someone with a specific moral position will hold that the attitude involves that belief, and this reflects perfectly well the point that I made earlier, that such a hypothetical is a statement of a standard, and if attacked is attacked as such and not, for example, as a sort of contradiction or empirical falsehood.

It may be thought at this point that too much weight is put upon the word 'involves'. For how can an attitude involve a belief (or a belief an attitude) in such a way? We recognize that people can hold the moral attitude without the belief and vice versa: what other involvement is there? To say that the attitude of approval to courage involves the belief that courage is a quality by which a man must act to achieve happiness is, as I said, to express a moral standard, to make a moral claim. The subtle thing is that the subject of the claim is now the attitude of approval of courage, and it is said that this *ought* to involve the belief that courage involves happiness. It is important to see that there is nothing in the least troublesome about this being a moral proposition: the object was not to show that such standard-giving hypotheticals are not moral propositions, but to show how they could be so. And they are quite straightforward moral propositions expressing the way in which attitudes ought to vary with beliefs.

This analysis has the further property that it enables us to deal with expressions of moral fallibility, in my opinion the hardest context of all for an anti-realist to understand. Consider 'I strongly believe that *X* is a good man, but I may be wrong'. Here we express an attitude to *X*, but then what happens? For a realist, we simply state the possibility that our belief does not accord with the facts, but what can an anti-realist say about it? It is easy to say that here I express an attitude to my moral attitude to X, and of course I do, but the question is whether this second-order attitude can be described consistently with anti-realism. For if we have to describe the second-order attitude just as 'belief in the possibility that the attitude of approval to X is unjustified', then we are in no better position than those who rest their analysis on attitudes being 'appropriate'. But let us consider what we envisage when we admit that we may be wrong in a moral belief. We envisage that we could, at some future date, want to change our attitude to the subject of the belief, not because the subject has changed, but because we realize that we have made a mistake. The mistake could be one of two kinds. Taking the example of 'X is a good man', we can envisage that we may have been mistaken about X: he isn't really kind, he only likes to appear so, and so forth. Or I can envisage a mistake in my standards. I think that a man's being kind is a reason for thinking that he is a good man. That is, I think that the belief that a man is kind ought to tend to create an attitude of approval towards him. This, as I explained above, is another moral belief, whose subject is the variation of an attitude with a belief. But I may be mistaken here, too: I can envisage, at least as a bare possibility, that some argument, or someone, or some event, should come along and show me that I am mistaken about kindness: some sorts of kindness kill the soul of the recipient, and so forth. Then I no longer think that the belief ought to tend to create the attitude. The propositional reflection of all these possibilities of errors is that the belief that something is good, although I may hold it, may be false. And thus, if I am right, a theory based upon attitudes can encompass those elements in moral thought that make us reflect on how difficult it is to know what is right and wrong, good or bad.

Finally we may consider tenses. Tenses can certainly provide extreme difficulty for analysis that concentrate upon what is done when something is asserted to be the case now: thus the Toulmin account of 'It is probable that P', according to which this is used to make a guarded assertion that P' provides no account of 'It was probable that P would happen'—or, at least, no account that does not confuse it with the very different 'It is probable that P happened.' And if we consider 'X was a morally fine man', it might appear that we have no option but to construe this as 'The attitude of approval toward X was appropriate'—an analysis of the form that I claimed to be totally unhelpful. However, a device is available that, although it may look unnatural, appears to me to take account of tensed assertions without having to view them as applying tensed predicates to attitudes. The question we must ask is whether anybody who asserts 'X was a morally fine man' is expressing a moral attitude. It is from the supposition that he is not that difficulty arises, just as difficulty arises when it is realized that by saying 'It was probable that P would happen' I am not guardedly asserting anything. But anybody asserting 'X was a morally fine man' is expressing a moral attitude. Not, it is true, to X as he is, for X may in the interim have degenerated. But he is expressing the attitude to X as he was. Quite clearly, anyone saying 'X was a morally fine man' is sincere only if he approves of X as he was, morally, and in making his assertion it is that approval which he expresses. The difficulty is thus averted by realizing that the subject of approval when a tensed assertion is made is not the object as it is now, but the object as it was then.

I have now given several examples of the device of propositional reflection, the ways in which expressions of attitude and propositions concerning the interrelations of attitudes with each other and with beliefs are given a syntax that makes them appear to relate to facts in a peculiar, unobservable, moral realm. It must in no way be considered surprising that this device should exist. For disagreement in moral attitude is one of the most important disagreements there is, and working out the consequences of moral attitudes, one of the most important subjects there is. The device of propositional reflection enables us to bring the concepts of propositional logic to this task. It enables us to use notions like truth, knowledge, belief, inconsistency, entailment, and implication to give moral argument all the structure and elegance of argument about facts.

But isn't the theory saying that there is really no such thing as moral truth, and nothing to be known, believed, entailed—only the appearance of such things? Not at all. It is a complete mistake to think that the notion of moral truth and the associated notions of moral attributes and propositions disappear when the realistic theory is refuted. To think that a moral proposition is true is to concur in an attitude to its subject: this is the answer to the question with which I began the essay. To identify this attitude further is a task beyond the scope of this essay, but it is the central remaining task for the metaphysic of ethics. To think, however, that the anti-realist results show that there is no such thing as moral truth is quite wrong. To think there are no moral truths is to think that nothing should be morally endorsed, that is, to endorse the endorsement of nothing, and this attitude of indifference is one that it would be wrong to recommend, and silly to practise.[15]

15. I comment further on the complex issues of this essay in the next, and from a recent perspective, in its Addendum.

7

Supervenience Revisited

A decade ago, in an article entitled 'Moral Realism', I presented an argument intended to show that two properties, which I called supervenience and lack of entailment, provided together an unpleasant mystery for moral realism.[1] This argument originally was suggested to me in a discussion with Casimir Lewy, which in turn was directed at a paper of G. E. Moore entitled 'The Conception of Intrinsic Value'.[2] The intervening decade has provided a number of reasons for revisiting my argument. First of all, it was couched in an idiom that subsequent work on modal logic—particularly the distinctions of various kinds of necessity and the general use of possible worlds as models—has made a little quaint. It would be desirable to see if the new notions allow the argument to stand. Second, we have seen a great deal of interest in supervenience as a notion of importance beyond moral philosophy. Thus, in conversation and correspondence I have heard it suggested that my argument must be flawed, because exactly the same combination of properties that I found mysterious occurs all over the place: for example, in the philosophy of mind, in the relationship between natural kind terms and others, in the relation between colours and primary properties, and so on. Since anti-realism in these other areas is not attractive, this casts doubt upon my diagnosis of the moral case. Last, moral realism is again an attractive option to some philosophers; although when I wrote I might have seemed to be shadow boxing, the argument is becoming relevant again. In any case, enough puzzles seem to me to surround a proper analysis of supervenience to warrant a fresh look at it.

Suppose we have an area of judgements, such as those involving moral commitments or attributions of mental states. I shall call these F judgments, and I shall also talk of F truths and F facts: this is not intended to imply any view at all about whether the commitments we express in the vocabulary are beyond question genuine judgements, nor that there is a real domain of truths or facts in the area. Indeed part of the purpose of my argument was to find a

1. S. Blackburn, 'Moral Realism', in *Morality and Moral Reasoning,* ed. J. Casey (London: Methuen, 1971); essay 6, this volume. More than a decade ago now, alas.
2. G. E. Moore, 'The Conception of Intrinsic Value', in *Philosophical Studies* (London: Routledge & Kegan Paul, 1922).

way of querying just these ideas. At this stage, all this terminology is entirely neutral. Now suppose that we hold that the truths expressible in this way supervene upon the truths expressed in an underlying G vocabulary. For example, moral judgements supervene upon natural judgements, or mental descriptions of people upon physical ones (either of the people themselves or of some larger reality that includes them). This supervenience claim means that in *some* sense of 'necessary' it is necessarily true that if an F truth changes, then some G truth changes, or, necessarily, if two situations are identical in point of G facts, then they are identical in terms of F facts as well. To analyze this more closely, I shall make free use of the possible-worlds idiom. But it must be emphasized that this is merely a heuristic device and implies no theory about the status of the possible worlds. Let us symbolize the kind of necessity in question by 'N' and possibility by 'P': for the present it does not matter whether these are thought of as logical, metaphysical, physical, or other kinds of modalities. We are now to suppose that some truth about a thing or event or state, that it is F, supervenes upon some definite total set of G truths, which we can sum up by saying that it is G^*. Of course, G^* can contain all kinds of relational truths about the subject, truths about other things, and so on. In fact, one of the difficulties of thinking about all this properly is that it rapidly becomes unclear just what can be allowed in our conception of a totality of G states. But intuitively it is whatever natural or physical states bring it about that the subject is F. I shall express this by talking of the set of G states that 'underlies' an F state. Belief in supervenience is then at least the belief that whenever a thing is in some F state, this is because it is in some underlying G state, or is by virtue of its being in some underlying G state. This is the minimal sense of the doctrine. But I am interested in something stronger that ties the particular truth that a thing is F to the fact that it is in some particular G state. We can present the general form of this doctrine as characterizing the relation 'U' that holds when one 'underlies' the other:

$$\text{(S)} \quad N\left((\exists x)(Fx \ \& \ G^*x \ \& \ (G^*xUFx)) \supset (y)(G^*y \supset Fy)\right)$$

The formula says that as a matter of necessity, if something x is F, and G^* underlies this, then anything else in the physical or natural (or whatever) state G^* is F as well. There is no claim that G^* provides the only way in which things can become F: intuitively, we know that something might be, say, evil in a number of different ways, and that something in one given physical state might possess some mental property that it could equally have possessed by being in any of a family of related physical states. The supervenience claim (S) is thus in no opposition to doctrines that now go under the heading of 'variable realization'. To get the claim that these doctrines deny, we would need to convert the final conditional: . . . $(y)(Fy \supset G^*y)$. But the resulting doctrine is not one in which we shall be interested.

I now want to contrast (S) with a much stronger necessity:

$$\text{(N)} \quad N(x)(G^*x \supset Fx)$$

Of course, (N) does not follow from (S). Formally they are merely related like this: (S) necessitates an overall conditional, and (N) necessitates the consequence of that conditional. So it would appear there is no more reason to infer (N) from (S) than there would be to infer Nq from $N(p \supset q)$. Hence also there is no inconsistency in a position that affirms (S) but also affirms:

(P) $P(\exists x)(G^*x \ \& \sim Fx)$

At least, this is the immediate appearance. In my original essay it was the nature of theories that hold both (S) and (P) (which I shall call the (S)/(P) combination) that occupied me. Such a theory would think it possible (in some sense commensurate with that of the original claim) that any given G state that happens to underlie a certain F state, nevertheless might not have done so. In other words, even if some G setup in our world is the very state upon which some F state supervenes, nevertheless, it might not have been *that* F state that supervened upon it. There was the possibility (again, in whatever modal dimension we are working) that the actually arising or supervening F state might not have been the one that supervened upon that particular G setup. My instinct was that this combination provided a mystery for a realist about judgements made with the F vocabulary, and that the mystery would best be solved by embracing an anti-realist (or as I now prefer to call it, a projectivist) theory about the F judgements.

To pursue this further, we might question whether there could be any motivation for holding the (S)/(P) combination. Consider the following possible doctrine about 'underlying', and about the notion of the complete specification of an underlying state, G^*:

(?) $N((\exists x)(Fx \ \& \ G^* \ \& \ (G^*x \ U \ Fx)) \supset N(y)(G^*y \supset Fy))$

The rationale for (?) would be this: Suppose there were a thing that was G^* and F, so that we were inclined to say that its being in the G state underlies its F-ness. But suppose there were also a thing that was G^* and $\sim F$. Then would we not want to deny that it was x's being G^* that underlies its being F, but rather that it was its being G^* *and* its being different from this other thing in some further respect—a property that explains why the other thing fails to be F? We can call that a *releasing* property, R, and then F will supervene only on G^* and $\sim R$. More accurately, G^* would denote a set of properties that do not really deserve the star. We would be wrong to locate in them a *complete* underlying basis for F.

This raises quite complicated questions about the form of these various doctrines. Let me put aside one problem right at the beginning. Since (S) is a conditional and contains an existential clause as part of the antecedent, it will be vacuously true if nothing is G^* and F; the necessitation will likewise be vacuously true if nothing could be G^* and F. So if (S) captured all that was meant by supervenience, we could say, for instance, that being virtuous supervened upon being homogeneously made of granite. Necessarily, if one thing homogeneously made of granite were virtuous, and this quality underlay the virtuousness, then anything so made would be. But this is just because it is impossible that anything of this constitution should be virtuous. I am going to sidestep this problem simply by confining the scope of F and G henceforth to cases where it is possible that something with a set of G properties, denoted by G^*, should be F. In fact, we are soon to deal with different strengths of necessity and possibility, and I shall suppose that this thesis is always strong enough to prevent the conditional being satisfied in this vacuous way.

The next problem of logical form is how we construe the denotation of a set of properties made by the term 'G^*'. First, we do not want the supervenience thesis to be made vacuously true through its being impossible that any two distinct things should be G^*—it then following that if one G^* thing is F, they all are. And the threat here is quite real. If, for instance, G^* were held to include all the physical properties and relations of a thing—if it were that and nothing less which some property F supervened upon—then assuming the identity of indiscernibles, we would have (S) satisfied vacuously again. To get around this I am going to assume a *limitation* thesis. This will say that whenever a property F supervenes upon some basis, there is necessarily a boundary to the kind of G properties that it can depend upon. For example, the mental may supervene upon the physical, in which case the thesis asserts that necessarily there are physical properties of a thing that are not relevant to its mental ones. A plausible example might be its relations to things with which it is in no kind of causal connection (such as future things). Again, the moral supervenes upon the natural, and the thesis will tell us that there are some natural properties that necessarily have no relevance to moral ones—pure spatial position, perhaps, or date of beginning in time. Given the limitation thesis, (S) will not be trivialized by the identity of indiscernibles. The last problem of form that arises is whether "G^*' is thought of as a name for some particular set of properties (which form a complete basis for F), or whether it is built into the sense of 'G^*' that any set of properties it denotes is complete. The difference is easily seen if we consider a very strong kind of necessity—say, conceptual (logical or analytic) necessity. It is unlikely to be thought analytic that being made of H_2O underlies being water. One reason for this is that it is not analytic that being made of H_2O exhausts the kind of physical basis that may affect the kind to which a substance belongs. That is a substantive scientific truth, not one guaranteed in any more *a priori* way. I am going to build into the sense of 'G^*' that in at least one possible world it denotes a set of properties sufficient to underlie F. I do not want it to follow that this is true in all worlds, although that is a very delicate matter. Fortunately, so far as I can see, it does not occupy the centre of the stage I am about to set.

If we accept (?) as a condition on what it is for a set of properties to underlie another, and hence on what it is for a property to supervene upon such a set, the relationship between supervenience and (E) changes. Suppose that there is something whose G^*-ness underlies its F-ness:

(E) $(\exists x)(Fx \ \& \ G^*x \ \& \ (G^*x \ U \ Fx))$

then we can now derive (N). In other words, (?) and (E) together entail (N). And as I have already said, (?) is an attractive doctrine. But it does mean that supervenience becomes in effect nothing but a roundabout way of committing ourselves to (N): the *prima facie* simpler doctrine that some set of underlying truths necessitates the F truth. This is in fact the way that supervenience was once taken by Kim; it enabled Kim to suppose that where we have super-venience, we also have reductionism.[3] Another way of getting at the attrac-tions of (?) would be to cease altogether from mentioning the requirement that there is something that is G^* and F. After all, surely some moral property might supervene upon a particular configuration of natural properties, regard-less of whether there actually is anything with that set. Or some mental property might supervene upon a particular physical makeup that nobody actually has. If we took this course, we would replace (S) by a doctrine:

$$(G^*x \ U \ Fx) \supset (y)(G^*y \supset Fy)$$

and then the doctrine that would give us (N) immediately would be

$$(G^*x \ U \ Fx) \supset N(G^*x \ U \ Fx)$$

Yet supervenience claims are popular at least partly because they offer some of the metaphysical relief of reductions, without incurring the costs; I want therefore to preserve any gap that there may be for as long as possible. This is particularly important in the moral case, where supervenience is one thing, but reductionism is markedly less attractive. So I am going to stick with the original formulation, subject to the caveats already entered, and while we should remain well aware of (?), I do not want to presuppose a verdict on it.

If we put (?) into abeyance, we should be left with a possible form of doctrine that accepts both (S) and (P): the (S)/(P) combination. It is this which I originally claim to make a mystery for realism. If there is to be a mystery, it is not a formal one, and I actually think that with suitable interpretations, there are relations between F and G vocabularies that are properly characterized by (S) and (P). It is just that when this combination is to be affirmed, I believe it needs explanation. In the moral case I think that it is best explained by a projective theory of the F predicates. But in other cases, with different inter-pretations of the modalities, other explanations are also possible. I shall argue this later.

Here, then, is a way of modelling (S) and (P) together. In any possible world, once there is a thing that is F, and whose F-ness is underlain by G^*, then anything else that is G^* is F as well. However, there are possible worlds in which things are G^* but not F. Call the former worlds G^*/F worlds, and the latter, G^*/O worlds. The one thing we do not have is any *mixed* world, where some things are G^* and F, and some are G^* but not F. We can call mixed

3. J. Kim, 'Supervenience and Nomological Incommensurables', in *American Philosophical Quarterly*, 1978, pp. 149–56.

worlds G^*/FvO worlds. These are ruled out by the supervenience claim (S): they are precisely the kind of possible world that would falsify that claim. My form of problem, or mystery, now begins to appear. Why should the possible worlds partition into only the two kinds, and not into the three kinds? It seems on the face of it to offend against a principle of plenitude with respect to possibilities, namely that we should allow any that we are not constrained to disallow. Imagine it spatially: Here is a possible world w_1 that is G^*/F. Here is another, w_2, that we can make as much like w_1 as possible, except that it is G^*/O. But there is no possible world anywhere that is just like one of these, except that it includes just one element whose G^* and F properties conform to the pattern found in the other. Why not? Or, to make the matter yet more graphic, imagine a time element. Suppose our possible worlds are thought of as having temporal duration. A mixed world would be brought about if w_1 starts off as a G^*/F world at some given time, but then at a later time becomes a G^*/O world. For then, overall, it would be mixed, and the supervenience claim would be falsified by its existence. This kind of world then cannot happen, although there can be worlds that are like it in respect of the first part of its history, and equally worlds that are like it in respect of the second part of its history.

This is the ban on mixed worlds: it is a ban on interworld travel by things that are, individually, at home. The problem that I posed is that of finding out the authority behind this ban. Why the embargo on travel? The difficulty is that once we have imagined a G^*/F world and a G^*/O world, it is as if we have done enough to also imagine a G^*/FvO world, and have implicitly denied ourselves a right to forbid its existence. At least, if we are to forbid its existence, we need some explanation of why we can do so. The positive part of my contention was that in the moral case, projectivists can do this better than realists. In the next section I rehearse briefly why this still seems to me to be so, if we make some important distinctions, and then I turn to consider related examples. And in time we have to return to the difficult claim (?), to assess its role in this part of metaphysics.

II

Necessities can range from something very strict, approximating to 'analytically true', through metaphysical and physical necessity, to something approximating to 'usually true'. Then anyone who sympathizes a little with the puzzle in an (S)/(P) combination can quickly see that it will remain not only if there is one fixed sense of necessity and possibility involved, but also in a wider class of cases. For whenever the supervenience claim (S) involves a strong sense of necessity, then it will automatically entail any version with a weaker sense of necessity. Hence, we will get the same structure at the lower level, when the possibility is affirmed in that corresponding, weaker, sense. Thus if (S) took the form of claiming that 'it is metaphysically necessary that . . .' and (P) took the form of claiming that 'it is physically possible that . . .', and if we also suppose (as we surely should) that metaphysical necessity entails physical necessity, then we would have the (S)/(P) combination at the level of physical necessity. On the other hand, we will not get the structure if the relation is reversed. If the possibility claim (P) is made, say, in the sense of 'possible as far as conceptual constraints go', this does not entail, say, 'metaphysically possible'. And then if (S) just reads 'metaphysically necessary', there is no mystery: we would have it just that it is metaphysically necessary, but not an analytic or conceptual truth, that F supervenes upon G^*; equally, it would not be an analytic or conceptual truth that any given G^* produces F, and there is no puzzle there. For the puzzle to begin to arise, we need to bring the modalities into line.

I mention this because it affects the moral case quite closely. Suppose we allow ourselves a notion of 'analytically necessary' applying to propositions that, in the traditional phrase, can be seen to be true by conceptual means alone. To deny one of these would be to exhibit a conceptual confusion: a failure to grasp the nature of the relevant vocabulary or to follow out immediate implications of that grasp. In a slightly more modern idiom, to deny one of these would be 'constitutive' of lack of competence with the vocabulary. We may contrast this with metaphysical necessity: a proposition will be this if it is true in all the possible worlds that, as a matter of metaphysics, could exist. Of course, we may be sceptical about this division, but I want to respect it at least for the sake of argument. For the (S)/(P) combination in moral philosophy provides a nice example of a *prima facie* case of the difference, and one that profoundly affects my original argument. This arises because someone who holds that a particular natural state of affairs, G^*, underlies a moral judgement is very likely to hold that this is true as a matter of metaphysical necessity. For example, if I hold that the fact that someone enjoys the misery of others underlies the judgement that he is evil, I should also hold that, in any possible world, the fact that someone is like this is enough to make him evil. Using 'MN' for metaphysical necessity, I would have both

$$(\text{S}_m) \quad MN((\exists x)(Fx \ \& \ G^*x \ \& \ (G^*x \ U \ Fx)) \supset (y)(G^*y \supset Fy))$$

and

$$(\text{N}_m) \quad MN(x)(G^*x \supset Fx)$$

and I would evade the original argument by disallowing the metaphysical possibility of a world in which people like that were not evil. This, it might be said, is part of what is involved in having a genuine standard, a belief that some natural state of affairs is sufficient to warrant the moral judgement. For, otherwise, if in some metaphysically possible worlds people like that were evil and in others they were not, surely this would be a sign that we hadn't yet properly located the natural basis for the judgement. For instance, if I did allow a possible world in which some people like that were not evil, it might be because (for instance) they believe that misery is so good for the soul that it is a cause of congratulation and rejoicing to find someone miserable. But then this fact becomes what I earlier called a releasing fact, and the real underlying state of affairs is now not just that someone enjoys the misery of others, but that he does so not believing that misery is good for the soul.

Because of this, the original puzzle does not arise at the level of metaphysical necessity. But now suppose we try analytic necessity. It seems to be a conceptual matter that moral claims supervene upon natural ones. Anyone failing to realize this, or to obey the constraint, would indeed lack something constitutive of competence in the moral practice. And there is good reason for this: it would betray the whole purpose for which we moralize, which is to choose, commend, rank, approve, or forbid things on the basis of their natural properties. So we might have

$$(S_a) \quad AN((\exists x)(Fx \ \& \ G^*x \ \& \ (G^*x \ U \ Fx)) \supset (y)(G^*y \supset Fy))$$

But we would be most unwise to have

$$(N_a) \quad AN(x)(G^*x \supset Fx)$$

For it is not plausible to maintain that the adoption of some particular standard is 'constitutive of competence' as a moralist. People can moralize in obedience to the conceptual constraints that govern all moralizing, although they adopt different standards and come to different verdicts in the light of a complete set of natural facts. Of course, this can be denied, but for the sake of this essay I shall rely on the common view that it is mistaken. So since we deny (N_2) we have

$$(P_a) \quad AP(\exists x)(G^*x \ \& \ Fx)$$

We then arrive at an $(S_a)/(P_a)$ combination, and my mystery emerges: why the ban on mixed worlds at this level? These would be worlds possible as far as analytic constraints go, or 'analytically possible' worlds. They conform to conceptual constraints, although there might be metaphysical or physical bars against their actual existence.

Of course, in a sense I have already proposed an answer to this question. By saying enough of what moralizing is to make (S_a) plausible, and enough to make (P_a) plausible, I hope to enable us to learn to relax with their combination. It is just that this relaxation befits the anti-realist better. Because the explanation of the combination depended crucially upon the role of moralizing being to guide desires and choices among the natural features of the world. If, as a realist ought to say, its role is to describe further moral aspects of the world, there is no explanation at all of why obeying the constraint (S_a) is constitutive of competence as a moralist.

Can this argument be avoided by maintaining (?)? No, because there is no prospect of accepting (?) in a relevantly strong sense. For (?) to help, we would need it to be read so that, necessarily (in some sense), if something is *F* and G^*, and the G^*-ness underlies its being F, then it is analytically necessary that anything G^* is F. And this we will not have in the moral case, for we want to say that there are things with natural properties underlying moral ones, but we also deny analyticities of the form (N_a). (?) would not help if the necessity of the consequent were interpreted in any weaker sense. For example, we might want to accept (?) in the form

$$(?_{MN})\quad MN((\exists x)(Fx \ \& \ G^*x \ \& \ (G^*x \ U \ Fx)) \supset MN(y)(G^*y \supset Fy))$$

Then there will be metaphysical necessities of the form of the consequent, that is, of the form (N_m), but they will not help to resolve the original mystery, since that is now proceeding at the level of analytical necessity. It is the possibility, so far as conceptual constraints go, of mixed worlds that is to be avoided.

III

The argument above works because we are careful to distinguish the status of the supervenience claim, and in this case its extremely strong status, from that of the related possibility claim. I have done that by indexing the modal operators involved: We have four different forms of modal claim: (S), (N), (P) and (?), and each of them can involve analytic or conceptual necessity, $(_a)$, metaphysical necessity $(_m)$, and we come now to physical necessity, $(_p)$. For now I want to turn to consider nonmoral cases of the same kind of shape. These examples are all going to start life as examples of the joint (S)/(P) combination. They may not finish life like that: it may become obvious, if it is not so already, in the light either of the plausibility of (?) or of the difficulty over banning mixed worlds, that either supervenience is to be abandoned, or (N) accepted. But here are some test cases:

First example. Suppose that in w_1 a physical setup G^* underlies some particular mental state F. Suppose G^* is possession of some pattern of neurones or molecules in the head, and F is having a headache. Nowhere in w_1 is there anything unlike x, in being G^* but not F. Next door, in w_2, however, there are things that are G^* but not F. Now we are told that w_1 is acceptable, and that w_2 is acceptable. But nowhere is there a world w_3 that is like w_1 but that changes to become like w_2, or that contains some particular individuals who are like those of w_2.

Second example. Suppose that in w_1 a particular molecular constitution G^* underlies membership of a natural kind, F. G^* consists of a complete physical or chemical breakdown of the constitution of a substance (e.g., being composed of molecules of H_2O), and F is being water. Nowhere in w_1 could there be a substance with that chemistry, that is not water. In w_2, however, this combination is found. Once again, although each of these possible worlds exists, there is no G^*/FvO, or mixed world, in which some substances with this chemical constitution are water and others are not.

Third example. Suppose that in w_1 a particular set of primary qualities, particularly concerning refractive properties of surfaces, G^*, underlies possession of a colour F. Nowhere in w_1 could there be things with that kind of surface, without that particular colour. However, there are possible worlds where this combination is found: G^*/O worlds. Again, there are no mixed worlds, where some things with the primary, surface properties are F, and others are not.

In each of these cases we have the (S)/(P) combination. And I hope it is obvious that each case is at least *prima facie* puzzling—enough so to raise questions about whether the combination is desirable, or whether we should make severe distinctions within the kinds of necessity and possibility involved to end up avoiding the combination altogether. How would this be done?

First Example

How should we interpret the supervenience of the mental on the physical? Perhaps centrally as a metaphysical doctrine, so we shall accept (S_m). Should we accept (S_a)? We should if we can find arguments as strong as those in the moral case for claiming that it is constitutive of competence in the mental language that we recognize the supervenience of the mental on the physical. But I doubt if we can do this. For whether or not we are philosophically wedded to the doctrine, we can surely recognize ordinary competence in users who would not agree. One day Henry has a headache, and the next day he does not. Something mental is different. But suppose he simply denies that anything physical is different (giving voice to Cartesianism). Is this parallel to the error of someone who makes the same move in a moral case? I do not think so: Henry is not so very unusual, and if his error is shown to be one because of the 'very meaning' of mental ascriptions, then whole cultures have been prone to denial of an analytic truth. In other words, it seems to me to be overambitious to claim that it follows, or follows analytically, from change in a mental state that there is change in an underlying physical state. It makes views conceptually incoherent when enough people have found them perfectly coherent (consider, for example, changes in God's mind).

Let us stick then with (S_m). It would seem to me plausible, if we accept this, to accept the correlative necessities (N_m) and $(?_m)$. We would then be forced to deny (P_m), and we just do not get involved with the problem of banning mixed worlds. (N_m) does the work for us, by disallowing the metaphysical possibility of G^* without F. However, there is the famous, or notorious, position of Davidson to consider, which accepts some form of supervenience of the mental on the physical, but also denies the existence of lawlike propositions connecting the two vocabularies.[4] Davidson is not very explicit about the strength of necessity and possibility involved in his claims, but it can scarcely be intended to be weaker than joint acceptance of (S_m) and of (P_p).

---

4. D. Davidson, 'Mental Events', in *Essays on Actions and Events* (Oxford: Clarendon Press, 1980).

And even if supervenience is taken as a matter not of metaphysical, but just of sheer physical necessity (in our physical world, there is no mental change without physical change, even if there *could* be), it does not matter. For from (S_m) we can deduce (S_p), so we have the $(S)/(P)$ combination, at the level of physical necessity. So, according to me, the position ought to be odd, and indeed it is. Why is it physically impossible for there to be a world that contains some w_1 characters with headaches, and some w_2 characters in the same physical state but without headaches? Once we have allowed the physical possibility of the w_2 type, how can we disallow the physical possibility of them mingling with w_1 types?

It does not appear to me that light is cast on this by Davidson's reason for allowing (P_p). This reason is that in some sense the mental and the physical belong to different realms of theory: ascriptions of mental properties answer to constraints different from ascriptions of physical ones, and hence we can never be in a position to insist upon a lawlike correlation of any given physical state with any given mental state (this is *not* just the variable realization point: here we are told not to insist upon a physically necessary physical-to-mental correlation; *prima facie* we might be allowed to do that in various cases, even if we could never insist upon lawlike connections the other way round). I do not accept that this is a good argument, for there can certainly be interesting laws that connect properties whose ascriptions answer to different constraints: temperature and pressure, or colour and primary properties, for instance. However, I do not want to insist upon that. For there remains the oddity that if Davidson's reasoning is good, it should apply equally to the supervenience claim. How can we be in a position to insist upon anything as strong as (S_p), let alone as strong as (S_m)? The freedom that gives us (P_p) is just as effective here. I may coherently and effectively 'rationalize' one person as being in one mental state and another as being in another, obeying various canonical principles of interpretation, regardless of whether they are in an identical G^* state: I might just disclaim interest in that. Of course, if (N_p) were true, it would be different, but it is precisely this which the anomalous character of the position denies.

So if the mental reality is in no lawlike connection with the physical, as (P_p) claims, I can see no basis for asserting that nevertheless it supervenes upon it. But, again, the word 'reality' matters here. *One* way of thinking that the mental must supervene upon the physical, in at least the sense of (S_m), is by convincing ourselves that the physical reality is at bottom the only reality: molecules and neurones are all that there are. And then there might be something about the way mental vocabulary relates to this—relates to the only reality there is—that justifies both (S_p) and (P_p). Perhaps there is some argument that obeying the supervenience constraint is required for conceptual coherence, or at any rate for metaphysical coherence; and perhaps Davidson's argument for (P_p) can be put in a better light than I have allowed. I do not want to deny this possibility. But I do want to point out that once more it is bought at the cost of a highly anti-realist, even idealist, view of the mental. The 'truth' about the mental world is not a matter of how some set of facts actually falls out. It is a matter of how we have to relate this particular vocabulary to the one underlying reality. If we thought like this, then we would begin to assimilate the mental/physical case to the moral/natural case. At any rate, it provides no swift model for arguing that anti-realism is the wrong diagnosis of the (S)/(P) combination in that case.

Why do I say that this is an idealist or anti-realist direction? Because the constraint on our theorizing is not explained by any constraint upon the way the facts can fall out. It is constrained by the way we 'must' use the vocabulary, but that 'must' is not itself derived from a theory according to which mental facts and events cannot happen in some given pattern; it is derived from constraints on the way in which we must react to a nonmental, physical world. I regard this as a characteristically idealist pattern: the way the facts have to be is explained ultimately by the way we have to describe them as being. Thus I would say that the explanation of moral supervenience is a paradigmatically anti-realist explanation. By way of contrast, and anticipating the third example, we can notice how there cannot be a strong, analytic version of the doctrine that colours supervene upon primary properties, precisely because it is so obvious that the only conceptual constraint upon using the colour vocabulary is that you react to perceived colour in the right way. Somebody who thinks that a thing has changed colour, but who is perfectly indifferent to any question of whether it has changed in respect of any primary property (or even who believes that it positively has not done so), is quite within his rights. His eyesight may be defective, but his grasp of the vocabulary need not be so.

Second Example

In order to avoid unnecessary complexity, I should enter a caveat here. I am going to take being composed of H_2O as a suitable example of G^*; an example that is of the kind of complete physical or chemical basis that results in stuff being of a certain kind, such as water. I am going to take it that this is known to be the case. So I shall not be interested in the kind of gap, which can in principle open up, in which people might allow that something is H_2O and is water, allow that wateriness supervenes upon the chemical or the physical, but deny that some other specimen of H_2O is water. This is a possible position, because it is possible to disbelieve that the facts registered by something's being H_2O exhaust the physical or chemical facts that may be relevant to its kind. I am going to cut this corner by writing as though it is beyond question that molecular constitution is the right candidate for a complete underlying property—a G^* property. I don't think that this affects the argument, although it is a complex area and one in which it is easy to mistake one's bearings.

Once more, it is natural to take the various claims involving the relationship of H_2O and water in a metaphysical sense. It is also natural, to me at any rate, to assert (S_m) only if we also assert (N_m), and ($?_m$). Being water supervenes upon being H_2O only because anything made of H_2O must be water.

And if we had an argument that it does not have to be water, perhaps because we imagine a world in which countervailing circumstance makes substances composed of that molecule quite unlike water at the macro-level (and more unlike it than ice or steam), then we would just change the basis for the supervenience. We would have argued for a releasing property, R, and the true basis upon which being water supervenes would be G^* (being H_2O) and being $\sim R$.

Might someone believe that the (S)/(P) combination arises at some level here? The argument would have to be that in some strong sense it *must* be true that being water supervenes upon physical or chemical constitution; but it need not be true, in this equally strong sense, that H_2O is the particular underlying state. Now, I do not think there is any very strong sense in which being water must be a property underlain by a physical or chemical basis. Of course, *we* are familiar with the idea that any such property must be a matter of chemistry. But there is no good reason for saying that people who fail to realize this are incompetent with the kind term 'water'. They just know less about the true scientific picture of what it is that explains the phenomenologically important, macro-properties of kinds. They are not, in my view, in at all the same boat as people who fail to respect the supervenience of the moral on the natural. This is because the latter fault breaks up the whole point of moralizing, whereas ignorance of the way in which wateriness is supervenient on the chemical or physical does not at all destroy the point of classifying some stuff as water and other stuff as not: uneducated people still need to drink and wash. However, it is now commonly held that there is no absolute distinction here: Quine has taught us how fragile any division would be between conceptual and 'merely' scientific ignorance. So someone might hold that there is an important kind of incompetence, half conceptual but perhaps half scientific, that someone would exhibit if he failed to realize the supervenience of being water upon chemistry or physics, and that this is a worse kind of incompetence than any that would be shown by mere failure to realize that it is H_2O which is the relevant molecule. So we might try a notion of 'competently possible worlds', $(_c)$, meaning those that are as a competent person might describe a world as being: then we would have an $(S_c)/(P_c)$ combination. Should this tempt us to an anti-realist theory of 'being water'?

Saying that there are no mixed possible worlds in *this* sense means only that any competent person is going to deny that there are worlds in which some things of a given chemical or physical structure are water and others of the same structure are not; but that competent people might allow worlds in which things are H_2O but are not water. The first is a kind of *framework* knowledge, which we might expect everyone to possess; but competence to this degree need not require the *specialist* piece of scientific knowledge, which we might not expect of everyone, and which might even turn out to be false without affecting the framework. We might even suppose that supervenience claims have, characteristically, this framework appearance, and suggest that this is why they do not trail in their wake particular commitments of the (N) form. And now the counterattack against my argument in the case of morals and mind gathers momentum.[5] For if an $(S_c)/(P_c)$ combination works in a harmless case like this, then the shape of that combination cannot in general suggest anti-realism, and something must be wrong in the arguments so far given.

One reaction would be to allow the parallelism, and to grasp the nettle. When I said that we could relax with the $(S_a)/(P_a)$ combination in morals, I tried to explain this by saying that the role of a moral judgement is not to describe further *moral* aspects of reality; it is because the vocabulary must fit the *natural* world in certain ways that the combination is explicable. I might try the same move here: it is because 'wateriness' is not a further aspect of reality (beyond its containing various stuffs defined in chemical ways) that the combination is permissible at the level of 'competently possible' worlds. But I think this will strike most uncommitted readers as weak: anti-realism has to fight for a place these days even in the philosophy of morals, and is hardly likely to seem the best account of the judgement that I have water in my glass. I think a better reaction is to remember well all that is meant by the notion of a 'competently possible world'. Remembering this enables us to say that an $(S_c)/(P_c)$ combination is harmless, and implies no problem of explanation that is best met by anti-realism. This is because the 'ban on mixed possible worlds' that it gives rise to is explicable purely in terms of *beliefs* of ours—in particular, a belief that we suppose competent people to share. We believe, that is, that no two things could be identical physically without also forming the same stuff or kind *and we believe that all competent people will agree*. While we suppose this, but also suppose that competent people may not agree that if a thing is H_2O then it is water (because this requires a higher level of specialized, as opposed to framework, knowledge), then we have 'competently possible' worlds of the two kinds, and the ban on mixed worlds. But this has now been explained purely by the structure of beliefs that can coexist with competence. There is indeed no further inference to a metaphysical conclusion about the status of wateriness, because the explanation which, in the other cases, that inference helps to provide is here provided without it. To put it another way, we could say that in the moral case as well, when we deal with analytically possible worlds, we are dealing with beliefs we have about competence: in this case the belief that the competent person will not flout supervenience. But this belief is only explained by the further, anti-realist nature of moralizing. If moralizing were depicting further, moral aspects of reality, there would be no explanation of the conceptual constraint, and hence of our belief about the shape of a competent morality.

It cannot be overemphasized that my original problem is one of *explanation*. So it does not matter if sometimes an $(S)/(P)$ combination is explained in some ways, and sometimes in others. I do not suppose that there is one uniform pattern of explanation, suitable for all examples and for all strengths of modality (particularly if we flirt with hybrids like the present one). The

5. I owe this objection to Michael Smith. I am also greatly indebted to conversations with David Bostock and Elizabeth Fricker.

explanation demanded in the moral case is, according to me, best met by recognizing that moralizing is an activity that cannot proceed successfully without recognition of the supervenience constraint, but this in turn is best explained by projectivism. In the present case, the best explanation of why competent people recognize the supervenience of kinds upon physical or chemical structure is that we live in a culture in which science has found this out. I don't for a moment believe that *this* suggests any metaphysical conclusions. If this is right, it carries a small bonus. It means that the argument in the moral case does not depend upon drawing a hard and controversial distinction between 'conceptual' and other kinds of incompetence. It merely requires us to realize that there can be good explanations of our beliefs about the things that reveal incompetence. Anti-realism is one of them, in the case of morals, and awareness of the difference between framework scientific beliefs and specific realizations of them is another and works in the case of natural kinds.

Third Example

The previous case posed the only real challenge that I know to the original mystery. By contrast, the case of colours reinforces the peculiarity in the case of morals. For it would be highly implausible to aim for colour/primary property supervenience as an analytic truth or one constitutive of competence with a colour vocabulary. Intuitively, we feel that it is very nice and satisfying that colours do indeed supervene upon primary properties, and that there would be scientific havoc if they did not. But anybody who believes that they do not (mightn't God live in a world where displays reveal different colours to him, although there are no physical properties of surfaces of the things displayed?) can nonetheless recognize colours and achieve all the point and subtlety of colour classification.

Recent empirical work casts doubt even on the fact that 'everybody knows' that colours of surfaces are caused by the wavelength of reflected light. Other relational properties may matter. So it is wise to be cautious before putting any advanced modal status on supervenience or necessitation claims in this area. Certainly we expect there to be *some* complete primary property story, G^*, upon which colour supervenes as a matter of physical necessity. But then we would also immediately accept the corresponding thesis (N_p), and there is no problem about mixed worlds. Similarly, if we bravely elevated the supervenience (S) into a metaphysical thesis, there would be no good reason why (N) should not follow suit. (N) will not rise into the realms of analytic necessity, but then neither will (S). So at no level is there a mystery parallel to the one that arose with morals, and with Davidson's position on the mental and the physical. Of course, an (S)/(P) combination could be manufactured at the level of 'competently possible worlds', as in the last example, but once more it would avail nothing, because it would be explained simply by the shape of the beliefs that we have deemed necessary for competence.

IV

I have now said enough by way of exploring the original argument and its near neighbours. It would be nice to conclude with an estimate of the importance of supervenience claims in metaphysics. Here I confess I am pessimistic. It seems to me that (?) is a plausible doctrine, and in every case in which we are dealing with metaphysical or physical necessity, it seems to me that we could cut through talk of supervenience and speak directly of propositions of the form (N). This makes it clear, for example, that we may be dealing with 'nomological danglers' or necessities that connect together properties of very different kinds, and it may lessen our metaphysical pride to remember that it is one thing to assert such necessities but quite another thing to have a theory about why we can do so. Like many philosophers, I believe many supervenience claims in varying strengths; perhaps unlike them, I see them as part of the problem—in the philosophy of mind, or of secondary properties, or of morals or kinds—and not as part of the solution.

Addendum

This essay and its predecessor have probably attracted more discussion than any others in this volume. But I am heartened by what I detect as a general impatience with easy acceptance of supervenience claims, either in the moral sphere, or in the philosophy of mind, or in the relations between the special sciences.[6] So at least my concluding paragraph has found an echo. Indeed, some philosophers have voiced mistrust of the whole notion, and it is easy to understand why. Supervenience is supposed to give us a great deal: the covariance of one set of properties (the F, or further properties) with another set (the G, or grounding properties); the dependence of the F properties on the G; these consistently with the absence of reduction of the F to the G properties; and, finally, all in a metaphysically innocent way. It is this last that makes the package almost too good to be true. Kim reminds us that when the same structure was discussed in the philosophy of biology, earlier in the century, Samuel Alexander, a leading emergentist, recommended that we accept emergence (in effect, the same thing as supervenience) with natural piety, and my 1973 essay pointed out the dark side of that: unless we can explain the supervenience, there is nothing metaphysically innocent about it at all.[7] Indeed, without further explanation we might be left with a nomological dangler, or

6. For instance, Stephen Schiffer, in *Remnants of Meaning* (Cambridge: MIT Press, 1987) claims that appeals to a 'special primitive' relationship of supervenience is 'obscurantist in the extreme'. Jaegwon Kim, in 'Supervenience as a Philosophical Concept' (*Metaphilosophy*, 1990) gives an extremely useful view of the various concepts that have been distinguished, and highlights the explanatory task that supervenience claims trail with them.

7. See Kim, p. 15.

worse if the supervenience is *a priori,* since then we are left with a nasty 'opaque isolated logical fact'. My strategy was to urge that the demand for an explanation is met much better by a quasi-realist story than by any other.

A number of writers challenged this perception. Some challenged whether supervenience of the moral on the natural is, as I claimed, analytic. One kind of counterexample might be divine command moralities, in which value is supposed to supervene upon the existence of a divine fiat, which presumably might deem some things good and then bad without there being natural change.[8] But apart from its doubtful coherence, I think the position would best be characterized as having a rather over-generous conception of the natural, by presenting divinities as well as humans to think of. Extreme axiarchism is a more threatening position, since it seems to reverse the order of dependency, making the natural world dependent on the ethical order. Again, the coherence of the thought is not all that evident, but a better response is to hand (here I am indebted to an unpublished paper, 'Moral Covariance', by Glenn Branch). We can jettison the 'dependency' element in supervenience without losing my argument. That is, so long as we have it analytic that the ethical *covaries* with the natural, or in Davidson's terms that *F* predicates cannot distinguish between any entities that *G* predicates cannot distinguish between, then we have the same demand for explanation, whether or not we think that *G*s sometimes depend upon *F*s. The whole business of dependence is very fraught in any event, as essays 11 and 13 testify, so it is probably wise to keep away from it as long as possible. This is one respect in which essay 6 may actually have posed the problem better than essay 7, whose asymmetric notion of 'underlying' introduces an element of dependency which, while present in most concepts of supervenience, may be better put on one side for the sake of this problem (although it will not leave the stage entirely, since it is worth realizing that it may pose a further explanatory demand of its own). That is, as well as explaining the status we give to the covariance of *F* predicates and *G* predicates, we must also explain why we think that the *F* properties are there 'in virtue of' an object's *G* properties, and this may not be all that easy. A quasi-realist will see both covariance and the asymmetry of dependency as a reflection of the fact that valuing is *to be done* in the light of an object's natural properties, and without that constraint nothing recognizably ethical could be approached at all.

Other writers have missed the point of the problem in other ways. Susan Hurley, for example, cites the fact that 'theories must supervene on descriptions of what they are theories about' and claims that this shows that there is no need for noncognitive underpining for supervenience, which is as well explained by her own theory-oriented view of ethics.[9] But the claim backfires, for the truth of theories need not at all supervene (let alone analytically) upon what they are theories about. The underdetermination of theory by data can be put exactly as the claim that it is logically possible that an identical body of

8. James Klagge, 'An Alleged Difficulty Concerning Moral Properties', in *Mind,* 1984.
9. S. Hurley, 'Objectivity and Disagreement', in *Morality and Objectivity,* ed. Ted Honderich (London: Routledge & Kegan Paul, 1985), pp. 56–57.

data might in one world be truly explained by one theory, and in another world by a different and incompatible theory.

Hurley goes on to 'make the point more formally' by making a distinction that seems to be equivalent to that between weak (intraworld) and strong (interworld) supervenience: 'in each logically possible world there may be some theory that does the requisite job, while there is no one theory such that in every logically possible world that theory does the requisite job'. 'Doing the job' here means being true by a coherentist conception of truth, so we have the idea that a theory may be true in one world but not in another, although in every world there will be some true ethical theory. This is no more than setting up the problem, giving us the distinction between

(1)   Necessarily, if anything x has property F in A, then there is a G such that x has G, and there is a theory true in A entailing that everything G has F.

and

(2)   Necessarily, if anything x has property F in A, then there is a G such that x has G, and there is a theory true at all worlds, entailing that everything G has F.

The ban on mixed worlds is given by the first, and the contrast with necessitation claims by its contrast with the second. The cost is that once we allow different theories of G/F relations true at different worlds, my question simply re-emerges: why shouldn't one of these theories be true of some objects in some world, for example at some place or time, and another be true of other objects at other places and times? Hurley tells us that there are to be no mixed worlds, but completely fails to engage the project of explaining why this has to be so, which is the problem I posed.

In general, I remain fairly happy with the argument. It does, I think, depend very heavily on the outside analyticity claim. If it is less than 'constitutive of competence' with the concepts that supervenience is recognized, the explanatory possibilities multiply. For example, 'Cornell' realism (see the addendum to essay 9) seems at first sight to have no trouble explaining supervenience: if ethical properties are natural properties, then of course they covary. But Cornell realism, I argue, is less successful in explaining what it is to have an ethical perspective on a natural property, and therefore not at all well equipped to say why it is crucial to that perspective that supervenience be respected. After all, water is H_2O, but it is not part of competence with attributions of wateriness that we respect a chemical supervenience claim. We make a scientific error, perhaps, but no conceptual error if we believe that wateriness depends on some other, perhaps unknown, properties.

A possible reaction to my problem is to press for 'strong', or interworld, supervenience, which is here called necessitation, whereas I pose the puzzle in terms of the weak, or intraworld, notion, which is why the ban on mixed worlds comes out oddly. Necessitation gives us the alternative posed in the first part of this essay, that there is some ground G^* such that, necessarily, if anything is G^*, it is F. It may be, as I hint in the essay, that this is a better notion to work with, and if so my problem disappears. But something in the texture of ethics is left out. For it is not evidently 'constitutive of competence' to recognize any instance of the conditional 'if anything is G^*, it is F' as necessary. It is not even clear that the competent must recognize that *there are* instances of such necessities. Yet supervenience (like universalizability) latched onto something quite obvious about ethics. This obvious thing seemed better captured by weak supervenience than by necessitation.

What this leaves us, however, is a rival explanation to mine. The analytic claim can be put weakly: it is entirely intraworld, as in (S_a) (p. 137), and this befits a condition on competent moralizing—which, after all, concerns what is true in this world rather than what might be true in exotic possible worlds. But then the proposition that there are no mixed worlds need not be analytic: it is no doubt true, and is recognized as true by the most capable people, such as philosophers. But the question of why philosophers think it true is answered another way: it is because we philosophers believe that there are instances of the necessitation, and that is where the authority behind the ban lies. Because if there cannot be things that are G^* and not F, then there cannot be worlds in which some G^* things are and others are not F.

If that is right, my original puzzle gets a solution without invoking any projective theory. But the explanatory demand must turn to the necessitations, and the realist must say why, for her, they do not amount to danglers best accepted in a spirit of natural piety. I know why I accept them, if I can find my ethical imagination simply baffled at trying to contemplate how not to approve or disapprove of things with particular natural properties. But the realist still seems left drawing a blank cheque on the synthetic *a priori,* which strikes me as worse, especially when, far from having examples of these necessities, we are so hard pressed to find examples where the unmodal conditionals are even true.

8

Errors and the Phenomenology of Value

Oh Is there not one maiden breast
That does not feel the moral beauty
Of making worldly interest
Subordinate to sense of duty?
W. S. Gilbert
The Pirates of Penzance

I

John Mackie described himself as a moral sceptic, and he described his theory of ethics as an error theory. The ordinary user of moral language wants to claim something that, according to Mackie, cannot be claimed without error: he wants to claim 'something that involves a call for action or for the refraining from action, and one that is absolute, not contingent upon any desire or preference or policy or choice, his own or anyone else's' (p. 33).[1] Again, someone in moral perplexity may want to know whether a course of action is wrong 'in itself' (p. 34), and 'something like this is the everyday objectivist concept', which is erroneous. For, according to Mackie, ordinary judgements and perplexities include an assumption that there are objective values, in a sense in which he denies that there are. This assumption is ingrained enough to count as part of the meaning of ordinary moral terms, but it is false.

Mackie did not draw quite the consequences one might have expected from this position. If a vocabulary embodies an error, then it would be better if it were replaced by one that avoids the error. Slightly more accurately, if a vocabulary embodies an error *in some use,* it would be better if either it, or a replacement vocabulary, were used differently. We could better describe this by saying that our old, infected moral concepts or ways of thought should be replaced by ones that serve our legitimate needs but avoid the mistake. Yet Mackie does not say what such a way of thought would look like, and how it would differ in order to show its innocence of the old error. On the contrary, in the second part of the book he is quite happy to go on to express a large number of straightforward moral views about the good life, about whether it is

1. Unless otherwise stated, page references are to *Ethics: Inventing Right and Wrong* (London: Penguin Books, 1977).

149

permissible to commit suicide or abortion, and so on. All these are expressed in the old, supposedly infected, vocabulary. Mackie does, of course, notice the problem. He explicitly asks (p. 49) whether his error theory rules out all first-order ethics, and when he returns to the question (p. 105) there is a real threat that ideally there would be no such activity as first-order moralizing. The threat is averted, supposedly, only by introducing the general Humean theme about the social function of morality: 'Morality is not to be discovered but to be made: we have to decide what moral views to adopt, what moral stands to take' (p. 106). Yet from the standpoint of an error theory, it is quite extraordinary that we should have to do any such thing. Why should we have to choose to fall into error? Surely it would be better if we avoided *moral* (erroneous) views altogether and contented ourselves with some lesser, purged commitments that can be held without making metaphysical mistakes. Let us call these 'shmoral' views, and a vocabulary that expresses them a 'shmoral vocabulary.' Then the puzzle is why, in the light of the error theory, Mackie did not at least indicate how a shmoral vocabulary would look, and why he did not himself go on only to shmoralize, not to moralize. And in my view this is enough of a puzzle to cast doubt back on to the original diagnosis of error. In other words, it would obviously have been a silly thing to do, to try to substitute some allegedly hygienic set of concepts for moral ones; but that in itself suggests that no error can be incorporated in mere use of those concepts.

In reply to this it may be said that appearances notwithstanding, Mackie did actually go on only to shmoralize. He rids himself of the error but uses the Humean reconstruction of practical needs and practical reasoning to advocate various shmoral views. These are only accidentally expressed in a vocabulary that looks like that of ordinary moralists: the identical shape of the words does not signify identical concepts, although there is sufficient overlap in function between moralizing and shmoralizing to justify retention of the same words. This is certainly possible. But it leaves an acute problem of identifying just where shmoralizing differs from moralizing: what shows us whether Mackie is moralizing or shmoralizing? Does it determine the issue that he will say things like 'there is no objective prescriptivity built into the fabric of the world'? Troubles multiply. First, it is clear that not all moralists will deny this (many moralists will not even understand it). Second, it seems gratuitous to infer that there are two different activities from the fact that there are two or more different theories about the nature of the activity. It would be much more natural to say that Hume and Mackie moralize, just as ordinary people do, but with a developed and different theory about what it is that they are doing. The error theory then shrinks to the claim that most ordinary moralists have a bad theory, or at least no very good theory, about what it is to moralize, and in particular that they falsely imagine a kind of objectivity for values, obligations, and so on. This may be true, but it does not follow that the error infects the practice of moralizing, nor the concepts used in ways defined by that practice.

Here, however, a fairly blanket holism can be introduced to rescue Mackie, or at least to urge that it is profitless to oppose him. Our theories infect our meanings; so a different theory about the nature of the activity of moralizing will yield a different meaning for the terms with which we do it; hence Mackie is right that the ordinary meanings do embody error. It becomes profitless to split things in two, so that on the one hand there is the error-free practice, and on the other hand a multiplicity of possibly erroneous theories about its nature. Indeed, the split appeals no more than the despised analytic-synthetic distinction, and if the opponents of an error theory need that, they will gain few supporters.

It is important, and not just to this philosophical issue, to see that this defence fails. To answer it, distinguish between the activity or practice of moralizing and the 'full meaning' of moral terms, where this is determined as the holist wishes, by both the practice and whatever theory the subjects hold about the nature of their practice. Then the holist may have the thesis about 'full meaning', with the consequence that Hume and Mackie may give a different full meaning to their terms, simply through having a different theory of their point and purpose. But it will not follow that their *practice* will differ from that of other people. Hence, it will not follow that other people's practice embodies error. For it is in principle possible that we should observe the practice of some subjects as closely as we wish, and know as much as there is to know about their ways of thinking, commending, approving, deliberating, worrying, and so on, yet be unable to tell from all that which theory they hold. The practice could be clipped on to either metaphysic. The holist will have it that this alters meanings throughout. But we can give him that, yet still maintain that no difference is discernible in the practice, and therefore that no error is embodied in the practice of those who hold the wrong theory. To use a close analogy, there are different theories about the nature of arithmetical concepts. Hence a holist may claim that a subject will give a different total meaning to numerals depending on which theory he accepts, and this difference will apply just as much when the subject is counting as when he is doing metamathematics. All that may be true, yet it would not follow that any practice of counting embodies error. That would be so only if one could tell just by observing it which of the competing metamathematical theories the subject accepts. In the arithmetical case this would not be true. Similarly, I maintain, in the moral case one ought not to be able to tell from the way in which someone conducts the activity of moralizing whether he has committed the 'objectivist' mistake or not; hence any such mistake is better thought of as accidental to the practice.

Obviously there is *an* answer to this. It is that the objectivist error does so permeate the practice that you can tell, from the way people moralize, that they are in its grip. It is as if a strict finitist theory of, say, arithmetic led someone to deny that you could count certain sets that others can happily enumerate. But which features of the practice show this? They are to be features that lie beyond the scope of what I have called 'quasi-realism': the enterprise of showing how much of the apparently 'realist' appearance of ordinary moral thought is explicable and justifiable on an anti-realist picture.[2]

2. 'Rule Following and Moral Realism', in *Wittgenstein: To Follow a Rule*, ed. S. Holtzman and S. Leich (London: Routledge & Kegan Paul, 1981), and chapter 6 of *Spreading the Word* (Oxford: Clarendon Press, 1984).

According to me, quasi-realism is almost entirely successful, and I do not think John Mackie provided reasons for thinking otherwise. In other words, proper shmoralizing is proper moralizing.

II

So far, I have tried to show that there is something fishy about holding an error theory yet continuing to moralize, and I have argued that the 'holistic' or Quinean defence of such a position would fail. The argument can now move in different directions. Let us call the Humean picture of the nature of morality, and of the metaphysics of the issue, projectivism. On this view we have sentiments and other reactions caused by natural features of things, and we 'gild or stain' the world by describing it as if it contained features answering to these sentiments, in the way that the niceness of an ice cream answers to the pleasure it gives us. Then we could say that Mackie is right about the metaphysical issue, and ought to have been more thoroughgoing in replacing moral terms and concepts by different ones—in other words, that the projectivist in ethics should conduct his practical reasoning in a different way: his shmoralizing would not be moralizing. Let us call this a revisionist projectivism. By contrast, there is the quasi-realist identification of shmoralizing with moralizing. In effect, the skirmishes in part I of this essay urge that quasi-realism be taken seriously, because even projectivists are going to find themselves indulging in a practice that is apparently identical with moralizing. Of course, in opposition to each of these views, there is the realist charge that projectivism is false in any case; finally there is the 'quietist' view, urged by Professor Hare, for instance, that no real issue can be built around the objectivity or otherwise of moral values.

If we are to say that the practices characteristic of moralizing are or are not available to a projectivist, we should be careful to identify the practices at issue. Elsewhere I try to show how the realist-seeming *grammar* of moral discourse can be explained on that metaphysic.[3] This involves, for instance, addressing the Geach-Frege problem of accounting for the unasserted occurrence of sentences using moral terms, explaining the propositional form that we give to moral utterances, explaining why we may legitimately worry whether one of our moral views is correct and hence explaining the role of a concept of truth in ethics, and so on. If this work is successful, there is no way of arguing that the grammar of moral discourse either refutes projectivism or forces it to take a revisionist course. This means, of course, that Mackie cannot properly use these aspects of our practice in support of the error theory. And sometimes he does just this. For instance, he cites Russell's feeling that on a particular moral issue (opposition to the introduction of bullfighting into England) one does not just express a desire that the thing should not happen, but one does so while feeling that one's desires on such a matter

3. See also essay 10.

are *right*.[4] Mackie thinks that this is a claim to objectivity, and as such errone-ous. The quasi-realist will see it instead as a proper, necessary expression of an attitude toward our own attitudes. It is not something that should be wrenched out of our moral psychology; it is something we need to cultivate to the right degree and in the right places to avoid the (moral) defect of indiffer-ence to things that merit passion. This actually illustrates a central quasi-realist tactic: what seems like a thought that embodies a particular second-order metaphysic of morals is seen instead as a kind of thought that expresses a first-order attitude or need. Perhaps the nicest example comes from coun-terfactuals that seem to assert an anti-projectivist mind-independence of moral facts: 'even if we had approved of it or enjoyed it or desired to do it, bear-baiting would still have been wrong' can sound like a second-order realist commitment directly in opposition to projectivism. But in fact, on the construal of indirect contexts that I offer, it comes out as a perfectly sensible first-order commitment to the effect that it is not our enjoyments or approv-als to which you should look in discovering whether bear-baiting is wrong (it is at least mainly the effect on the bear).

For the rest of this essay I shall suppose that this aspect of quasi-realism is successful. So projectivism can accommodate the propositional grammar of ethics; it need not seek to revise that. On the contrary, properly protected by quasi-realism, projectivism supports and indeed explains this much of our ordinary moral thought. But in my experience this explanation is apt to leave a residual unease. People feel uncomfortable with the idea that this is the true explanation of our propensity to find and to respect values, obligations, du-ties, and rights. This unease is perhaps rather like that of nineteenth-century thinkers who found it so difficult to do ethics without God. It is located in a tension between the subjective source that projectivism gives to morality and the objective 'feel' that a properly working morality has. It is this objective feel or phenomenology that people find threatened by projectivism, and they may go on to fear the threat as one that strikes at the core of morality. We may scoff at those who thought that if God is dead, everything is permitted. But it is harder to really shake off the feeling that if duties, rights, and so forth come down to *that*—to the projectivist earth—then they do not have quite the power or force, the title to respect, that we were brought up to believe.

It is, I think, particularly the side of morality associated with *obligation* that is felt to be subject to this threat. Obligation needs to be 'peremptory and absolute', as George Eliot famously said; it often needs to be perceived as something sufficiently external to us to act as a *constraint* or bound on our other sentiments and desires. The chains and shackles of obligation must come from outside us. Can anything both be felt to have this power, and yet be explained as a projection of our own sentiments? The charge will be that projectivism falsifies this aspect of morality; projectivism will be unable to endorse this kind of perception of obligation, but must explain it away as a phenomenological distortion. This perception will be seen as the result of an

4. P. 34.

error, and realist opponents of projectivism will join with revisionists to urge that it marks a point at which quasi-realism fails.[5] The realists will trust the phenomenology, and the revisionists will regret it. We can notice in this connection that when Mackie identifies the error of ordinary thought, he often points to the 'intrinsic' or 'absolute' to-be-done-ness that certain actions are felt to possess.[6] It is not just the 'intrinsic' value of happiness or pleasure, because it is less surprising that these values should receive a projective explanation. It is as if the objectivist's error is to think of certain things as obligatory in a way that has nothing to do with us, and about which we can do nothing: a way that could in principle stand opposed to the whole world of human desire and need.

Now, admittedly, it might seem from this that the error is to adopt a deontological rather than a teleological first-order morality. But surely this is wrong, for Mackie did not want the error to be purely one of adopting a defective or nonconsequentialist first-order morality. Doing that may be a natural consequence of a metaphysical mistake, but it is not in itself an 'error' intrinsic to the very nature of morality. I think instead that Mackie chose the word, and chose to concentrate upon, *obligation* because of the absolute and external 'feel' that he wanted to indicate, and that he felt was not explicable or defensible on a projective metaphysic. And if he were right, then by threatening this part of the feeling of obligation, projectivism would indeed threaten one of the most important and characteristic parts of morality. But is there any reason to believe that he is right?

The issue will look rather different, depending on whether the difficulty is supposed to concern the explanation of moral psychology, or its justification. Consider a very pure case of someone in the grip of a duty. Mabel and Fred want to marry each other. The opportunity is there, the desires are aflame, the consequences are predictably acceptable or even desirable. There is only one thought to oppose it: they have a duty to do otherwise, so it would be wrong. And this feeling that it would be wrong can wrestle with and sometimes even overcome all the rest. Isn't this mysterious? Called conscience, it used to be mysterious enough to suggest an internal voice of God standing outside the natural world of sentiments and desires. On the present line of thought, it is mysterious enough to suggest perception of an external or objective moral fact, also standing outside the natural world of sentiments and desires. Unfortunately, neither of these explanations is more than a gesture. It is trivial to point out the gaps they leave. But there is a better explanation: Fred has been brought up in a certain way, and a consequence of this upbringing is that he looks on certain courses of action with horror. He will keep his self-respect, be able to live with himself, only if he conducts his life in a particular way, and this prompts a range of feeling that is sufficiently strong to oppose immediate desire and that gains expression when he describes the conduct as 'wrong.' Whether it was a good thing that Fred was brought up like

5. See for instance the first paragraph of John McDowell's 'Values and Secondary Qualities', in *Morality and Objectivity,* ed. T. Honderich (London: Routledge & Kegan Paul, 1985).

6. *The Miracle of Theism* (Oxford: Clarendon Press, 1982) pp. 104, 115 ff.

that is a matter of judgement, but it can hardly be doubted that it is a good thing that people should sometimes feel like that, for otherwise they are more likely to do the most awful things. It is of course a brute fact about human beings that our sources of self-respect are malleable in this way, but that is a matter of common observation. Equally, it is a matter of common observation that there are cultural ways of reinforcing such feelings in elements of the population that may be in particular need of them: traditionally soldiers and girls get strong injections of honour and duty.

At the level of explanation, then, it is hard to see why there is any problem for the projectivist. Indeed, it is hard to see how there *could* be. For many of the ingredients of his account will be needed by any other account. For instance, his observations on the plasticity of our sensibilities, and on the various devices that lead people to respect different sets of obligations and to value different aspects of things, will simply be copied by a realist, who will need to say that our perceptions of moral facts are similarly trained and adapted. As usual, however, the extra ingredients the realist adds (the values or obligations which, in addition to normal features of things, are cognized and the respect we then feel for these cognized qualities) are pulling no explanatory weight: they just sit on top of the story that tells how our sentiments relate to natural features of things. If Fred poses a problem, then, it cannot be one of the explanation of moral psychology but must be one of justification.

If Fred is rational, can his virtue survive his own awareness of its origin and nature? If Mabel throws into her wooing a whole projective plus quasi-realist explanation of what Fred is doing when he maintains that it's wrong, and if Fred is rational, will this not destroy his resolve? Shouldn't he think something like this: that although he has been brought up to use moral categories and to think that there are moral obligations and so forth, *there are none really*—they are a fiction, or a useful, regulative myth: hence, forget them? Once again we are reminded of those thinkers who felt that if there were no God or no afterlife, then it would be rational to ignore the claims of morality whenever self-interest suggested it. Their anxiety was grounded on a mistake about rationality, for the altruistic or principled man is no more nor less rational than the self-interested—he is just different in ways that affect his happiness and the happiness of communities composed of people like him. Rationality in itself does not force one sensibility or another on us *just* because we have some belief about the origin of that sensibility. This is obvious if we take a parallel: Mabel may be tempted to laugh at Fred's moustache; Fred may seek to dissuade her by telling a projectivist story about the judgement that something is funny, but there is no reason for him to succeed. Finding things very funny is perfectly compatible with believing that it is a tendency to laugh which we project on the world when we do so. It is not uniquely rational to try to smother our sense of humour because of this belief about its nature. So Mabel is not irrational if she accepts Fred's theory of laughter and continues to laugh at his moustache, and by analogy he may be perfectly rational to accept the projectivist account of morality, and to maintain his resolve just as forcefully as before.

I say that he may be rational to do this. But it is possible that he is not, for an explanation of the origin of a sentiment can diminish its force. For example, psychologists sometimes connect humour with sublimated or concealed aggression. Believing this explanation, and being ashamed of aggressive instincts, it would be rational for me to find fewer and fewer things funny. The explanation *coupled with* other values undermines the sentiment. Similarly, a morality might contain values whose effect, coupled with a projective explanation, is to diminish a subject's respect for some obligations. For example, a child may be brought up to believe that things really matter only in so far as God cares about them; learning not to think of conscience as the voice of God would couple with this attitude to diminish the force with which the child feels obligations. Or someone might suppose that only commitments that describe the constitution of the real world have any importance and that all others are better ignored: a projective explanation of morality may then diminish the attention that person is prepared to pay to it.[7] This latter attitude is actually quite common. For example, when people feel uncomfortable about trying to impose a morality on other people, what troubles them is the idea that moral commitments lack real, objective truth values certified by an independent reality. The hope of rehabilitating morality by making it an object of perception or reason, and thereby giving it a better claim on our attention, bears witness to the same idea. In each case, however, it is not the explanation of the practice *per se* that has the sceptical consequence, it is the effect of the explanation on sensibilities that have been brought up to respect only particular kinds of thing. So when people fear that projectivism carries with it a loss of status to morality, their fear ought to be groundless, and will appear only if a defective sensibility leads them to respect the wrong things.

So far I have considered this problem only as it affects obligations. But similar remarks can be apposite in connection with values. It is not initially so surprising that we can go on valuing the good things of life while knowing that the valuing is an expression of our own subjective sentiments. This need be no more odd than that we should go on finding things funny, or painful, or worthwhile, or beautiful, although God is dead, or although we accept subjective responses as the source of these reactions. However, David Wiggins has found a problem even here for the position that he called noncognitivism, which shares with projectivism the Humean theme that 'ends are supplied by feeling or will, which are not conceived either as percipient or as determinants in any interesting way of perception'.[8] The core of the charge is, I think, that projectivism cannot coexist with the way in which we perceive values as residing in things outside ourselves. It is not entirely clear, because Wiggins associates with projectivism the repugnant (first-order) doctrine that the only things that possess any intrinsic value are human states of consciousness. But a projectivist's sensibility need not, and in my view should not, take this shape. He can admire features of things regardless of their effects on us: his first-

7. Mackie mentions this kind of psychology on p. 24.

8. 'Truth, Invention and the Meaning of Life', British Academy Lecture (Oxford: Clarendon Press, 1976).

order morality need be anthropocentric no more than it need be egocentric. Remember here that a projectivist who avails himself of quasi-realism can assert those tantalizing expressions of apparent mind-independence: it is not my sentiments that make bear-baiting wrong; it is not because we disapprove of it that mindless violence is abominable; it is preferable that the world should be a beautiful place even after all consciousness of it ceases. The explanation of what we are doing when we say such things in no way impugns our right to hold them, nor the passion with which we should do so. But if we dissociate ourselves from this target, then at this point Wiggins seems to threaten projectivism no more than the attack deflected in the last paragraph. It might be that there are people who cannot 'put up with' the idea that values have a subjective source; who cannot put up with the idea that the meaning of their life and their activities is ultimately something they confer, and that even critical reflection on how best to confer them conducts itself in the light of other sentiments that must be taken simply as given. But this will be because such people have a defect elsewhere in their sensibilities—one that has taught them that things do not matter unless they matter to God, or throughout infinity, or to a world conceived apart from any particular set of concerns or desires, or whatever. One should not adjust one's metaphysics to pander to such defects.

There is still that nagging feeling that on this metaphysic 'there are no obligations, and so on, *really*' (otherwise, why call the position anti-realist?). But urging this as a problem confuses two different contexts in which such a remark might occur. Protected by quasi-realism, my projectivist says the things that sound so realist to begin with—that there are real obligations and values, and that many of them are independent of us, for example. It is *not* the position that he says these for public consumption but denies them in his heart, so to speak. He affirms *all that could ever properly be meant* by saying that there are real obligations.[9] When the context of discussion is that of first-order commitment, he is as solid as the most virtuous moralist. It is just that the explanation of why there are obligations and the rest is not quite that of untutored common sense. It deserves to be called anti-realist because it avoids the view that when we moralize we respond to, and describe, an independent aspect of reality. Again, mathematics provides a useful model for understanding this. There are anti-realist views of what we are doing when we practise arithmetic. But they need not and should not lead to anyone wondering whether 7 + 5 is 'really' 12, for that would be an expression of first-order doubt that would not be a consequence of the second-order theory. Arithmeti-

---

9. Compare Evans on the unintelligibility of one way of thinking of colours as real ('Things Without the Mind', in *Philosophical Subjects*, ed. Z. van Straaten [Oxford: Clarendon Press, 1980]). I want to maintain that any genuinely anti-projective attempt to think of obligations or values as 'real' either is similarly unintelligible or marks a mistake about explanation. This is why I would deny that there is an aspect of moral *phenomenology* that gives morality an objective appearance that quasi-realism must regard as illusory (as McDowell claims in note 4 to 'Values and Secondary Qualities'). For there is nothing in the appearances of morality to force us to make the mistake about explanation. Obligations and so forth appear in exactly the way I would predict.

cal practice would remain as solid and certain as could be, but explained without reference to an independent mathematical reality.

III

Thus far I have been using quasi-realism to protect the appearance of morality: to urge that there is no error in our ordinary ways of thought and our ordinary commitments and passions. This enterprise will interest a projectivist most, because it defends him against the most forceful attack he faces, which is that he cannot accommodate the rich phenomena of the moral life. But realist opponents of projectivism need to notice quasi-realism as well, since otherwise they do not know how to launch an attack on projectivism. They would not have correctly located its strengths or weaknesses. Nevertheless, they could concede that its defence is successful on these fronts, yet still maintain their hostility. They can urge that the metaphor of projection fails, or is better replaced by a comparison between our knowledge of ethics and our knowledge of other things, such as mathematics or colours. It is this latter comparison that I now wish to explore. It is not, in my view, right to suppose that there is immediately an issue between two rival theories of morality. This is partly because some of the writers I shall mention, who might seem to be offering a perceptual account of morality, are at least half-inclined to deny that they wish to offer a theory at all, although that does leave the status of some of their remarks regrettably unclear. At any rate, as I see it there are in the beginning two invitations, but they are not so much rivals as complementary to each other. The one is to explore the idea of a projection upon the world of a sentiment that we feel; the other is to explore the idea of a perception of a real property, but one that is intimately related to our own sensibilities. These mark different directions of exploration, and it should not be obvious at first sight which will prove the more profitable. I believe that at the end the first provides illumination where the second runs into obstacles, disanalogies, and an ultimate inability to say anything. I also believe that the first can explain and soothe away the fears that lead people to the second—the fear I addressed in part II, for example, that without obligations of a reality to which a person cannot aspire, everything is permitted. I shall try to make good these claims by presenting the 'perceptual' direction in the light of the writings of David Wiggins, Thomas Nagel, and John McDowell, and more recently Hilary Putnam,[10] but as I mentioned, I am conscious that it is not easy to extract one theory, or just one theory, from those writings. However, at least they suggest a direction of thought, and it is this direction which I want to block.

The opposition understands that projectivism is an explanatory theory that maintains that moral values are projections of sentiment because we have a

10. Wiggins, op. cit.; T. Nagel, 'Subjective and Objective', in *Mortal Questions* (Cambridge: Cambridge University Press, 1979); J. McDowell, 'Are Moral Requirements Hypothetical Imperatives?' (*Proceedings of the Aristotelian Society, Supplementary Volume*, 1978); H. Putnam, *Reason, Truth and History* (Cambridge: Cambridge University Press, 1981).

better explanation of moral practices if we see ourselves as responsive only to a value-free world. But according to the opposition, a number of considerations make this an insufficient basis for projectivism. Disquiet can perhaps be focused under three headings.

(1) Consider secondary properties. Colours (etc.) are real properties of objects, and this is true even if the best causal explanation of how we detect them proceeds by mentioning primary properties. Colours really exist, although the reality that contains them is not independent of the fact that there also exist human modes of perception.

(2) The thesis just put forward will appear surprising only because (i) of a prejudice that only primary properties, or the properties of some 'ultimate' scientific theory of things, are real, or (ii) we forget the truth that the world cannot be 'prised away from' our manner of conceiving it, nor from our interests and concerns when we do so. Since neither of these motives is legitimate, there is no obstacle to (1), and to using the parallel with colours to allow a reality to values and so forth.

(3) It is true that a training of a particular kind is needed to enable people properly to perceive values and so forth, but this is harmless: people need training to detect, for example, features of tunes or shades.

I do not suppose that each of the writers I have mentioned would assent to each of these. For example, although the work of Nagel is prominent in opening up the idea of a reality that is yet subject-dependent, his own work on moral motivation is much more concerned with rationality than with any analogy to the perception of secondary qualities. And Wiggins thinks that the question of the truth of moral commitments looks very different if we consider values and if we consider obligations. But I shall put questions of attribution to one side, simply taking these three themes to form the core of a *perceptual* model of moralizing that at least appears to be a rival to projectivism. *Is* it a rival, and if it is, then how are we to tell which is better?

Wiggins writes that he has 'long marvelled' at the fact that philosophers have dwelt frequently upon the difference between 'good' and 'red' or 'yellow'. I do not think he should have, unless indeed it is marvellous that philosophers should emphasize things that are banal and basic. At any rate, it is very easy to rattle off significant differences between secondary properties and those involved in value and obligation. Here are half a dozen.

(a) Moral properties supervene upon others in a way quite different from any in which secondary properties do. It is a scientific fact that secondary properties supervene upon primary properties. It may even be a metaphysical fact, at least inasmuch as it would offend deep metaphysical commitments to imagine secondary properties changing while primary properties do not. But it is not a criterion of incompetence in the ascription of secondary properties to fail to realize that they must supervene upon others. On the other hand, that moral properties supervene upon natural ones is not a scientific fact, and it *is* criterial of incompetence in moralizing to fail to realize that they must do so.[11]

11. See also essays 6 and 7.

(b) The receptive mechanisms whereby we are acquainted with secondary properties are well-known objects of scientific study. For example, the kinds of damage to the retina or the ear or the taste buds that result in defective perception of secondary qualities can be studied. These studies are not at all similar to studies of defects of character that lead to moral blindness: these latter studies have no receptive or causal mechanisms as their topic. This is just as well, for we need to put things in a particular moral light after we are told about their *other* properties; we do not *also* have to wheel a particular sensory mechanism up against them. Connected with this, and with (a), is the thought that if our secondary-property-detecting mechanisms fail, we might expect to know that immediately: it presents itself as a loss of immediately felt phenomenal quality, just as it does when light fails or we stick cotton wool in our ears. There is no such loss when we become, say, corrupt. We cannot become corrupt overnight, and usually we cannot tell when we have done so. Indeed, it would be a hallmark of many kinds of moral blindness that this is so. The really coarse man thinks that he is perfectly in order, but that other people are too fastidious (recognizing that you have become really coarse is in this way self-refuting: the realization itself shows some residual delicacy).

(c) It is not altogether simple to characterize the 'mind-dependence' of secondary qualities. But it is plausible to say that these are relative to our perceptions of them in this way: if we were to change so that everything in the world that had appeared blue came to appear red to us, this is what it would be for the world to cease to contain blue things, and come to contain only red things. The analogy with moral qualities fails dramatically: if everyone comes to think of it as permissible to maltreat animals, this does nothing at all to make it permissible: it just means that everybody has deteriorated.[12]

(d) The way in which moral practices vary with the forms of life of a society is not at all similar to the way, if any, in which perceptions of secondary qualities can vary with those forms of life. Roughly, we expect such perceptions to vary in acuity depending on whether the property perceived is important to a culture. But once a predicate is located as expressing such a property, there is no prospect of finding that it has a radically different extension, whereas many things are evaluated quite differently in different groups or at different times. Similarly, apart from rare borderline cases, there is nothing in secondary quality ascription parallel to the 'essentially contested' character of many moral verdicts.

(e) It is up to a subject whether he cares about any particular secondary property in any way. If morality consisted in the perception of qualities, there would be a theoretical space for a culture that perceived the properties perfectly, but paid no attention to them. But however it is precisely fixed, the practical nature of morality is clearly intrinsic to it, and there is not this theoretical space.

(f) Evaluative predicates are typically attributive: a thing may be good *qua*

12. I stressed this in 'Rule Following and Moral Realism' in *Wittgenstein: To Follow a Rule*, ed. S. Holtzman and S. Leich (London: Routledge & Kegan Paul, 1981). McGinn concentrates upon the point in *The Subjective View* (Oxford: Clarendon Press, 1983), p. 150.

action of a commander-in-chief, but bad *qua* action of a father, just as a man may be a good burglar but a bad batsman. Secondary properties just sit there: a red tomato is a red fruit and a red object just bought at the grocer's. (Wiggins notices this asymmetry after the passage quoted.)

Of course, the extent to which these constitute disanalogies can be debated. But perhaps by way of illustrating their strength in the moral case, we can notice that sometimes they will not present such a clear picture. For example, it is very doubtful whether they apply with equal force to the perception of physical *beauty*. For at least (a), (c), (e), and (f) can be queried in this case. And this in turn connects with the sense we can have that sometimes the beauty of a thing must be perceived and cannot be told. Whereas when it cannot be told how *good* something was, this is always because some *other* fact about it resists communication—how happy we were, or how brave we needed to be. So, unlike John Mackie, I incline to find the projective nature of morality much better motivated than the projective theory applied to aesthetic evaluation. But applied to ethics, the cumulative effect of this considerations seems to me to be great enough that expecting a theory of moralizing to look very much like a theory of secondary quality perception appears a severe error of philosophical taste. Nevertheless, we cannot depend entirely upon this cumulative effect. For it will be retorted that mention of secondary qualities just provided an illustration of a combination, a shape of theory, that can also apply to ethics, however different the subject matter is in other respects. This is the combination or shape of theory illustrated by (1), (2), and (3). So the disqualification of secondary properties wins one battle, but it does not by itself win the war against a 'perceptual' direction.

I will now try to show that once they are properly distanced from other perceptual analogues, (1), (2) and (3) provide no theory of ethics at all, let alone one capable of standing up against projectivism. The first thing to realize is that there is nothing to prevent a projectivist from *speaking of* the perception of moral properties, of the world containing obligations, and so on. We speak of the perception of every single category of thing and fact that we ever communicate. We speak of perception of numerical truths, truths about the future, truths about the past, possibilities, other minds, theoretical entities of all kinds. We speak of perception whenever we think of ourselves as properly indicating the truth: in other words, whenever we feel able to say that 'if it hadn't been the case that p, I would not be committed to p'. But this is not the end of epistemology, but its beginning, for the theorist's job is to reflect upon our right to hold such conditionals. Merely reporting that we hold them is not doing this. Now, in the ethical case, the projectivist, protected again by quasi-realism, has a story to tell about this: he can explain why people who are satisfied that their moral sensibilities are functioning well express themselves in this way. But genuine cases of perception standardly demand stories with different ingredients. 'If it hadn't been the case that the shape was square, I would not have believed that it was' can be said because we are causally affected by shapes and can use those effects to deliver verdicts on them. 'If it hadn't been red, I would not have believed that it was' can be said because I know enough of my normality in relation to other people to know that only when a thing disposes most people, in good light conditions, to say that it is red, do I say that it is red. And of course I can be wrong about that on an occasion of bad light or bad brain state or whatever.

The important point is that speaking of moral perception by itself provides no theory whatsoever of such conditionals. It provides only a misleading sense of security that somewhere there is such a theory. The theory is not causal, as in the case of shape, nor can it be a matter of conformity with a community, for that just misplaces moral reality, which is not created by community consensus, as (c) reminds us. So what is it? It just doesn't exist. But this means that the invitation to explore the perceptual direction has simply petered out. It is as if someone thought that they could seriously provide a theory of mathematical truth that based itself on the idea that we perceive that $7 + 5 = 12$, and then simply turned its back on the disanalogies between such knowledge and ordinary sense perception. It is obvious that until the question of the status of these conditionals, and our right to believe them, is prosecuted nothing has been said, or at any rate nothing that cannot be tacked on to the end of any genuinely successful account of arithmetic. Similarly with ethics.

The nub of the matter, then, is that the projectivist provides an explanation making moralizing an intelligible human activity with its own explanation and its own propriety, and the opposition provides none, but gestures at an evidently lame analogy. John McDowell has countered both by claiming that the explanatory pretensions of projectivism are 'spurious', and by mounting an opposition case for being able to do something better.[13] I take this last claim first. In effect it uses the 'interest-relative' nature of explanation to cite contexts in which proper explanations of various verdicts can be given by citing supposedly projected states of affairs. 'Why did I find that frightening/funny/appalling?' It can satisfy the interest behind such questions to answer 'Because it *merited* fright/mirth/horror'. 'Why do we find human happiness good?' 'Because it *is* good'. Citing the supposedly projected state of affairs here plays a part in an explanation, and one that in certain contexts can meet the need behind the question.

This is true, but by itself it is quite inert. Compare: 'why do we say that the cube root of 1728 is 12?' 'Because it *is* 12'. At least if the motive behind the question is fear that this is an anomalous, surprising thing for us to say, then the answer can allay it: we are, as it were, only running true to form in such a verdict. We are not in the grip of strange or local arithmetical error. This provides an explanation relative to an interest in whether the thing that we say shows us making a mistake: the reply says that it does not. Similarly in the first cases: a suspicion that there is something odd about, say, finding the dark frightening can be allayed by saying that it is what you would expect, that darkness merits fear. But of course allowing all this goes no way to disallowing another, wider, explanatory interest that these answers quite fail to engage.

13. McDowell, 'Values and Secondary Qualities,' p. 118ff.

This questioner may be asking why we find something frightening because he finds any such reaction puzzling: why do human beings ever feel fear, or get as far as supposing that anything merits fear? No doubt there is an answer to hand: one which talks of the behavioural consequences of the emotion, and their evolutionary advantages to creatures that have it. In a similar vein we try to place the activity of moralizing, or the reaction of finding things funny, or the practice of arithmetic. In particular we try to fit our commitments in these areas into a metaphysical understanding of the kinds of fact the world contains: a metaphysical view that can be properly hostile to an unanalysed and *sui generis* area of moral or humorous or mathematical facts. And relative to this interest, answers that merely cite the truth of various such verdicts are quite beside the point. This, again, is because there is no theory connecting these truths to devices whereby we know about them—in other words, no way of protecting our right to the conditionals I identified.

Could it be held that this explanatory interest is somehow unjustified: that explanations of a certain type cannot be had, or that the desire for them is the desire for an illusory, 'external' viewpoint outside of all human standpoints and perspectives? This is the justification for not having or wanting to have an explanatory theory along my lines at all. There are two reasons to resist this 'quietist' idea (again, I hesitate to attribute it directly, because the opponents to projectivism that I have mentioned tend to ride both the perceptual, explanatory line and the suggestion that we need no line at all, in uncomfortable tandem). The first reason for rejecting it is that we know that it is a common human option to moralize about more or fewer things in greater or lesser strengths. The scope of morality can wax and wane, and this makes it urgent to find an explanation of the practice that goes some way to defining its *proper* scope. Secondly, there can never be an *a priori* right to claim that our activity in making judgements X permits of no explanation (except the gesture that says that we perceive X-type states of affairs). You just have to try the various explanations out. And of course it is particularly perverse to say that any explanatory attempt in a direction must fail when many appear to have succeeded well. (I myself think that there is precious little surprising left about morality: its metatheory seems to me pretty well exhaustively understood. The difficulty is enabling people to appreciate it.) Could it be said that although these wider explanatory interests are legitimate, they mark a boundary between the philosopher and the natural scientist? The evolutionary explanation of the emotion of fear is not only empirical, but marks a recognizable divide between any enterprise of understanding fear as we all feel it and know it and understanding it discursively, in terms of its origins or function. Can the philosopher rest with the phenomenology, and dismiss the rest as sociology, psychology, or someone else's science? The trouble then is that the philosopher gets to say nothing: Hobbes and Hume and Mackie become classified as natural scientists, and the only philosophical activity left is playing variations on the theme of everything being what it is and not another thing. The philosophical spade becomes by definition the one that is turned on the first shove.

IV

There is one final question I would like to raise, but not to settle. So far I have discussed the metaphysics as if it were exclusively a second-order issue, with no necessary consequences for first-order moral theory. But we saw in part II that when Mackie characterizes the mistake that according to my kind of projectivism need not be made, he finds it natural to describe it by using a deontological moral vocabulary. And it is, I think, not a mistake to expect that a projective theory will consort with consequentialist first-order views. Since those views are generally downgraded today, it will be important to get that connection a little bit further into focus, lest projectivism be damned by association.

It should be said at the outset that there is no essential connection between projectivism and a consequentialist view in ethics. It could be that all human beings found it natural to feel certain sentiments, which gain expression as approval, when faced with some features of action, although those features have no consequences that explain the approval. This would be parallel to the way in which certain gestures or timings of actions are hugely funny, although for no apparent reason. If we had this kind of propensity, it would not alter the metaphysics—it would not in itself make a realistic theory easier to define properly, or more likely to be true. But we would say that those features are good (or right, or whatever) and perhaps we would be unable to envisage admirable moralities that did not do so: we would have a deontological ethics. As a metaphysical view, projectivism explains what we are doing when we moralize. It does not follow that it can explain, or be asked to explain, all the features of the particular way we moralize. First-order quirks would be as mysterious to a Humean as they are to anyone else. Nevertheless, it is natural to associate projectivism with consequentialist moralities, in the following way. A projectivist is unlikely to take the moral sentiments as simply given. He will fill out the story by attempting an explanation of the practice of moralizing. This turns to its function, and particularly to its social function. In Mackie's terms, morality is an invention that is successful because it enables things to go well among people with a natural inheritance of needs and desires that they must together fulfil. Moral thought becomes a practice with a purpose. Saying this goes beyond the metaphysical view, as I have tried to explain, but it is a natural addendum to it. And if it is right, there must be at least a limit to the extent to which moral thought can oppose consequentialist, teleological reasoning. It will be unclear how wholeheartedly a moralist who understands this second-order theory can endorse deontological views that stand in the way of all human purpose or fulfilment. Perhaps this is part of the trouble with Fred and Mabel. Perhaps Fred has a psychology that motivates him one way, when his and Mabel's happiness would be found another way. So should he not regard this as an encumbrance: isn't he the victim of an upbringing, and should he not see his particular psychology as a defect, whether or not he can effectively work to change it?

This is another version of the problem of part II, except that this time it is the peculiarly deontological cast of mind that is threatened. But Fred need not regard himself as a victim, so long as he can endorse the general policy of producing human beings whose motivational states are like his. What we then have is a 'motive consequentialism'—a grown-up brother of rule-utilitarianism.[14] The motivations people obey are good in proportion as the consequences of people being like that (and knowing that other people are like that) are good.[15] Actions are then judged either in the light of the motivations that prompted them, or in the different dimension of their actual effects in the world, depending on the purposes for which we are judging them. But the position does not collapse into ordinary act-consequentialism, because for well-known reasons one would expect a society of people motivated solely by consequentialist considerations to do pretty poorly. Nor need any such position share the other prominent feature of utilitarianism that causes dislike: the idea that all values are ultimately commensurable. The features of human life that we value, and that would be drawn into any remotely plausible sketch of human flourishing, very probably represent a bundle of ultimately incommensurable goods, among which there is no systematic way of making choices. In any case, there is ample room for a projectivist to respect the reasons that make this seem plausible. His explanatory project can start from the heterogeneity of ways in which life can flourish or fail. On the whole, then, I regard the alliance with consequentialism as a strength; to put it another way, it is an alliance with only the best features of that direction in ethical thought. Of course, there may be features of some people's moralities that even this diluted motive-consequentialism cannot well explain, and these it will regret. But I hope I have said enough to show that none of them could possibly count as integral to moral thought itself.

14. And, fairly clearly, the one that Hume endorsed. Talking of motives is better than talking of rules (rule-utilitarianism can be charged with 'rule worship' when it tries to give the verdict to a rule rather than to utility in a hard case. But what charge is there of motive worship?), and as explained in the text, consequentialism is not subject to at least some of the main objections to utilitarianism.

15. Rule-utilitarianism is falsely supposed to collapse into act-utilitarianism partly through neglecting this qualification (e.g., B. Williams, *Utilitarianism For and Against* [(Cambridge: Cambridge University Press, 1973), p. 118 ff]). I am contesting what Williams calls the 'act-adequacy premise'. The consequences of a rule being embedded in a society go well beyond the consequences of definite commissions or omissions for which the rule is responsible. There is also the consequence of mutual knowledge that the rule is likely to order action. To illustrate the effect of this, consider a rule that promises made to dead people should be respected. The main part of the good such a rule does lies not in any surplus utility of acts performed in accordance with it, but in the dignity with which one can approach old age or death in a society where it is known that people have such respect. This value resides not in acts, but in states of mind for which respect for the rule is responsible.

15. There is a subtle discussion of this relationship in A. Gibbard, *Wise Choices, Apt Feelings* (Cambridge: Harvard University Press, 1990), esp. chapter 17.

9

How To Be an Ethical Anti-Realist

Some philosophers like to call themselves realists, and some like to call themselves anti-realists. An increasing number, I suspect, wish to turn their backs on the whole issue.[1] Their strengths include those of naturalism, here counseling us that there is none except a natural science of human beings. From this it follows that there is no 'first philosophy' lying behind (for instance) physics, or anthropology, enabling the philosopher to know how much of the world is 'our construction' (anti-realism) or, on the contrary, 'independent of us' (realism).

This naturalism bestows small bouquets and small admonishments to each of the previous parties. The anti-realists were right to deny that there exists a proper philosophical (*a priori*) explanation of things like the success of physics, which some people were acute enough to discern from their armchairs, while others did not. A scientist can say that there was a certain result because a neutrino or electron did this and that, but a philosopher has nothing to *add* to this. If she tries to say, 'Not only did the result occur because of the neutrino, but also because neutrino theory depicts (corresponds with, matches, carves at the joints) the world,' she adds nothing but voices only a vain, and vainglorious, attempt to underwrite the science. This attempt may have made sense in a Cartesian tradition, when the mind's contact with the world seemed so problematical, but its time has passed. On the other hand, anti-realists, sensing the futility of this road, stress instead the dependence of the ordinary world on us, our minds and categories, and again the additions they offer are unacceptable.[2] Characteristically, if realism fails because it is vacuous, anti-realism fails because it strays into mistakes—making things dependent on us when they obviously are not, for example.[3] Again, and perhaps even more clearly, it is plausible to see anti-realism as attempting to theorize where no theory should be—in this case, making the unnatural, Cartesian mind into a source of worlds. These theories are naturally described as 'transcendental', and the word reminds us that for all his hostility to rational psychology, Kant himself failed to escape this trap.

1. For example, see Arthur Fine, 'Unnatural Attitudes: Realist and Instrumentalist Attachments to Science', in *Mind*, 1986.

2. On Putnam in this connection, see Ruth Garrett Millikan, 'Metaphysical Anti-Realism', in *Mind*, 1986.

3. My favorite example is Putnam, *Reason, Truth and History* (Cambridge: Cambridge University Press, 1981), p. 52.

The transcendental aspect can be seen if we put the matter in terms of what I call 'correspondence conditionals.' We like to believe that if we exercise our sensory and cognitive faculties properly and end up believing that p, then p. What kind of theory might explain our right to any such confidence? If p is a thesis from basic physical theory, only the theory itself. To understand why, when we believe that neutrinos exist, having used such-and-such information in such-and-such a way, then they probably do, is just to understand whatever credentials neutrino theory has. That is physics. Any attempt at a background, an underwriting of the conditional from outside the theory, is certain to be bogus.

When considering such global matters as the success of our science or the nature of our world, it seems that naturalism ought to win. But in local areas, it seems instead that the battle can be joined. In this essay I would like to say in a little more detail why I think this is so. The main problem which I leave dangling is that of seepage, or the way in which anti-realism, once comfortably in command of some particular area of our thought, is apt to cast imperialistic eyes on neighboring territory. The local anti-realist faces the problem of drawing a line, which may prove difficult, or that of reneging on naturalism and allowing that global anti-realism must after all make sense. The second part of my essay is an exploration of this specific problem.

Why can battle be joined in local areas? What I said about physics might be retorted upon any area. To understand how, when we believe that twice two is four, we are probably right requires arithmetical understanding. To understand why, when we believe that wanton cruelty is wrong, we are also right requires ethical understanding. Where is the asymmetry?

Let us stay with the example of ethics. Here a 'projective' theory can be developed to give a satisfying way of placing our propensities for values. According to me, the surface phenomena of moral thought do not offer any obstacle to this theory. They can be explained as being just what we should expect, if the projective metaphysics is correct. (I call the doctrine that this is so 'quasi-realism'—a topic I return to later.) I have also argued that this package contains various explanatory advantages over other rival and alleged rival theories. The projectivism is not, of course, new—the package is intended indeed to be a modern version of Hume's theory of the nature of ethics, but without any commitment to particular operations of passions such as sympathy. Emotivism and Hare's prescriptivism are also immediate ancestors. Anything new comes in the quasi-realism, whose point is to show that, since projectivism is consistent with, and indeed explains, the important surface phenomena of ethics, many of the arguments standardly used against it miss their mark. These arguments allege that projectivism is inadequate to one or another feature of the way we think ethically; the quasi-realism retorts that it is not, and goes on to explain the existence of the features. Such features include the propositional as opposed to emotive or prescriptive form and the interaction of ethical commitments with ordinary propositional attitude verbs, talk of truth, proof, knowledge, and so forth. Here, it is the relationship of that programme to naturalism that is to be determined.

I

The first link is this. I think that naturalism demands this view of ethics, but in any case it motivates it. It does so because in this package the fundamental state of mind of one who has an ethical commitment makes natural sense. This state of mind is not located as a belief (the belief in a duty, right, value). We may *end up* calling it a belief, but that is after the work has been done. In fact, we may end up saying that there really are values (such as the value of honesty) and facts (such as the fact that you have a duty to your children). For in this branch of philosophy, it is not what you finish by saying, but how you manage to say it that matters. How many people think they can just *announce* themselves to be realists or anti-realists, as if all you have to do is put your hand on your heart and say, 'I really believe it!' (or, 'I really don't')? The way I treat the issue of realism denies that this kind of avowal helps the matter at all. The question is one of the best theory of this state of commitment, and reiterating it, even with a panoply of dignities—truth, fact, perception, and the rest—is not to the point.

The point is that the state of mind starts theoretical life as something else—a stance, or conative state or pressure on choice and action. Such pressures need to exist if human beings are to meet their competing needs in a social, cooperative setting. The stance may be called an attitude, although it would not matter if the word fitted only inexactly: its function is to mediate the move from features of a situation to a reaction, which in the appropriate circumstances will mean choice. Someone with a standing stance is set to react in some way when an occasion arises, just as someone with a standing belief is set to react to new information cognitively in one way or another. It matters to us that people have some attitudes and not others, and we educate them and put pressure on them in the hope that they will.

So far, two elements in this story are worth keeping in mind, for it will be important to see whether a projective plus quasi-realist story can do without them. These are: (1) the fundamental identification of the commitment in question as something other than a belief and (2) the existence of a neat, natural account of why the state that it is should exist.

Obviously, the emergence of cooperative and altruistic stances is not a mere armchair speculation. It can be supplemented by both theoretical and empirical studies.[4] It is noteworthy that the account will insist upon the nonrepresentative, conative function for the stance. The evolutionary success that attends some stances and not others is a matter of the behaviour to which they lead. In other words, it is the direct consequences of the pressure on action that matter. Evolutionary success may attend the animal that helps those that have helped it, but it would not attend any allegedly possible animal that thinks it ought to help but does not. In the competition for survival, it is what the animal *does* that matters. This is important, for it shows that only if values are intrinsically

---

4. R. Axelrod, *The Evolution of Cooperation* (New York: Basic Books, 1984).

motivating is a natural story of their emergence possible. Notice, too, the way the evolutionary success arises. Animals with standing dispositions to cooperate (say) do better in terms of other needs like freedom from fleas or ability to survive failed hunting expeditions by begging meals from others. No right, duty, or value plays any explanatory role in this history. It is not as if the creature with a standing disposition to help those who have helped it does well *because* that is a virtue. Its being a virtue is irrelevant to evolutionary biology. There is no such naturalistically respectable explanation.

The commitment may have psychological accretions consistently with this being its core or essence. The precise 'feel' of an ethical stance may be a function of local culture in its scope, or of some of its interactions with other pressures and other beliefs. A pressure toward action can be associated variously with pride, shame, or self-respect, and there is no reason to expect a simple phenomenology to emerge. The essence lies in the practical import, but the feelings that surround that can vary considerably. There is no reason for a stance to feel much like a desire, for example. Consider as a parallel the way in which a biological or evolutionary story would place attraction between the sexes, and the culturally specific and surprising ways in which that attraction can emerge—the varieties of lust and love (whose imperatives often do not feel much like desire either, and may equally be expressed by thinking that there are things one simply *must* do; I say more about this later). So, if a theorist is attracted to the rich textures of ethical life, he need not, therefore, oppose projectivism. No 'reduction' of an ethical stance to one of any other type is needed.

Now contrast the kind of evolution already sketched with any that might be offered for, say, our capacity to perceive spatial distance. Again, what matters here is action. But what we must be good at is acting according to the very feature perceived. A visual-motor mechanism enabling the frog's tongue to hit the fly needs to adapt the trajectory of the tongue to the place of the fly relative to the frog, and an animal using perceived distance to guide behaviour will be successful only if it perceives distances as they are. It is because our visual mechanisms show us far-off things as far-off and near things as near that we work well using them. That is what they are *for*. We can sum up this contrast by saying that although the teleology of spatial perception is spatial, the teleology of ethical commitment is not ethical. The good of spatial perception is to be representative, but the good of ethical stances is not.

The possibility of this kind of theory, then, provides the needed contrast between the general case of science, where an attempt to provide a further, background theory is transcendental, and the local particular case of ethics, where there are natural materials for such a story ready at hand. It also means that philosophers wanting a general realism versus anti-realism issue cannot take comfort from the local case; the materials to generate theory there exist, as it were, by contrast with anything that can be provided in the general case.

These simple naturalistic points are not always respected. Consider, for example, the position associated with John McDowell and David Wiggins. This goes some way in the same direction as projectivism, at least in admitting that a person's ethical outlook is dependent on affective or conative aspects of his makeup. But it takes those aspects as things that enable the subject to do something else—to perceive value properties. It is only if one is moved or prone to be moved in a certain way that one sees the value of things, just as it is only if one is prone to be moved in some way that one perceives the sadness in a face.[5] This is supposed to do justice to the obvious point that sentiments have something to do with our capacity to make ethical judgements, yet to retain a 'perceptual' and cognitive place for moral opinion.

Let us suppose that this is a substantial theory and different from projectivism (in the light of what is to come, neither supposition is beyond doubt). The view is substantial if it holds that changes in one's sensibilities enable one to do something else: *literally* to perceive ethical properties in things. Or if the 'something else' is not literal perception, then at least its kinship with perception must be very close—so close that it cannot be explained as projection of a stance. For the view is no different from projectivism if this 'something else' is nothing else at all, but merely a different label for reaching an ethical verdict because of one's sentiments. In other words, it is only different from projectivism if this literal talk of perceiving plays a theoretical role, and not just a relabeling of the phenomena. This is not at all obvious. Theoretically low-grade talk of perception is always available. Everyone can say that one can 'see' what one must do or what needs to be done, just as one can 'see' that 17 is a prime number. When I said that it is not what one finishes by saying that is important, but the theory that gets one there, this is one of the crucial examples I had in mind.

Literal talk of perception runs into many problems. One is that the ethical very commonly, and given its function in guiding choice, even typically, concerns imagined or described situations, not perceived ones.[6] We reach ethical verdicts about the behavior of described agents or actions in the light of general standards. And it is stretching things to see these general standards as perceptually formed or maintained. Do I see that ingratitude is base only on occasions when I see an example of ingratitude? How can I be sure of the generalization to examples that I did not see? (I could not do that for colour, for instance. Absent pillar-boxes may be a different colour from present ones; only an inductive step allows us to guess at whether they are.) Or do I see the timeless connection—but how? Do I have an antenna for detecting timeless property-to-value connections? Is such a thing that much like color vision? Perhaps these questions can be brushed aside. But in connection with naturalism, the question to ask of the view is why nature should have bothered. Having, as it were, forced us into good conative shape, why not sit back? Why should this be merely the curtain-raiser for a perceptual system? It seems only

5. John McDowell, 'Non Cognitivism and Rule Following', *Wittgenstein: To Follow a Rule,* ed. by S. Holtzman and C. Leich (London: Routledge & Kegan Paul, 1981). Also, Sabina Lovibond, *Realism and Imagination in Ethics* (Oxford: Blackwell, 1983). Other writers influenced by the analogy include Mark Platts, *The Ways of Meaning* (London: Routledge & Kegan Paul, 1979) and Anthony Price, 'Doubt about Projectivism', in *Philosophy,* 1986.

6. John Locke, *An Essay Concerning Human Understanding,* Book IV, chapter IV, pp. 6–7.

to engender dangerous possibilities. It ought to make us slower to act, for we must process the new information perceived. Worse, it might be that someone moved, say, by gratitude comes to see the goodness of gratitude and then has, quite generally, some other (negative) reaction to what is seen. Perhaps typically, the conative pressure opens our eyes to these properties, about which we then have a different, conflicting feeling. Or is it somehow given that what comes back is what went in—that the property perceived impinges on us with the same emotional impact required for perceiving it? How convenient! But how clumsy of nature to go in for such a loop! And why did we not evolve to short-circuit it, as projectivism claims? In other words, we have here the typical symptoms of realism, which not only has to take us *to* the new properties but also has to take us back *from* them, showing how perception of them contrives to have exactly the effects it does.

This extravagance came from taking literally the talk of perception made possible by changes of sensibility. But the theory seems to be meant literally. Wiggins, for example, thinks that although projectivism can be dismissed (values 'put into [or onto, like varnish] the factual world'), the right view is that there are value properties and sensibilities for perceiving them 'made for each other' as 'equal and reciprocal partners'.[7]

Can this be understood? Projectivism, from which the theory is supposed to be so different, can easily embrace one half of the doctrine—that the properties are made for the sensibility. The embrace ought to be a bit tepid, because we shall see better ways of putting the view that value predicates figure in thought and talk as reflections or projections of the attitudes that matter. But it is the other half, that the sensibilities are 'made for' the properties, that really startles. Who or what makes them like that? (God? As we have seen, no natural story explains how the ethical sensibilities of human beings were made for the ethical properties of things, so perhaps it is a supernatural story.)

Wiggins, I think, would reply that nothing extraordinary or unfamiliar is called for here. Refinement or civilization makes both sensibility and property. It is the process of education or moral refinement that makes sensibilities end up in good harmony with values. 'When this point is reached, a system of anthropocentric properties and human responses has surely taken on a life of its own. Civilization has begun'. The implicit plea that we get our responses to life into civilized shape is admirable, but is it enough to locate a view of the nature of ethics, or is there a danger of confusing uplift with theory? Certainly, it is true that when we have gone through some process of ethical improvement, we can turn back and say that now we have got something *right*—now we appreciate the value of things as they are, whereas before we did not. This Whiggish judgement is often in place, but it is, of course, a moral judgement. Is it not pertinent to explaining *how* sensibilities are 'made for' values. Is it a good theoretical description or explanation of the fact that we

7. D. Wiggins, *Truth, Invention and the Meaning of Life* (British Academy Lecture, 1976), p. 348.

value friendship that, first, it is good and, second, civilization has 'made' our sensibilities 'for' the property of goodness? It seems overripe, since it goes with no apparent theory of error (what if our sensibilities are unluckily not made for the properties?), no teleology, and no evolutionary background. Its loss of control becomes clear if we think how easy it is to generate parallels. Perhaps something similar made our arithmetical powers for the numbers, or our tastes for the niceness of things. Or, perhaps, on the contrary, the talk of our sensibilities being made for the properties is theoretically useless and the more economical remainder is all that is really wanted.

Might there still be room for a view that the properties are 'made for' the sensibility, which avoids projectivism? The analogy with colours, for all its many defects, might be held to open such a possibility. But colour at this point is a dangerous example. If we ask seriously what colour vision is made for, an answer can be found—but it will not cite colours. Colour vision is probably made for enhancing our capacities for quickly identifying and keeping track of objects and surfaces, and this asymmetry with, for instance, spatial perception remains the most important point of the primary-secondary property distinction.

Any analogy with colour vision is bound to run into the problem of dependency. If we had a theory whereby ethical properties are literally made by or for sensibilities, ethical truth would be constituted by and dependent on the way we think. This might not repel Wiggins. It agrees with the analogy with colours, and in the course of discussing Russell's worry ('I find myself incapable of believing that all that is wrong with wanton cruelty is that I don't like it'), Wiggins freely asserts that 'what is wrong with cruelty is not, even for Bertrand Russell, just that Bertrand Russell does not like it, but that it is not such as to call forth liking given our *actual* responses.'[8] But is it? I should have said not. It is because of our responses that we *say* that cruelty is wrong, but it is not because of them that it is so. It is true that insertion of the 'actual' into the sentence makes it wrong to test the alleged dependence by the usual device of imagining our responses otherwise and asking if that makes cruelty any better.[9] But our actual responses are inappropriate anchors for the wrongness of cruelty. What makes cruelty abhorrent is not that it offends us, but all those hideous things that make it do so.

The projectivist can say this vital thing: that it is not because of our responses, scrutinized and collective or otherwise, that cruelty is wrong. The explanation flows from the way in which quasi-realism has us deal with oblique contexts. It issues an 'internal' reading of the statement of dependence, according to which the statement amounts to an offensive ethical view, about (of course) what it is that makes cruelty wrong. Critics of this explanation allow the internal reading, but complain that the quasi-realist is being wilfully deaf to an intended 'external' reading, according to which the depen-

8. 'A Sensible Subjectivism', in *Needs, Values, Truth* (Oxford: Blackwell, 1987), p. 210.

9. The use of 'actual' to make rigid the reference to our present attitudes and thereby fend off some natural objections to dispositional subjective analyses is exploited in this connexion by Michael Smith.

dency is a philosophical thesis, and one to which the projectivist, it is said, must assent.[10] The crucial question, therefore, is whether the projectivist wilfully refuses to hear the external reading. According to me, there is only one proper way to take the question 'On what does the wrongness of wanton cruelty depend?': as a moral question, with an answer in which no mention of our actual responses properly figures. There *would* be an external reading if realism were true. For in that case there would be a fact, a state of affairs (the wrongness of cruelty) whose rise and fall and dependency on others could be charted. But anti-realism acknowledges no such state of affairs and no such issue of dependency. Its freedom from any such ontological headache is not the least of its pleasures. A realist might take this opportunity for dissent. He might say, 'I can just *see* that the wrongness of cruelty is a fact (perhaps an external one) that needs an ontological theory to support it—no theory that avoids providing such support is credible'. In that case I gladly part company, and he is welcome to his quest—for what kind of ontology is going to help? The Euthyphro dilemma bars all roads there.[11]

It is tempting to think: on this metaphysics the world contains nothing but us and our responses, so the fact that cruelty is bad *must* be created by our responses. What else is there for it to be dependent upon? The prejudice is to treat the moral fact as a natural one, capable of being constituted, made, or unmade, by sensibilities. The wrongness of wanton cruelty does indeed depend on things—features of it that remind us how awful it is. But locating these is giving moral verdicts. Talk of dependency is moral talk or nothing. This is not, of course, to deny that 'external' questions make sense—the projectivist plus quasi-realist package is an external philosophical theory about the nature of morality. But external questions must be conducted in a different key once this package is brought in. We may notice, too, how this undermines a common way of drawing up the realist versus anti-realist issue, according to which anti-realism asserts that truth in some or all areas is 'mind-dependent' and realism denies this. For here is the projection, as anti-realist a theory of morality as could be wished, denying that moral truth is mind-dependent in the only sense possible.

The point can be made as follows. As soon as one *uses* a sentence whose simple assertion expresses an attitude, one is in the business of discussing or voicing ethical opinion. Such sentences include 'The fact that *cruelty is wrong* depends on . . .' or 'Our refined consensus makes it true that *cruelty is wrong*'. And so on. If one generalizes and says things like 'moral facts depend on us,' the generalization will be true only if instances are true or, in other words, if one can find examples of truths like those. Since these ethical opinions are unattractive, they must be judged incorrect, as must generalizations of them. If one attempts to discuss external questions, one must use a different approach—in my case, a naturalism that places the activities of ethics in the realm of adjusting, improving, weighing, and rejecting different senti-

10. Quassim Cassam, 'Necessity and Externality,' in *Mind*, 1986.
11. As essays 1 and 3 attest.

ments or attitudes. The projectivist, then, has a perfect right to confine external questions of dependency to domains where real states of affairs, with their causal relations, are in question. The only things in this world are the attitudes of people, and those, of course, are trivially and harmlessly mind-dependent. But the projectivist can hear no literal sense in saying that moral properties are made for or by sensibilities. They are not in a world where things are made or unmade—not in this world at all, and it is only because of this that naturalism remains true.

The charge that projectivism refuses to hear an explanatory demand as it is intended can be returned with, I suggest, much more effect. I was severe earlier with Wiggins's theoretical description of us as indulging in a kind of coordination of responses and properties as we become civilized. But it is telling that the Whiggish appeal to a value ('civilization') is introduced at that point. For the introduction of values into explanatory investigations is echoed in other writings in this tradition, notably in those of John McDowell.[12] The strategy is that in a context purportedly comparing explanations of a practice—the practice of ethical judgement—we allow ourselves to invoke the very commitments of that practice. Why are we afraid of the dark? Because it is fearful. Why do we value friendship? Because it is good and we are civilized. Why do I dislike sentimentality? Because it merits it. And so on.

The refusal to stand outside ethics in order to place it is supposed to tie in with one strand in Wittgenstein. This is the thought that there is characteristically neither a reduction nor an explanation of the members of any major family of concepts in terms of those of another. Ethical notions require ethical sensibilities to comprehend them. Similarly, why should it not require an ethical sensibility to comprehend an explanation of the views we hold? Only those who perceive friendship as good will understand why we do so, and to them it can be explained why we do so by reminding them that it is good, or making them feel that it is so. The rest—aliens, outsiders, Martians—cannot be given the explanation, but this is as it must be. What I said about the explanation of our spatial capacities will make it apparent that the circularity exists there in exactly the same way. Only those who appreciate distance can understand the distance-centered explanation of visual perception.

This returns us to a theme that has been touched at many points in this essay. The insistence on hearing explanatory demands only in a way in which one can invoke values in answering them had a respectable origin. We agreed earlier that the parallel would be true of thinking about the correspondence conditionals in the case of physics. But I hope I have said enough to show that nature and our theory of nature surround our ethical commitments in a way that gives us a *place* from which to theorize about them. No thing and no theory surround our physics. In other words, the difference in the ethical case comes in the theses I labeled (1) and (2)—the brute fact that an external explanatory story is possible. We already know that in even more local cases,

---

12. For instance in his 'Values and Secondary Properties', in *Value and Objectivity, Essays in Honour of J. L. Mackie,* ed. T. Honderich (London: Routledge & Kegan Paul, 1985).

where what is at question is not 'the ethical' in a lump but particular attitudes and their etiologies. Social anthropology is not confined to explaining the rise of puritanism to puritans or the evolution of polygamy to polygamists. Similarly, nothing in Wittgenstein offers any principled obstacle to explaining the general shape and nature of ethical attitudes and their expressions in projective terms.

Indeed, much in Wittgenstein is sympathetic to doing so. Not only is Wittgenstein himself an anti-realist about ethics, he is in general quite free in admitting propositions or quasi-propositions whose function is not to describe anything—the rules of logic and arithmetic, for instance. It is clear that what he wants to do is to place mathematical practice, not as a representation of the mathematical realm, but as 'a different kind of instrument', commitment to which is not like central cases of belief but much more like other kinds of stance. It is also interesting that some of the apparently irritating or evasive answers he gives when faced with the charge of anthropocentricity are exactly those that a projectivist can give if quasi-realism has done its work, and that according to me, no other philosophy of these matters can give. For example, when Wittgenstein approaches the question whether, on his anthropocentric view of mathematical activity, mathematical truth is yet independent of human beings, he says exactly what I would have him say:

> "But mathematical truth is independent of whether human beings know it or not!"—Certainly, the propositions 'Human beings believe that twice two is four' and 'twice two is four' do not mean the same. The latter is a mathematical proposition; the other, if it makes sense at all, may perhaps mean: human beings have *arrived* at the mathematical proposition. The two propositions have entirely different *uses*.[13]

The proposition expresses a norm that arises in the course of human activities, but it does not describe those activities, and it has no use in which the correctness of the norm (the truth of the proposition) depends upon the existence or form of those activities. *That* question simply cannot be posed; it treats what is not a dependent state of affairs belonging at all to the natural world as if it were.

I have tried to show that naturalism, which turns away from realism and anti-realism alike in the global case, turns toward projective theories in the ethical case. This theory is visibly anti-realist, for the explanations offered make no irreducible or essential appeal to the existence of moral 'properties' or 'facts'; they demand no 'ontology' of morals. They explain the activity from the inside out—from the naturally explicable attitudes to the forms of speech

13. Ludwig Wittgenstein, *Philosophical Investigations* (Oxford: Blackwell, 1953), p. 226. In 'Wittgenstein and Realism' (in *Wittgenstein: Eine Neubewehrung,* eds. J. Brandl and R. Haller, Vienna: Holder-Richler-Temsky, 1990), I cite Wittgenstein's nondescriptive treatment of philosophical propositions (grammatical rules), religious propositions (expressions of ways of life), many apparent descriptions of oneself (avowals), expressions of certainty, as well as modal and arithmetical commitments. In each case—and these are the only cases in which his later philosophy is seen at full tilt—his quasi-realist leanings are obvious, so it is a pity that he is usually pressed into the service of blanket minimalism or soggy pluralism.

that communicate them, challenge them, refine them, and abandon them, and which so mislead the unwary.

So far I have talked of the issue of mind-dependency in fairly abstract terms, and relied upon a relatively subtle move in the philosophy of language to defend my view. I now want to discuss these points in practical terms. It is evident that a more fundamental mistake underlies some discomfort with projectivism. The mistake is visible in Wiggins's critique of 'non-cognitive theories' in his British Academy Lecture.[14] It results in the charge that projectivism cannot be true to the 'inside of lived experience'. Other writers (I would cite Nagel, Williams, and Foot) seem to illustrate similar unease. The thought is something like this: it is important that there should be some kind of accord in our thinking about ethical stances from the perspective of the theorist and from that of the participant. Our story about ethical commitment is to explain it, not to explain it away. But projectivism threatens to do the latter (many people who should know better think of Hume as a skeptic about ethics, and, of course, John Mackie saw himself as one). It threatens to do so because it shows us that our commitments are not external demands, claiming us regardless of our wills or in direct opposition to our passions. It makes our commitments facets of our own sentimental natures; this softens them, destroying the hardness of the moral must.

From the inside, the objects of our passions are their *immediate* objects: it is the death, the loved one, the sunset, that matters to us. It is not our own state of satisfaction or pleasure. Must projectivism struggle with this fact, or disown it? Is it that we projectivists, at the crucial moment when we are about to save the child, throw ourselves on the grenade, walk out into the snow, will think, 'Oh, it's only me and my desires or other conative pressures—forget it'?

It ought to be sufficient refutation of this doubt to mention other cases. Does the lover escape his passion by thinking, 'Oh, it's only my passion, forget it'? When the world affords occasion for grief, does it brighten when we realize that it is we who grieve? (The worst thing to think is that if we are 'rational', it should, as if rationality had anything to tell us about it.)

There is an important mistake in the philosophy of action that, I think, must explain the temptation to share Wiggins's doubt. The mistake is that of supposing that when we deliberate in the light of various features of a situation we are *at the same time* or 'really' deliberating—or that our reasoning can be 'modeled' by representing us as deliberating—about our own conative functioning. Representing practical reasoning as if it consisted of contemplating a syllogism, one of whose premises describes what we want, encourages this mistake. But just as the eye is not part of the visual scene it presents, the sensibility responsible for the emotional impact of things is not part of the scene it takes for material. Nor is our sense of humor the main thing we find funny. This does not mean that our sensibility is hidden from us, and when we reflect on ourselves we can recognize aspects of it, just as we can know when we are in love or grieving. But it does mean that its own shape is no part of the

14. *Truth, Invention, and the Meaning of Life,* section 4, note 6.

input, when we react to the perceived features of things. Furthermore, even when we reflect on our sensibility, we will be using it if we issue a verdict: when we find our own sense of humor funny, we are not escaping use of it as we do so.

This misconstruction leads people to suppose that on a projective theory all obligations must be 'hypothetical' because they are properly represented as dependent upon the existence of desires. But the lover who hears that the beloved is present and feels he must go, or the person who receiving bad news feels he must grieve, has no thoughts of the form 'if I desire her/feel sad then I must go/grieve'. Nothing corresponds to this. The news comes in and the emotion comes out; nothing in human life could be or feel more categorical. In ordinary emotional cases, of course, a third party may judge that it is only *if* he desires her that he must go; this is not so in ethical cases. One ought to look after one's young children, whether one wants to or not. But that is because we insist on some responses from others, and it is sometimes part of good moralizing to do so.

Once these mistakes are averted, is there any substance left to the worry about failure of harmony of the theoretical and deliberative points of view? I think not. Sometimes theory can help to change attitudes. One might become less attached to some virtue, or less eager in pursuing some vice, after thinking about its etiology or its functioning. One might qualify it a little (we see an example in what follows). But sometimes one might become more attached to the virtue, and sometimes everything stays the same. Does the story threaten to undermine the promise that the stances cited in this theory of ethics make good natural sense (does it take something divine to make the claims of obligation so pregnant with authority)? Not at all—I have already mentioned the 'musts' of love and grief, and those of habit and obsession are just as common.

There is one last charge of the would-be realist. This claims that projectivism must lead to relativism. 'Truth' must be relative to whatever set of attitudes is grounding our ethical stances; since these may vary from place to place and time to time, truth must be relative. The very analogies with other conative states press this result: what to one person is an occasion for love or grief or humor is not to another. Consider a young person gripped by the imperatives of fashion. The judgement that people must wear some style, that another is impossible, has its (naturally explicable and perfectly intelligible) function; it appears quite categorical, for the subject will think that it is not just for him or her that the style is mandatory or impossible (it was so in the parents' time as well, only they did not realize it). Yet, surely this is a mistake. The verdict is 'relative', having no truth outside the local system of preferences that causes it. The image is plain: a projectivist may inhabit a particular ethical boat, but he must know of the actual or potential existence of others; where, then, is the absolute truth?

The answer is that it is not anywhere that can be visible from this sideways, theoretical perspective. It is not that this perspective is illegitimate, but that it is not the one adapted for finding ethical truth. It would be if such truth were natural truth, or consisted of the existence of states of affairs in the real world.

That is the world seen from the viewpoint that sees different and conflicting moral systems—but inevitably sees no truth in just one of them. To 'see' the truth that wanton cruelty is wrong demands moralizing, stepping back into the boat, or putting back the lens of a sensibility. But once that is done, there is nothing relativistic left to say. The existence of the verdict, of course, depends on the existence of those capable of making it; the existence of the truth depends on nothing (externally), and on those features that make it wrong (internally). For the same reasons that operated when I discussed mind-dependency, there is no doctrine to express relating the truth of the verdict to the existence of us, of our sentiments, or of rival sentiments.

What, then, of the parallel with the other emotions, or with the fashion example? The emotions of grief and love are naturally personal; if the subject feels they make a claim on others, so that those unstricken somehow *ought* to be stricken, then she is nonrelativistically, absolutely wrong. Similarly with fashion: the underlying story includes the need for a self-presentation that is admirable to the peer group, and if what is admirable changes rapidly as generations need to distance themselves from their immediate predecessors, then the teenager who thinks that her parents were wrong to like whatever clothes they did is mistaken in the same way as the subject of an emotion who imputes a mistake to those who cannot feel the same. But the strongest ethical judgements do not issue from stances that are properly variable. They may sometimes be absent, from natural causes, as if a hard life destroys a capacity for pity. But this is a cause for regret; it would be better if it were not so. In the variations of emotion, and still more of fashion, there is no cause for regret. In saying these things I am, of course, voicing some elements of my own ethical stances, but, as I promised, it is only by doing this that ethical truth is found.

II

If projective theories have everything going for them in ethics, how much can they jettison and still have *something* going for them? The two ingredients I highlighted are the possibility of identifying the commitment in a way that contrasts it usefully with belief, and a 'neat, natural account' of why the state that it is should exist. In the case of ethics we have conative stances and a visible place for them in our functioning. But what of other cases?

Colour commitments might attract attention, because not everybody will be happy that the agreed story about what colour vision is and why we have it leaves realism as a natural doctrine about colours. Here the second ingredient is present. There is a neat, natural story of our capacity for colour discrimination, and in its explanatory side, both physically and evolutionarily, it makes no explanatory use of the *existence* of colours. But there is no way woefully to contrast colour commitments with *beliefs*. Their functional roles do not differ. So there will be no theory of a parallel kind to develop, explaining why we have propositional attitudes of various kinds toward colour talk, or why we speak of knowledge, doubt, proof, and so forth in connection with them. If anything can be drawn from a realism versus anti-realism debate over colour (which I rather doubt), it would have to be found by different means.

Modal commitments are much more promising. Our penchant for necessities and possibilities, either in concepts or in nature, is not easy to square with a view that we are representing anything, be it a distribution of possible worlds or (in the case of natural necessity) a timeless nomic connection between universals.[15]

First, consider the case of logical necessity. A theory insisting on a nonrepresentative function for modal commitment is clearly attractive. Here, however, although I think the first desideratum is met—we can do something to place the stance as something other than belief in the first instance—the second is not so easy. The kind of stance involved is insistence upon a norm, an embargo on a trespass. Saying that 2 + 2 is anything other than 4 offends against the embargo, and the embargo in turn makes shared practices, shared communication possible. So far so good, but what of a 'neat, natural theory' of the emergence of the embargo? That shared practice should exist is good—but do they so clearly depend upon such policing? If they do, it appears to be because of something else: because we can make no sense of a way of thinking that flouts the embargo. It introduces apparent possibilities of which we can make nothing. This imaginative limitation is, in turn, something of which no natural theory appears possible, even in outline. For when we *can* make sense of the imaginative limitation, we do find it apt to explain away or undermine the original commitment to a necessity. If it seems only because of (say) confinement to a world in which relative velocities are always slow compared to that of light that we find a relativistic view of simultaneity hard to comprehend, then that already shows how we would be wrong to deem the theory impossible. If it is only because of the range of our colour vision that we cannot imagine a new primary colour, then we would be unwise to rule out the possibility that some natural operation might result in our admitting one. Natural explanation is here the enemy of the hard logical must.

It is not obviously so in the case of natural necessity. Once more the paradigm is Hume—not the Hume of many commentators, but the real Hume, who knew that talk of necessity was irreducible but gave a projective theory of it. The explanation here has us responsive to natural regularity, and forming dispositions of expectation (we might add, of observing boundaries in our counterfactual reasoning), which in turn stand us in good stead as the regularities prove reliable. Here, once we accept the Humean metaphysics, the naturalism seems quite in place. The upshot—talk of causation—is not undermined but is explained by this interpretation. This accords exactly with the case of ethics. There is a difference, however. I do not think metaphysical obstacles stand in the way of the conception of nature that does the explanatory work in the example of ethics. But many writers have difficulty with the conception of nature that is supposed to do it in Hume's metaphysics of

15. David Armstrong, *What Is a Law of Nature?* (Cambridge: Cambridge University Press, 1983), chapter 6.

causation. Regularities—but between what? Events—but how are these to be conceived, stripped of the causal 'bit' (to use the computer metaphor)? Events thought of as changes in ordinary objects will scarcely do, for as many writers have insisted, ordinary objects are permeated with causal powers. Nothing corresponds to the easy, sideways, naturalistic perspective that strips the world of values.

What is the option? All sides carry on talk of causation in whichever mode they find best. The new realists like to produce apparent ontologies— universals, timeless connections, and the rest. The Humean does not mind, so long as the explanatory pretensions of these retranslations are kept firmly in their place (outside understanding). Is there scope for a debate here? It is a place where the ghosts are hard to lay, and I for one do not like being there alone in the gloom.

Addendum

Since this essay was written, an influential marker in the debate has been its nominal mirror-image, entitled 'How To Be an Ethical Realist', by Richard Boyd (in *Essays on Moral Realism,* ed. Geoff Sayre-McCord, Ithaca: Cornell University Press, 1988). Readers of that paper may expect this essay to be a reaction not so much to Oxford, Wittgensteinian, realism, but to the newer, naturalistic, Cornell variety. That is unfortunate, but in addition to essay 11 in this volume, I can here add some brief remarks about that theory.

Cornell realism highlights the possibility of a property identity: to be good is to be something-or-other natural. The theory may cite sophisticated clusters of natural properties, or whatever natural properties best satisfy some alleged folk theory of The Good, but its essence is equally visible if we consider a simple equation: to be good is to produce human happiness, for instance. The equation is protected from Moore's open question argument, by being pre- sented not as any equation of meaning, but as a substantive metaphysical identity, conceived along the lines of 'water is H_2O' or 'heat in gases is molecu- lar motion'.

I find this approach puzzling, because it is unclear what probems it solves. It does not speak to moral psychology, because it does not tell us what the difference is between those who equate creating human happiness with the good and those who do not. That is, it does not address the question of whether seeing the creation of happiness *under the heading* of the good is possession of an attitude, or a belief, or something else, or whether it connects with action in one way or another, or with emotions such as guilt and shame (for a parallel point in connexion with modality, see the Addendum to essay 3). It does not speak to issues of meaning, because we do not know whether those who resist the equation flout some (hidden) principle of meaning that governs ethical concepts, and it does not speak to issues of proof and objectiv- ity, because we do not know whether denying the equation is making an objective or cognitive mistake or something else. If the equation does not help with issues of moral psychology, or motivation, or meaning, or epistemology, what good does it do? It seems to be an agreeable afterthought of those particular people whose ethics allows them to accept the creation of human happiness as a standard.

One way of missing these questions is to think that realism, at least so far as a predicate is concerned, is essentially the doctrine that the predicate refers to a property, or a real property. If we have reference to a real property, then any sentence in which the predicate is concerned can be given a standard truth-theoretical semantics; its truth is guaranteed in the way that any more straightforward truth is guaranteed, and the contrasts that anti-realism tried to open up are smoothed out. Michael Dummett has expressed this conception of realism, but he himself appears to go on to point out that unless reference plays some role in the theory of meaning, it remains possible that the meaning we give to some set of remarks deserves an anti-realist construction. Here it is a question of what states of mind *end up* with the theorist announcing the identity of reference, and if those states are either covertly or visibly 'noncognitive', no advance in a realist direction is made.

The crucial point, as far as 'reference' goes, is that in ordinary cases it ties with meaning: to understand an expression is to have a grasp, explicit or implicit, of what its reference is. Here, without further argument (which then bears all the burden), there is no such equation, since people with aberrant standards understand ethical terms, yet there is no apparent link to the properties that the naturalist highlights. One might be tempted to think that if there is a real property identity, anyone missing it must be making an objective, metaphysical error. But this is not so, since all it takes to miss it is a defective ethical sensibility.

Once this is understood, property identity drops out of the picture. There is no harm in saying that ethical predicates refer to properties, when such properties are merely the semantic shadows of the fact that they function as predicates. A quasi-realist protection of ethical truth protects ethical predicates, and if our overall semantic picture is that predicates refer to properties, so be it. But ethical *predication* remains an entirely different activity from naturalistic predication, and this is only disguised by thinking of the world of properties as one in which hidden identities may be revealed by the philosopher-as-scientist.

10

Attitudes and Contents

I. General Considerations

G. F. Schueler's article puts in a forceful way various reservations about my treatment of indirect contexts, on behalf of the position I have called 'quasi-realism.'[1] His opposition is, I think, as complete as could be: it is not only that my treatment has been incomplete, which I happily concede, or that its formulation has been defective, which I am prepared to believe, but also that nothing like it could possibly succeed. That at least is the proper consequence of some of his views—on logical form, on validity, and on the nature of commitment. For example, if showing that an inference has 'the logical form' or 'is an instance' of *modus ponens* involves taking it as 'the realist picture' has it, then no attempt to explain it in other terms will be compatible with its having that form. Again, if validity is ('as it is used in logic') defined in terms of the impossibility of premises being true and conclusions false, then persons reluctant to apply truth and falsity to any of the elements of an inference will have to admit that the inference is not valid, as the term is used in logic. Third, if 'talk of "commitments" is problematic for the antirealist', then anti-realism will make no headway by thinking of a class of commitments more general than those with representative or realistic truth conditions. Fortunately, none of these contentions seems to me correct. Since the survival of quasi-realism even in spirit demands their rebuttal, I shall start by considering them in turn.

1. It is not too clear what it is for an argument to have the logical form of *modus ponens*. If it is a diagnosis of its syntactical form, then obviously having that logical form is compatible with any number of deep and different semantics for the components. To show this, compare 'P, $P{\rightarrow}Q$, so Q' with the implication taken as truth-functional, with the same seeming argument taken as some suppose the English take it: $P{\rightarrow}Q$ is the commitment of one who attributes a high probability to Q conditional upon P. Which is the true *modus ponens*? If we plump for either exclusively, we face the uncomfortable consequence that it becomes controversial whether natural English contains any inferences of the form. If we embrace both, then being of the form *modus ponens* is compatible with any number of deep and different *explanations* of

1. G. F. Schueler, 'Modus Ponens and Moral Realism,' in *Ethics*, 1988, pp. 501–517.

the semantics of the components: how it comes about that we have here elements describable as true or false, or a connective properly represented by some → or other. The same point could be made with any connective: knowing even when to interpret the negation sign of a logic as meaning negation is no easy matter.[2] If quasi-realism, in the form in which I tried to develop it, is right, the 'deep' semantics of a surface example of *modus ponens* is to be explained in a particular, and perhaps initially surprising, way. But it is *modus ponens,* for all that. Or, if we say it is not, then we have no effective procedure for telling when anything is.

2. Perhaps the best way to answer the restrictive view of validity is by appeal to authority. One might cite imperative logic. Or one might cite the approach to propositional inference in terms of coherent subjective probability functions, where validity corresponds to there being no coherent function attributing a lesser probability to the conclusion than to the premises, and coherence is defined in terms of immunity to Dutch book.[3] (This is the approach that would best marry with the probabilistic view of conditionals above.) Or one could cite the view of Stig Kanger, that in interpreting a deontic logic, the extension of the truth predicate to the formulae, which could equally be regarded as imperatives or expressions of attitude, is a conventional matter.[4] A further reply would draw the usual distinction between an algebraic, mathematical, pure, or uninterpreted semantics—itself sufficient to yield notions of satisfaction, validity, and completeness—versus an applied or interpreted semantics, in which the valuation clauses reflect something about the use or meaning of the connectives.[5] Formal studies are content with the first, so that truth-in-a-structure, or satisfiability defined in terms of (for instance) sets of open sets in the topology of the real line, defines validity.[6] But even when we turn to the second, the question of priorities still arises. It does not go without saying that we interpret the propositional connectives by drawing on an antecedent understanding of (classical) truth and falsity. Falsity and negation go hand in hand, and it should not be obvious which is the dominant partner. The view that it is by knowing how to *use* the connectives in proofs that we come to understand them, and hence gain what understanding we have of the truth tables, is perfectly open. In Prawitz's words, 'Presumably, the observational consequences that can be drawn from the assumption that a person knows the condition for the truth of a sentence can also be drawn from the assumption that he knows how to use the sentence in proofs'.[7] The whole

2. B. J. Copeland, 'What Is a Semantics for Classical Negation?', in *Mind,* 1986, p. 478.

3. Hartry Field, 'Logic, Meaning and Conceptual Role,' in *Journal of Philosophy,* 1977.

4. Stig Kanger, 'New Foundations for Ethical Theory', in *Deontic Logic: Introductory and Systematic Readings,* ed. R. Hilpinen (Dordrecht: Reidel, 1971), pp. 55–56.

5. M. Dummett, 'The Justification of Deduction,' in *Truth and Other Enigmas* (London: Duckworth, 1978), p. 293. A. Plantinga, *The Nature of Necessity* (Oxford: Oxford University Press, 1974), pp. 126 ff.

6. H. Weyl, 'The Ghost of Modality,' in *Philosophical Essays in Memory of Edmund Husserl* (Cambridge, Mass.: Harvard University Press, 1940).

7. D. Prawitz, 'Meaning and Proofs: On the Conflict between Classical and Intuitionistic Logic,' in *Theoria,* 1977.

philosophy of intuitionistic interpretations of the logical constants and of those who give priority to sequent calculi and natural deduction systems opposes the simple assumption that an antecedent understanding of 'representative' truth and falsity affords the only road to understanding validity. A more plausible view, and one that nicely fits quasi-realism, is that attributions of validity and application of the truth predicate go hand in hand: I expand on this below.

3. Schueler finds the very notion of a commitment 'problematic for the anti-realist.' His argument that it is one of 'those terms which seem to entail a realist picture' is this: 'If I am committed to, say, paying my nephew's way through school, or to the claim that a Republican succeeded Carter, then this seems something objective, forced on me by a promise I have made or other views I hold'. Well it might be, if we could suitably cash the metaphor of forcing, and suitably interpret objectivity—although whether the objectivity forced by, say, promises has anything to do with realism is another matter. But equally, the commitment might not be forced by anything, like the commitment to go for a jog once a week or to improve one's golf. It does not matter, because I use 'commitment' as a general term to cover mental states that may be beliefs, but also those that gain expression in propositional form, but which for various reasons philosophers such as Hume, Ramsey, Wittgenstein, Stevenson, Ayer, Hare, and I have seen in terms of such things as acceptance of rules, changes in disposition, and possession of attitudes, which are worth separating from beliefs. Some commitments will have nothing to do with approval: these include the change in one who accepts a rule of inference, or treats a proposition as necessary, or accords a high subjective probability to Q upon P, and so on, as well as Schueler's example of his belief that a Republican succeeded Carter. In the sphere of ethics, approval and attitude are natural terms to work with, but it would not matter if neither fitted exactly or if better terms for the state in question existed. What is important is the theoretical issue of whether and why the state is worth distinguishing from belief, or at least from belief with representational truth conditions thought of realistically.

II. Fast-Track and Slow-Track Quasi-Realism

So far, I have simply dissented from Schueler's reasons for general pessimism about the approach, intending to show that the ideas behind quasi-realism survive his onslaught. But he is on stronger ground in attacking the detail of my treatment. I shall turn to that after taking stock for a moment.

The problem is that of the embedding of sentences that primarily express attitude, in contexts that might appear to admit only sentences that, in some contrasting way, express propositions. When I say that these sentences primarily express attitude, I have never intended to deny that they can be regarded as expressing beliefs or propositions. This opposition would be going beyond anything I embrace. But I do mean that the right way of theorizing about them identifies them, in the first instance, as expressing states of mind whose function is not to represent anything about the world. They express something more to do with attitudes, practices, emotions, or feelings arising in contemplating some kinds of conduct, with goal seeking, with insistence upon normative constraints on conduct, and they express nothing to do with representing the world. In the familiar metaphor, their 'direction of fit' with the world is active—to have the world conform to them—rather than descriptive or representational. I call someone who approves of both this contrast, and this direction of theorizing, a projectivist. Projectivism may seem to be automatically opposed to the view that in saying that something is good (etc.) we give voice to a real belief about it, and it is often so introduced (as labels like 'noncognitivism' suggest). But this opposition is not automatic. Subtlety with the concept of belief, or with the concept of truth or of fact, may enable the expressivist to soften this opposition. Theory may enable us to understand how a commitment with its center in the expression of subjective determinations of the mind can also function as expressing belief, or be capable of sustaining the truth predicate—properly called 'true' or 'false'. I tried to herald this development with the notion of a 'propositional reflection' in the older essay, 'Moral Realism' [essay 6], and it was the point of the last pages of chapter 6, and of all of chapter 7, in *Spreading the Word*.[8] It means separating truth (in this application at least) from 'represents' and its allies, but nobody has ever pointed out the harm in that.

It did, however, seem to me that before this happy result could be secured, work had to be done. It had to be shown *why* a sentence with this role could *properly* function in the ways ethical sentences do—why it sustains a fully propositional role. I now think we should distinguish both a slow track and a fast track to this result. The slow track involves patiently construing each propositional context as it comes along. This is the line I took in trying to meet Geach's problem. Its advantage is that of honest toil over what might seem like theft; its disadvantage, if Schueler is right, is that it does not work. But before judging that, I should admit not only that it threatens to look Ptolemaic but also that it seems not to correspond to any obvious cognitive processes we go through. It is not as though construing (say) conditionals with evaluative components comes harder to us than construing them with ordinary components, and this will need explanation.

Fast-track quasi-realism would get there in better style. It would make sufficient remarks about truth to suggest that we need a comparable notion to regulate evaluative discourse (even though this is nonrepresentational) and then say that our adherence to propositional forms needs no further explanation than that. The adoption of propositional form and style meets our need to share and discuss and dissent from attitudes or other stances. It involves only philosophers in error, and little more need be said. That sounds cavalier, but it was the line of, for instance, Kant and Nietzsche and probably Wittgenstein,[9]

8. Simon Blackburn, *Spreading the Word* (Oxford: Clarendon Press, 1984).

9. I. Kant, *The Critique of Judgement*, trans. J. C. Meredith (London: Oxford University Press, 1927). Although Kant believes that the judgement of taste is not a cognitive judgement (p. 41) and is determined by subjective sensation, he also thinks that since we wish to demand similarity of feeling from others, we 'speak of beauty as if it were a property of things' (p. 52);

none of whom found any particular trouble in imagining the emergence of a predicate with a nondescriptive role. Nietzsche puts it roundly:

> The pathos of nobility and distance, as aforesaid, the protracted and domineering fundamental total feeling on the part of a higher ruling order in relation to a lower order, to a *below*—*that* is the origin of the antithesis "good" and "bad" (the lordly right of giving names extends so far that one should allow oneself to conceive the origin of language itself as an expression of power on the part of the rulers: they say "this *is* this and this," they seal every thing and event with a sound, and, as it were, take possession of it).

Perhaps our general propensity to seal things with sounds needs no detailed explanation or justification (cf. 'this is nice' as a way of voicing pleasure, and immediately giving rise to compounds, 'if it's nice, two would be nicer', etc.). But compromises are possible: the fast track can benefit from some of the security achieved on the slow, and the slow track can make use of some of the short cuts of the fast. Or so I shall argue. Notice that, whichever track we favor, the point is to *earn* our right to propositional forms—including the use of a truth predicate. If this is done, any conventional concept of validity tags along—there is a level of analysis at which *modus ponens* and the rest are no different when their components are evaluative from when they are not.

III. Embedding

A parallel to the idea that a certain sentence expresses an attitude ('Hooray for the Bears') would be the obvious truth that some others express commands ('Go to see the Bears') and questions ('Are the Bears doing well?'). Now, when imperatives and questions give rise to subordinate clauses, the linguistic forms typically maintain an indication of the original mood, even if there is another syntactic change: 'he told me *to* go to see the Bears', 'he asked me *whether* the Bears are doing well', 'if *I am to* go to see the Bears, I had better have some tea first'. Here the right thing to say is that the subordinate clause maintains the mood of the original, but that it is not uttered with the *force* that a direct utterance of the sentence has (nothing is commanded or questioned). Nevertheless, mood is in some sense primarily an indicator of force. It is only by understanding what a question or command is that one understands the function of the interrogative or imperative mood.

There is a *prima facie* puzzle here: Mood is primarily an indicator of force; force is lost in subordinate clauses, but mood is not. I do not think, however, that the puzzle is very deep, although its formal representation can be difficult. The subordinate clause in 'he said that *P*' identifies which proposition he

---

Nietzsche, *The Genealogy of Morals*, first essay, II; L. Wittgenstein, *Remarks on the Foundations of Mathematics* (Oxford: Blackwell, 1956), p. 163, contains a particularly clear statement of the view that statements of mathematics mislead philosophers by their descriptive form. See also essay 9, note 13.

asserted; the clauses in 'he told me to go to see the Bears' or 'he asked whether the Bears are doing well' identify which order he gave or which question he asked. Mood indicates that a question or command is still part of the topic, even when the overall communication is not itself a question or command. Technically, I therefore agree with Michael Pendlebury that mood (or at least the presence of the indicator 'to go . . .' , 'whether . . .') affects the sense of such clauses: the embedding does not cancel the semantic significance of the mood indicator, which is to maintain some connection with an original command or question.[10] It can matter that a question or command is still in this sense part of the *topic*. Perhaps the nicest illustration of this is the difference between 'he knew that the Bears had won' and 'he knew whether the Bears had won': the first gives us simply the content of his knowledge, while the mood in the second shows that what he is said to have known is the answer to a question, which might have been yes or no. Of course, saying that in this way a command or question is part of the topic is not implying that one was ever actually uttered—one can know the answer to questions that have never been asked.

We do not have a mood that indicates in this way that an attitude is part of the topic. The nearest approximation is in indirect reportage of wishes expressed in the optative: 'would I were in Grantchester!' can perhaps be reported: he said that he would be in Grantchester, but there is at least a slight sense of strain. Normally, if I make plain to you what I feel, say about the Bears, I will most probably do so using a sentence with an 'expressive' predicate: 'the Bears are great!' The report of what I said in indirect speech is then easy: 'he said that the Bears are great'. According to projectivism, the item of vocabulary shows that the original utterance was expressive of attitude. In the subordinate clause, the item remains to make attitude the topic, just as overt mood indicators do. The person who said that the Bears are great expressed just that attitude about the Bears. Saying that this is what he did is not of course endorsing or subscribing to the view, any more than reporting a command or question involves reissuing it in *propria persona*.

Suppose we spoke an 'emotivist' language, in which expressions of attitude wore this function on their faces. We would not have the predicative form, to keep such expressions in the indicative mood, but an ejaculatory mood, corresponding to that of 'Hooray for the Bears'. It would then be necessary to have a construction of subordinate clauses corresponding to words such as 'that . . .', 'to . . .', and 'whether . . .', that marks the original attitude as the topic. There seems no problem of semantic principle about this: 'that!', 'whether!', and so on might be introduced, so that 'he said that! hooray for the Bears' tells us which attitude he expressed, 'he wondered whether! hooray for the Bears' tells us which attitude he was pondering, and so on.

If natural languages have chosen not to register expressive force by a particular mood, they may have chosen to do it in other ways. And taking

---

10. M. Pendlebury, 'Against the Power of Force: Reflections on the Meaning of Mood', in *Mind*, 1986, pp. 361–73.

other cases of mood and force as our model, there might be no great difficulty about imagining it done by an expressive mood and yielding a smooth interpretation of at least some subordinate clauses. Here there is room for the compromise between fast- and slow-track quasi-realism: see how far you get in imagining an overtly expressive language developed in such ways, and diminish (even if not to zero) the gap between what it achieves and what we do with predication, and talk of truth.

IV. A Logic

In his original article, Geach concentrated upon the special case of the antecedent of conditionals. My suggestion involved, first, describing what we are up to in embedding what is primarily an expression of attitude in a context, making it intelligible that the context should have a function. Second, it involved giving sufficient semantic theory to show why we have the way we do of meeting that need. Thus, in the case of Geach's original conditional, my suggestion of what we are up to involved taking up an attitude to an involvement of attitude with attitude, or attitude with belief. Such 'second-order' stances seemed to me both needed in themselves and plausible candidates for the import of a conditional with evaluative elements. If we use '$\Rightarrow$' to signify the *involvement* of one mental state with another, the result was that a simple conditional, 'if lying is wrong, then getting your little brother to lie is wrong', came out as:

$H! (\backslash B!L\backslash \Rightarrow \backslash B!GBL\backslash)$

where the $\backslash \ldots \backslash$ notation shows that our topic is the attitude or belief whose normal expression occurs within the slashes. Involvement is not a logical notion, but neither should it seem mysterious. I tried to explain it by introducing the idea of a sensibility as a function from belief to attitude, attitude to attitude, and so on: it is what we would overtly talk about by saying things like 'I really approve of *making* approval of an action depend on its consequences' or 'believing that *should* increase your approval of this'. Endorsing or rejecting such an involvement of commitments one with another is an important thing to do; it is therefore not surprising that we have a simple English form with which to do it.

Let us now consider *modus ponens*. We have

$B!L$
$H!(\backslash B!L\backslash \Rightarrow \backslash B!GBL\backslash)$
So: $B!GBL$.

Schueler and others rightly raise doubts about the kind of inconsistency in avowing the two initial attitudes and refusing endorsement of the conclusion.[11] In *Spreading the Word,* I talked of a 'fractured sensibility' that could not be a proper object of approval. Schueler reasonably asks why it could not be an object of approval and whether in any case this smacks more of a moral or evaluative problem than of a logical one. Yet *modus ponens* with these components is surely logically valid, and a proper semantics for expressions of attitude ought to explain why.

How do attitudes become things that enter into logical relationships, that *matter* in the theory of inference? It is well known that logical relationships between imperatives can be studied by thinking of joint satisfiability—seeing whether there is a consistent world in which each of a set of imperatives is obeyed. Similarly, deductive relationships between norms can be studied by thinking of ideal or relatively ideal worlds in which the norms are met. If we have here the basis for a logic, it extends to attitude. For $H!p$ can be seen as expressing the view that p is to be a goal, to be realized in any perfect world—a world in which $\sim p$ is less than ideal, according to this commitment. The contrary attitude $B!p$ would rule p out of any perfect world, and corresponding to permission we can have $T!p$, which is equivalent to not hooraying $\sim p$, that is, not booing p.

Putting attitude to the fore, instead of the more usual obligations and permissions of deontic logic, promises two gains. The first is that writers on deontic logic usually interpret 'Op' and 'Pp' as purely propositional by making them describe what is obligated or permitted by some supposed background set of norms (the most notable exception to this generalization is Hector-Neri Castañeda).[12] But this divorces them from their ordinary expressive use, which is not to describe what some (possibly alien) system of norms yields but to insist upon or permit various things. If the apparatus of deontic logic can be taken over while this use is kept primary, so much the better. But there is another gain in taking the portmanteau term 'attitude' rather than the particular, restricted notion of 'obligation' and 'permission'. This is that the logical apparatus should apply wherever we have the idea of a goal or aim and the corresponding idea of something to be avoided or not to be avoided. We need not be in the realm of the obligatory, or of *requirements,* but merely in that of the needed or even just the desirable. Consistency in goals is still a desideratum whose logic needs development. And in fact the deductive apparatus of deontic logic does not depend in any way on taking obligations and permissions as fully fledged deontic notions. The same structure exists if 'Op' is interpreted as any kind of view that p be true ideally and 'Pp' as any kind of toleration of p.

There is nothing surprising about using realization of goals or ideals as the final test for consistency. The ordinary way of finding whether recommendations are consistent is to imagine them carried out and see if that can be consistently done. But Schueler rightly raises a problem that might affect the extension to attitude. This is that consistency in attitude is not a particular

11. Bob Hale, 'The Compleat Projectivist', in *Philosophical Quarterly,* Spring 1986, pp. 65–85, anticipates the difficulties with validity.

12. H-N. Castañeda, *Thinking and Doing* (Dordrecht: Reidel, 1975), esp. chapter 2.

virtue. I may wish that p and wish that $\sim p$ without particular shame. I may desire that p, and desire that q, but not desire that p & q: I want to spend the evening at the theater, and I want to read my book, but I do not want to read my book at the theater. There is a sense in which my goals are inconsistent—they cannot all be realized—but, if this does not matter, then it is not sufficiently *like* the vice of inconsistency in belief to form the basis of a logic.

My comment on this is threefold. First of all, I think part of the objection comes from confusing desires with wishes. Inconsistent wishes may not matter because in wishing or daydreaming we are spinning fictions, and inconsistent fictions do not matter. This is because there is no connection with action. But for all that, inconsistency in real desire may matter. Incompatible and therefore unrealizable goals are bad in a way quite analogous to the way in which inconsistent beliefs are bad. The latter cannot represent the world properly; but the former cannot represent how to behave in the world properly: they cannot mate together with beliefs, in the usual belief-desire psychological framework, to direct effective action. The man who believes both that it is raining and that it is not is badly placed to act if he wants, say, to avoid getting wet. But so is the man who believes that it is raining but wants both to get wet and not to get wet.

The second point to notice is that attitude and desire are capable of qualification. I may be subject to some desires, or some pressures (tiredness, mood) that suggest reading a book and others that suggest visiting the theater. Do I want both to read a book and to go to the theater? It is a crude way of representing my state. Perhaps I want to read a book *inasmuch as* I am tired, and want to go to the theater *inasmuch as* I like company. I feel the different pressures, but it is at least as natural to say that I don't know what I want to do as it is to say that I want to do both. I can indeed say that I would like to do both, but that takes us back to the realm of wishes (I would like them not to conflict somehow). So one way of diminishing the attraction of inconsistent desires is to remember the difference between full-scale, all-in desires, and attractions or pressures that are not yet resolved.

Even if this point were contested, a third defense is waiting. Although I have urged the advantage of thinking in terms of a catholic conception of attitude rather than of strict deontological notions, we could restrict ourselves to concepts of being for or against or neither for nor against things where consistency *does* matter. If this is a more limited range than the full spectrum of desire, this need not matter. If, for instance, it embraced only desires that one was inclined to submit to public scrutiny or translate into practical advice, then there would be a corresponding restriction of the interpretation of notions such as 'goal' or 'ideal'. That is fine, provided the relevant attitudes satisfy the constraints when it comes to interpreting the logic in a domain such as ethics. Since ethics is at bottom a practical subject, this is to be expected.

In the usual metaphor, the direction of fit between desires and the world is opposite to that between beliefs and the world. The desire that p dictates action if it is deemed likely, but avoidable, that $\sim p$, whereas the belief that p

needs abandoning if it is deemed likely that $\sim p$.[13] But since belief and desire do each have a direction of fit and a content, then each should be fitted to play a role in a logic of consistency. A person may flout the demand of consistency in complicated or demanding situations, but only at the cost of tension: his goals cannot be realized, or if he has inconsistent beliefs, the world cannot be as he represents it. It may be admirable that we sometimes get into states where we feel that tension, but this is so for belief as well as desire. It could not be admirable in general, and it could not be true in general, for these states are essentially characterized by responsibility either to the world, in the case of beliefs, or in our response to the world, in the case of attitude.

I therefore reject Schueler's contention that there is no legitimate notion of inconsistency. But it remains to be seen whether it ratifies my assault on *modus ponens,* or any other natural inference pattern. Meanwhile, there is another natural worry about my proposal. As it stands it yields no smooth extension to other propositional contexts. For instance, simple disjunction with an evaluative component does not yield an obvious second-order attitude. 'Either Johnny has done something wrong, or Freddy has' is not well represented as $H!(\backslash B!J\backslash$ OR $\backslash B!F\backslash)$ where 'OR' introduces a kind of disjunctive relation between attitudes. Because even if the idea of a disjunctive relation between attitudes makes sense, one might know that one of them has done something wrong but quite disapprove of taking up a negative attitude toward *either* of them—if neither has yet been proved guilty, for instance. The stance that $H!(\backslash B!J\backslash$ OR $\backslash B!F\backslash)$ expresses seems to be that of someone who endorses only psychologies that contain at least one of the embedded attitudes (this would be the natural interpretation of disjunction), but this is not at all the same as the stance of someone who thinks that either Johnny has done something wrong or Freddy has. One could interpret disjunction by first translating it into the associated conditional and then using the account of conditionals on that. But there is something *ad hoc* about such procedures. They take the theory too far from anything that seems necessary for the ordinary truth-functional disjunction, and their very unnaturalness raises again the question of adequacy. Even if the notion of involvement gives a reasonable surrogate for implication, there may be no such notion naturally available in each case of potential embedding.

Suppose then we take the theory of inference as primary. If we ask what these embeddings are *for,* the immediate answer is that they mediate inference. They show us the deductive relationships between our commitments, and between our commitments and our beliefs. So rather than *replace* logical constants, as in the approach I just gave, we might try to *retain* them and to provide an interpretation of embeddings of attitude in the contexts the deductive system is to treat: in the first place, contexts provided by the truth functors.

We know, or think we know, what the negation, disjunction, and conjunction of an ordinary proposition is. It needs showing that we have any right to

13. Michael Smith, 'The Humean Theory of Motivation', in *Mind,* 1987, pp. 36–61.

extend those notions to cover expressions of a different kind. Thus, in the language to come, $H!p$ is to be treated as a well-formed formula capable of entering the same embeddings as p. Even if this provides a language that is formally workable, it still needs showing that it provides one which is interpretable—in which $H!p$ can still be regarded as fundamentally expressive of attitude.

Consider first negation. What can $\sim H!A$ mean? Schueler might say: nothing much to do with truth or falsity, and since that reversal is the fundamental effect of negation, it cannot mean anything to apply the notion here. But I have already remarked that it might go the other way round: falsity of p is the truth of the negation of p. Ordinary negation is expressive of denial: $\sim p$ is that proposition whose expression denies p. There is a clear corresponding relation between attitudes: there exists that attitude that 'denies', or rejects, having p as an aim or goal. If $H!p$ expresses the attitude of endorsing the goal p, $\sim H!p$ then expresses that of opposition: tolerating $\sim p$ or allowing it as consistent with an ideal world. So we can say that $T!A$ is substitutable for $\sim H!A$, and $H!A$ for $\sim T!A$. Such a conversion drives external 'negations' on attitudes inward. So even if the original occurrence of the external negation made us uneasy, the unease is dissipated *formally* by the conversion and *philosophically* by recognizing sufficient analogy between conflict of attitude and conflict of belief.

What of other truth-functional contexts? An important feature of inference using propositional calculus embeddings is that they can all be represented by the normal forms of conjunction and disjunction. In a tableau development each move either adds to the string (as when A, B, are appended under A & B) or divides the string (as when A makes one branch, and B another, under A v B). Now let us suppose that we are involved with an evaluative commitment, $H!A$ or $T!A$ in a propositional calculus embedding. We can see what this means if we can interpret the strings in which it issues. This reduces then to the problem of interpreting these two elements in a tree structure. But it is easy to see what a string represents if, underneath this embedding, we get $H!p$ occurring alone (e.g., under p & $H!p$ we get $H!p$). This means that the initial complex commits us to the attitude, and this is not hard to interpret. Being against clergymen and for free love commits one to being against clergymen, and the notion of consistent realization of aims or goals shows us why.

There remains the case in which a tableau under a complex branches, and $H!p$ belongs to one of the branches. The interpretation is that one potential route to drawing out the consequences of the complex involves this commitment, although another may not. Thus p v $H!q$ issues in a branch; it is the commitment of one who is what I shall call *tied to a tree*—that is, tied to (either accepting that p, or endorsing q), where the parentheses show that this is not the same as (being tied to accepting p) or (being tied to endorsing q). Rather, the commitment is to accepting the one branch should the other prove untenable. The essential point is that this is a quite intelligible state to be in. Philosophically, we justify the procedure by analogy with the ordinary notion of accepting a disjunction, which similarly ties one to a tree of possibilities, and formally, the language admits of identical deductive procedures.

How does this relate to the original proposal for treating the conditional? Under a material conditional $A \rightarrow B$, we get the tree with $\sim A$ in one branch and B in the other. Suppose then we treat Geach's conditional 'if lying yourself is wrong, getting your little brother to lie is wrong' this way. Someone asserting it is tied to the tree of (assenting either to 'lying yourself is not wrong' or to 'getting your little brother to lie is wrong'). What was right about my original proposal is that being so tied is in this case characteristic of a particular value system or set of attitudes. Only someone with a certain view of the relation between doing things directly and doing them indirectly is apt to assent to the conditional. This represents the reason for his being tied. What was inelegant about the original proposal, I now think, was putting that directly into the content of the conditional itself. The assent to the conditional itself does not tell us why someone is tying himself to that tree, it tells us only that he is tied and that we can use this fact in assessing the consistency of his position. I return to this below, after detailing the logic a little.

I do not want to claim finality for the semantics I shall now sketch, but it illustrates how a logic might be developed, and it shows that notions of inconsistency and satisfiability can be defined. (It also bears out Kanger's remarks mentioned above.) It uses Hintikka's notion of a set of 'deontic alternatives'.[14] In Hintikka's semantics, the central notion is that of norms obtaining in a possible world, and of the deontic alternatives to that world being the possible worlds that are in accordance with those norms. Hintikka compares this notion to Kant's 'Kingdom of Ends' (*Reich der Zwecke*): it represents a 'mere ideal' (Kant: '*freilich nur ein Ideal*') that is not realized but that we nevertheless must be able to think of consistently.

In Hintikka's development we work in terms of a model system or set of model sets. A model set is a partial description of a possible world or alternative. A set of sentences including oughts and permissions will be satisfiable if it is embeddable in such a set. This means that a set of sentences L is satisfiable if and only if there is a model system S and a model set $m \in S$, such that L is a subset of m. Logical truth of A is unsatisfiability of the negation of A; B is a logical consequence of A if and only if $A \rightarrow B$ is valid, that is, $(A \& \sim B)$ is unsatisfiable.

Where we are not concerned with attitudes, the notion of a model set m is defined in a standard way:

If $p \in m$, then not $\sim p \in m$;

if $p \& q \in m$, then $p \in m$ and $q \in m$;

if $p \lor q \in m$, then $p \in m$ or $q \in m$ or both;

if $(Ex)p \in m$, then $p (a/x) \in m$ for some individual constant a;

14. J. Hintikka, 'Deontic Logic and Its Philosophical Morals', *Models for Modalities* (Dordrecht: Reidel, 1969).

if $(Ax)p \in m$ and if the free singular term b occurs in the sentences of m, then $p\ (b/x) \in m$;

$p\ (a/x)$ is the result of replacing the variable x by the singular term z everywhere in p.

Henceforth I shall depart somewhat from Hintikka's terminology, in order to separate some of the main ideas more obviously. Suppose that to a standard first-order language we add operators $H!$ and $T!$ subject to the condition that if A is a well-formed formula, $H!A$ is well formed and $T!A$ is well formed. Suppose now we start with a set of sentences L, which may contain sentences with these operators among them. We begin by defining a *next approximation to the ideal, L^*, of L.*

(Ii)   If $H!A \in L$, then $H!A \in L^*$;

(Iii)   If $H!A \in L$, then $A \in L^*$;

(Iiii)   If $T!A \in L$, then a set L^* containing A is to be added to the set of next approximations for L.

(Iiv)   If L^* is a next approximation to the ideal relative to some set of sentences L, then, if $A \in L^*$, $A \in$ subsequent approximations to the ideal $L^{**}, L^{***} \ldots$

We can say that a set of *final ideals*, $\{L^{***} \ldots\}$ of L, is obtained when further use of these rules produces no new sentence not already in the members $L^{***} \ldots$ of the set.

The set of sentences L may contain disjunctions or conditionals ready to be treated as disjunctions in the deductive apparatus. We can say that to each branch of a disjunction there corresponds a *route* to an ideal.

We can then define

A set of sentences L is unsatisfiable iff each route to a set of final ideals S results in a set of sentences S one of whose members contains both a formula and its negation.

These rules need a little gloss. Obviously, Iii embodies the aim that an ideal relative to a starting set of attitudes is obtained by specifying that the goals expressed are met. Rules Ii and Iii merely ensure that the attitudes specified originally remain in the subsequent realizations (if it is good that people are kind, it remains good in a world in which they are kind). The statement $T!A$ gets handled slightly differently. It sees A as compatible with, but not mandatory to, perfection. When tolerations are in play we have to consider both developments in which they are realized and also developments in which they are not. One next approximation for $(T!p\ \&\ T!\sim p)$ should contain p, and another $\sim p$, but the fact that they are inconsistent with each other does not reflect back on the original sentence. So to assess consistency, we need to think of formulae as producing a *set* of next approximations. The rule is that if $T!A$ is present in a set, there must be *a* next set in which A is present, although it is not to be in all. This means that we shall have to consider sets of next approximations to the ideal and sets of final idealizations. Intuitively, what is to matter is whether each such set is consistent.

It may be that modifications of Iiv would be desirable. What is obtained by realizing a toleration might not automatically feed through to subsequent approximations. The intuitive idea would be that something may be tolerated now, whereas were some ideal to become realized, it would no longer be tolerable: in that case, Iiv would need qualification.[15]

We want to iterate the procedure of generating a next ideal. This can be done by repeated use of these rules. If L^* is already a next approximation to the ideal and contains a sentence A, then except where A derives from realization of a toleration, it must transfer to further approximations to the ideal L^{**}. . . . This is not so in general, if A belongs to an original set L (for it may be a pity that A: A & $H!$ $\sim A$ is consistent). Here the idea is that once we are following out what is so in the progressive approximations to a perfect world, any realized ideal remains realized. The denizens of paradise do not move.

To get a feel for such a semantics, consider the formula $H!p{\rightarrow}p$. This is not valid: $\{H!p, \sim p\}$ is satisfiable. The next approximation is $\{H!p, p\}^*$, and this is a final ideal and is consistent. (As the gloss of Iiv showed, p does *not* transfer through to L^*—as far as the original set goes, p may be a pity, and this is reflected in its absence from the final ideal.) Now however consider $H!$ $(H!p{\rightarrow}p)$. This is valid, for $T!$ $(H!p$ & $\sim p)$ is not satisfiable. By Iv, $(H!p, \sim p)^*$ must be added as a next ideal. But the ideal under that is $\{H!p, p, \sim p\}^{**}$, which is inconsistent. Here is the operation of Iiii: it was already in this working out of the ideal that $\sim p$, so it stays there when we further consider the ideal obtained by realizing $H!p$, and it generates inconsistency.

15. In his 'Moral Quasi-Realism' in *Reality, Representation, and Projection*, eds. J. Haldane and C. Wright (New York: Oxford University Press, 1993), Bob Hale shows that this is too strong as it stands. It gives us that $T!H!p$ yields $H!p$, whereas intuitively tolerating admiring p is not the same as admiring p. On the other hand, we need that $T!(H!p$ & $\sim p)$ is inconsistent since otherwise $H!(H!p{\rightarrow}p)$ would not be valid. The rule that is wanted needs to be that when (but only when) what you tolerate is a wide scope $H!$ . . . this may fairly be taken as realized in assessing you for consistency. I discuss this further in 'Realism: Quasi or Queasy', in the same volume. Technically, the rule that emerges is that if L^* is a next approximation relative to some set of sentences L, then if L^* contains $H!(X)$, then a subsequent approximation L^{**} contains X and all the other sentences of L^*.

In chapter 5 of *Wise Choices, Apt Feelings* (Cambridge, Mass.: Harvard University Press, 1990), Allan Gibbard gives an elegant account of indirect contexts based on a possible world semantics. Instead of the consistency of realization of a set of attitudes, Gibbard relies on the consistency of a set of norms, and this undoubtedly makes it easier to generate a smooth logic, since the multiple embeddings that loom rather large in this essay are not a problem. It would be possible to urge that starting with an abstract structure, such as a set of norms that is itself already in the space of logic, being subject to norms of consistency, is starting with more Fregean baggage on board than one ought to be allowed. But Gibbard and I are agreed that in the end this is not an important charge, since he gives a functional story for the emergence and propriety of norms of consistency parallel to that which I give for sets of attitudes.

Transferred to these terms, Hintikka's main worked example is this. Prior once took it as a 'quite plain truth' of logic that

$$H!p \ \& \ (p \rightarrow H!q) \rightarrow H!q$$

But $\{H!p, p \rightarrow H!q, T! \sim q\}$ is perfectly satisfiable. In tree form and using the notion $=0\Rightarrow$ to signify adding the next approximation to the ideal, we get

$$H!p$$
$$T! \sim q$$

The right-hand route is bound to contain the inconsistent set, but the left yields none—reflecting the fact that if something that ought to be so is not, obligations or norms or goals consequential on its being so need not be held either. As in the first example, something here is a pity, and this is reflected by the fact that $H! \ [H!p \ \& \ (p \rightarrow H!q) \rightarrow H!q]$ is indeed valid.

The possibility of valid formulae with wide scope $H!$ suggests a notion of 'deontic validity' (Hintikka's term): in other words, although A may be consistent, $H!A$ need not be. In turn this gives us a needed notion: a person may be something worse than 'immoral', or possessing contingently defective attitudes, but not be 'inconsistent' in the sense of believing anything logically false. He may simply have ideals or goals which admit of no consistent realization.

This logic yields one reduction principle immediately: $H!H!p$ yields $H!p$. What about $T!T! \rightarrow T!p$? $\{T!T!p \ \& \ H!\sim p\} =0\Rightarrow\{T!p \ \& \ H!\sim p\}$, and this too is inconsistent. This reflects the 'one-dimensional' way in which realizations of goals are treated: we look through $H!$ and $T!$ to see what happens when they are realized, and this transparency extends to iterations of them. Many complexities could be introduced at this point and in connection with iterations generally.

The semantics also generates interesting sidelights on the original proposal for treating *modus ponens*. Suppose we took as an example 'X is good, if X is good Y is good, so Y is good'. Then a treatment like my original might render it

$$H!p; \ H! \ (H!p \rightarrow H!q) \ \text{so} \ H!q$$

And this is indeed valid. But the satisfaction is short-lived, for if we turn instead to 'Giving makes happiness; if giving makes happiness, then Christmas is a good thing, so Christmas is a good thing' a parallel treatment renders it

$$p; \ H! \ (p \rightarrow H!q) \ \text{so} \ H!q$$

This argument is invalid. There is no way of reimporting the original p into the set of final ideals. Clearly a treatment that makes a big asymmetry between these two arguments is suspicious. However, my old proposal did not quite have this form—it involved no propositional calculus embedding of $H!p$. Now that such a form is available, obviously we short-circuit these proposals simply to get $H!p$, $H!p{\rightarrow}H!q$, so $H!q$, and similarly for the second version. Each of these is valid.

So is Schueler right that my original proposal shows no inconsistency in the set containing the premises of a *modus ponens* inference, but a denial of the conclusion? As I mentioned, the original proposal for conditionals took seriously the idea that they create an indirect context—one where the propositions or attitudes normally expressed become, in some sense, the reference or topic of the utterance. In the present development conditionals are treated as disjunctions and broken open for example by tableau methods. Is there essential opposition here? Not necessarily. The issue is whether we can interpret endorsement of $(\backslash A\backslash{\Rightarrow}\backslash C\backslash)$—the original interpretation—as equivalent in strength to $(\mathord{\sim}A \vee C)$—the place conditionals now have in the logic. Only a little leeway with 'endorsement' and 'involves' ('$\Rightarrow$') is needed; as much, in fact, as gives the material implication its usual right to be thought of as rendering a conditional. Say: endorsing the involvement is tying oneself to the tree: in other words, tying oneself to restricting admissible alternatives to those in which $\mathord{\sim}A$, and those in which C. You have one or the other. And the effect of this on the theory of inference, when A or C or both are evaluative, is brought out in the model theory.

V. Conclusion

Slow-track quasi-realism will want to say that these proposals analyze or give us the logical form of the arguments we are considering. Fast-track quasi-realism need not say this. It can say: 'all this is very interesting'. It shows how *little* is involved if we imagine us jumping ship—changing from an expressivist language to our normal forms. But it is unnecessary to claim that we make no jump at all. That would involve, for instance, defending the claim that negation is absolutely univocal as it occurs in $\mathord{\sim}H!p$ and in $\mathord{\sim}p$, and similarly for the other constants. But this need not be claimed. All we have is sufficient similarity of logical role to make the temptation to exploit *ordinary* propositional logic quite irresistible—and that is what we naturally do. The expressivist language serves as a model showing us why what we do is legitimate—but that may be all. This is what I meant by saying that fast-track quasi-realism can benefit from the security provided by slow-track. I like this methodology. We bootstrap our way into appreciating how propositional expression, the arrival of indirect contexts, and the arrival of the truth predicate, meet our needs, without in any way betraying the original, economical, metaphysical vision. At times we may have taken steps, benefiting from what are only analogies between these kinds of commitments and beliefs, in order to treat the former as we treat the latter. But if so, these steps are little and natural.

11

Just Causes

In this essay I reflect mainly upon some difficulties that have been urged against a 'projective' explanation of ethical discourse. These difficulties in turn introduce wider problems about explanation and natural kinds, and perhaps indicate further things to be said about the ongoing realism versus anti-realism debate in ethics and elsewhere.

There are two kinds of difficulty I have in mind, both urged by Nicholas Sturgeon in his paper 'What Difference Does it Make Whether Moral Realism Is True?'[1] The first I shall call the argument from sense, and the second the argument from explanation. The first points to some aspect of moral communication that a theory, such as mine, might find it difficult to construe. The second does the same for explanations.

The essential structure of the argument from sense is this: A projective theory has two items at its disposal in its sketch of a moral psychology. There is the *input* side, or natural features of the world to which the subject is responsive in forming an ethical commitment. And there is the *output* side, or kind of commitment formed—the attitude or pressure upon action or choice. It is important to projectivism that it can usefully identify these, initially at least, without relying upon a moral vocabulary. It must be able to pin down the input without saying (for example) that it is a perception of justice or obligation or value. And it should pin down the output without saying that it is just the ethical response, the 'kind of reaction we have when we approve of something'. I put in the caveat that this should be so *initially,* for it is not true that this austerity has to go on forever. If a projectivist can, as I put it, earn the right to think in terms of an ethical truth and ethical features of things, then he can talk of us responding to them and responding ethically, when he works within the system. It is just that he thinks he has an explanation of what this amounts to that gives no ground to realism.

Now as we look at the individual members of a community, we will find a great deal of variety on each count. I shall take the case of social justice as an example. Then holding constant a given output, say, one of active approval

1. Nicholas Sturgeon, 'What Difference Does It Make Whether Moral Realism Is True?', in *Spindel Conference: Moral Realism, Southern Journal of Philosophy Supplement,* 1986. Similar points are made in a variety of ways by many contributors to *Essays on Moral Realism,* ed. Geoff Sayre-McCord (Ithaca: Cornell University Press, 1988).

and encouragement, we find that people differ in the kinds of arrangements that prompt it. And holding constant a given input—say, belief that a society is governed by Rawls's difference principle—we find a variety of outputs, ranging from adoration to execration. We find too attitudes that some people take, and that others never take: white-hot indignation, for instance. And some people respond to features that others are pretty much incapable of noticing: male patronization or racial stereotyping, for example.

Against this heterogeneous background, one constancy stands out and now appears odd. This is that we allow almost anyone, whatever the input and whatever the output, who so expresses herself, to be talking about *justice*. In Professor Sturgeon's example, Socrates and Thrasymachus disagree about what justice *is*—but they are not talking at cross-purposes. They are not doing so, even if one of them finds in it arrangements that leave the other cold, and finds in it an object of concern and respect while the other scorns it. The challenge now is plain: how can the projectivist find a single topic for such a debate? How can he explain the intuition that the two protagonists in such a debate are both talking about justice, but disagree about its nature?

As Sturgeon notes, this a resurgence of an old objection to naturalistic reductions in ethics. In this form of theory, if my standards for a thing being just are that it is X, and yours are that it is Y, then in saying that it is just I am saying that it is X, and in saying that it is not just you are saying that it is not Y; the decisive objection is that both these remarks might be true, so that the disagreement has disappeared. And one good reason for emotivism was that it restored the clash, as one of attitude and policy. What is now claimed is that this form of solution is itself subject to the same objection. It restores disagreement in cases where the same reaction is in play: you being *for* something and I being *against* it. But it can find no identity of content if both standards and reactions are fluid. Yet this is apparently something we manage to do.

There are of course limits to our charity. Suppose you claim to find it unjust that I start walking more often than not on the right foot, but furthermore add that this is one of those cases of injustice that actually deserves either no attention or even commendation. We cannot well get on terms with this: the diagnosis has to be either that you are joking, or that you misapprehend the term. A Satan who wants evil to be his good is one thing; a Satan who wants this, but also has bizarre standards for evil, perhaps applying the term mainly to acts of fairness and benevolence, would be best reinterpreted.[2] Thrasymachus himself faces this peril: if he sticks to the view that justice is what is in the ruler's interest,[3] perhaps he is not best seen as discussing justice at all. Add the quirk that he is contemptuous of whatever it is that he is thinking of, and the difficulty increases.

However, even if we chop off some of the more extreme cases by this means, there will be plenty of variation both of standard and of response, and

---

2. Milton, *Paradise Lost,* Book IV, 1.108. It is notable that Satan actually makes this exclamation in the course of bidding farewell to hope, fear, and remorse—it is not a *mere* change in standards, or a kind of existentialist experiment with a new fashion in values, that is in play.

3. *Republic* 339a.

the challenge to find the one content within it still remains. The other resource the projectivist has is clearly more promising. This is to remember other examples of our determination to find uniformity in sense, even in the face of massive differences of cognitive shape. Consider a straightforward belief—say that some tree is an elm. Any two people are likely to differ in some way in the evidence that will prompt them to think this and in the significance they attach to it. But we will again allow sameness of content, even embracing the most idiosyncratic input side (the person who cannot tell elms from beeches) and bizarre output side (the person who thinks that if it is an elm it will house a witch). So there is the same challenge to pin down sameness of belief given wide idiosyncrasy of conceptual role.

There is a well-known solution to this problem. That is that a group speaking a language holds itself together with what Putnam called 'division of linguistic labour' and what in *Spreading the Word* I called 'deferential conventions'.[4] In the clearest cases, we institutionalize an authority, and anyone using a term is *liable* to be regarded as having used it with the meaning vested in it by the authority. The familiar cases include deference to a deposit of usage or to scientific authority or dictionary authority. Anyone using a term is therefore in principle up for being *told* what it means, and his own peculiar configuration of knowledge and ignorance is not the arbiter of it. We might say that in this picture sameness of meaning or content is something that is imposed, although only on someone who himself abides by, or recognizes the authority of, the convention. We would not find someone liable in this way if they belonged to a genuinely different social group, and as in the interpretation of dialect we can show some flexibility here. But the reason for deeming meaning to be common is clear enough: for the purposes of smooth communication we need to look past the idiosyncrasy and take away as much of a common, communicable content as we can. Of course, this imposition can seem like a myth. We can remain impressed by the endless divergence of cognitive architecture even within a small group at one time, and lose any sense that we are *right* to impose a common meaning. But two thoughts should dispel this vertigo. One is that we need the imposition for communication. And the other is that we probably need it, or something like it, for any thought at all. If the content of a person's remarks were read straight back from her actual dispositions to application and withholding, then any standard of correctness and incorrectness vanishes, and with it the possibility of truth or falsehood.[5]

If this is the way to think of sameness of meaning, how will it apply to ethics? In ethics we have no single authority, and we are dealing with 'essentially contestable concepts'—ones where we predict the differences of input and output so far described. But the basic mechanism remains the same. We need to see disagreement where it exists, and for what it is. We do so by presuming a common, communicable topic. The 'default' position in any

---

4. *Spreading the Word* (Oxford: Clarendon Press, 1984), pp. 130 ff.
5. The modern *locus classicus* is Saul Kripke's *Wittgenstein on Rules and Private Language* (Oxford: Blackwell, 1982).

conversation is that we are discussing the same issue, even if we have different opinions about it. Only wild idiosyncracy overturns the default.

The question now is whether the projectivist can simply take this over. It seems that he can. He should do so by imposing as much identity of content as the need for communication and debate requires, hence, respecting the possibility of a common topic through different standards and responses. This means that the initial presumption in any debate about justice will be well seen as doubly quantificational. We presume that the subject responds to *some* aspect of a society's structures with *some* response of favour or disfavour. The evidence that can be cited may have to fall within a certain range, but it may not be the same as mine. That is what makes arguing with each other worthwhile. Similarly, the responses must fall within a certain range—they must have something to do with a taste or distaste, with encouragement or acquiescence versus rejection and regret—but, again, they may not be the same as mine. Some words delimit the range more closely than others. The so-called 'thick' ethical terms—courageous, courteous, fair-minded, and so on—delimit the input side closely, but leave open quite a variety of responses. Output-oriented terms— outrageous, intolerable, squalid—express relatively specific responses, but might be applied to a wide range of subjects.

A great deal of effort goes into locating the responses. Is what we value what we desire to desire?[6] Or what we fully or finally desire to desire to . . . ? Or is it something else altogether? The perspective I am urging will not see these issues as definitional. What may be needed is not a swift, *a priori* boundary, but a longer exploration of the possible contours of desire, remorse, higher order desire, and other pressures on choice and action. Milton's Satan can be represented as wanting to make evil his good because of his actual self-disgust, indeed his suffering, at being forced (by the need to have something over which to reign) to make such a choice. For this reason it would be absurd to see him as using the term only in an 'inverted commas' sense. He knows that it is *evil* he is choosing. But if his strategy is successful, and he succeeds in driving out not only remorse but all the other elements that enable him to see his own plight as desperate, then indeed the interpretation would start to waver. He would no longer be *seeing* evil as his good, but merely *doing* evil and seeing it as good.

We might be tempted to separate only some desires as values—ones that arise from or survive some process of universalization, for example. But we then face the need to conduct a dialogue with people who reject any such process. We should not see them as having no values at all, thereby closing off the vocabulary for dialogue or dispute.

For an example of indeterminacy of interpretation, consider the prisoners' dilemma. Suppose we face the need to educate people to obtain the highest social good from such situations, and do so by putting various pressures on them in childhood. Suppose this works for someone sufficiently well that he

---

6. For a defence of this choice, see David Lewis, 'Dispositional Theories of Value', in *Proceedings of the Aristotelian Society, Supplementary Volume*, 1989.

feels motivated to cooperate. But suppose too that he desires to desire not to cooperate (he thinks cheats get more out of life). We might say that he desires not to have the cooperative values he has. Or we might say that he fails to act on his real (egoistic) values. My attitude is that we do not have to choose: whichever way we put it, the task of getting him back into feeling comfortable with the cooperative choice (seeing it as *better*) remains the same. Saying anything further about the responses, just as saying more about the standards, will be entering into an essentially first order, *moral* debate. It will be a matter of assessing the *right* importance to give to various kinds and configurations of desire or other pressure, and views on that can differ. This in turn makes it important to frame the conversation as one around a common topic, the aim being to explore differences of sensibility, and to promote improvement and agreement. Words like 'justice' stand exactly where they need to, as the focus for the exploration.

This simple story may seem strange to anyone conditioned to expect a theory of meaning to take a certain form. We may have been led to expect talk of 'descriptive meaning', located by the input side, and 'prescriptive' or emotive meaning, located by the output. Yet here is a view that acknowledges neither. This seems to me pure advantage. Meaning is properly talked of only where we have *convention*. But there is no convention governing the selection of standards in ethics: someone who approves of the wrong things is not unconventional in the way of someone who uses a word wrong. A group cannot put pressure on an isolated moral view by claiming that it is a convention that other things are good or bad. Nor is there a convention governing the actual output: someone who feels a different way about the importance of something (that may be described as justice or virtue) cannot be brought into line by citing meaning. This is why, in my view, Professor Hare's battle to make universalizability, and hence perhaps utilitarianism, emerge from the meaning of ethical terms is quixotic. The reason is that the upshot would be only that there is a convention that anyone reasoning without (roughly) abstracting away from her own position is not to be described as reasoning 'ethically'. If this is true, we may still prefer and campaign for other ways of reasoning. But it is unlikely to be true, for that very reason: we will need to emerge with such a preference or campaign. And the terms in which to do so best are obvious: one side thinks that universalizing is the way to find out which things are good, and the other side thinks something else is. Any theory on which the terms have been ('by definition') coopted by just one side lacks the ordinary means to locate this debate. Things would be easier if words enforced ethics, but they will not do so, any more than reason will.

The points I have made also diminish the force of one attack often made on projectivism. This is its difficulty in defining, in other than ethical terms (approval, guilt, etc.), the state of mind projected. I reply that, because of the mechanisms given above, we would not want a definition serving only to rule out cases that we need to 'rule in'. It would be damaging if the rich textures of ethical response were somehow visibly *sui generis*, incapable of being explained as developments from less particular responses of desire, or of willingness to bow to pressure or to conform to group observances. But there is no reason to believe that the natural history of ethics witnesses any inexplicable leaps of psychology.

It is always necessary, in discussing moral realism, to press the question of how realists escape the traps laid for their opponents. Why exactly does the existence of a 'real' moral property help to restore sameness of sense to differently functioning participants in a debate? Thrasymachus and Socrates have to be brought into some kind of relationship with any such property. But their different standards and different views of the importance of the issues they are discussing make that just as hard for the realist as for anyone else. Suppose, for example, that justice in a state really supervenes upon the existence of the difference principle governing distributions of wealth, and suppose further that rightness belongs to the person in whom justice trumps all other practical considerations. Then consider Thrasymachus, who thinks, or expresses himself as thinking, that justice is whatever is in the interests of the strongest, and (let us say) that in any case it is right to pay no attention to the claims of justice when you can get away with it. How does 'realism' help us to see his words as possessing the same sense that they do in the mouth of a Socrates? *Prima facie* he is talking of something other than the real thing, something that arises differently and makes different claims altogether.

The usual answer draws on the analogy with natural kind terms. Two theorists may equally be talking of water, although differing about its nature; why should two theorists not be talking equally of justice, although differing about its nature? But the solution to the problem in the case of natural kinds is quite different. A man may be known to be talking of water, in spite of making misguided claims, because we can trace the causal line: we know the stuff that prompts his claims, and toward which his actions are directed. But there is no analogous procedure in the case of justice—no independent tracing of the *focus* of attention that can counterbalance the impression that he is talking of something else entirely.

A 'naturalistic' realist, still working with the 'water = H_2O model', must reply to this objection by filling out the contact we have with the real properties. Perhaps there is some explanatory role for the property with which he identifies goodness or justice, whereby we all touch the right property in spite of other differences. But this suggestion falls to an unpleasant dilemma. There are two ways we might be locked onto moral properties, through being in contact with natural ones with which they are identical. We may be in contact cognitively (thinking of such properties, or in terms of them), or it may be that they, or more accurately instantiations of them, are in some favoured way explanatory of our thought and practice. The water/H_2O case indicates the latter model. But it then meets the fatal objection that someone might surely be thinking and talking of justice even in a world in which it is not to be found. Suppose justice in society *is* the instancing of the difference principle. Suppose no societies do this. Then no such instancing is causally or in any other way responsible for any of my thoughts, and on the natural kinds model, just as it is said that Twin Earthers do not think of water as they splash around in

XYZ, so it would have to be said that nobody in a bad world can think or dream of justice. The essence of this argument is that it is always tokens or instances of properties, rather than properties *tout court,* that play explanatory roles independently of the content of thought. I can certainly change my behaviour through thinking of a chiliagon. But 'chiliagonhood' or the property of being a chiliagon cannot influence me otherwise, except through being instanced. I cannot change my behaviour or thought 'because of the property of being a chiliagon' unless this means either that I suddenly started to think in terms of such a property, or was influenced by the existence of an instance, for example by bumping into one.

On the other hand, if the contact is thought of more cognitively, so that someone can indeed think of a justice that is never found, the issue of interpretation remains moot. Suppose a Nozick strenuously insisting that justice in society has to do with transfers of ownership, and has nothing whatsoever to do with the embedding of the difference principle. What is the story saying that he is 'really' well seen as thinking and talking of justice (the instancing of the difference principle) in spite of his views? How do we see him as actually concerned with this property, in spite of the disavowal? I see no independent reason for doing this, and the realist falls victim to the same argument—from different standards to different sense—that he used to overturn his Moorean and Fregean ancestors. In short, for the realist to deem him to be talking of the favoured property involves just as much of an imposition, or policy of looking past the differences of standard and conceptual role, as it does for the anti-realist: here as elsewhere the reality of the property is quite idle. In fact, if anything it makes matters worse, since for the realist there may be a hidden right or wrong, depending on the explanation of the subject's thought, where for the anti-realist our purposes give us automatic standards of right imposition. For all I can see, on the realist picture, one person may be misguided in standards and motivations, but 'locked onto' the right property; another with the same functioning may be 'locked onto' the wrong one, so although we engage them equally and accuse them both of mistakes about justice, we might be wrong to do so. For the anti-realist there is no such possibility: the interpretation is, as it were, downwind of our interpretative needs.

Although I think the above dilemma is fatal to this kind of realism, it does introduce the whole issue of explanations involving moral properties, and brings us to the second of Professor Sturgeon's objections. As examples in which the moral feature of a situation is attributed an explanatory role, he reminds us that poverty and injustice may be cited in the same breath as explanations of human events such as revolutions and cites the plausible truth that children thrive when treated with decency and humanity. And the projectivist, he believes, cannot tolerate this, since according to him there is no feature there to play any causal role at all.

There are, I think, three compatible lines that a projectivist might use to explain these explanations. The first would be to query whether the explanations are elliptical. Someone citing injustice as the cause of revolution might be adverting to the population's *perception* of injustice, or belief that they are victims of injustice. And there is nothing surprising in this having effects (if the projectivist is still avoiding talk of perception and belief, then substitute the population's attitude toward their arrangements). This is a plausible construction of the revolutions case: at least, I cannot readily think of mechanisms whereby injustice brings about revolutions except through the population's awareness of it. However, the children case is different: we might explain a child thriving by mentioning the decency and humanity with which she was brought up, without supposing that the child perceived the upbringing as decent and humane. The child might thrive because of it even at a time when she lacks the concepts to recognize the upbringing as decent and humane. This brings us to the second projectivist line, which is that the explanation points downward to the properties upon which the moral verdict depends. According to me, an upbringing is decent and humane *in virtue of* other features—meeting the child's needs, engaging with its attempts at action and communication, and so on—and I may simply point toward those other, causally powerful properties by using the moral predicate. An education will have to be decent and humane in virtue of other properties, and those other properties will bring it about that children thrive (indeed, that's largely why they get the honorific titles).

This may seem *ad hoc* at first sight, so it is worth dwelling a little on other cases where the same pattern is found. In what Jackson and Pettit call 'programme explanations' we mention some *supervening* feature of a state in order to point to the existence of some other, underlying property, whose instancing is the causally powerful event.[7] Thus Fred's coughing at a particular place and time in the concert irritated the conductor. But it is quite proper to explain the conductor's annoyance by mentioning that someone coughed. We do not have to pick out the individual event: it may be enough to say that it was an event of some sort. Or we may explain opium's effect, if not very helpfully, by saying that it has a dormitive virtue, or in other words possesses *some* property that causes sleep. The actual chemical property responsible may be unknown to us, but by saying that there is one there we at least rule out other kinds of explanation. Again, I may explain the appearance of a letter on the screen when I press a key by saying that the computer is running Word, and again it is plausible that this explanation works merely by telling us that there is *some* property in the electronics correlating keystroke and letter.

The presence of quantification in these explanations is important, given what I said earlier about the attribution of content to the moral remarks of others. If you tell me that injustice caused the revolution, I understand that there is some property that you take to give rise to injustice, and that caused the revolution. I must, in my own assessment, separate the truth of the causal story you are pointing toward, from my own verdict on whether it amounts to injustice. Knowing your devotion to Rawls I may have a good idea of the first, and I may agree, for instance, that the absence of the lexical priority of liberty indeed caused the revolution. Perhaps I would not myself call that unjust, but

7. F. Jackson and P. Pettit, 'Functionalism and Broad Content', in *Mind,* 1988.

I can assent to the explanation without endorsing the verdict you pass on the feature. Of course, it can work the other way round, if I assent to the injustice but deny the causation. And finally there is scope for misunderstanding, if I am not privy to the kinds of feature you take to justify the verdict. We might each say that injustice caused the revolution, but be completely at cross-purposes: I am pointing to the absence of government by the differing principle, and you to the Right have in mind the punitive top taxation rate of 30 percent.

I cannot readily think of an explanation citing a moral property that will not succumb to one of these two diagnoses. But I would like to introduce the third, more speculative strategy, even if we do not have to rely upon it. This *allows* that there exists a moral feature, injustice, and even allows that it can itself be causally relevant, in spite of having a projected origin. It will not be obvious that this position is available to the projectivist. But here is a sketch of the way it might be. The first part is to establish our right to talk of the moral feature or property. Now, if the projectivist adopts quasi-realism, he ends up friendly to moral predicates and moral truth. He can say with everyone else that various social arrangements are unjust, and that it is true that this is so. Once this is said, no further theoretical risks are taken by saying that injustice is a *feature* of such arrangements, or a quality that they possess and that others do not. The first step, in other words, is to allow propositional forms of discourse, and once that is done we have the moral predicate, and features are simply abstractions from predicates.

The second part is to explain how such a feature might be causally relevant. This is not easy, because we have deep problems in thinking out how *any* features are causally relevant. Strictly speaking, we want to say that it is their instances that are relevant, but when we think in detail of instantiation, we tend to lose sight of the way the property itself relates to the causal powers of the instance. This is the problem that prompts writers following Lewis and Davidson to equate mental events with physical events, or in general 'supervening' events with subvening realizations, generally thought of in terms of particular physical states or mechanisms. Thus in Jackson and Pettit's example, the causally powerful event is a particular disturbance of Fred's coughing and also the realization of someone coughing. In their handling of the case, mentioning that someone coughed is a 'programme explanation' for us, the causally relevant feature being its 'realization' on the occasion in a particular sequence of events. The idea is that we look down from its being someone coughing, to find its being that particular sequence of physical events, and it is only then that we find causal power.

I do not regard this diagnosis as compulsory.[8] We might well want to say that the causally relevant feature was just someone coughing—why is this not a property whose instancing actually made the conductor angry? One way, of preserving our right to say this will be via identifying the event of someone coughing with the event of molecules moving. But there may be other ways. I

8. See also essays 13 and 14.

do not need to adjudicate that here. On any view, the conductor, we suppose, is apt to explode when anybody coughs, so making somebody cough gives us a control over him: it is a feature of the audience that we can pick out and work upon, regardless of its particular 'realization', and when this is so we want to talk about causal relevance. This is so whether the causal chain works via the conductor's *thought* that someone is coughing, or whether the coughing simply acts on his emotional system regardless of his recognizing it as a cough.

The same might be true in the moral case. If we can talk of a feature of a situation, via the development above, we can also use it in controlling events. Thus, suppose a variety of social arrangements qualify, in our view, for injustice. Suppose I want to promote a revolution. Working from within my moral view I can issue the instruction that you bring about injustice, as a means to doing it: I need not care which particular realization of events you go in for, if I think that any will do equally. In the same way I can raise the temperature or get someone to cough, without caring which particular distribution of kinetic energies of molecules, or which particular person, realizes the state. So, similarly, I may want you to be controlled by the moral reaction: to create a state of affairs that merits disapprobation, since I believe that if you do that revolution will follow on, perhaps as others come to share the same reaction. To sensibly issue the order I must suppose that your standards for injustice are roughly the same as mine. It will not be much good if you think that socialist utopias are intrinsically unjust, whereas I had in mind something more to the right. But similarly, it is no good using a badly calibrated thermometer to control the central heating.

It may be instructive to compare the case of colour. We know enough about the physics of colour to know that the best explanation of our colour classification is the upshot of a complex function of the energy levels of the three different kinds of receptor.[9] Without endorsing a dispositional view of the term, it is nevertheless true that as far as science is concerned, coloured things share only a disposition to activate the same classification from (creatures like) *us*. If this peculiar instrument, the visual system, did not exist, no physicist would find anything but a shapeless disjunction of different physical states in all the things we see as red. Nevertheless, we can certainly cite colours in causal explanations: the butterfly escapes being eaten because its colour matches the branch; the picture did not sell because the colours were too bright. Colour may be what we need to use, as evolution does, to control a certain effect, and again, where this is so we talk happily of causal relevance. It should, however, be noticed that the only straightforward example of such causal power is *via* perception (conforming to the first kind of case above).

It seems to me, then, that there is nothing in our explanatory use of moral properties that lies beyond a projectivist's grasp. But by now many readers will be wondering what remains that is distinctive of projectivism. In the old days (they will complain) it was easy: we knew what emotivists and prescriptivists stood for. But this new, conciliatory position is harder to pin down,

9. C. L. Hardin, *Colour for Philosophers: Unweaving the Rainbow* (Indiana: Hackett, 1986).

harder to recognize as a position. My view has always been that it is a question of explanation, of 'placing' our propensity for ethics within a satisfactory naturalistic view of ourselves. I distinguish then between the ingredients with which you start, and what you can legitimately end up saying as you finish. To place ethics, I deny that we can help ourselves to moral features and explanations from the beginning. We have to see them as constructions, or, as I call it, projections, regarding ourselves in the first instance as devices sensitive only to natural facts and producing only explicable reactions to them. The aim is to explain and make legitimate the emergence of full-blown ethics on this austere basis. But there is no need to deny, as the error theorists did, that the full-blown system is in order as it is. Nor is there any need to regret apparently realistic features of it, if these can be earned from the slender basis. Among these will be a propensity, when we are working from within the system, to use ethical predicates in the ways that Sturgeon highlights.[10] But, as I say, I can see no sellout to any other metaphysic of ethics in the fact that we do so.

There is a final, much less easily dissected aspect of the matter that I should like to end by mentioning. It is, I think, undeniable that moral anti-realism is often seen as a dangerous doctrine, a more or less surreptitious denial of the importance of ethics or of the possibility of genuine first-order ethical theory. It is thought to consort with lack of real seriousness, just as relativism is felt to undermine any real commitment. Nearly all writers who currently incline to promote real first-order theory—Parfit, Foot, Nagel, Mc-Intyre, Dworkin, and many others—find it important to eschew anti-realism, and those who embrace it in one form or another—Mackie and Williams come to mind—are less enthusiastic about the possibilities of substantive ethical theory. I incline to a historical or cultural diagnosis of this piece of false consciousness. It seems to me that there is always a temptation to absorb ethics into the most convenient example of respectable inquiry. In the heyday of theology, the will of God determined ethics. When 'logic' held sway, philosophers conceived of themselves as investigating the logic of moral discourse, and in those who wished to promote substantive views (Hare is paramount here), the goal became one of showing how those views were really consequences of that logic. When logic loses ground and naturalism is in the ascendant, the model is that of the scientist: just as the analytic chemist breaks open the hidden nature of water, so the philosopher as scientist breaks open the hidden nature of the good. His equations—justice is the difference principle, goodness is happiness, or whatever—then derive authority from their similarity to the respected scientific activities on which they are modelled. But any authority so derived is hollow, of course, and the models serve merely to disguise the fact that in advancing such equations we are *just* moralizing, no more and no less. We may be doing it well or poorly, of course, but the activity itself, rather than neighbouring paradigms, is the judge of that.

By all means we may urge and argue that all and only societies that embed

10. Those interested can follow the dialectic through a rejoinder by Professor Sturgeon, and a reply by me, in *Philosophical Studies*, 1990.

the difference principle are just, or that all and only actions that promote happiness are good. But we should remember that only a loss in understanding what we are doing comes from thinking of ourselves as thereby identifying, in a scientific spirit, the property that is justice or goodness, as opposed to describing, from a moral perspective, the properties of just and good institutions or actions.

III

MIND AND MATTER

12

The Individual Strikes Back

In this essay I address some of the points Saul Kripke makes in his treatment of the 'rule-following considerations' in the later Wittgenstein ('LW').[1] There are two different quarries to track down. There is the question of whether Kripke's exegesis of Wittgenstein ('KW') is correct—whether KW is LW. And there is the distinct question of the real significance of the considerations, as they are put forward by KW. Kripke himself is carefully agnostic about this second issue.[2] KW is not Kripke *in propria persona*. And Kripke is also careful to distinguish the exegetical issue from the question of significance. The two issues only connect like this: If KW's arguments have some property that we are convinced cannot belong to any argument that LW would have used, we shall suppose that KW is not the real LW. And admirers of Wittgenstein will suppose that significance is such a property: if KW's considerations are faulty, then for that reason alone KW cannot be LW; LW would not have used faulty considerations. But without commenting on this optimism, I want to discuss two other properties that might distinguish KW from LW: KW's use of scepticism and his attitude to facts. Each of these aspects may legitimately raise worries about his identity with LW. And I shall also offer some thoughts about the significance of KW's arguments for our conceptions of meaning.

Our topic is the fact that terms of a language are governed by rules that determine what constitutes correct and incorrect application of them. I intend no particular theoretical implications by talking of rules here. The topic is that there is such a thing as the correct and incorrect application of a term, and to say that there is such a thing is no more than to say that there is truth and falsity. I shall talk indifferently of there being correctness and incorrectness, of words being rule-governed, and of their obeying principles of application. Whatever this is, it is the fact that distinguishes the production of terms from mere noise, and turns utterance into assertion—into the making of judgement. It is not seriously open to a philosopher to deny that, in this minimal

---

1. Saul Kripke, *Wittgenstein on Rules and Private Language* (Oxford: Blackwell, 1982). All page references are to this work. Paragraph references in the text are to the *Philosophical Investigations*.
2. Page 5.

sense, there is such a thing as correctness and incorrectness.[3] The entire question is the conception of it that we have.

KW pursues this issue by advancing a certain kind of scepticism. As Kripke is well aware, this might provoke immediate protest. Surely LW is consistently scornful of scepticism? But this reaction misunderstands the function of scepticism in a context such as this. The function is not to promote a conclusion about knowledge or certainty, but to force a reconsideration of the metaphysics of the issue. That is, we begin with a common-sense or unrefined conception of some kind of fact. We think we have an understanding of what that kind of fact consists in. The sceptic tries to show that on that conception we would have no way of distinguishing occasions when the fact obtains from those when it does not. Now, we might conclude from this that our conception was correct and that there is therefore a definite kind of proposition whose truth value we can never reliably judge. This would be a traditional sceptical conclusion. But we might alternatively conclude that since we do know the truth about the kind of thing in question, the conception was at fault. The things we know do not have the kind of truth condition we took them to have; the facts are not quite the kind of thing we took them to be. This is a metaphysical conclusion, and the sceptical dialogue is an instrument for reaching it. LW may have had no time for sceptical conclusions. But he may well have had thought processes that can be revealed by using a sceptical instrument to reach a metaphysical conclusion. This is what KW does. So, as far as the issue of using a sceptical weapon goes, KW may well be LW.

It is clear that on this account there are two parts to the business; attacking the old conception and producing a replacement. The negative part might be successful, although the positive part is not. If LW was successful, then in the positive part he produced a conception on which public rule-following (in some sense of 'public') is possible, whereas private rule-following is not. I shall be arguing that KW is not successful in doing this. He does not succeed in describing what it is for there to be a rule in force, with the property that this can obtain in a public case but not in the private case.

I. Sceptical Solutions

Kripke describes KW as adopting a 'sceptical solution' to the sceptical considerations, modelled upon Hume's sceptical solution to his own doubts. To assess this idea it is important to separate various strands in Hume's extremely complex position. If KW is understood to be taking over the wrong parts of Hume, he may too easily be rejected as a pretender. I suspect that parts of Kripke's presentation will encourage this—particularly those where he talks of the sceptical solution.

3. Crispin Wright comes close to denying it in *Wittgenstein on the Foundations of Mathematics* (London: Duckworth, 1980), e.g., pp. 21–22, where he seems to attribute to Wittgenstein an error theory of determinacy of the correctness of saying anything.

Hume calls section V of the First *Enquiry* the 'Sceptical Solution of these Doubts'. The doubts in question were introduced in Section IV; they concern operations of the understanding. In particular they concern our ability to reason *a priori* about what must cause what, and the impossibility of justifying inductive reasoning. The sceptical solution of section V consists in denying that processes of reasoning have the power and the place hitherto assigned to them. They are replaced by processes of custom. This is why we have a sceptical solution: Hume offers a view of ourselves which in part he shares with traditional sceptics. The shared part is the denial that we can justifiably reason to our beliefs. (Hume differs from tradition in his estimate of the consequences of that.) When Kripke introduces the analogy with Hume, this is what he first mentions. But this is not the aspect of Hume (nor the section of the *Enquiry*) that actually matters. What matters is his reinterpretation of the concept of causation—the topic of section VII of the *Enquiry*.[4] It is here that Hume has a (fairly) pure example of the process I described: a sceptical argument forcing us to revise our conception of a kind of fact. It is here that he parallels KW. But the reinterpretation does not deserve to be called a 'sceptical solution' to anything, nor did Hume so call it. It is at most a proposal prompted by sceptical problems. But in principle it might have been prompted by other considerations altogether. And in fact Hume's reinterpretation of causation is motivated only partly by scepticism. It is at least as firmly seated in the theory of understanding: problems with our Idea of the causal nexus. In this part of Hume, scepticism is subsidiary, even as a tool.

Kripke can rejoin that Hume's reinterpretation of causation is, in itself, deservedly called sceptical for a further reason. It denies that there is a 'fact' of whether there is a causal connexion between two events. At least, that is how Kripke takes Hume.[5] But here too, there are subtleties in the offing, and they matter to the parallel with KW. This is because LW's attitude about 'facts' is going to be crucial, and crucial to many philosophers' belief that KW differs from him. The philosopher we have described ends up reinterpreting some kind of fact. This leaves various options. The first might be called 'lowering the truth-condition'. This asserts that sentences in the area can only, legitimately, be given such-and-such a truth-condition. This can be combined with the view that in our ordinary thought we confusedly attempt to do more, or misunderstand what we are actually doing enough to make mistakes (although there is always a problem about how we can attempt to do more, if we are supposed to have no conception of anything more to do). Lowering the truth-condition is then a reforming view, and entails an 'error' theory of ordinary thought. But it can be combined with the view that the lowering really reveals what we meant all along; this gives us reductionism. Often it does not matter very much which combination is offered, and indeed, since a decision depends on a fine detection of ordinary meaning, we would expect some degree of indeterminacy.

---

4. Similarly in the *Treatise*, esp. Book I, part 3, section 14.
5. Pages 68, 69.

Quite distinct from lowering the truth-condition, there is the option of denying one altogether. The sentences in question are given some other role than that of asserting that some fact obtains. This option is familiar from expressive theories of moral commitment or from views that try to see arithmetical theses as rules rather than descriptions or propositions, and so on. Now I say that this option is distinct from lowering the truth-condition, and indeed in its initial stages it certainly is. It is a confusion, for instance, to muddle together expressive theories of ethics with naive subjective theories that give moral commitments a truth-condition but make it into one about the speaker. Arguments against this latter view often have no force against the former. But Hume is responsible for the very complication that makes it so hard to keep these options properly separated. This is the view that the mind spreads itself on the world: the view I call projectivism. According to projectivism we speak and think 'as if' the world contained a certain kind of fact, whereas the true explanation of what we are doing is that we have certain reactions, habits or sentiments, which we voice and discuss by such talk. Hume was quite clearly a projectivist in moral philosophy, and it is plausible to see his metaphysics of causation as in essence identical.[6]

Like the option of lowering the truth-condition, the option of denying that there is one can be combined with either of two attitudes to our ordinary practice. One would be that it embodies error. Ordinary talk is conducted as if there were facts, when there are no such facts. The talk is 'fraudulent' or 'diseased'. The other option is less familiar, but much more attractive. It holds that there is nothing illegitimate in our ordinary practice and thought. The respects in which we talk as if there are, for instance, moral facts, are legitimate. (I have called this view 'quasi-realism'.) If LW were a projectivist, he would have to be this kind, for it preserves the doctrine that ordinary talk and thought, before we start to philosophize about the nature of our concepts, are in perfect order as they are.

Kripke acknowledges the strand in LW that matters here. He also realizes that it goes far—far enough to stop LW from endorsing any such judgement as this: 'there is no fact of the matter whether a term is rule-governed or not'. But KW expresses himself differently: KW believes that there is 'no such fact, no such condition in either the "internal" or the "external" world' (p. 69). This talk will outrage friends of LW. KW denies the existence of a certain kind of fact altogether; LW would never so express himself, *ergo* one is not the other. But now recall that Hume himself says that 'those who deny the reality of moral distinctions may be reckoned amongst the most disingenuous of disputants'.[7] Why? Because insisting on this reality is part of normal thinking. It is part of the way of life, or way of thought or talk, that quasi-realism can protect for us. So there must be room for a different version of LW. This one would abandon his hostility to facts. He should accept that talking of facts is

---

6. For typical statements compare the appendix to the *Enquiry*, and *Treatise*, p. 167.
7. *Enquiry Concerning the Principles of Morals*, section I.

part of our legitimate way of expressing ourselves on the difference between terms that are rule-governed and terms that are not. He has to do this if he doubles for LW. For recall that the very passage (*Investigations* §137) that begins these considerations is a version of the redundancy theory of truth. And on that theory (whatever else it holds), there is no difference between saying that it is true that *p* and that *p* or between saying that it is a fact that *p* and that *p*. So anybody prepared to assert that terms are rule-governed—and as I explained initially, that must mean all of us—can equally be heard saying that there are facts, truths, states of affairs of just that kind.

Kripke says something strange about this. On p. 86 he imagines someone saying that it cannot be tolerable to concede to the sceptic that there are no truth-conditions or corresponding facts to make a statement about someone's meaning true: 'Can we not with propriety precede such assertions with "It is a fact that" or "It is not a fact that"?' But Kripke puts this complaint in the mouth of an *objector* to LW. He then reminds us that LW accepts the redundancy theory of truth, and says that this gives him a short way with such objections. The dialectic seems to be the wrong way round. *Because* he accepts the redundancy theory, LW can assent to the locutions of fact and truth. They add nothing to the fact that we judge other people not to be following rules and applying terms in accordance with standards of correctness.

I don't know that the redundancy theory of truth should have this soothing power. It may be that there are explanations of why we make some judgements, and why we apply the calculus of truth-functions to the judgements we make, that still leave us queasy when we consider whether there are facts in the case. The quasi-realist construction of ordinary moral discourse is a good example. Even if it protects everything we do, it can still leave us uneasy when we contemplate the question: 'Yes, but are there any moral facts on this account?' I shall not consider that question further in this paper. I just want to note that on a redundancy theory, it is a bad place to become puzzled, and that LW held a redundancy theory. Hence it seems that there is space for a *persona* who profits from KW's arguments but draws a rather different conclusion from them. With due humility, I shall call this character BW. He is going to share a great deal of the argumentative strategy of KW. In part his difference is relatively cosmetic: the belief that scepticism is only in play, if at all, as an instrument, and that the eventual conception of rule-following that must emerge does not deserve to be called sceptical. But in part he differs more substantially, because he hopes to preserve the implications of the redundancy theory in LW, and he hopes to cement a more particular relationship between LW and the real Hume, who matters to metaphysics. If he can preserve our right to talk of the fact that words obey principles of application, this may be as much because he forces us to revise our conception of a fact as anything else. Alas, however, BW has one radical flaw. On his philosophy, there is no particular reason to discriminate against the would-be private linguist. But before advertising his intended end point further, it is necessary to review some of the arguments by which he gets there.

II. The Critique of Rule-Following

It may seem outrageous to the touchy friends of LW that anything in Hume could be a model for LW's attitude to rule-following. But perhaps we can stem some of the outrage by reminding ourselves that it is an essentially normative judgement that we are chasing. It is the judgement that something is correct or incorrect. When this fact proves fugitive, as KW shows that it is, its normative nature is largely the problem. So it cannot be that outrageous to apply our best explanations of value judgements to it, and this is what BW hopes to do. But why is the fact fugitive in the first place?

In Kripke's development, we start by considering the understanding I had of some term at some time in the past, which we can arbitrarily call 'yesterday'. Suppose the term is some arithmetical functor, 'plus' or '+'. I understood it by grasping a principle of application. We then consider my position today. When I come to do a calculation, which we suppose I have never done before, I certainly believe myself to follow a principle. I believe myself to be *faithful* to yesterday's rule, by adopting the same procedure or principle in determining answers to problems expressed using the functor. Thus I believe that if I am faithful to yesterday's principle, I should say '57 + 68 is 125'. Notice that this is not quite the same as claiming that I should say this unconditionally. I may wish to change my allegiances. There's no impropriety in deciding that yesterday's principle of application is not the best one for this term, and to consciously start to use it according to different rules. It is just that *if* I am faithful, then I *ought* to give that answer. I most certainly should not say that 57 + 68 is 5. Nor should I say that there is more than one answer to that problem, or that the problem is indeterminate, so that there is no answer at all. The sceptical dialogue then commences. The sceptic asks me to point to the fact that I am being faithful to yesterday's rule by saying only one thing, and not these others. And this proves hard to do. For any fact that I tell him about myself seems compatible with the 'bent-rule' hypothesis, as I shall call it: the hypothesis that the rule that was really in force yesterday was a Goodman competitor. In other words, the kinds of fact I am apt to allege are compatible with a story in which I really understand by 'plus' a function with a particular singularity at $x = 57$ and $y = 68$. For example, I might yesterday have meant what we should now express by saying

$x + y =$ the sum of x, y, except when $x = 57$ and $y = 68$ and 5 otherwise

This hypothesis is not refuted by my present staunch denial that I had any such thought in mind yesterday, or that if asked I would have used words like these to explain myself. For the sceptic will urge that as well as having had a bent interpretation of '+' yesterday, I could have had a bent interpretation of these other terms as well. So pointing out that I would have presented no such explanation to myself does not refute the sceptic. It would really be a question of my using another rule to interpret the first (e.g., the rule for interpreting various synonyms for '+' or for interpreting terms that would have occurred in any explanation of the functor that I would have proffered). So the fact that yesterday I would have said, for instance, '$x + y$ is always a number greater than either x or y, with $x = 57$ and $y = 68$ no exception' is consistent with my having been a secret bent rule user. The singularity, by current lights, would have been there in the way I took the words involved in such an affirmation. Perhaps 'exception' meant . . .

This argument (which is much more forcefully and thoroughly presented in Kripke) undoubtedly corresponds to a central negative point of LW's. The point is that taking a term in a certain way is something different from *presenting* anything as an aid to understanding it, or from *accepting* anything as aids to understanding it. He says in §201 that he has shown 'that there is a way of grasping a rule which is *not* an *interpretation* but which is exhibited in what we call "obeying the rule" and "going against it" '! The negative point, that we gain no approach to the required fact by embarking on a potential regress of interpretations, is quite clear. The more positive claim, that the fact is exhibited in what we call obeying a rule, must wait.

When presenting the sceptical challenge this way, we should not lose sight of the fact that the case can be made without instancing a rival principle of application, a bent rule, at all. A sceptic might just doubt whether there was, yesterday or today, any principle at all behind my application of '+'. Perhaps all that happened was that I would look at things, such as triples of numbers, and after a process that was phenomenologically just like one of being guided by a rule, declare '$z = x + y$' I would be in the same case as a lunatic who thinks he is doing sums, when all that is happening is that he is covering pages with symbols. Or, I would be like the man whom Wittgenstein considers at §237, who with great deliberation follows a line with one leg of a pair of dividers, and lets the other leg trace a path, but one whose distance from the original line he varies in an intent but apparently random way. He might think he is tracing a path determined by a rule relating its course to the first line. But his thought that this is what he is doing does not make it true. In some ways this is the primary weapon that LW uses against the private linguist. He forces him back to saying that he has only his own conviction that he is following a rule at all, and this private, phenomenological conviction that one is following a rule is not enough to make it true.

I have followed Kripke in concentrating upon the normative aspect of the fact we are looking for. So I agree with him that the answer to the problem is not going to be given just by talking of dispositions we actually have. However, and crucially for what follows subsequently, I do not think the dispositional account falls to all of Kripke's objections. The analysis he considers (p. 26) says that I mean some function ϕ by my functor if and only if I am disposed, whenever queried about the application of the functor to a pair of numbers, to give the answer that actually is that function, ϕ, of them. Kripke attacks this on the grounds that my dispositions are finite. 'It is not true, for instance, that if queried about the sum of any two numbers, no matter how large, I will reply with their actual sum. For some numbers are simply too large for my mind—or my brain—to grasp' (pp. 26–27). So, according to

Kripke, my dispositions fail to make it true that I mean addition by '+' and not 'quaddition'—a function that gives different results just when x and y are so big that I cannot do sums involving them.

There are difficulties here. It is not obvious that dispositions in themselves are either finite or infinite. The brittleness of a glass is a respectable dispositional property. But there is an infinite number of places and times and strikings and surfaces on which it could be displayed. Does this glass have a disposition that covers, for example, the fact that it would break if banged on a rock on Alpha Centauri? What if scientists tell us that this glass couldn't get there, because it would have decayed within the time it takes to be transported there? Perhaps I am not disposed to give the answer faced with huge sums. But perhaps also I have dispositions that fix a sense for the expression 'the answer I would accept'. The answer I would accept is the one that *would* be given by reiterating procedures I *am* disposed to use, a number of times. (The notion is *doubly* dispositional.) The fact that I am not disposed to follow those procedures that number of times seems like the fact that the glass cannot get to Alpha Centauri. Now, a sceptic might maintain that we do not know of a dispositional fact about me that is described in this way. Perhaps I am only disposed to say that '3 + 5 = 8' when the calculation is not embedded in really huge calculations. But this is just scepticism about dispositions. It is like supposing that the glass may be not brittle but 'shmittle', where x is shmittle if it breaks when struck except. . . . In effect, this is inductive scepticism about the concept of a disposition, querying whether we can legitimately take dispositions to cover what would have happened on unobserved occasions. So it cannot be used to argue that even if we accept the concept, it permits no answer to the problem of huge calculations. A similar complication might answer Kripke's second objection (pp. 28–29). This is that what I mean cannot be read off from what I am disposed to do, since I may be disposed to make mistakes. The dispositionalist would have to read off what I meant from a table of answers I actually give, and this might involve saying that I was computing (correctly) a bent function—'skaddition'—and not making a mistake in attempting to add. But this seems to ignore surrounding dispositions. Kripke rightly dismisses any view that simply takes for granted a notion of the function it was intended to compute, or that defines user's competence, since it presupposes the ideas we are looking for. But at least it is true that a calculator can have, in addition to dispositions to give answers, dispositions to withdraw them and substitute others. And it is possible that putting the errant disposition into a context of general dispositions of this sort supplies the criterion for which function is meant. The equation would be: By '+' I mean that function ϕ that accords with my extended dispositions. An answer $z = \phi(x,y)$ accords with my extended dispositions if and only if (i) it is the answer I am disposed to give and retain after investigation, or (ii) it is the answer I would accept if I repeated a number of times procedures I am disposed to use, this being independent of whether I am disposed to repeat those procedures that number of times.

Kripke's point about mistakes can be illustrated if we consider a calculating machine. There is no physical or dispositional difference between a machine that is 'supposed' to compute addition but because of a mistake in the hardware computes a bent function, and one that is designed to compute the bent function in the first place. The two may be perfectly identical. This strongly suggests that the notion of correctness, the notion of *the* rule to which we are to be faithful, has to come from outside the thing itself. In the case of the calculator, it certainly does. But this need not entirely destroy a dispositional account, provided it can look for dispositions outside the simple disposition to give answers.

So is it a real truth that the right rule for '+' is in force among us? My own answer would be that we do have dispositions that enforce this judgement. They make it the only possible judgement about ourselves, when we describe each other's thoughts. The concealed bent-rule follower is a theoretician's fiction. Whenever we try to fill out the story of a person or a community that really adopts a bent rule, it turns out that the singularity in the rule (by our lights, of course) must affect the dispositions to behave that the community or individual shows. I have argued this elsewhere in connexion with Goodman's paradox.[8] The concealed bent-rule follower is often thought of as though nothing about him is different until the occasion of bent application arises. But this is wrong. Someone who has genuinely misunderstood a functor is different, and the difference can be displayed quite apart from occasions of application. Consider, for instance, the bricklayer told to add bricks to a stack two at a time. If this means to him 'add 2 up to 1000, and then 4', his reaction to the foreman may be quite different. Perhaps he cannot carry four bricks at a time.

However, I am not going to pursue this defence of dispositions. I share Kripke's view that whatever dispositions we succeed in identifying could at most give standards for selection of a function that we mean. They couldn't provide us with an account of what it is to be faithful to a previous rule. It is just that, unlike Kripke, I do not think dispositions are inadequate to the task of providing standards. Indeed, I think they *must* be adequate. For notice that the problem of finitude applies just as much to any community as to any individual. If the finiteness of an individual's dispositions leaves it indeterminate whether he means one function or another by some functor, then so must the finiteness of community disposition. So although communities induct their members into '+' using community practices and go through all the corrections and imitations that constitute community use, still, all that is consistent with the 'skaddition' hypothesis too. We don't find communities disposed to calculate numbers that are just too big. But prosecuting this point takes us into BW's divergence from KW.

III. The Community and the Individual

The individual has a hard time against Kripke's sceptic. How does the public fare better? The individual couldn't make the sceptic appreciate the kind of

---

8. *Reason and Prediction* (Cambridge: Cambridge University Press, 1973), chapter 4, and *Spreading the Word* (Oxford: Oxford University Press, 1984), chapter 3.

fact it was—that he was being faithful to a principle, or rule, or previous intention, when he gave some answer. The sceptic charges that there is no fact of the matter whether the bent rule or the natural rule was the one intended, or whether one principle of application or another was in force yesterday. And if there is no fact of the matter of this sort, then there is really no fact of the matter that any principle at all was in force. Any answer to the new sum can be regarded as equally 'right', and that means that we cannot talk about 'right'. Faced with this impasse, the individual thankfully turns to the community. He can point to his inculcation in a public practice, his gradual conformity to patterns of behaviour accepted by others, and his acceptance as a competent operator with '+'.

The sceptic might allow all this to make the difference. But he has suddenly gone very soft if he does. He can easily specify bent principles, with points of singularity where neither I nor anybody else used the terms yesterday. If such points worried the individual, then they should equally worry the community. So how does mention of the community give us the determinate rule?

KW's answer is that in a sense it doesn't (see, for instance, p. 111). The community is as much at a loss to identify the fugitive fact as the individual was. The position is supposed to be no different metaphysically. The difference is that the community endorses or accepts the competent operator. They or 'we' *allow* him to be using '+' to mean addition. He is 'seen' or *dignified* as a rule-follower. We, the community, have justification conditions for doing this. To gain the title, the individual's practice (on the finite number of occasions when it will have been shown) must accord in some suitable way with the community practice (on the finite number of occasions when *it* will have been shown).

Now, merely citing the fact that we 'see each other as' obeying the same principle of application makes no headway at all. Remember that the point of the original worries about rule-following was not epistemological. The aim was not to suggest that we cannot provide a foundation of some sort for the judgement that a rule is in force, or that we cannot provide principles for inferring such judgements from other, more basic principles. If this were the aim, then replying that there is no inference and no foundation, but just a basic fact that we make such judgements of each other, 'seeing each other as' following principles might be relevant—at any rate, as relevant as this move is in other areas of epistemology. But making this point does nothing to suggest *how* we are seeing each other when we say such a thing. We know well enough what it is to see something as a duck, because we know what ducks are. But we don't know what it is to see someone as obeying a principle of application, unless we know what it is to follow one, and so far we still have no conception of this. To put it another way, we do not know what a community would be lacking if its members failed to see each other this way, or if they continually saw each other in the light of potential bent-rule followers.

So the sceptic is still liable to feel short-changed. He has pointed out bent rules that might have been in force yesterday, compatibly with all that the individual could point to. He has pointed out that for all that the individual could show, there might be nothing but his onward illusion that rules are in force and that his dispositions to respond are correct or incorrect. The individual now links arms with others. The sceptic attempts to point out the same two things to them: for all they can describe about themselves, bent rules (and perhaps differently bent rules) might have been in force, underlying their fortuitous coincidence of behavior over the finite samples they have come across. Since this means that any answer to a new problem might be as correct as any other, the sceptic suggests that again there is just the onward illusion that there is correctness or incorrectness. The community replies that it has a practice of dignifying its members as saying things correctly or incorrectly, and in the light of this practice it says that all its members do mean the same, and that what they mean provides a principle of application of a term.

We can see one way in which this could silence the sceptic. If the mutual support itself provides the standard of correctness, then a community can answer him. To understand this, consider the analogy with an orchestra. Suppose that there is no such thing as an individual playing in accord with instructions coming down from the past, by way of scores or memory. Suppose too that on an individual instrument there is no standard for the way a piece ought to go (all melodies are equally acceptable). Then an individual cannot play well or badly in isolation. Nevertheless, the orchestra may have standards of harmony across instruments. And at a given time most instruments are playing, say, notes from the chord of C major, then the individual who hits a dissonant C# is incorrect by the standards of the orchestra. They can turn on him. Unfortunately, this provides only a poor analogy for communities and their relations to their own rule-following. For in the orchestra, harmony with others provides a direct standard of correctness. This is not so with judgement. My community may all suddenly start saying that $57 + 68 = 5$, but this does not make me wrong when I continue to assert that it is 125. I am correct today in saying that the sun is shining and daffodils are yellow, regardless of what the rest of the world says. Obviously, any solution to these problems must avoid the disastrous conclusion that it is part of the truth-condition of any judgement that a community would make it (unless of course the judgement is itself not about the sun and daffodils and so on, but about the community).

If the community cannot turn to the orchestral metaphor, then how have they answered the sceptic? And why cannot their answer be taken over by the isolated individual? Remember that there is a distinction between the overall practice of a community, thought of as something defined by principles and rules, and the exposed practice, thought of as only a partial, finite segment of applications. If a community practices addition, meaning one thing and not another by some functor '+', then the exposed practice will cover only a small proportion of the applications whose correctness follows from the overall practice. As the possibility of bent functions is supposed to show, the exposed practice does not logically determine the question of which overall practice is in force. Then we can imagine what we might call a 'thoroughly Good-manned community' in which people take explanations and exposure to small samples—yesterday's applications—in different ways. The sceptic who won against Kripke's individual will now win against a community, showing that they have no conception of the fact that makes it true that they do not form a thoroughly Goodmanned community.

It may be helpful to think of it like this: The members of a community stand to each other as the momentary time-slices of an individual do. So just as the original sceptic queries what it is for one person-time to be faithful to a rule adopted by a previous person-time, so the public sceptic queries what it is for one person to be faithful to the same rule as that adopted by another. Now if the public sceptic can be bypassed by, in effect, saying that this is what we do—we see each other as mutually understanding the same rule, or dignify or compliment each other as so doing, provided the exposed practice agrees well enough—then the private sceptic can be bypassed in the same way. His doubts admit of the same projective solution. When LW denies that 'we have a model of this superlative fact' (§192), we can, as far as the metaphysics goes, shrug and say that this is how we see ourselves. Then, as I have already explained, the entire problem is to explain how we are seeing ourselves when we go into this mode. In particular we need to cite some *standard* for saying this—and, if LW is to win through, a standard that separates the public from the individual. For when I write the sensation term in my diary I can and will see myself as being faithful to a previous intention to apply it only in a determinate range of circumstances. And, paying me the compliment (as it were), you can do so too. It might be different if it somehow were natural for us to dignify fellow members of the same public with the title of rule followers, and natural to hesitate over any purely private attempt at self-description. But generally speaking, there is little difference in naturalness. Until LW supposedly argues that we shouldn't do so, most people would find it quite natural to believe that a putative private linguist might be following or failing to follow previously formed intentions to apply principles of application.

The dilemma so far is this. If the presence or potential presence of a community of persons practising the same way enters as part of the truth-conditions, part of the analysis, of what it is to follow a rule, the sceptic who won against the private individual looks equally set to win against a community that has the benefit of mutual support. But if mention of the community comes as part of a Humean or projective solution, allowing us to bypass troubles over our conception of the superlative fact, then a similar side-step is in principle available to the individual. To split the individual from the public we need enough understanding of how we are regarding ourselves to be able to specify standards that need to be met by a candidate for rule-following, and we have not yet got this.

The simple move, endorsed by KW and, for instance, by Peacocke, is to say that in the case of the individual there is no distinction between it seeming to him that a rule is in force, and there being a rule in force. The trouble with this is that in any sense in which it is true (see next section), it is equally true

9. *Enquiry,* section I.

that there is no distinction between a community being thoroughly Good-manned but seeming to itself to have a unified practice, and its actually having a unified practice. And when the community says 'well, we just see ourselves as agreeing (dignify or compliment ourselves as comprehending the same rule)', the individual just borrows the trick, and compliments himself on his rapport with his previous times. The community needs to say that the compliment is *empty* in the case of one individual but meaningful in the case of a set of them. How is this to be argued?

IV. Public and Private Practice

Peacocke writes:

> In the end, Wittgenstein holds, the only thing that must be true of someone who is trying to follow a rule, so long as we consider just the individual and not facts about some community, is that he is disposed to think that certain cases fall under the rule and others do not. But this is something which is also true of a person who falsely believes that he is conforming to a rule. His general argument is that only by appealing to the fact that the genuine rule-follower agrees in his reactions to examples with the members of some community can we say what distinguishes him from someone who falsely thinks he is following a rule.[10]

The lynch-pin of this interpretation is the absence of a 'distinction', in the case of an individual, between the case where he believes that there is a rule when there is none and the case where he believes it and there is one. And my question has been: do we think we have yet been given a 'distinction' between a thoroughly Goodmanned community accidentally agreeing in exposed practice and a real community of understanding? And then, if the distinction is given using materials from Hume—the projection upon one another of a dignity—I ask what the standards are whereby it takes several people to do this, when one cannot do it to himself. I shall now try to exhibit the force of this question by considering the individual further. This is to illustrate the gap between anything that has happened in LW, at least as far as §202, and the application to exclude the private linguist.

Let us recall the basic point that giving an explanation, either in words or using other aids, such as pictures or models, does not logically determine the rule that governs one's understanding of a term: 'Any interpretation still hangs in the air along with what it interprets, and cannot give it any support' (§198). To avoid the threatening paradox that nothing can accord nor conflict with a rule, because anything can be made out so to do, LW introduces the positive suggestion that our rules are anchored in practice. In the remainder of this paper I shall assume that this is along the right lines. That is, dignifying each other as rule-following is essentially connected with seeing each other as

---

10. C. Peacocke, 'Rule Following: The Nature of Wittgenstein's Arguments', in S. Holtzman and S. Leich, eds., *Wittgenstein: To Follow a Rule* (London: Routledge & Kegan Paul, 1981), p. 73.

successfully using techniques or practices. This at least begins to isolate the nature of the judgement. It suggests a direction from which to find standards for making the judgement, and in my view it connects interestingly with pragmatic and coherence aspects of judging. Now, having introduced the notion of a practice or technique. LW immediately goes on to draw two famous conclusions: that to think one is obeying a rule is not to do so, and that it is not possible to obey a rule privately. These are not the same, and the second is not warranted. The question is, what kind of thing does a practice have to be if it is to block the sceptical paradox? Perhaps, for instance, the concept of a practice can include that of someone setting out to describe his mental life, even on a highly private conception of the mental. The basic negative point certainly does not rule that out. To do so we would need further thoughts about what a practice must be, and the connexion it is supposed to need with actual or possible publics. It is therefore a great pity that, with one eye cocked on the later applications, commentators simply assume that by §202 the publicity of practice has been satisfactorily argued (Peacocke, for instance, just announces that 'by "practice" he here means the practice of a community' [p. 72]). Of course, many believe that the later discussion of sensation *S* and so on justifies the restriction. But that is another issue; to invoke it is to abandon the hope that the rule-following considerations provide wider, more general thoughts from which the anti–private language conclusion independently emerges. To illustrate the gap, we can consider the halfway house (to full privacy) provided by Robinson Crusoe cases.

Consider the example (due to Michael Dummett) of a born Crusoe who finds a Rubik's cube washed onto his island, and learns to solve it. The fact is that he does it. He certainly doesn't solve it randomly, for he can do it on demand. It is natural to say that he follows principles ('when there is a last corner left, do *x* . . .'). Perhaps he has some rudimentary diagrams or other mnemonics that he consults. With these he can do it, and without them he cannot. Kripke considers what LW's attitude should be to such a case. The attitude he offers, on behalf of KW, is that we can think of Crusoe, in such a case as this, as following rules. But, 'If we think of Crusoe as following rules, we are taking him into our community and applying our criteria for rule-following to him'. The sceptical considerations are supposed to show 'not that a *physically isolated* individual cannot be said to follow rules; rather than an individual *considered in isolation* (whether or not he is physically isolated) cannot be said to do so'.[11] Again there is a nice parallel (although not quite the one Kripke makes) with Hume. One conclusion that might be drawn from Hume is *not* that a pair of events in a universe with no others cannot be related causally (which is how Kripke takes Hume); rather, if we suppose that they are, we are thinking of them as members of a (potential) family of other regularly related events. We are not considering them in isolation, but, for instance, are thinking of what would happen if there were others like them.

Still, it is not clear what the compromise is. Certainly I, or we, are doing

11. Kripke says useful things about this, pp. 90 ff.

the thought-experiment. I have to consider whether Crusoe is a rule-follower by using the normal, community-wide way I make the judgement. But that would be true of any situation I seek to describe. And then, just as (*contra* Berkeley) I might conclude that an island considered in isolation has a tree on it, might I not conclude that Crusoe, considered in isolation, was following a rule? How does the phrase 'considered in isolation' bring the community further into the picture in this case than in the case of the tree? We are apt to retort that Crusoe would have been a rule-follower in this situation whatever I or we or any other community in the world had thought about it—just like the tree. And the reason is that all by himself he had a technique or practice.

Now reconsider the private linguist, meaning someone who believes that he has given an inner state a semantically essential role. Suppose he believes that yesterday, in the presence of the state, he defined for himself a qualitative similarity that other states might bear to it; that he is on the lookout for recurrence and involved in the practice of judging whether such a recurrence takes place. We seek to show that this is not a real practice. Let our private linguist accept the basic point, admitting that the mere offering of words, images, and so on does not determine a rule of application, or principle, that is really in force. But he does not accept that his candidate practice is unsatisfactory. What has LW got to show him?

'Whatever is going to seem right is right'—there is no distinction between his seeming to himself to follow a rule and his genuinely doing so. It has often been suggested that this charge is unargued, or, if argued, only supported by overtly verificationist considerations. My endeavour has been to show how difficult it is to release the public from its attack. In the light of this, let us reconsider the projective and naturalistic elements that assisted the public: the point that we naturally and perhaps usefully regard ourselves as mutual possessors of the same understanding. We see ourselves so, and this attitude is, in Humean vein, immune from sceptical destruction. Furthermore, there is no lowering of the truth-condition of this judgement. It sits with its own vocabulary and scorns any 'account' of it in other terms. It is just that if a public failed to see itself in this light, it would mean that it could only see the ongoing patterns of noise and reaction, in which no principle, no genuine judgement, no truth and falsity, is visible.

My criticism of the flat reply to the sceptical problem ('this is how we see ourselves') was, in effect, that it gave no account of what a community would be missing if it failed to see itself in this light. Following LW we have accepted that the clue to what is missing is to come from the notion of a practice. BW therefore uses this thought and the fact that dispositions provide satisfactory standards for the making of the judgement. As with other judgements with normative elements, there is no attempt to make a lowering of the truth-condition. The judgement can be seen perfectly well in terms of the projection of an attitude (this cannot be uncongenial to LW). But that left us unclear about the standards for applying it. BW therefore accepts most of what emerges from LW, doing less violence to the redundancy theory and to the preparedness to talk of facts, even when the underlying metaphysic is not what that might suggest. But however well BW matches LW, Blackburn insists on asking: is there any reason why the private linguist should not so regard himself? And in that case *whose* is the attitude 'whatever is going to seem right is right'? Not the subject's own, for he dignifies himself as a genuine believer, as having a principle of application and making a judgement with it. In doing so he *allows* the possibility of mistake (it is not something there in the things going on in his head or in his behaviour; it is something arising as a projection from an attitude he takes up to his own projects). It is a component of his attitude that a particular judgement might turn out better regarded as mistaken.

How can this attitude be appropriate? A technique is something that can be followed well or badly; a practice is something in which success *matters*. Now in the usual scenario, the correctness or incorrectness of the private linguist's classification is given no consequence at all. It has no use. He writes in his diary, and, so far as we are told, forgets it. So when LW imagines a use made of the report (e.g., to indicate the rise of the manometer) he immediately hypothesizes a public use. He thereby skips the intermediate case where the classification is given a putative private use. It fits into a project—a practice or technique—of ordering the expectation of recurrence of sensation, with an aim at prediction, explanation, systematization, or simple maximizing of desirable sensation. To someone engaged on this project, the attitude that whatever seems right is right is ludicrous. System soon enforces recognition of fallibility.

I conclude then that it is no mistake to see the latter sections, from §240 onward, as integral to the anti–private language polemic. BW simply cannot separate the private from the public with any considerations that are in force earlier on. But I have tried to suggest other things as well. Following through the problem of answering the paradox leads to sympathy with a basically 'anti-metaphysical' conception of rule-following. We simply cannot deliver, in other terms, accounts of what constitutes shared following of a rule, or what the fact of a rule being in force 'consists in'. In my view this invites a projectivist explanation of these kinds of judgement, although also in my view we cannot conclude that it is improper to talk of 'facts of the case'. In any event, we are left searching for standards whereby to make the judgement. It is possible that those standards should exactly separate the public from the private (on some vulnerable conception of the private, of course). But there is no particular reason to expect them to do so. The problems with dispositions, either as giving us the missing kind of fact, or as providing standards for allowing that a rule is in force, failed to separate the public and the individual. So we cannot now simply *demand* from the putative private-linguist an 'account of what the distinction [between genuinely following a rule and only seeming to himself to do so] amounts to'. He can reply, 'It amounts to all that it does in the case of the public'. Just as a public dignifies itself as producing more than an interminable flood of words and noise, and sees itself as making mutually comprehensible judgements, capable of truth and falsity, so does he. The public doubtless has a purpose in doing this, and is right to do it. When his putative discriminations are part of a practice, so does he.

13

Losing Your Mind: Physics, Identity, and Folk Burglar Prevention*

In this essay I introduce a paradox in much current thinking about physics. The paradox is that physics (and indeed any human thought) never identifies causes—real causes. It may give us causal explanations, but these are only ways of pointing toward the real causes, or features in virtue of which effects follow causes. The paradoxical conclusion is that the predicates we use do not express or refer to the causally powerful properties or states. We can head toward the engine room, perhaps, but never get there. I diagnose current eliminativism in the philosophy of mind as largely the upshot of the paradoxical way of thinking. If I am right, its proponents have done a great service, giving us an outward and visible sign of an inner spiritual tangle. I start by saying a little about eliminativism, by way of introducing the way of thinking about physics that, according to me, it depends upon, and thence identifying the paradox.

The prophets of eliminativism may follow one of two models in their attitude to the categories whereby we understand ourselves and each other in terms of what we feel, think, believe, intend, desire. One model is the prophet Isaiah ('from the sole of the foot even unto the head there is no soundness in it'), and the other is John the Baptist ('there cometh one mightier than I after me'). The frequent comparisons of commonsense psychology to caloric theory, phlogiston theory, or demonology suggest the first, whereas the mere belief that in the future something better may turn up, by some standards of accurate prediction, completeness, simplicity, or capacity to deal with borderline cases, gives only the second. It is only on the first model that there is something false in commonsense psychology. The second attitude no more suggests that commonsense categories falsify things than belief in Newtonian mechanics falsifies the folk view that it is harder to lift a heavy stone than a light one, or belief in hydrodynamics falsifies the view that there are rivers.

In this essay I oppose only the stronger doctrine. What is wrong with

*This essay owes an unusual amount to discussion and correspondence. I particularly want to thank Ned Block, Mark Rowlands, Philip Pettit, and Marianne Talbot, as well as Jay Rosenberg and the other symposiasts at the Greensboro Colloquium in 1988. An especial debt is due to David Lewis, whose patient incredulity enabled me to avoid many errors.

strong eliminativism is not its saying that a particular mode of description may one day be replaced. I have no quarrel (how could one quarrel?) with the bare possibility of future modes of understanding that somehow improve on those of folk psychology. Equally I have no quarrel with the bare possibility of future modes of understanding that similarly improve on those of folk geography or furniture classification. Again, many of the arguments against common-sense categories detail particular hard cases of belief ascription and cases where attribution of content is underdetermined.[1] I shall not be concerned with these; there is, after all, no general doctrine that denies a term any application because it is polycriterial or gives rise to difficult or borderline cases. Finally, there is the issue of norms of rationality versus the natural—the issues concerning correctness that burgeon into the rule-following consider-ations; but I shall not be centrally concerned with these either. Instead I shall argue that what is wrong with current eliminativism is its claim to see how commonsense psychological description conflicts with science.

I. The Theory-Theory

To engage with eliminativism, I shall make one concession at the outset. This is that 'commonsense psychology' should be identified as being, in some suitable sense, a 'theory'. For the purposes of this paper I shall accept that the terms of commonsense psychology get their meaning from an implicit func-tional definition, or a network of sayings, platitudes even, connecting beliefs, desires, and the rest with typical causes, typical interrelations, and typical effects. Saying that commonsense psychology is a theory, in this weak sense, is not inconsistent with allowing that it is used to do many things, nor with allowing that we often know by observation, or direct access to our own states, what we ourselves and others believe, desire, and so on.[2] If we are to reject the view that it forms a theory, this ought, I believe, to be on the grounds that it suggests an unsustainable asymmetry between my own case (observational, direct knowledge) and the third-person case (theoretical, indi-rect knowledge), but in this paper I shall not pursue that problem.

For eliminativism, the term 'theory' in fact functions as a staging post: because of some considerations, commonsense psychology is well regarded as a theory, but theories are corrigible, hence *it* is corrigible, and the question of its replacement may be raised. The view that terms are introduced by implicit functional definition, which I shall call the role or network model of them, does not itself immediately carry implications of corrigibility. Its doing so depends on the corrigibility of the elements of the network—the generaliza-tions that keep commonsense psychological terms in place and enable them to

---

1. Stephen Stich, *From Folk Psychology to Cognitive Science* (Cambridge, Mass.: Bradford Books, 1983), especially chapters 4 and 5.

2. This point is well made by Patricia Churchland, 'Replies to Comments', in *Inquiry*, 1986, p. 254. But I am now much more sceptical of the virtues of the 'theory' idiom: see my 'Theory, Observation and Drama', in *Mind and Language*, 1992.

be used in explanation and prediction. It is not obvious how corrigible these
are. A sample list includes such things as

- Barring self-control, anger causes impatience and antisocial behaviour.
- Barring a stronger contrary purpose, hunger causes eating.
- Barring pathological personality or circumstance, the apprehended loss
  of loved ones causes grief.[3]
- People generally do what they say they will do.
- Intending *P* & *Q* is normally sufficient for intending *P* and intending *Q*
  (from Fodor).[4]

Suppose we agree that such generalizations underlie commonsense practice, in the sense that if they are denied, commonsense psychology will have
no explanatory and predictive use, and no terms with any meaning. Still the
examples do little to show us how commonsense theory is corrigible. For we
may have very little idea indeed how scientific progress, or any other, could
tempt us to abandon any of them, let alone sufficient of them to count as
abandoning the overall commonsense perspective (nobody is concentrating
on small adjustments in this debate).

The real danger in using the word 'theory' is supposing that it does this
work for us. Stich and Churchland frequently remind us of other 'folk theories' that might once have inspired similar certainties, but turned out wrong
root and branch: folk demonology, folk cosmology, folk dynamics. As Stich
roundly puts it: 'Nor is there any reason to think that ancient camel drivers
would have greater insight or better luck when the subject at hand was the
structure of their own minds rather than the structure of matter or of the
cosmos.'[5] But the question will be whether the certainties—the platitudes
exampled above—of commonsense psychology could be relevantly similar to
the mistakes early scientific theory made about force, inertia, demons, or
motion. It is certainly overplaying anything gained by introducing the word
'theory' to suppose that it guarantees such a similarity. Since the role or
network view applies to any term, the right point of comparison may be not
early cosmology and dynamics, but those other things that camel drivers
doubtless got quite right as they skilfully coped with their world: such unpretentious certainties as that generally it takes more effort to lift a heavy
stone than a light one, that sunshine warms and dampness chills, that people
may safely drink water but also can drown in it, that a long journey takes
more time than a short one, and so on without end. The very generality of
holistic considerations and the network model shows that these may be much
nearer the right points of comparison than anything more overtly 'theoretical'. So we have nothing to support the vision of likely error.

The same trap of overplaying what is achieved by introducing the term
'theory' is fallen into by Paul Churchland when he charges that commonsense

---

3. Patricia Churchland, op. cit., p. 256. See also Paul Churchland, 'Eliminative Materialism
and Propositional Attitudes', in *Journal of Philosophy*, 1981, p. 71.
4. J. Fodor, *Psychosemantics* (Cambridge, Mass.: Bradford Books, 1987), chapters 1–3.
5. Stich, *Folk Psychology*, p. 229.

psychology is likely to be bad theory, since it is both incomplete in its domain and stagnant.[6] Whether or not these are bad signs in science, or at least in research science, they certainly need not be in the loosely knit body of platitudes connecting hunger and attempts to get food, or anger and bad behaviour. Nothing in the network model shows that if concepts are suitable for stating truths, the generalizations of the network must be complete by any standard. Nor need they be under pressure to evolve. Perhaps they remain unchanging through the generations because they are certain, like the platitudes about sunshine, rain, and longer journeys taking more time: one man's stagnation is another man's certainty. It is also relevant to point out that the impression of stagnation may be largely an artefact of the philosophical tendency to abstraction—to talking as if the only relevant concepts are belief and desire. If one looks instead at the richer textures of psychological understanding that inform our lives, change is much more readily visible (it is also noticeable that change typically does not bring falsification: in a future culture people may not think in terms of, for instance, 'falling in love', and may not do so, but that would not refute the fact that *we* do both).

On the other hand, it will not help to press the other way—to say, for example, that the sample generalizations are incorrigible because close to tautologous, or, if we prefer, 'criterial' for the states of anger, hunger, intention. For this meets the familiar point that if the criteria for the existence of a state, in terms, say, of what causes it, are *a priori,* and if there are similar *a priori* criteria for its consequences, then to avoid a pretended *a priori* status for what is all too visibly a contingent and *a posteriori* matter—the correlation between the antecedents and the consequences—it must be contingent and *a posteriori* that any such state exists. Better then not to award too grand a status to arbitrary elements of the network. Our success in understanding one another is at least a success in putting behaviour into familiar patterns, and it is a contingent fact that those patterns are not disrupted, in one or many instances, sufficiently to baffle the attempt.

II. The Sovereignty of Physics

We now engage the essential part of the position: the idea that there is sufficient tension between the claims of folk psychology and the increasing body of knowledge of the sciences for it to be on the cards that the sciences undermine it. The general eliminativist strategy is to try to say something specific about the kind of state that having a belief or desire must be taken to be, and then to argue that there may be no possibility of evolving science countenancing that state.

Within that general strategy there are two ends to work from. One might have a precise and exclusive sense of the states that science countenances, and do relatively little to show that psychological states fail. Or one might think

6. Paul Churchland, op. cit., p. 74.

that there is something very specific about psychological states such that, without too much precision about science, one can nevertheless see that science cannot countenance them. Of course, one can work from both ends at once. Because it is physical thinking that centrally troubles me, I consider the first end the more important.

Let us accept the sovereignty of physics. I take this sovereignty to be an ontological thesis best stated in terms of supervenience: we suppose that fixing all the facts discernible to physics fixes everything.[7] This does not deny the existence of things, states, and perhaps properties that supervene on the physical. But it ought to deny that there is a dimension of freedom in the way these things supervene: it should not be contingent whether, given the physical truth, there is also this or that further truth, of chemistry, or biology, or psychology. David Lewis believes that supervenience will be contingent upon the absence of 'alien' properties, but I hope that their absence will be a truth of our physics. If the way the supervening facts overlaid the total physical truth were contingent, God would have to fix something else than the physics: he would have to fix the possible relations that the overlying truths bear to the physics. Real sovereignty should mean that there is not this extra thing to do. Only if real sovereignty exists is everything physically fixed. Otherwise the ways in which extra states overlie the physical states would amount to further contingencies, ineradicable 'nomological danglers'. We could well mark the difference by saying that the sovereignty of physics cannot countenance emergent properties, where emergence is thought of as a brute contingent extra, but can countenance supervenient properties. Supervenience is physically fixed emergence.

If there is supervenience, is there to be physical explicability? Clearly the natural or best explanation of a physical thing having a physical property need not belong to physics. In most contexts, the best explanation of this chair being within three miles of Carfax may be that it belongs to me, and this is where I live. The doctrine of the sovereignty of physics implies only that the position of the chair is physically fixed, not that the explanation is the most natural or quickest to give, or the one asked for in any particular context. But there should be this connexion with explanation: another God, who knew how the creating God has fixed the physics, could explain why the chair is where it is.

The doctrine of the sovereignty of physics does not entail determinism over time. It does not entail that if God has fixed the physics and the laws at t, he has thereby fixed the states of the world at t'. He may or may not have. Sovereignty is a synchronic doctrine, not a diachronic one. But it should not be read as implying that fixing the physics at a snapshot time t fixes all the facts at t. It might not fix the historical facts at t, such as how big the tree was three years ago, and in principle this might matter to the evolution of physical states after t. To allow for indeterminism and external facts of this sort, it is best to

---

7. This definition is also given by, e.g., John Haugeland, 'Weak Supervenience', in *American Philosophical Quarterly*, 1982.

use two temporal quantifiers: read the doctrine as saying that anything that fixes all the physical facts *at every time* fixes all the other facts that obtain *at any time*.

We are looking for argument implying that the sovereignty of physics threatens the existence of psychological states. So which states does a science like physics countenace? The question is ambiguous. It may be asking which states physics allows and which it disallows. Or it may be asking which states physics describes—which it is concerned with. It is one thing for any science to imply that some state cannot exist, and a quite different thing for it simply to work in other terms. Physics may deny, for instance, that some kind of causation exists ('ghostly mental causation', perhaps) because it would break conservation laws. But it does not deny that chairs exist, just by working in other terms. Chairs are physical things.

Matters apparently stay the same when we think of properties, or states of affairs: chairhood, or being a chair or a chiliagon. Singular reference introduces more freedom in our descriptions of fact: physics does not work with the predicate 'being within three miles of Carfax'. Yet surely its sovereignty is consistent with truths of the form 'this chair is within three miles of Carfax'.

There is a seductive answer to the question of which states physics countenances, which goes like this: Since physics is sovereign, a true theory must be reducible to physics. Folk psychology is a theory; hence, if it is true it must reduce to physics. But reduction implies coextensive predicates to give us an 'image' of the theory taken over in the larger theory. However, there is no real prospect of there being physical predicates coextensive with those of psychology. Hence, there is no real prospect of psychological theory being true.[8] In this argument the sovereignty of physics is taken to imply that all truths can be given an extension-preserving mapping into truths of that science. The implication is that if 'thinking that the ornaments need dusting' cannot be made to correspond to a kind of physical theory, it cannot be true that people think that the ornaments need dusting. But why is this argument more plausible than an equivalent proof that there are no chairs within three miles of Carfax?

I shall come at this problem by considering the dialectic with which Patricia Churchland supports one part of her position. Her concern is to deny that functionalism defends psychology against the requirement of reduction. (Functionalism is here not much more than a label for the role theory, talking of what we do because of our psychological states and what typically gets us into them.) Functionalism famously deflects the demand for reduction because in talking of functional identities between things we remain indifferent to sameness or difference of underlying physical states and mechanisms. This is true within a science: in physics, radios, resistors, thermometers, and batteries can be made of many different kinds of thing. In biology, birds and bees both fly, but the material constitution of their wings and muscles is different. This

---

8. This is my phrasing of the view I take to be implicit in Patricia Churchland's *Neurophilosophy* (Cambridge, Mass.: Bradford Books, 1986), chapter 7.

suggests the possibility of benign cross-classification between psychology and physics. As it is often put, there are 'role states' and variable 'realizing states'. Churchland opposes this rapprochement with two arguments.

Considering the equation of temperature with mean kinetic energy of molecules, she rightly points out that the identity is inapplicable to the temperature of solids, of plasmas, and of empty space. It is unattractive to deny that there is a reduction of temperature to mean kinetic energy of molecules, so the moral she draws is that reduction can be domain-specific: temperature can be one thing in a gas, another in other things. 'Though this is called "multiple instantiability" and is draped in black by the functionalist, it is seen as part of normal business in the rest of science . . .'[9] The moral is that reduction may be relative to a domain: 'we may, in the fullness of time and after much co-evolution in theories, have one reductive account of, say, goals or pain in vertebrates, a different account for invertebrates, and so forth'. The implication is that wherever the predicates cross-classify, there is still to be found a physical state which 'is' the property (of believing that *p* or being in pain or whatever) in one thing, and another which 'is' the same property in another thing.

The dialectical position is a little confused here. If reduction is allowed to go on in this way, then it will not require extension-preserving translations of predicates of the old theory into those of the reducing theory. It simply will not matter whether one physical kind (and term) or many exist that correspond to the old term. If there are many, we just say that temperature (or whatever) is one thing in the one case, and another in the others. This gives us a very relaxed attitude to the relation between the old predicates and their physical partners, and one would have thought that far from draping such a thing in black, the functionalist is happily celebrating the freedom thus offered. It becomes no argument either against functionalism or against the reduction by these standards of any folk theory to physics, that no extension-preserving mappings can be found. So how does Churchland see this claim as difficult for the functionalist, and good for the eliminativist? Surely it is because she sees the underlying classifications as the only real ones, so that the concept of temperature turns out to lack 'empirical integrity' once this many–one relationship to underlying physics emerges. It is as if God, to know everything, can now avert his eyes from old-style temperature, the original role state, and look at only the differing energies or realizing states. He would need to frame no claims involving temperature to know everything. Temperature has lost 'empirical integrity'. In this view, physics as it were absorbs the role state into the realizing state, and thus eliminates it.

The same attitude to physics is visible in the second thing that Churchland says. Following Enç, she makes the point that mean kinetic energy of molecules in a gas may itself be 'variably realized' since identity of mean kinetic energy is compatible with quite different distribution of molecules and directions of motion: a given volume of gas may stay the same temperature as its

9. Op. cit., p. 357

molecules change position. 'To be consistent functionalists should again deny reductive success to statistical mechanics since, as they would put it, temperature of a gas is differently realized in the two cases. If, on the other hand, they want to concede reduction here but withhold its possibility from psychology, they need to do more than merely predict hardware differences between species or between individuals.'[10] Again, the implication is that with the expanded vision that enables us to see the endless variation in molecular position, the overlying role state becomes invisible: reduced, eliminated.

III. Physical Thinking

Many readers will be protesting that the last two words of the last section should not go together. The identification of role state with realizer state, they say, is certainly a reduction, but certainly not an elimination. Before commenting on that, I shall say a little about whether we should accept Churchland's description of the case in physics.

If a bright learner asks the teacher why we can talk of the temperature of a solid, when temperature is mean kinetic energy of molecules, and those in the solid are not moving, it is hardly satisfactory to reply that temperature is one thing in gases and another thing elsewhere. The learner wants to know what justifies us in talking of the same property at all, so that a solid and a liquid each can be at 100° Celsius, for instance. And there had better be an answer.

Of course there is. Physics can explain how gases, liquids, solids, and space can be at the same temperature. In equilibrium thermodynamics the concept of temperature is justified in the first place by the zeroth law, that if two bodies are in thermal equilibrium with each other, and one is in equilibrium with a third, then the other is also in equilibrium with the third.[11] This is what allows for the definition of an equivalence class of systems in thermal equilibrium. The definitions allow for gases, solids, and any other physical system to be in thermal equilibrium with one another. They are in equilibrium when no net energy transfer arises from their thermal contact (e.g., from placing the body in the space or gas or liquid). This will be because of a relation between the mean kinetic energy of molecules in the gas, and whatever makes up the thermal energy of the other system: the vibration energies of molecules in some solids, of molecules and electrons in metals, and so forth.

Should we identify temperature with these 'realizations'? Why should we want to? We already have it down as the property two systems have in common when they are each capable of thermal equilibrium with a third. In other words, the fundamental thing to be said about temperature, as about number and most concepts of physics, is that what is needed is a definition of the equivalence relation of having the same temperature as . . . ; this and the

10. Op. cit., p. 357
11. See, e.g., C. J. Adkins, *Equilibrium Thermodynamics* (New York: Cambridge University Press, 1983).

further relations necessary to produce a scale are provided, and nothing further need be said about what temperature is, although a great deal can be said about the kind of energy involved and its source in the kinetic energy of molecules or other property of the body, gas, space, and so on. We also see why the consequence Churchland is drawing, that propositions about temperature become invisible to science, is undesirable, to put it mildly: why should we reject the salient equivalences as unreal just because we have found a mechanism for them?

So one must beware of rewriting the relation between thermodynamics and kinetic theory as if a question of identity and its answer were the main point. In physics, as opposed to philosophical glosses on it, there is simply no use for a statement like 'the temperature in this system is . . .' that implies, for instance, that over a phase change the temperature has to change (it was one thing, e.g., the kinetic energy of moving molecules, and is now another, e.g., the vibration energy of static molecules). On the contrary, the only use physics has for the form 'the temperature is . . .' insists that the temperature of a solid and a gas in equilibrium is the same: 0°C, for instance.

It may help to see this if we reflect that the equivalence between two volumes of gas at the same temperature is an equivalence visible to the kinetic theory. Sharing mean kinetic energy of molecules is a concept of the theory and defines an equivalence class of volumes of gases. In fact, given the gas laws it follows from the equation of pressure with transferred momentum that temperature in a perfect gas must vary with mean kinetic energy—the concept as it were forces itself on the subject. Enç is therefore wrong to say that mean kinetic energy is a kind term of kinematics 'only by courtesy'.[12] One might as well say that energy is a concept of classical dynamics only by courtesy, or (since things of different constitutions each do it) that being in a state of uniform motion in a straight line is a concept of physics only by courtesy. Physics is not at all confined to constitutional kinds (as if it were not a physical truth that differently composed material things might share mass or charge or velocity).

To use a different example, finding what is the same about a closed system of objects at different heights and moving at different velocities in a gravitational field was a great achievement of classical dynamics. It was only by doing this that dynamics identified the equivalence of potential and kinetic energy. The whole point of the concept is that it classifies across difference of 'state', where that is conceived in terms of mere spatial array and velocity of constituent particles. For just this reason it would be a misdescription of two such systems to say that energy is 'one thing' in one system and another in another, merely because the positions and velocities of the particles are different.

I now present the first part of my paradox. It is essential to physical understanding that its predicates unify. They classify across differences of realization, for the following reason: The basic concept is that of a system in a state. The state is characterized by intensive and extensive magnitudes: pres-

12. Berent Enç, 'In Defence of the Identity Theory', in *Journal of Philosophy*, 1980, p. 279.

sure, force, and density are intensive (local) magnitudes, and mass, volume, and internal energy extensive ones. These magnitudes take possible values (the number that are capable of independent fix defines the number of degrees of freedom of the system); the art of the physicist is to find the right variables and the right laws connecting them to give a function for the evolution of one state into another. Now it is absolutely vital to doing this that concepts emerge that cover systems with different forms of thermal energy, or cover changes of 'realization'—that allow, for example, for something such as temperature or entropy which applies indifferently across changes of phase from solid or liquid to gas. If there is no unification, there is no scope for conservation across changes, and the central concept of physical thinking disappears.

I sum up this truth about physics in the thesis (T): physical thinking is essentially a question of finding the one state that covers many realizations. It is forever a question of finding a unifying feature, a pattern in the particular evolutions of systems. If this is finding a role state that permits different realizations, physics only ever deals in roles: it is role seeking 'all the way down'. No harm in that: thesis (T) is bland enough, only perhaps serving to avert a lay misunderstanding of physics as essentially concerned only with microscopic facts, or concerned only with identity. Thesis (T) opposes the idea that the 'states' that physics countenances are to be thought of as literally spatial items, morphologically identified. Nothing could be less true to physics. It requires no controversial functionalism to see that is simply false that accelerating at 25m per second per second 'is one thing in this car and another in that cannonball' or that being able to pass petrol at 25cc per sec is 'one thing in this tube of circular cross-section and another in that one, which is square'. Remember too that even causal favourites like solidity are only the possession of some property that precludes occupancy of the same space by other things with some properties.

The view of physics that (T) warns against could be called the Tractarian view, although in calling it this I am conscious of pointing to a cluster of thoughts, or images determining thoughts, rather than a clear unique doctrine. In its simplest form, it is the view that physics itself is incapable of describing equivalences between systems that differ in some microscopic configuration—in the spatial array of constituent particles. The idea is that identity of a physical state consists in the spatial configuration of particles, and evolutions of state are changes in this over time. Every state is then what it is and not another thing—a unique combination of a value for each physical parameter at each place. But for it to explain at all, physics must find the one in the many. This means finding properties that do not answer only to configurations of constituent particles (although of course it may also, at some level, find properties that do so answer). The moral drawn from temperature and energy is quite general, and must be if physics is to explain.

I hope now that the reader feels the first stirrings of unease. It is the unique state, the realizing state, or array of magnitudes or tropes or instances of properties at points, that causes. It is here that the 'making happen' happens: how, then, can we identify the cause by citing the relational, dispositional or role-given properties with which physical thinking leaves us? At least in the seventeenth century the condensation seemed to yield something solid, and (people wrongly thought) something that leads us to intelligible point-by-point causation. But we cannot have that thought any more. We are left only with point-by-point magnitudes for things that are essentially dispositional—electrical charge, for instance—but we are not left with a 'quality' that underlies the 'power', or with a 'ground' that underlies the disposition, or with a state that finally realizes the role. If the property is not identified as a power, or equivalently, if the 'state' of it being realized is not identified as a role state, then the categorical, pure presence of an instance at a point will be unknowable to physics.[13]

An especially interesting example of the lure of the microscopic, Tractarian physical state is given by John Haugeland's excellent paper, 'Weak Supervenience'. Haugeland is arguing as I am against the need for identity theory. But his example of the problem of identifying the 'robust' events of common description with the 'mathematical events' of physical theory depends eventually on a Tractarian view of what these events are. His example is the crossing of a pair of waves generated from different ends of a tank. Imagine that as they cross each crest hits a cork. Haugeland asks which event describable in the language of ultimate physics is identical to the wave-hits, and finds none: 'when we turn up our microscope, however, and look at the positions and velocities of the water molecules, there isn't a trace of either wave-hit to be found anywhere. . . .'[14] But why should one expect to find the events and states of interest to physics by 'turning up our microscope'? If fluid dynamics is treated in kinetic theory, the magnitudes characterizing a liquid at a point and time (velocity, viscosity, density, pressure, temperature) are not associated with the specific detail of microscopic states. They are associated with averages of properties of many microscopic entities. The 'mathematical events' of physics are therefore quite large-scale enough to map onto the events of waves travelling and crossing. It is the individual events and magnitudes that are not.

Does a Tractarian vision infect eliminativism? Consider Stephen Stich's discussion of the relation between mind and brain.[15] Trouble arises because, via the notion of a state, commonsense psychology becomes landed with rather specific commitments to the nature of neurophysiological workings. So Stich can urge that the notion of a belief state is undermined if it turns out that one part of the brain is causally responsible for my saying that there is a cat under the bed, and another part for my reaching down to lift it out. The idea is that, according to folk psychology, one belief state (that the cat is

---

13. I am here grateful to Robert Kraut and George Pappas. The difficulty over solidity is heralded in Locke's ambivalent attitude to the possibility of knowing the qualities, as distinct from just the powers, of things (including microscopial things): compare, for instance, *Essay*, Book II, chapter IV, sections 1 and 6. See also essay 14.

14. Haugeland, op. cit., p. 100.

15. Stich, op. cit., p. 237 ff.

under the bed) is responsible for both the saying and the doing; neuroscience finds two different states separately responsible for the saying and the doing; hence folk psychology was wrong. Notice, however, that typically people tend to say only that there is a cat under the bed when they are disposed to act in whichever way is appropriate to that information, so presumably there typically exists some connection between any different areas of the brain that are involved, ensuring that one area goes into a cat-behaving state only if the other area goes into a cat-reporting state. Hence there is room to find a single fact or feature such as that of having the action and the speech area coordinated. But this will be simply a fact about the organization of the brain (it is not a fact that is 'located' anywhere). I suspect that Stitch failed to see this counter because of implicit Tractarianism: a count of located neuro-physiological states would be blind to that kind of state. In short, unless we are in the grip of the Tractarian vision, the argument is out of court from the beginning. The single belief state of folk psychology involves no commitment to one or many genuinely internal mechanisms, any more than the single kinematic state of a motor car—being in uniform motion in a straight line, say—requires that anything, let alone any given number of things, is happening inside it.

If predicates are taken in the resolutely functionalist way I am commending, then we are not finding that F-ing is one thing in one object and another in a second, because they do it by different mechanisms. It might be a different thing, but only if it is a different thing that they are doing. From the functionalist's point of view, this would be because it is impossible to find a functionally equivalent state across the divide. But that would be a different matter, although English is unfortunately cavalier at the crucial point.[16] For the English question 'what is flying?' permits either a (quick and easy) role-state answer, or a (long, and variable) realizing-state answer. It may be right too that in many contexts the latter is the more interesting. What is not true is that this undercuts role-state explanation, nor that it threatens the causal efficacy of such states.

Notice, however, that impatience with traditional ('analytical') philosophy of mind might lead a forward-looking eliminativist to resurface here. Perhaps traditionally there were two questions, one scientific and explanatory, and the other more analytic. But why respect the second? Perhaps in a modern climate the question 'what is thought (belief, desire)?' admits only of a scientific construction: either we are asking for underlying mechanisms and need to sit at the feet of neurophysiologists, or we back to playing with concepts that lack empirical integrity. Alas, there is no escaping metaphysics without doing more of it than the mere hymning of science involves. The eliminativists believe that the sovereignty of physics and the rise of neurophysiology pose a distinct threat to psychological categories. But they cannot make this claim look plausible without giving or presupposing some account of how science threatens role states. They retain responsibility for showing how the undermining

16. I owe David Lewis thanks for pointing out the need for caution here.

works: in round terms, what belief and desire explanation was, that it should be shown to have had its day.

IV. Role States and Causation

Thesis (T) says that physical thinking is essentially a matter of finding the one feature that covers many realizations. One might call this the one state, but it is dangerous. We envisage states, very naturally, as things with positions and boundaries, and this spatial imagining is surely responsible for part of the problem. With this caveat in place, I now turn to the idea that finding the causes—the real causes—of events cannot be a matter of identifying a role state or feature covering variable realizations. I shall illustrate the difficulty— although it is of far greater generality—by thinking of the trouble we have fitting psychology together with causality.

Folk psychology has little overt to say about states. If it talks of them at all, it is to talk of us who get into psychological states, not of any states that get into us. If I get into a state of believing that I am Jesus, no doubt things will have gone on in my brain. But there is no first-order project of finding whether the state I have got into is some very state that has got into this part of me. Commonsense psychology gives no reason to think of the states we get into as spatial arrays. None of the platitudes defining folk psychology talks in these terms: as with physics, it is philosophical gloss, not first-order theory, that insists. So why impose talk of states and then reify and locate them? The ruling answer goes like this: Folk psychology may confine itself to using predicates such as '. . . believes (desires, etc.) that *p*'. But we need a view of the conditions making such ascriptions true. Functionalism is a start. But we want our psychological states to have causal powers, enabling them to affect the real world, and we want them to do so in ways we can see as conforming to the sovereignty of physics. The best way to do this is to identify the states making the ascriptions true, first with neurophysiological and then, hopefully, with physical states. If those states will not go into that shape, then so much the worse for them.

This is the heart of the issue, set forth with his usual clarity and force by Lewis, who wrote that his argument for identity theory (the identification of role with realizer states) parallels the following, 'which we will find uncontroversial':

> Consider cylindrical combination locks for bicycle chains. The definitive characteristic of their state of being unlocked is the causal role of that state, the syndrome of its most typical causes and effects: namely, that setting the combination typically causes the lock to be unlocked and that being un-locked typically causes the lock to open when gently pulled. That is all we need know in order to ascribe to the lock the state of being or not being unlocked. But we may learn that, as a matter of fact, the lock contains a row of slotted discs; setting the combination typically causes the slots to be aligned; and alignment of the slots typically causes the lock to open when

gently pulled. So alignment of the slots occupies precisely the causal role that we ascribed to being unlocked by analytic necessity, as the definitive characteristic of being unlocked (for these locks). Therefore alignment of slots is identical with being unlocked (for these locks). They are one and the same state.[17]

Lewis claims three advantages for so thinking. First, the states become recognized as 'real and efficacious'. Second, 'unrestricted natural interdefinition of the state and others of its sort becomes permissible'. Third, it becomes intelligible that the state may sometimes occur despite prevention of its definitive manifestations. The alternative he considers preserves the separation of role state and realizer state. But, according to Lewis, this denies efficacy to the former, for a pure disposition is an inefficacious entity.

The last two advantages are not central to my problem, but I shall briefly register a query about each of them. First then, mutual definition seems to go on just as well if we stay with the role predicates of commonsense theory: if there is a definition of belief or desire to be had, it will be had whether we think of it as saying what an underlying mechanism is, or instead as defining the truth that someone is believing or desiring. A definition of flying can be had (roughly: staying aloft in a gravitational field without external support) without adverting to any particular mechanism whereby some particular thing does it.

Second, the identification of role and realizer state may seem to solve problems over externally prevented manifestations of state. But this is not clear, for these problems arise as much with the identification in place as without it. This is easy to overlook, since once we think of the state as an inner spatial presence, it seems evident that it can be there regardless of whether its effects are its typical effects. But what will not be evident is that the internal, realizing state is on this occasion the original role state, for this is now contingent. Consider the lock again. Another lock might share a whole physical part with the original: five disks coming into line, for instance. But it may have a device that prevents this from being enough to open it (you also have to whisper the magic word that triggers the minute relay). The five disks are in line, but the lock is not unlocked. If we talk the identity way, we have to say that its being unlocked is a composite: its five disks getting into line and its relay tripping. For this lock, it is not true that its being unlocked is its five disks getting into line. Calling the state of being unlocked *UL*, and that of having five disks in line *S*, we learn that the following is not a valid argument:

Lock 1 is unlocked iff it is in state *S*,

so State *UL* is state *S*. Lock 2 is in state *S*,

so Lock 2 is in state *UL*,

so Lock 2 is unlocked

17. David Lewis, 'An Argument for the Identity Theory', *Philosophical Papers,* Volume 1 (New York: Oxford University Press, 1983), p. 100.

because Lock 2 is not unlocked. Such an argument trades on forgetting that the identity 'state UL is state S' must be relativized to locks for which it is true that when the five disks are in line, they are unlocked. How to tell which locks these are? Easy, provided we know when something is unlocked. But any difficulties in telling when a lock with five disks in line but unopenable is unlocked remain. For example, if there is a disruption of the typical workings of the first lock, preventing the chain opening, we may say that it is unlocked but jammed. But we may prefer to say that it is still locked. Or there may be an accidental disruption to the first kind of lock preventing it from getting into the state S, although it now opens when lightly tugged (it is a raped lock: the fifth disk is damaged, and the other four give it its function). Here we are hardly likely to say that it cannot get into the state of being unlocked. The role state theorist who avoids the identity has exactly this freedom, or (if we want principles for settling the description) this problem. Of the first lock he can say that the thing is unlocked but jammed. He can say this because he can say that if the occasion were right for manifestation of its disposition (e.g., if the rust were out of the way), it would open. Or, he can say that it can't be unlocked, because this is the right occasion for display of the disposition, and the thing will not open. Similarly, if it opens although the state S has not come about, the role state theorist can deny that it is unlocked (forced, rather) if unlocking implies responding by opening to the right kind of input (a key, not a drill).

In other words, indeterminacies over what to think when we would expect a disposition or other functional trait to be manifested, but it is not (or not to be manifested, when it is), need handling in the same way whether or not the identity is flourished. If there is a disruption between the physical state that normally explains the disposition and its exercise on an occasion, the identity theorist simply confronts the open question of whether to say that the state 'is' on this occasion the original state. His penchant for identity does not tell him the answer. And the role state theorist faces the question of whether this is the 'right' occasion for exercise of the role. The same is true of the more urgent case in which paralysis prevents beliefs and desires from becoming manifest. There are some facts about the paralysed agent that would be expected to lead to his acting some way, but others that prevent it. Is he disposed so to act? He would be if the occasion were right (i.e., if the disability disappeared), but the occasion will not be right; he will not talk or act as things are. If this leaves us not knowing what to say, try bringing on the identity theory. Does he possess a state that (in him) is the belief or desire? This is just as hard to tell. There are difficulties in knowing what to say of such cases: the contingent or kind-relative identification with underlying state makes it no easier.[18]

18. Lewis reminds me (private correspondence) that his target in the paper was not this kind of role-state theory, but a behaviourism that thought it did know what to say: it had to say that if there was no display of the disposition, the psychological state was absent. I quite accept that this position is unhappy, but my point remains that it is not necessary (nor, as Lewis of course knows, sufficient, since you have to find a principle for selecting locks for which the identity holds) to insist on the identity by way of refuting it.

Of course, these were two subsidiary arguments for making the identity-arguments parallel to the famous Davidsonian argument for event-identity between the mental and the physical. In each development the most important issue is the first that Lewis cites: that of causation, and the intuition that role states do not cause, whereas realizer states do. Alongside the thesis (T) we now have the antithesis (A):

> *Thesis (T)*: Physical thinking is essentially a question of finding the one state that covers many realizations.

> *Antithesis (A)*: If one state covers many realizations, it is they and not it that are causally relevant (powerful, active).

These are not incompatible, of course, but together they do give us the conclusion (C):

> *Conclusion (C)*: Physical thinking is not a question of finding states that are causally relevant.

And this is sufficiently strange to count as paradoxical. If physics is not the discovery of causally relevant states, what is?

So far I have merely introduced (A) and done nothing to defend it. First, we need to be clear what it says and does not say. It does not say that role states cannot be cited in causal explanations. They may be if causal explanation 'points toward' causally active states, without itself citing them. Thus, to take Jackson and Pettit's example, the fact that someone coughed may be mentioned in explaining why the conductor got angry.[19] But it features in such an explanation, according to them, by pointing us toward the particular state that actually made the conductor angry—Fred's coughing, or perhaps some feature of Fred's coughing on this occasion. We mention role states, on such an account, in order to shrink the domain from which causally relevant particular states must come. In the same way we might cite a power or disposition, not because in mentioning these things we are actually giving the relevant feature, but because it confines the domain within which such a feature exists. Thus we can mention the dormitivity of the opium and provide an explanation of someone sleeping, but what we are saying is that there is some other property the opium has, that causes sleep.[20]

For a similar reason (A) is not denying that role states may be nomologically connected with effects. A causally relevant property will bring about an effect. It will also bring it about that other higher-order, relational, and dispositional properties are instanced, and they may then be in a lawlike correlation with the effect. Thus in a gas the increase in kinetic energy of these molecules in this configuration will transfer energy to the thermometer; it also will give

19. F. Jackson and P. Pettit, 'Functionalism and Broad Content', in *Mind,* 1988, p. 394.
20. Ned Block, 'Can the Mind Change the World', in *Meaning and Method: Essays in Honour of Hilary Putnam,* ed. G. Boolos (Cambridge: Cambridge University Press, 1990).

the gas new powers. The increase in kinetic energy brings it about that the gas has some property responsible for extra available thermal energy, and it thereby also brings it about that the gas bears a different energy-exchange relationship to many other things. These changes in role state are, however, epiphenomenal: the molecules do the pushing, and the other properties, supervening upon the first, come along for the ride.

Except, of course, remembering the discussion of physics, it will not really be the molecules doing the causing, but (in the first instance) distributions of other parameters of energy and force within them. And if thesis (T) is right, then for all we shall ever know there will be other magnitudes and realizing states beyond those again, all the way down. If our physics stops at some level—say with electrical charge—then there will still be a quality or qualities realizing that charge. But, as with Cartesian egos, it will be forever hidden how many there are, or what it is, or whether it is the same on odd dates and even dates.

There are other arguments in favour of (A). Writing of the second-order property of being provocative to a bull (i.e., having some property that causes the bull to react) Block says: 'supposing that provocativeness provokes the bull would be supposing a strange and gratuitous sort of overdetermination of the bull's anger. . . . [T]o suppose that it always happens would be to suppose a bizarre systematic overdetermination'.[21] And our dislike of this can be fortified by remembering how easy it is to generate supervening states. To use an example of Lewis's: if the steam in the cylinder is at 190 pounds per square inch, then it is also in the state of being either at 190 psi, or full of suspended particles of gold dust. We think the former causes the piston to move, but its being in the latter state does not. Disjunctive states are bad candidates for causal relevance; quantificational states (someone coughing) and higher-order states (having some property that causes sleep) seem just as doubtful.

If thesis (T) characterizes physical thinking, and antithesis (A) is not short of defence, can we live with conclusion (C)? Perhaps we can. After all, lawlike explanatory relevance is left to us. There is nothing wrong with saying that the thermometer went up because the temperature is rising, even if ('strictly speaking') what made it go up was a succession of microscopic impingings, or rather, the instancing of the properties that ultimately realize all the powers we can ever know about. We might even take a Humean pleasure in reflecting that the ultimate causes of things are forever obscured from us, so that all we can do is mark the patterns they reliably create as events unfold. And it draws some of the sting from the epiphenomenalism of the mental if its causal inefficacy is on all fours with that of changes of temperature or energy levels. Nevertheless, it would be good to put into place some other route to a solution. We ought to reflect that in spite of the shift in our understanding of causation that Newton and Hume brought about, it is not compulsory to describe it by saying that we never identify real causes. It is hard to believe that 'being a feature in virtue of which things happen' is itself a transcendental

21. Block, op. cit.

property, forever defying identification. There ought to be a humanly accessible notion of what it is that makes things happen—one we can rely upon in making recipes and controlling events.

V. Higher-Order Causal Relevance

Things with the same temperature form a certain equivalence class, although the thermal energy can be created by many different means. Sameness of temperature is therefore a higher-order property: the having of some energy source ensuring that no heat is transferred when in thermal contact with any of a class of other things. Now imagine a chain of events as follows. A thermometer is affected by its thermal contact with something, and records a temperature. Suppose it is connected to a further system—a current flows in a wire if the reading is below a certain level. The current in turn triggers a switch, and lights the boiler, raising the temperature. Then there is a good sense in which the system 'looks through' which realization of thermal energy caused the reading. It is sensitive equally to the different creations of thermal energy (if the thermometer is flexible enough, by moving molecules, vibration energies, electromagnetic energies and so on). That is, the current flows regardless of any particular realization of the temperature, and in the same way the boiler lights regardless of any particular configuration of the electrons in the wire carrying the current. The boiler raises the temperature today as it did yesterday. We ought to have a humanly applicable conception of causal relevance, enabling us to say that the system works the same on each occasion: the same features cause the same effect.[22]

Consider now a lock. Think of a burglar as an instrument. The lock being unlocked can be responsible for the burglar getting in: it is the feature to cite, and to use if we wish to control the movements of burglars. Its being unlocked is the upshot of its having four disks in line, on this occasion. But that is not the feature the burglar detected, or is perhaps even capable of detecting. Nor is this only a problem about burglars. A much simpler instrument can be sensitive to whether there is no force on the chain, without being sensitive to whether this is because there are four disks in line, or five, or anything else. Again, the upshot 'looks through' the preceding realization.

---

22. An excellent discussion of the issues that trouble me, in the Davidsonian context of event identity, is the interchange between Ted Honderich and Peter Smith: Ted Honderich, 'The Argument for Anomalous Monism', in *Analysis,* 1982, p. 59; 'Anomalous Monism: Reply to Smith', in *Analysis,* 1983, p. 147; and 'Smith and the Lover of Mauve', in *Analysis,* 1984, p. 86. Peter Smith: 'Bad News for Anomalous Monism?' in *Analysis,* 1982, p. 220; and 'Anomalous Monism and Epiphenomenalism: A Reply to Honderich', in *Analysis,* 1984, p. 83. Honderich's original instinct is also found in F. Stoutland, 'The Causation of Behaviour', in *Essays in Honour of G. H. von Wright,* ed. J. Hintikka (Dordrecht: Reidel, 1976). Another good discussion is Davidson, 'Thinking Causes', in *Mind and Brain: Perspectives in Theoretical Psychology and the Philosophy of Mind* (Bielefeld: Zentrum für Interdisziplinäre Forschung, 1991), with the accompanying sceptical comments by Kim and Sosa. My position is most similar to that of Peter Menzies, 'Against Causal Reductionism', in *Mind,* 1988, p. 551.

A vivid case of this 'looking through' is indifference of a physical result to the question of which instance of a quantification is realized. The burglar alarm goes off because someone is in the room. It was Bill: Bill (or more: some particular result of Bill being in some particular place at some particular time) caused it to go off, but it is still true that it went off because someone was in the room. That is what makes it go off; that is what is supposed to make it go off. It is not as if it malfunctioned. You cannot take it back saying that it is supposed to go off because someone is in the room, whereas it actually was made to go off by Bill being in the left hand corner of the room standing on one foot. Is this giving in to a 'bizarre causal overdetermination', since on a given occasion the instrument will have responded both to some highly particular flux of energy and to someone being in the room? Surely there is nothing bizarre about it. We simply do not have to choose between these properties as ones whose instancing makes things happen, ones with causal power and relevance.[23]

But does citing anything less than the particular, as we do when we find a common feature in causal transitions, leave us with just a signpost to something else, which alone has 'real' causal relevance? I say not. In finding causal relevance we are finding features, like rising temperature, or carrying current, that are essentially repeatable, but whose presence can be registered, and brought about, by mechanisms that function in the same way on each of numerous occasions. The one we find in the many can also be a one whose being there makes things happen.[24]

So far then I am insisting on having my cake and eating it: separating the role and realizer states, but keeping genuine causal efficacy for the role state. It might occur to some to wonder whether this challenges the sovereignty of physics. Again, I say not. The sovereignty of physics requires only that the connexion between the role or disposition and the underlying state be explicable. Its sovereignty would be challenged only if there were something it could not explain in (say) the fact of the five disks coming into line enabling the lock to be opened. But there need not be. In this lock, when the five disks are in line, there is no force opposing the tension of a pull on the chain. So the chain moves. In other locks, when the five disks are in line, there might still be a force opposing the tension of such a pull. In them, the chain will not move. The property or fact of being locked or unlocked is thus explained, and physical explicability does not require that we work in terms of states and their identity at all. We do not have to 'identify' the velocity of the car with the

23. Lewis rightly reminds me that his original example was a bicycle lock, and that cylindrical locks are not commonly used on houses. But 'folk burglar prevention' sounded better to me than 'folk bicycle theft prevention', so I have let it stand.

24. It is only the particular instance, not the feature, that causes things to happen. Instead of 'the instancing of a feature', we get the event in its full (transcendental) particularity. Pondering this intuition, I find myself reminded of Bradley's hostility to abstraction: the view that only a picture of reality that involves no abstraction (i.e., reality itself) is (really) true strikes me as very like the view that only the total Tractarian particular causes. But I cannot explore the relationship here. See Stewart Candlish, 'The Truth about F. H. Bradley', in *Mind*, 1989, for the 'identity' theory of truth.

application of the energy to the wheels in order for the velocity to be explicable by the energy.

The intuition I am opposing is probably this: If there is anything other than identity, then there are two things (two states) to be connected—on the one hand, the underlying physical configurations, and on the other hand, the fact that the lock opens when gently pulled. But unless we can squeeze these together, as it were, there is then bound to be a gap for physics to cross, and it will never explain the exact landing point: the very way the categorical state matches up to the disposition. And my rejoinder is that any intuition that there is an explanatory gap here simply transposes into the same intuition that there is an explanatory gap on the identity story: a gap in understanding why or when state S is state UL. If we know why the configuration gives rise to the disposition, we know this, but otherwise we do not. Nothing is made more intelligible by the identity.

My claim then is that being unlocked is not an epiphenomenon, rendering literally false folk burglar prevention—the theory in which we say 'because it was unlocked, the bicycle rolled downhill'; 'because it was unlocked, the burglar could push it open'. The fact that no force opposed the tension on the chain is in perfectly good standing as a fact that matters. It was because of that fact (which in turn *may* be because the five disks were in line) that gravity or the burglar met no resistance. Would it be somehow better not to cite the fact of it being unlocked, and only to cite the disks being in line? Not at all: gravity and the burglar 'look through' the reason why it was unlocked.

If (A) was at fault, what of the degenerate cases, such as disjunctive states, or dormitivity? Here I can only sketch an approach. Arbitrary disjunctions? The disjunctive state of 'having the steam at 190 psi or being full of suspended particles of gold dust' is not a state that any natural causal system 'looks through' to. A cylinder would be in that state by being full of suspended particles of gold dust. But there is (I take it) no normal effect common to that state and to the state of being full of steam under pressure. Only if there were would the state begin to stand in the same relation to having the steam as temperature does to a particular molecular distribution, and thence to look like a candidate for causal efficacy. There is no genuine nomological connection between satisfying this predicate and doing anything (perhaps I should say: anything whose unity is visible to a non-Goodmanian, well-behaved categorization of the world). Quantification? A conductor, like a burglar alarm, may be sensitive to someone coughing. Making someone cough gives us control over his temper, a recipe for making him seethe, and a causally relevant state of an audience. We have here a system that looks through its realizations, and I see no objection to causal efficacy. Higher-order properties, like the provocativeness of the cape? A bull is certainly a good instrument—the best going—for detecting whether a stimulus is one that provokes bulls. If a change in temperature is causally relevant to the thermometer, why isn't a change in provocativeness causally relevant to changing demeanour in the bull? My own answer to this would be to reverse Block's. What is wrong with citing this feature is not that it is causally irrelevant but that it is explanatorily such a dud: it provides no basis for prediction and no useful recipe for doing things that control bulls. Being told to wave something provocative at the bull is indeed merely being given a signpost: it points me toward the need to discover the properties that cause the reaction. Whereas there is virtue in citing temperature: I can control the rise of the thermometer by controlling temperature, without needing to discover anything about the realization of temperature at all.

It may be said that in all these examples, the causal efficacy of the role state, like the role state itself, supervenes upon the Tractarian particulars and their evolutions through time. I do not want to deny this, provided we are comfortable with such a property—provided it is not a subtle invitation to denying that the causal power, the relevance and efficacy of the feature, is real enough.

VI. Physical States

If we have a good idea of how the thermometer can be made to act by the temperature, can we immediately see how we can be made to act by beliefs and desires? Obviously there is a huge gap: sameness of temperature is at least visible to physics; sameness of belief arguably not.[25] Still working, as it were, from the physical end, the question will be one of defining a more realistic concept of a physical state or property. Presumably physical states include the possession of a physical property by a physical thing; the bearing of physical relations by n-tuples of physical things; the being in complexes of physical states or bearing of amalgams of physical properties by conglomerations of physical things. There is nothing in the sovereignty of physics that forbids (physically explicable) complexity, amalgamation, or conglomeration.

It is sometimes thought that there should be, because of the following argument. Physics explains by citing laws; there may be a law covering the transition from A to B, and one covering the transition from C to D, but this would not entail that there is one covering the transition from $(A \& C)$ to $(B \& D)$. This may be true about laws. But physical explicability is agglomerative and transitive, even if law is not. Thus when a system composed of A and B evolves to a subsequent state C and D because of a law L determining C from A, and another L' determining D from B, then even if there is no single law covering this evolution, there is still nothing physically unexplained about it. For an example, consider a body of known weight, position, and temperature $<p,T>$ in a gravitational field of known strength and direction. Suppose a kinematic law K will give a position p' for it after t seconds. Suppose the body consists in a battery passing current through a circuit, and a law of electromagnetics L determines a temperature T' for it after the same interval. At t it will be in a certain position and at a certain temperature, and nothing in this

25. For recent scepticism, see Hilary Putnam, *Representation and Reality* (Cambridge, Mass.: Bradford Books, 1988), p. 84 ff.

evolution is physically unexplained. The transition from $<p, T>$ to $<p', T'>$ is both determined and explained by physics—even if physics uses two different laws to do it. It is a transition in which nothing is physically inexplicable. God did not have to do anything extra to secure this evolution of state.

Churchland's vision of the relation between special sciences and physics demands coextensions of terms. Will the sovereignty of physics require anything so strong? In the example given, it does not matter if physics has no interest in the particular evolution, and no kind term to pick out the complex states involved. Further examples suggest a two-stage analysis of this phenomenon. The first part allows for 'token-token' identity, but the second is less familiar. Consider (to use Fodor's example) the physical process summed up in the geological 'law' that meandering rivers erode their outside banks. A physical process, and one in principle explicable by fluid hydrodynamics. Yet neither river nor meander nor bank is a term of physics. All that the 'reduction' of the law to one of physics, in this relevant sense of the word, requires, is that rivers are (each of them) some, but not necessarily the same, kind of flowing liquid; that meanders are (each of them) some, but not necessarily the same, kind of curved configuration; and that banks are (each of them) some, but not necessarily the same, kind of material liable to lose its cohesion under transverse forces. Each token of the type is an event describable in terms of hydrodynamics. If we think these kinds are invisible to physics, then the fact that a kind is thus invisible is no bar to reductive physical explanation. *A fortiori* it is no motive to 'eliminativism' or rejection of the truths expressed in terms of the kind, even given the sovereignty of physics. The coming of hydrodynamics does not prove that there are no folk rivers.

The example takes us only halfway. We are already prepared to believe that bank erosion is a physical process, and we do not mind saying that rivers and meanders are, each of them, something physical. But we might still worry how physical explicability transfers from any given token of the type to the overall explanandum. Would it not require seeing a physical 'shape' in what is perhaps invisible to physics: the reason the disjunction of tokens all count as examples of the same type—river, meander, or bank? It is here that the demand for an 'image' of the predicate in the explanatory science (physics) reemerges. It is as if it may be all very well explaining each token of the type, but unless there is a physical explanation of the tokens constituting and exhausting examples of the type, the original explanandum is not yet touched. Thus it is that more impressive cross-classification is typically introduced via examples like chairs, ornaments, money, and so on. These kinds correspond even less well to physical boundaries. Whether or not they think it undermining, writers generally agree that there is a distinction between classifications that carve nature at the joints and those that do not, and these kinds, reflecting as they do the particular interests of human beings, surely do not.

This thought needs a little attention. Of course it is true that we discriminate things by other than physical properties, we 'look through' things like mass, velocity, shape, conductivity, constitution, and so on. And a bullheaded attempt to find disjunctive physical kinds underlying most terms of classification, including those that enter into some laws, is fruitless. Again using Fodor's example, it is a law that bad money drives out good, but an attempt to 'define' a term like 'money' by thinking of the enormous (limitless) potential disjunction of physical kinds of stuff that might serve as money, and then framing 'laws' covering that disjunction, is a hopeless way to try to make the law 'physically explicable'. Even if such a disjunction were somehow created, it is doubtful whether we could think of it as making anything explicable. It would not be the 'physical' properties of the members of the disjunction that are responsible for them being there (round bits of metal, printed pieces of paper, cowrie shells . . .): there is nothing visible to physics tying the bundle together. Since the disjunction threatens to be quite shapeless, we might insist that it still plays no role in helping us to understand why things of that kind drive out other things of that kind.

But this is the wrong way to go. Instead we must enlarge our gaze to think of the wider system: us-using-money, or us-discriminating-chairs. It does not follow from the cross-classification of chairs with respect to properties like mass, material constitution, shape (up to a point), and so on that there is anything invisible to physics in the wider system. It would be possible, for instance, to construct a physical system including various receptors that selects objects in its environment by properties other than weight, mass, constitution. Think of a robot capable of 'sitting'—taking up some position, and sensitive to feedback telling it whether some of its parts are under mechanical stress in that position. Then think of it discriminating likely objects on which it can 'sit', capable of selecting further among them on the basis of feedback from its own states, and eventually able to mimic our own chair-selecting practices (if it is complained that we discriminate chairs by features other than whether we can sit on them without strain, imagine the robot endowed with other sensitivities—e.g., to the history of production or whatever else matters). Of course it will be by physical means that its sensors and feedback mechanisms work. But given the sovereignty of physics, the same is true of us. The whole system of chair discrimination by robot would be physically explicable. Hence there is no *a priori* reason why the same is not so of us. In this development the physicalist explanation does not try to complete an inventory of the woods, plastics, metals, and other things that chairs are and might be made of. Nevertheless the explanation proceeds by finding what is physically common to occasions on which a classification is effected. Notice too that the physical explicability of the classification in turn does not imply that the robots are built identically. As already emphasized, physics is capable of being quite relaxed about what makes two occasions physically similar. A circuit diagram gives a perfectly good physical description of a device, although there are endless different things that can serve as wires, resistors, or capacitors.

Similarly with money: nobody of course has the least idea how it would go in detail, because social facts are one stage further from physics than psychological ones. But if there is physical explicability of people desiring things and exchanging things, then there will be physical explicability of Gresham's law, and again without providing the shapeless list of things that can serve as money. The upshot is that it should not be barely asserted that 'chair' or 'money', let alone 'river' or 'bank' is a kind invisible to physics, even though it cross-classifies with respect to many physical properties of its members. The supervenience requirement is satisfied in the following sense: by creating the entire physical system, God had done enough to create the use for the kind term. He has also done enough to create a physical relation, with chairs the things in its domain—the things disposed to elicit and sustain the chair verdict from us.

VII. Psychological States

With this much understanding of physical states behind us, the task of this paper is nearly finished. But I shall end by saying a little about the other end of the relationship.

The subordinate clauses in propositional attitude psychology mention content; the object of the demonstrative is a thought or proposition, not a sentence, nor words nor utterances.[26] Folk psychology is quite silent over implementation. It makes no claim that there is some 'level' of explanation of our thinking that fruitfully relates us to sentences or words. It is therefore not affected by discoveries, such as seem likely to come in the wake of the successes of parallel distributed processing architecture for recognitional and other systems, that there is no fruitful level of explanation that sees such things as involved with rules, or words, or syntactically complex instructions and subcognitive processing. Just as a parallel distributed processing network can 'recognize' a sound or a pattern without anything that ought to be called computation, so, perhaps, we can think that our friend is coming down the street equally without literal computation. There is no *a priori* reason to suppose that because the skill is great, the mechanisms explaining it involve real, but quick and unconscious, cognitive processes. On the other hand, there is no *a priori* reason against this: the fruitfulness of such a level of analysis is a matter of scientific, not philosophical, speculation.

Will psychology, granted this much independence, ever make a cognitive science? Some see the hostility to treating psychological states as natural objects as implicit in Frege's antipsychologism. It is certainly present in Collingwood, in whom the capacity of a thinker for self-critical change of his own beliefs and desires blocked the pretensions of psychology, or anything else, to be a 'science' of thought.[27] Similarly Putnam argues that the business of

26. Of course, there is a huge literature trying to deny this. Some arguments are canvassed in my 'The Identity of Propositions', in Blackburn, ed., *Meaning, Reference and Necessity* (Cambridge: Cambridge University Press, 1975). Paul Churchland has been active in allowing that intentional predicates can enter causal relations although the relata are abstract, by drawing the parallel with 'numerical attitudes' (e.g., *Matter and Consciousness,* op. cit., 2nd ed. [Cambridge, Mass.: Bradford Books, 1988], chapters 3, 4). Contrast Stich, ibid., p. 243.

27. R. G. Collingwood, *An Introduction to Metaphysics* (Oxford: Oxford University Press, 1940), chapters XI and XII. I discuss this further in 'Theory, Observation and Drama' in *Mind and Language,* October 1992.

attributing a mental state, with a certain content, to another always involves issues of judgement seamlessly bringing to bear any of a formless class of cultural, historical, or hermeneutic pressures, and the prospects for the outcome of such a process being a scientifically respectable predicate seem very poor.[28] Allied to this are the normativity or rationality constraints governing psychological attribution and the resulting suspicion that we have an essentially dramatic, rather than descriptive, activity. But the catholicism that I have been urging enables physical respectability to gobble up this too: in principle, a norm-wielding system is not more invisible to physics than a chair-detecting one or a money-using one.

If we make the role-realizer identity, we can say that redescription of states under predicates that reveal their lawlike connections makes good any preceding causal explanation: it is the fund that backs up what is otherwise only a promise. It is essential to this idea of 'making good' that the thing described in the initial, lawless way is the thing that can also be described in the later, lawlike way: this is the model common to Davidson and Lewis. Sometimes this is plausible. The stone balances the scale, not because there is a law that stones do, but because the stone is the thing of mass x at distance d from the fulcrum. But with unnecessary identities out of the way, there is no analogy to this in the case of psychological explanation. We can be agnostic about whether psychological explanations can aspire to the condition of laws (even if they do not for us, it is hard to see why they could not for a more simple animal). Whether there is psychological law or not, no redescription of mental states that succeeds in introducing a lawlike connection missing from psychology would make good the psychological explanation. In other words, all we would get would be something citing a different fact about me or my neural states. We might find that 'as I believe' or 'when I believe' or 'upon coming to believe' that p, such-and-such changes happen, and they are lawlikely correlated with others. But we will not thereby get a new lawlike correlation between 'a state that is the mental state' of coming to believe that p, and the other changes. Such a filling out changes the subject. It substitutes mention of something different.

It will be said again that I want it both ways: I want both to stress the separateness of role states (role features) and to award them the causal accolade that (it will be said) properly belongs only to realizer states. I reply that it is the opposition that wants it both ways: both to preserve the causal power belonging to the presence of features wide and small, and to succumb to the Tractarian vision, by insisting that the real engine of change is the irredeemably particular configuration of things. And this, I have argued, renders it invisible to physics, and indeed to all human thought.

Folk psychology is a wonderful thing. It is no wonder that we are baffled by the prodigious knowledge and abstraction, the sheer instrumentation, that enables us to look through the particular features of ourselves and others that might otherwise get in the way, and type us all by our beliefs and desires. The

28. Putnam, op. cit., passim.

difficulty lies in seizing and sustaining the idea that in so doing we are identifying real features whose instantiation is causally effective in producing events in the world. In this essay I have not addressed all the obstacles to doing this, but I hope I have removed some.

14

Filling in Space

Why do people think that dispositions must have categorical grounds underlying them? Well, the clock tells the time because there is such-and-such an arrangement of little bits inside it; Sandy barks because her vocal chords vibrate; the light glows because electrons whizz around in its filament. The explanations are excellent, but do they illustrate the doctrine?

They do if they bring us to categorical grounds that indeed underlie the dispositions. But they do not if they bring us to something else. For instance, they might only bring us to a point where the possession of some disposition by something is explained by the possession of other dispositions by the same or different things. Or they might bring us only to the instancing of a power (disposition) at some region of space explained by the instancing of some other power at some related region of space.[1]

When we think of categorical grounds, we are apt to think of a spatial configuration of things—hard, massy, shaped things resisting penetration and displacement by others of their kind. But the categorical credentials of any item in this list are poor. Resistance is *par excellence* dispositional; extension is of use, as Leibniz insisted, only if there is some other property whose instancing defines the boundaries: hardness goes with resistance, and mass is knowable only by its dynamical effects. Turn up the magnification and we find things like an electrical charge at a point, or rather varying over a region, but the magnitude of a field at a region is known only through its effect on other things in spatial relations to that region. A region with charge is very different from a region without: perhaps different enough to explain all we could ever know about nature. It differs precisely in its dispositions or powers. But science finds only dispositional properties, all the way down.

Evans talked of a prejudice against bare ungrounded dispositionality, 'equally offended by the idea of two places alike in what occupies them between visits, yet of which one is such that if one goes to it, one will have certain experiences, and the other is not'.[2] He wanted as well a 'relatively

---

1. To avoid clutter I should say that from now on I shall talk indifferently of powers, dispositions, and 'counterfactuals' to describe the features on the noncategorical side of the fence; it is their contrast with the other side that matters, not possible differences between them.

2. Gareth Evans, 'Things Without the Mind', in *Philosophical Subjects*, ed. Zak van Straaten (Oxford: Clarendon Press, 1980), p. 102.

abiding property' that fills out the intervals in the exercise of dispositions. Physics can give him this only in a backhanded way that will not satisfy the demand. An electrical field can abide, certainly, but that means just that there is a period of time over which various counterfactuals are true. It does not give us reason to think of a different property, quietly persisting, as it were, even when the disposition is not exercised.[3]

Perhaps I have been unduly verificationist. True, you might say, things like fields and masses are known by their effects on other things. But this should not prevent us thinking of them as *in themselves* categorical. There will be a categorical ground, G, for the (multitrack) disposition D whereby we know of mass or charge. It will be in virtue of the instancing of such a G that an object has the mass that it does, or a region of space the charge. When we think this, I believe we surreptitiously imagine an improvement in science that would enable us to identify G: a new theory about something true of charged regions of space, for example, rather like the molecular theory of gases. But this road leads only to the same place. Just as the molecular theory gives us only things with dispositions, so any conceivable improvement in science will give us only a better pattern of dispositions and powers. That's the way physics works.

Is it the way it has to work? I believe so. A quick route to this conclusion is to see the theoretical terms of a science as defined functionally, in terms of their place in a network of laws.[4] A slower route is to reflect on what is needed from physical thinking. What is needed is the use of concepts—energy, temperature, entropy—that cover changes of state, permitting the formulation of conservation laws. Such concepts in effect tell us what is the same about a changing system, in terms precisely of its powers and dispositions.[5]

G will remain, therefore, entirely beyond our ken, a something-we-know-not-what identified only by the powers and dispositions it supports. And then the possibilities multiply. Perhaps there is a possible world just like ours, not only in surface appearance, but in all that physics could ever discover, in which the dispositions have a different categorical ground, G'. Perhaps in our own world G' supports dispositions on Mondays and Wednesdays, while G supports them on the other days. But the real problem arises with the nature of the underlying and support that G provides for D. Is it logically necessary that G support D? Presumably not—what could logic have to say about it? And since we know nothing of G, it can hardly be *a priori* in any other way that it does what it does. Presumably then there is a law whereby G supports D, and this law imputes a power to G. So it ought to need a separate categorical ground, G^*, it being in virtue of G^* that G gives rise to D in the worlds that obey this law. But then the power of G^*, to bring it about that G gives rise

3. Cf. Strawson's reply to Evans, van Straaten, op. cit.,, p. 280. 'If it seems true of the sensory properties in general that they all dissolve together, under reflective pressure, into dispositions, this seems even more certainly true of the "physical" properties which are held to constitute their categorical base'.
4. David Lewis, 'How to Define Theoretical Terms', in his *Philosophical Papers,* volume I (New York: Oxford University Press, 1983).
5. I tell this story at greater length in essay 13.

to *D*, will itself need a ground, and so forever. To stop the regress we need a brute or bare power without a categorical ground: better in that case not to insist on grounds in the first place.

Are we in danger of proving too much? It seems as though we have excised categorical properties from nature altogether, leaving only features that, as Russell said, are each other's washing.[6] The problem is very clear if we use a possible-worlds analysis of counterfactuals. To conceive of *all* the truths about a world as dispositional is to suppose that a world is entirely described by what is true at *neighbouring* worlds. And since our argument was *a priori,* these truths in turn vanish into truths about yet other neighbouring worlds, and the result is that there is no truth anywhere.[7] Here is a good analogy. Early philosophers such as Whitehead and Collingwood, reflecting on modern physics, saw that it resolved substance into function and drew the consequence that there is no such thing as a state of nature at a literal timeslice: processes take time. 'There is no nature at an instant'.[8] The present problem is that processes take possibilities as well as actuality, so there is no nature at an actual world.

In Lewis's exploration of these issues, categoricity comes in the 'Humean mosaic' or pattern of 'perfectly natural intrinsic properties which need nothing bigger than a point at which to be instantiated'.[9] It seems as though we need them, but it now also seems as though we cannot have them—our best physical understanding of the world gives us no conception of what they might be. But the mention of Hume is suggestive. We can think of the Humean mosaic in experimental terms: a colour here, a tactile sensation there, a sound somewhere else. Categoricity in fact comes with the subjective view: there is nothing dispositional, to the subject, in the onset of a pain or a flash in the visual field. Such events come displayed to us as bare, monadic changes in particular elements of experience. In this perspective a change in perceived colour is as categorical as a change in shape or a twinge of toothache, even if, from the objective standpoint, 'all that goes on' when such changes occur is that a change of functional (dispositional) state arises, the subject being disposed to act and think differently as a consequence of changes in the dispositions of surrounding things.

The trouble now is that such events, conceived of as categorical, play no role in a scientific understanding of the world; they certainly do not serve to

6. *The Analysis of Matter* (London: Kegan Paul, 1927), p. 325. 'There are many possible ways of turning some things hitherto regarded as "real" into mere laws concerning the other things. Obviously there must be a limit to this process, or else all the things in the world will merely be each other's washing'.

7. I have subsequently found this point made in very similar terms by Howard Robinson, *Matter and Sense* (Cambridge: Cambridge University Press, 1982), chapter 9. Robinson uses it to attack any conception of matter, whereas I leave the issue in Hume's hands rather than Berkeley's.

8. See for example, R. G. Collingwood, *The Idea of Nature* (Oxford: Oxford University Press, 1945), Introduction, sections 4 and 5. The saying is quoted from Whitehead, *Nature and Life* (Cambridge: Cambridge University Press, 1934), p. 48.

9. David Lewis, *Philosophical Papers,* volume II (New York: Oxford University Press, 1986), Introduction, p. x.

ground anything. The question remains whether we can live with a concept of objectivity that leaves us only powers without end, and escape from the discomfort this causes by somehow retreating to a subjective point of view. Strawson counsels that we can, self-consciously shifting perspectives to avoid the contradiction of thinking of the same event as both categorical and dispositional.[10] But the problem remains that this gives us no help in understanding what, except counterfactuals, is true of the objective order of nature, unless, heroically, we see that order as a kind of construct from the categorical point-instances of properties available to the subjective view—a kind of neutral monism. It almost seems that carelessness and inattention alone afford a remedy—the remedy of course of allowing ourselves to have any idea at all of what could fill in space.

10. Strawson, in van Straaten, op. cit., pp. 280–81.

Index